Thomas Paul Urumpackal, ORGANIZED RELIGION
ACCORDING TO DR S. RADHAKRISHNAN

Analecta Gregoriana

Cura Pontificiae Universitatis Gregorianae edita
Vol. 184. Series Facultatis Theologicae: Sectio B, n. 59

THOMAS PAUL URUMPACKAL

ORGANIZED RELIGION ACCORDING TO DR S. RADHAKRISHNAN

UNIVERSITÀ GREGORIANA EDITRICE

ROMA 1972

THOMAS PAUL URUMPACKAL

ORGANIZED RELIGION ACCORDING TO DR S. RADHAKRISHNAN

Università Gregoriana Editrice

ROMA 1972

Quest'opera di Thomas Paul Urumpackal: ORGANIZED RELIGION ACCORDING TO DR S. RADHAKRISHNAN è stata pubblicata con l'approvazione ecclesiastica (Vicariato di Roma 15 marzo 1972) dalla Università Gregoriana Editrice, Roma 1972, e stampata dalla Tipografia della Pontificia Università Gregoriana.

TO
THE MEMORY OF
ARCHBISHOP MAR MATHEW KAVUKATT

CONTENTS

INTRODUCTION

A tendency to foster mutual understanding and co-operation is a remarkable feature of our time. Everywhere barriers are breaking down, frontiers are losing their meaning and nations are coming together, discarding their isolationist policies. The great achievement of Pope John XXIII and the Second Vatican Council lies in the fact that they realized this desire for fellowship, were able to adjust themselves to the changing times and even to lead the change itself. Thus, they succeeded in channelling the course of Church history in a new direction. A friendly approach, readiness to understand, willingness to engage in dialogue, collaboration in matters of common interest and an acceptance of whatever is true and good are always possible and certainly praiseworthy.

Scholars observe that it is the first time that a Pope and an Ecumenical Council have expressed such a positive and open attitude towards other great religions of the world[1]. The Church, in fact, has never refused to recognize whatever is true and good in other religions, although hitherto her teachings were often indirectly formulated. The Second Vatican Council states the attitude of the Church towards other religions extremely clearly, perhaps as never before. After declaring that the « perception of that hidden power which hovers over the course of things and over the events of human life »[2] instils into the lives of non-Christian peoples a profound religious sense, the sacred Council continues:

---

[1] Cf. ROBERT A. GRAHAM, Introduction to *Declaration on the Relationship of the Church to Non-Christian Religions,* in WALTER M. ABBOT *et al.* (eds), *The Documents of Vatican II* (New York 1966) 659. « Through the centuries, however, missionaries often adopted the attitude that non-Christian religions were simply the work of Satan and the missionaries' task was to convert from error to knowledge of the truth ... Now for the first time, there is recognition of other religions as entities with which the Church can and should enter into dialogue » (Cf. WALTER M. ABBOT *et al.* (eds), *The Documents of Vatican II,* p. 662, n. 11).

[2] *Declaration on the Relationship of the Church to Non-Christian Religions,* art. 2.

« The Catholic Church rejects nothing which is true and holy in
these (non-Christian) religions. She looks with sincere respect
upon those ways of conduct and life, those rules and teachings
which, though differing in many particulars from what she holds
and sets forth, nevertheless often reflect a ray of that Truth which
enlightens all men » [3]. Showing a remarkable respect for other
religions, the Church, 'Mother and Teacher of all nations' exhorts
us through the Second Vatican Council: « prudently and lovingly,
through dialogue and collaboration with the followers of other religions, and in witness of Christian faith and life, to acknowledge,
preserve, and promote the spiritual and moral goods found among
these men (non-Christians), as well as the values in their society
and culture » [4]. These good elements are to be « healed, enobled,
and perfected unto the glory of God, the confusion of the devil,
and the happiness of men » [5].

Therefore, a deeper study of other religions and a fresh
scrutiny of the relationship of our own with them becomes necessary. « Theological investigation must necessarily be stirred
up in each major socio-cultural area, as it is called. In this way,
in the light of the tradition of the universal Church, a fresh
scrutiny will be brought to bear on the deeds and words which
God has made known, which have been consigned to the sacred
Scripture, and which have been unfolded by the Church Fathers
and the teaching authority of the Church » [6]. Only with such
an investigation will we be able to see more clearly « in what
ways faith can seek for understanding in the philosophy and wisdom
of these peoples » [7]. Then « avenues will be opened for a more
profound adaptation in the whole area of Christian life » [8].

The Church in India is in duty bound to investigate and as
far as possible, make a clear assessment, of the religious values
found in Hinduism, the religion of the great majority of the Indian
people which embodies the « most searching quest in the natural
order of the Divine that the world has known » [9]. The results
of this investigation will show the way, we hope, towards an

---

[3] Ibid.

[4] Ibid.

[5] Second Vatican Council, *Dogmatic Constitution on the Church*, ch. II,
art. 17.

[6] Second Vatican Council, *Decree on the Missionary Activity* of the
Church, ch. III, n. 22. Cf. also Ibid., ch. II, n. 11.

[7] Ibid.

[8] Ibid.

[9] P. JOHANNS, *Hinduism* (London 1934) 28.

indigenous theology, which is a pressing need of Christianity in India.

In India we are experiencing in every walk of life a peaceful revolution; in economics and politics the old views are giving way to new ones; in religion, ancient monistic views are re-interpreted and are posing a challenge to every other religion with renewed vigour and self-confidence. Many influential Hindu theologians today favour some kind of monism.

Dr Sarvepalli Radhakrishnan is undoubtedly the best known of all these modern Hindu thinkers. His position has become significant to resurgent Hinduism because he has attempted, with considerable success, to modernize Śaṅkara who is the universally accepted St Thomas of Hinduism. Like Śaṅkara he is trying to restate the eternal meaning of the Hindu religion. If Śaṅkara's mission was to the Hindus alone, Radhakrishnan's is to the entire world. In recent years Christian intellectuals of India are showing a growing interest in him, because he evaluates every point in Christian theology in the light of the re-interpreted religion of the Upanishads. Therefore a study on him will help us to become acquainted not only with the modern Hindu view of life but also with the modern Hindu view of the Christian life. A study of the Hindu attitudes towards life, especially Christian life, has suddenly become imperative after the Second Vatican Council which declared: « Christ Himself searched the hearts of men, and led them to divine light through truly human conversation. So also His disciples, profoundly penetrated by the Spirit of Christ, should know the people among whom they live and should establish contact with them » [10]. It is in response to this declaration that this our study on Dr Radhakrishnan's Idea of Organized Religion, got under way.

Christianity and Hinduism, according to Radhakrishnan, stand at the opposite poles in the matter of organization. If Christianity is the type of the organized religion, Hinduism is the type of ' open religion '. While organized religions stress their external elements, Hinduism insists only on internal experience. According to Radhakrishnan, spiritual experience is the hallmark of all authentic religions. All genuine religions, therefore, are diverse expressions of a single eternal evolving religion. Just as life on

---

[10] *Decree on the Missionary Activity of the Church*, ch. II, n. 11. Cf. also *Declaration on the Relationship of the Church to Non-Christian Religions*, art. 2.

earth, the religion of man is in a continuous evolution, ever realizing greater and greater perfection. It has passed from naturalistic polytheism to monotheism. Now it has to leave out the institutional elements and pass from belief in God to the realization of the Godhead, from monotheism to monism. Thus religion must become a pure spiritual experience of the Absolute. That stage of religion would coincide with the ultimate evolutionary stage of man.

In this dissertation we have followed a simple method: to find out the main elements of Radhakrishnan's idea of organized religion, to collect and co-ordinate them and draw the necessary conclusions. Following this method we have tried to develop Dr Radhakrishnan's concepts of the intimate nature (chapter V) and different aspects (chapters III and IV) of organized religion. We shall also determine his idea of the eternal basis of religions (chapter II) and of a religion which is above and beyond organized religions (chapter VI). This, we believe, will help us to see his views on organized religion in their right perspective. In the critical section of our thesis we are not asking if this or that particular statement of Radhakrishnan is valid or not. We take up the basis of his theology of religion and his most basic reasons for it and evaluate them; finally we give the basic lines of our own approach to the matter.

We are greatly indebted to Rev. Fr. Mariasusai Dhavamony, S. J., Professor of Hinduism and History of Religions at the Pontifical Gregorian University, Rome, and an expert in classical as well as modern Hinduism, whose critical sense, clear judgment and profound knowledge of Hinduism have been of unfailing help in bringing this work to its present form. We thank him most sincerely for his constant encouragement and invaluable help.

Rome, 7th March, 1969.

THOMAS PAUL

ABBREVIATIONS

A Source Book	=	*A Source Book in Indian Philosophy,* London 1957.
BG	=	*The Bhagavdgītā,* 2nd ed., London 1949.
D	=	DENZINGER-RAHNER, *Enchiridion Symbolorum* (1960).
EPW	=	*Education, Politics and War,* Poona 1944.
ERWTh	=	*Eastern Religions and Western Thought,* 2nd ed., London 1940.
EWR	=	*East and West in Religion,* London 1933.
EWS	=	*East and West Some Reflections,* London 1955.
Fragments	=	*The Religion of the Spirit and the Wordl's Need: Fragments of a Confession,* in PhSR, pp. 5-82.
FS	=	*Fellowship of the Spirit,* Cambridge, Massachusetts 1961.
GB	=	*Gautama the Buddha,* 2nd ed., Bombay 1946.
HVL	=	*The Hindu View of Life,* Unwin Books ed., London 1960.
IC	=	*India and China,* 2nd ed., Bombay 1947.
Ind. Ph. I	=	*Indian Philosophy* v. I, 2nd ed., London 1929.
Ind. Ph. II	=	*Indian Philosophy* v. II, 2nd ed., London 1929.
IVL	=	*An Idealist View of Life,* Unwin Books ed., London 1961.
K	=	*Kalki or the Future of Civilisation,* 2nd ed., London 1948.
MG	=	*Mahatma Gandhi: Essays and Reflections in His Life and Work,* 2nd ed., London 1949.
MST	=	*My Search for Truth,* Agra 1949.

OSW, October 1952 - January 1956 = *Occasional Speeches and Writings October 1952 - January 1956,* Delhi 1956.

OSW, February 1956 - February 1957 = *Occasional Speeches and Writings February 1956 - February 1957,* Delhi 1957.

OSW, October 1952 - February 1959 = *Occasional Speeches and Writings October 1952 - February 1959,* Delhi 1960.

OSW, July 1959 - May 1962 = *Occasional Speeches and Writings July 1959 - May 1962,* Delhi 1963.

OSW, May 1962 - May 1964 = *President Radhakrishnan's Speeches and Writings May 1962 - May 1964*, Delhi 1965.

PhRT   = *The Philosophy of Rabindranath Tagore*, London 1918.

PhSR   = PAUL ARTHUR SCHILPP (ed.), *The Philosophy of Sarvepalli Radhakrishnan*, New York 1952.

Pr. Ups.   = *The Principal Upanishads*, London 1953.

RC   = *Reply to Critics*, in PhSR, pp. 787-842.

RCW   = *Religion in a Changing World*, London 1967.

RF   = *Recovery Faith*, London 1956.

RR   = *The Reign of Religion in Contemporary Philosophy*, London 1920.

RS   = *Religion and Society*, 2nd ed., London 1948.

RWN   = *The Religion We Need*, London 1928.

The Brahma Sūtra = *The Brahma Sūtra: The Philosophy of Spiritual Life*, London 1960.

The Spirit in Man = *The Spirit in Man*, in *Contemporary Indian Philosophy*, 2nd ed., London 1952, pp. 475-505.

ThWN   = G. KITTEL and G. FRIEDRICH (eds), *Theologisches Wörterbuch zum Neuen Testament*, Stuttgart 1933ff.

I

FORMATION OF DR. S. RADHAKRISHNAN'S
IDEAS ON RELIGION

All innovators are inheritors too. Past traditions play an important rôle in our conduct and manners. The past is constantly flowing into the present [1]. Every genius has an indebtedness to the past. Radhakrishnan is intensely aware of this fact. He says:

> « Human minds do not draw up sudden stray thoughts without precedents or ancestors ... There is no such thing as utterly spontaneous generation. Philosophic experiments of the past have entered into the living mind of the present ... Life goes on not by repudiating the past but by accepting it and weaving into the future in which the past undergoes a rebirth. The main thing is to remember and create anew » [2].

Moreover, he agrees that he has learned a great deal from others though he is not a follower of any [3]. Therefore to understand clearly how far the theological experiments of the past have entered into the dynamic mind of Radhakrishnan and in what way he has created them anew, it is necessary to delve a little into his theological ancestry.

Radhakrishnan has two ancestral lines in theology, one in India, the other in the West. First we shall see the main Indian traditions which he has inherited; secondly his education and intellectual career and lastly the influence of Western thinkers on him. Accordingly this chapter is divided into three parts. 1) Indian Traditions. 2) Education and Intellectual Career of Dr S. Radhakrishnan. 3) Influence of Western Thinkers on Dr S. Radhakrishnan.

---

[1] Cf. RCW, p. 145. For the sake of brevity we are making use of some abbreviations, which are explained on pp. xix-xx.

[2] *Fragments,* p. 10.

[3] Cf. Ibid; RC, p. 842.

1) INDIAN TRADITIONS

i. *Ancient Indian View of Religion*

The known history of Indian religious thought begins with the *Vedas* (ca. 1000 B. C.)[4]. In them « man is seen groping in the dark at first but becoming ever more sure in his quest for the Eternal, the Real, and the Light, both in himself and in the world that surrounds him »[5]. Scholars see five distinct religious currents running through the Vedic period: vague primitive monotheism[6], phenomenal polytheism[7], philosophical monotheism[8], pantheism[9] and monism[10]. In the *Brahmanas* sacrifice was considered the most important aspect of religion. But there appears also a monistic tendency. The ultimate goal was said to be to reach the Absolute, the primordial principle. With *Aranyakas,* sacrifice lost its importance, and meditation and asceticism substituted it.

In the *Upanishads, Brahman* was considered the ultimate principle which spontaneously manifests itself as the universe. *Atman* was conceived of as the inner principle in man. All logical searches to understand the ultimate principle were futile. « It is a mystery beyond human understanding, which can be known only by direct intuition. Then the supreme discovery of the *Upanishads* was made. The ultimate ground of reality in nature (Brahman) is one with the ultimate ground of being in the soul (Atman) »[11]. This identification of *Atman* and *Brahman* is one of the essential teachings of the *Upanishads*[12]. This is expressed in the great sayings « *Tat tvam asi* » (That art thou) and *Aham Brahma asmi* (I am Brahman). Our inborn ignorance hides from us this su-

---

[4] The escavations of Mohenjo-daro and Harappa give indications of Hindu practices as early as 3000 B.C. (Cf. SIR JOHN MARSHALL, *Mohenjo-daro and Indus Civilization* I (1931) 52f.

[5] R. C. ZAEHNER, *The Catholic Church and World Religions* (London 1964) 23.

[6] Cf. DASGUPTA, *A History of Indian Philosophy I* (Cambridge 1961) 17.

[7] Cf. SHARVANANDA, *The Vedas and Their Religious Teachings,* in *The Cultural Heritage of India,* I, p. 24.

[8] Cf. *Rig Veda,* III, 55; Cf. SHARVANANDA, *The Cultural Heritage of India,* I, p. 25.

[9] Cf. *Rig Veda,* X, 129, 2; FR. ZACHARIAS, *An Outline of Hinduism* (Alwaye 1956) 35.

[10] Cf. SHARVANANDA, *The Cultural Heritage of India* I, p. 25.

[11] B. GRIFFITHS, Hinduism: New Catholic Encyclopedia VI (1967) 1125.

[12] Cf. M. DHAVAMONY, *Indian Philosophy*: New Catholic Encyclopedia VII (1967) 458.

preme identity. So our liberation and goal of life consist in discovering this identity. But knowledge is beyond sense and reason. Only in a direct intuition, where the distinction between *Ātman* and *Brahman* disappears, this discovery is made and spiritually realized. So the seers of the Upanishads were not seeking a speculative knowledge of the truth but a mystical and spiritual experience of it. Ever since the dawn of the Upanishadic period (700-600 B. C.) Indian genius has taken a firm stand on mystical experience. Since mystical experience is beyond logic and reason, it is capable of varied interpretations. Thus, an awakening to intuition became the main thing and the doctrine derived from it secondary. Religious experience has to be interpreted in a way that will awaken intuitive experience. Radhakrishnan sums up the whole thing in these words : « The Hindu attitude to religion is interesting. While fixed intellectual beliefs mark off one religion from another, Hinduism sets no such limits. Intellect is subordinated to intuition, dogma to experience, outer expression to inward realization » [13].

The *Bhagavadgītā* is the most popular of the Hindu sacred books. It is later than the *Upanishads,* and forms part of the *Mahābhārata*. Its authorship is attributed to Vyāsa.

The Gītā synthesizes the different elements of the Vedic cult of sacrifice, the Upanishadic teaching of the Absolute Brahman, the Bhāgavata theism, the Sāṁkhya dualism and the Yoga meditation. It takes up the Upanishadic concept of the Brahman as the Absolute; but goes beyond and says that impersonality of the Absolute is not its whole significance. It develops the theistic side of Upanishadic teaching. The Supreme is conceived as the transcendental, the cosmic and the individual reality [14]. Hence it has been described as both "metaphysics and ethics, *brahmavidyā* and Yoga-śāstra, the science of reality and the art of union with reality" [15]. It is a religious classic.

The *Bhagavadgītā* is written in the form of a dialogue between Krishna, the incarnation of God, and Arjuna. In the course of dialogue Krishna reveals to Arjuna much concerning the self, Brahman and the incarnate God that he himself is [16].

First, Krishna tells Arjuna that the soul lives again in future incarnations and that it is a timeless essence which of its nature

---

[13] HVL, p. 13.
[14] Cf. *A Source Book,* p. 101.
[15] Cf. Ibid., p. 101.
[16] Cf. RC. ZAEHNER, *The Catholic Church and World Religions,* p. 34.

can in no way be affected by the life or death of the body. This leads Krishna to discuss the ways and means by which the soul can achieve liberation, and the meaning of liberation. He shows "that to experience Brahman or *nirvāna* as the timeless principle in the soul is the prelude, subject to God's grace, to sharing in the Being of God himself who is the source from which both Brahman and *nirvāna* proceed; and the soul now realizes that the infinite dimension it has experienced in itself it has not of itself but because it is indwelt by God"[17]. Accordingly, in the Gita, Bhakti or loving devotion attains its full significance after liberation. So it is beyond the realization of one's transcendent self as Brahman. The personal union with God is thus the end. Krishna's final and most important message is not about becoming Brahman! it is a message that God loves man and man's salvation is in a passionate love for God that leaves room for nothing else. "Greatly do I desire thee", says Krishna, "therefore will I tell thee thy salvation. Bear me (ever) in mind, love me, worship me and reverence me. Thus shall thou come to me. I promise thee truly; for thou art dear to me"[18].

There are six orthodox schools of Hindu thought. The most important of them is the Vedanta, founded by Badarāyana. This system takes up the true spirit of the *Upanishads*. Scholars in Hinduism are of opinion that "it is perhaps the truest exponent of the habits of thought of intellectual Hindus for all time"[19]. Of all the six orthodox systems the Vedanta had the greatest influence on Radhakrishnan. In the course of time this system was interpreted differently by different authors. Śaṅkara (788-820) gave a non-dualistic interpretation to it. Rāmānuja (1050-1137) based his qualified non-dualism on the Vedanta. Madhva (1198-1278) interpreted the Vedanta in a dualistic way. Of these interpreters Śaṅkara seems to have influenced Radhakrishnan more than others. According to Śaṅkara, Reality is One (Brahman) without the second. Brahman is pure Being (*sat*), pure Knowledge (*cit*) and pure Bliss (*ānanda*). This Absolute is identified with the *Ātman* of man. Brahman cannot be known by reasoning. By and in direct intuition (*anubhava*) the self knows its identity with Brahman. Śaṅkara, indeed, used logic, but maintained that there is a higher knowledge which reason cannot attain.

---

[17] Ibid., p. 36.
[18] *Bhagavadgītā*, XVIII, 64-65.
[19] M. DHAVAMONY, *Indian Philosophy*, art. cit., p. 459.

ii. *Reform Movements in Hinduism*

Reform in Hinduism began with the foundation of Brahmo-Samaj in 1828 by Rām Mohun Roy (1772-1833). He tried to free Hinduism from polytheism and image worship and to construct a monotheism in the light of Christian and Moslem teachings for which he found support in the *Upanishads*. It was he who first preached that the basic principles of all religions are the same and that they only need to be stressed [20]. Ram Mohun's reform work was continued by Devendranath Tagore (1817-1905) and Keshub Chandra Sen (1838-1884). The Brahmo Samaj became divided under Keshub, because of his rational approach to the *Vedas*. In 1875 Dayananda Saraswati (1824-1883) founded Arya Samaj. He preached that the *Veda* is the key to the solution of all problems, and that truth, wherever found, is of the *Veda*. The ideas of the Theosophical Society, which was started in New York in 1875 by Madame Blavatsky and Colonel Olcott had also an appeal for the reformers. The Theosophists believe that no religion is an exclusive way to salvation and that the soul is divine by nature. The soul in its earthly life is unaware of this fact. Through some prescribed disciplines, it is said, the soul can realize its divine nature. All such realized souls together form a great Brotherhood [21].

Meanwhile, Ramakrishna Paramahamsa (1836-1886), a priest at the Dakshineswar temple outside Calcutta claimed to have attained direct experience of the Ultimate Reality by his ascetical discipline. He believed that he had realized the identity of his self with Brahman. For some time he deliberately meditated as a Christian and as a Moslem in order to realize God in these religions too. Finally he came to the conclusion that all religions are essentially one. Ramakrishna's disciple, Vivekananda (1862-1902) who founded the Ramakrishna Mission, spread these doctrines not only in India but also in Europe and America. He seems to have greatly influenced Radhakrishnan [22]. So perhaps, we should list here the main doctrines of Vivekananda [23]. 1) Man

---

[20] Cf. KALIDAS NAG., *The Brahmo Samaj,* in *The Cultural Heritage of India* IV (Calcutta 1956) 618.

[21] Cf. C. JINARAJADASA, *What Theosophists Believe?* in *The Cultural Heritage of India,* IV, pp. 647f.

[22] Cf. MST, p. 14; OSW, May 1962 - May 1964, p. 123.

[23] For a brief account of Vivekananda's religious ideas Cf. SWAMI NIRVEDANANDA, *Sri Ramakrishna and Spiritual Renaissance,* in *The Cultural Heritage of India,* IV, pp. 711ff.

is potentially divine. 2) Religion is the manifestation of the Divinity that is already in man. 3) The salvation of man is through the realization of his identity with the Absolute. 4) There is a unity underlying all religions. Therefore, all religions are equally good as means for salvation. 5) Quarrels among religions arise from over-emphasis on secondary details. 6) The fundamental elements of all religions, divested of all their external forms, constitute a universal religion which alone needs to be insisted upon.

Later Rabindranath Tagore laid special emphasis on the ideal of one world built on a universal religion. Mahatma Gandhi added non-violence and social service to the essentials of religion. Thus among the intellectuals "There was a conscious revolt against social, political and religious institutions" [24].

In short, the unity of mankind of Rām Mohun, the vedism of Dayananda, the scientific spirit of Keshub, the mystical experience of Ramakrishna, the harmony of faiths of Vivekananda, the universalism of Tagore, and a general uneasiness about the Christian missionary activities were the general characteristics of renascent Hinduism.

Such were the religious movements that Radhakrishnan encountered in his search for the universal religion. Many of these surging currents went straight into the impressionable mind of young Radhakrishnan.

2) EDUCATION AND INTELLECTUAL CAREER OF DR S. RADHAKRISHNAN

About the life and the works of the saints and sages of modern India any amount of literature is available. But we may not find an elaborate biographical work on Dr S. Radhakrishnan. He has constantly refused to write a descriptive autobiography. Even when well known editors requested him to do so, he politely declined. However an intellectual autobiography of Dr Radhakrishnan, significantly described as "My Search for Truth" can be found in *Religion in Transition* which Vergilius Ferm edited in 1937 [25]. Even in this, the description of his life abruptly ends after a few pages. Later, Paul A. Schilpp requested him to write some au-

---

[24] OSW, July 1959 - May 1962, p. 139.
[25] An off-print of this was brought out by Shiva Lal Agarwala and Co. Ltd., Agra (in 1946).

tobiographical notes in order to include them in the volume, *The Philosophy of Sarvepalli Radhakrishnan,* which he was editing. Here also Radhakrishnan gives an intellectual autobiography under the title, " The Religion of the Spirit and the World's Need: Fragments of a Confession ".

i. *Birth and Early Life*

Radhakrishnan was born on September 5, 1888, at Tirutani a small town, in the Chittoor District, forty miles North-West of Madras; he was the second child of Telugu Brahmin parents, who were orthodox in their religious outlook [26]. Tirutani was, and is even today, a famous pilgrim centre. There he lived his early years. The religious life around him might have influenced his religious outlook in some measure [27]. He had a strong faith " in the reality of an unseen world behind the flux of phenomena " [28], for which he could not account. This faith has remained in him even when he was faced with grave difficulties [29]. He had a meditative frame of mind and loved solitude. After finishing his early schooling, he studied for twelve years in Christian missionary institutions. From 1896 to 1900 he was in the Lutheran Mission High School at Tirupati. Tirupati had also shrines which attracted many pious pilgrims. He studied from 1900 to 1904 in Voorhees' College, Vellore and then from 1904 to 1908 at Madras Christian College. Thus he grew up " in an atmosphere where the unseen was a living reality " [30]. This early training, especially in Madras Christian College, " with its atmosphere of Christian thought, aspiration and endeavour " [31], determined his approach to the problems of Philosophy " from the angle of religion as distinct from that of science or history " [32]. He was the first recipient of the gold medal awarded in honour

---

[26] MST, p. 1. Only two years after the death of Ramakrishna, the great Hindu saint, Swami Vivekananda had begun his excellent career. Tagore was twenty seven. All were great Hindu reformers.

[27] Cf. SAMARTHA, *Introduction to Radhakrishnan: the Man and His Thought* (New Delhi 1964) 2.

[28] MST, p. 1.

[29] Cf. Ibid.

[30] Cf. *Fragments,* pp. 6f.

[31] Cf. *The Spirit in Man,* p. 475.

[32] *Fragments,* p. 7. Cf. also OSW, July 1959 - May 1962, p. 195.

of Dr Samuel Satyanathan by the Madras University by obtaining
the highest marks in Ethics in the B. A. Degree examination [33].

Although he was "essentially shy and lonely" he passed for
a social and sociable man [34]. He loved books. The vistas they
unveiled and the dreams they awakened inspired in him profound
emotions [35].

His religious temperament was nourished by protracted education in the religious and theological atmosphere of Christian institutions. The religious motive became stranger in every aspect of
his life. But the direction which his religious enthusiasm took
was determined mainly through the criticism of Hindu beliefs and
practices by Christian missionaries [36]. These criticisms led him
to marshal counter arguments to defend his own faith by all means.
He describes his reactions in *My Search for Truth*:

> "At an impressionable period of my life, I became familiar
> not only with the teachings of the New Testament, but with
> the criticisms levelled by the Christian missionaries on Hindu
> beliefs and practices. My pride as a Hindu roused by the
> enterprise and eloquence of Swami Vivekananda was deeply
> hurt by the treatment accorded to Hinduism in missionary
> institutions. It was difficult for me to concede that Hindu
> ascetics and teachers who preserved for our world a living
> contact with the classical culture of India, which is at the
> root of much that we know and almost all that we practise,
> were not truly religious " [37].

He was really annoyed to see that truly religious people should
treat as subjects for derision the doctrines that others held sacred [38].
In *Fragments* he criticizes them for not being genuine seekers of
truth and for having disturbed his faith and shaken the traditional props on which he leaned [39].

Those were times of change in India. " The Indian mind

---

33 Cf. OSW, October 1952 - January 1956, p. 387.

34 Cf. MST, p. 2.

35 Cf. Ibid., p. 1.

36 Cf. DHIRENDRA MOHAN DATTA, *Radhakrishnan and Comparative Philosophy,* in PhSR, p. 668.

37 MST, p. 14.

38 Cf. Ibid., p. 44; RC, pp. 806-807; JOACHIM WACH, *Radhakrishnan
and Comparative Study of Religion,* in PhSR, p. 448.

39 Cf. *Fragments,* p. 9. But on October 3, 1962, speaking at the Madras
Christian College, Radhakrishnan recalled the names of all his teachers
and said, « It is difficult to imagine a better team of European and Indian
members of the staff » (Cf. OSW, July 1959 - May 1962, p. 194).

had already tested the cultural and spiritual values of the Western World. The mood which ruled now was one of exploiting that creed if that were possible "[40]. With Vivekananda the tidal waves of neo-Hinduism had reached as far as America. The current of the time was to deliver conscientiously the wisdom of India to the Western world. Radhakrishnan admits that the spirit of the times strengthened his resolve to defend the Indian culture and religion[41]. In this way the Christian apologists made him an Hindu apologist. He says: " The very multiplicity of these absolutisms makes it difficult for us to assume, if we are honest, that our absolutism is true and all others false ... A critical study of Hindu religion was thus forced on me "[42]. Thus he gradually became a defender of Hinduism[43]. This accounts for his critical views on whatever is Western and Christian in his contributions to periodicals like, *International Journal of Ethics, The Monist, Quest* and in his books like *East and West in Religion, Eastern Religions and Western Thought.*

ii. *Intellectual Career*

Radhakrishnan's first published work was his thesis for his M. A. Degree: *Ethics of the Vedanta,* which was a reply to the charge that the Vedanta system had no room for ethics. The publication of a book with his name on the title page excited young Radhakrishnan a great deal. The thrill was augmented by the praise of Professor Hogg[44]. This essay indicates the general trend of his thought: religion must establish itself as a rational way of living.

In 1909 he became a teacher of Philosophy in the Presidency College, Madras. He studied the Hindu classics, *the Upanishads, the Bhagavadgītā, the Brahma Sūtra;* the works of Sankara, Ramanuja, Madhva, Nimbarka etc., and works on *Hinduism, Buddhism, and Jainism.* Among the Western thinkers Plato, Plotinus, Kant, Bradley, and Bergson ' influenced him a great deal '[45]. His

---

[40] Cf. B. K. MALLIK, *Radhakrishnan and Indian Civilization,* in *Radhakrishnan: Comparative Studies in Philosophy Presented in the Honour of His Sixtieth Birthday* (London 1951) 259.

[41] Cf. MST, p. 10.

[42] *Fragments,* p. 9.

[43] Cf. DHIRENDRA MOHAN DATTA, *Radhakrishnan and Comparative philosophy,* in PhSR, p. 668.

[44] Cf. MST, p. 10f.

[45] Cf. *Fragments,* pp. 9-10.

studies revealed to him the defects of present-day Hinduism. He says :

> " I remember the cold sense of reality, the depressing feeling of defeat that crept over me as a causal relation between the anaemic Hindu religion and our political failure forced itself on my mind during these years. What is wrong with Hinduism? How can we make it somewhat more relevant to the intellectual climate and social environment of our time? Such were the questions which roused my interest " [46].

He became Professor of Philosophy at the Presidency College, Madras, in 1916. In 1917 he was appointed Lecturer in Philosophy at the Arts College, Rajahmundry. The following year he was appointed Professor of Philosophy in the University of Mysore, and held the post for three years, during which he contributed articles to well known reviews such as the *International Journal of Ethics, Monist,* and *Quest.* He was a follower of Saṁkara, but did not hesitate to restate some of the theories of Saṁkara, the theory of *māyā* for example. He found support for his views in Rabindranath Tagore, which led him to study more closely the latter's works. The result was his first important book, *The Philosophy of Rabindranath Tagore,* which secured a friendly reception and was praised by Tagore himself.

At this period, he held a spiritualistic non-dogmatic view of religion. He explains it thus : « It is not a private revelation or what is imposed by the public authority, but what springs naturally from the light of reason and the insight of experience. I was persuaded that Philosophy led us to a spiritual or what I called, an absolutist view of religion » [47]. In a series of articles contributed to *Mind,* he pointed out that Bergson was an absolutist. From a similar point of view he examined the philosophical views of many other writers such as Leibniz, William James, Rudolf Eucken, Bertrand Russell, and argued that religion had interfered in their philosophical pursuits and therefore their conclusions were not wholly philosophical. He set forth his own views at the same time and published *The Reign of Religion in Contemporary Philosophy* [48]. This is his first major work and many great philosophers praised him highly for it. He became known as an idealist

---

[46] *The Spirit in Man,* pp. 475-476.
[47] MST, p. 15.
[48] in 1920.

philosopher. Professor Hinman even coupled him with Bosanquet, calling them two representative idealists.

In 1921 the Vice Chancellor of Calcutta University, Sir Asutosh Mookerjee, offered him the King George V professorship of philosophy in his university. He occupied that chair for the next twenty years. Meanwhile, J. H. Muirhead requested him to write a book on Indian philosophy for his series: " Library of Philosophy ". In 1923 the first volume of Radhakrishnan's monumental *Indian Philosophy* appeared. In this he makes a lucid survey of the philosophy of the *Vedas and Upanishads,* the theism of the *Bhagavadgita,* the pluralistic realism of Jainism, the ethical idealism of Buddha and the later divergencies of Buddhist philosophy. The second volume of *Indian Philosophy* saw the light in 1927. In this he discusses the six schools of Hindu philosophy.

Radhakrishnan's articles in the *Hibbert Journal* brought him into contact with its editor, Dr L. P. Jacks, the Principal of the Manchester College, Oxford. Dr L. P. Jacks invited him to deliver the Upton Lectures for the year 1926. At the same time the University of Calcutta deputed him to represent it at the Congress of Universities of the British Empire in June 1926 and at the International Congress of Philosophy at Harvard University in September 1926. Thus he came into direct contact with the living philosophers of the West. His lectures at the Manchester College were published under the title *" The Hindu View of Life "*. In this he gives a rational account of Hindu Dharma [49]. The Harvard lectures came out in book form as *Kalki* or *The Future of Civilisation.*

In 1929 he was invited to occupy the chair of Comparative Religion at Manchester College, Oxford. The first of his lectures at Manchester College, together with four others, was published in 1933 under the title *East and West in Religion* [50]. He was also requested to give the Hibbert Lectures for 1929. These lectures were published in book form in 1932 under the title *An*

---

[49] D. S. Sarma says that this is « the most popular of Radhakrishnan's books » (Cf. D. S. Sarma's Introduction to *Great Indians*, p. 8).

[50] The other lectures are 1) The Jowett Lecture on March 18, 1930 at Mary Ward Settlement, London; 2) Sermon at Manchester College in November 1929; 3) Sermon at Manchester College Chapel in June 1930; and 4) The Presidential address at the general Conference in connection with the seventieth birth day celebrations of Rabindranath Tagore in Calcutta, December 1931. This is reproduced as the last essay in *Great Indians.*

Idealist View of Life. This, according to D. S. Sarma, is the " most important of Radhakrishnan's books, for it is here that we get his original contribution to the religious thought of his time " [51]. The book received a cordial welcome from great men like Bertrand Russell, Samuel Alexander, and W. R. Inge.

On his return to India he was appointed Vice Chacellor of Andhra University in 1931. In the same year he was nominated a member of the International Committee of Intellectual Co-operation of the League of Nations. He remained a member till the League was dissolved.

In 1936 he became the Spalding Professor of Eastern Religions and Ethics at Oxford. Till 1938 he was teaching, one term at Calcutta University and two terms at Oxford. The lectures at Oxford were published in one volume in 1939 under the title *Eastern Religions and Western Thought.* In this book the main intention of Radhakrishnan was to prove that the Upanishadic mysticism has been a continuous influence in Western thought from the time of Pythagoras and Plato down to our own times. Although this book is not an example of structural perfection, it is not lacking a unity of outlook. With this book, it seems, his religious views reached maturity.

While Radhakrishnan was at Oxford he was invited to give the Master Mind Lecture. He spoke on ' Gautama the Buddha '. His treatment was so excellent that it was described as a lecture on a master mind by a master mind. This lecture is the content of his *Gautama the Buddha.*

In 1939, at the request of Madan Mohan Malaviya, he accepted the Vice Chancellorship of the Benares Hindu University. Two years later he was appointed to the Sir Sayaji Rao Chair of Indian Culture and Civilisation. In 1942 he gave the Kamala Lectures at the Calcutta University, which were published in 1947 under the title *Religion and Society.* In 1944 he got an invitation from China to give a series of lectures in that country. These lectures constitute *India and China.* The same year saw the publication of *Education, Politics and War.* A year later he published *Is This Peace?*

In 1946 he led the Indian delegation to UNESCO's first conference held at Paris. From the beginning he was a member of the Executive Board of UNESCO and its Chairman for 1948-1949. Later he became President of the General Conference of UNESCO in 1952, 1954, 1958 and of its Tagore Centenary Celebrations in 1960. Meanwhile in 1948 he became Chairman of

the Indian Universities Commision. In the same year he published
a translation of the *Bhagavadgītā* with an Introductory Essay and
Notes, and in the following year *Great Indians* and *Report of
the University Education Commission*[52]. In 1949 he was appointed
India's Ambassador to the U.S.S.R. A year later his translation
of *Dhammapada,* with Introduction and notes, was published.

By this time he was universally acclaimed. His sixtieth and
seventieth birthdays were honoured by memorial books. In 1952
Paul A. Schilpp published a collection of essays on Radhakrishnan
under the title *The Philosophy of Sarvepalli Radhakrishnan.* In
the same year he became Vice Presidente of India. He was re-
elected to the same office in 1957. *The Principal Upanishads,* was
published with Introduction and notes in 1953. In 1954 he gave
the Sir Edward Beatty Memorial Lectures at McGill University.
These were published in 1955 under the title *East and West, Some
Reflections,* in which he tried to show the influence of the East on
the West. In the same year was published his *Recovery of Faith*
in which he insists on the importance of spiritual experience in
religion and the need for inter-religious friendship. In 1960
appeared his translation of *The Brahma Sūtra* with Introduction
and notes. The Book bears a suggestive subheading *The Philosophy of the Spiritual Life.* In 1961 he gave a lecture on the
Fellowship of the Spirit at Harvard University which appeared
under the title, *Fellowship of the Spirit.*

In May 1962 he was elected Presidente of India for five
years. Even in this period of high office his pen was not idle.
His latest work, *Religion in a Changing World,* was published
in 1967. In this book he envisages a world community united by
a single world religion as the order of the future. As Vice President and President of India he made a number of occasional
speeches and wrote prefaces to many books. The Publications
Division of the Government of India collected these occasional
speeches and writings and published them in three volumes[53].

---

[51] D. S. Sarma, Introduction to *Great Indians,* p. 9.

[52] Jointly with Sir James Duff and others.

[53] The first volume contains occasional speeches and writings from
October 1952 to February 1959. Originally those from October 1952 to
January 1956 were in one volume and those from February 1956 to February
1957 were in a second volume. Now these together are put in a combined
volume. The second volume contains occasional speeches and writings from
July 1959 to May 1962; and the third those from May 1962 to May 1964.
The occasional speeches and writings from May 1964 on are in the press.

3) THE INFLUENCE OF WESTERN THINKERS ON DR S. RADHA-
KRISHNAN

As Radhakrishnan belongs to the intellectual circle at Oxford of this century, it may be useful to outline briefly the philosophical and religious movements at Oxford and in England while he was a professor there. These movements of thought did certainly influence him in some measure [54]. As his sympathies were with the idealists, we shall first examine the position of that school in England. Then, we shall indicate the religious currents prevalent in England at that time.

i. *The Oxford Semi-Hegelians*

When George Berkely, the Bishop of Cloyne (1685-1753) declared in his church "*esse est percipi*", Dr. Johnson refuted it by "striking his foot with mighty force against a large stone, till he rebounded from it" [55]. All the same, idealism, in one form or another, had gained sufficient footing among the intellectuals of England from the time of the Oxford Hegelian, Thomas Hill Green (1836-1882). He believed that in an important sense consciousness can be said to be the principle of objectivity. The supreme consciousness is the Absolute, and man is a subject in whom the eternal consciousness reproduces itself as the spiritual principle [56].

The most important of Green's disciples was F. H. Bradley (1846-1924). According to him all the inconsistencies seen in the appearance vanish in the Ultimate Reality. The contradictions they expose come from our incomplete perception. Truth must be experienced, and what cannot be experienced is not truth. "Sentient experience, in short, is reality, and what is not this is not real" [57]. He recognises the soul, or a finite centre of immediate experience, which transcends the given moment and raises itself into the world of eternal verity. This finite centre is not an object but a "basis on and from which the world of objects is made" [58]. The immediate intuition of this centre furnishes no consistent view about

---

[54] Cf. P. T. RAJU, *Idealistic Thought of India* (London 1953) 342.

[55] G. B. HILL and L. F. POWELL (eds.), *Boswell's Life of Johnson* I (Oxford 1934) 471.

[56] *Prolegomena*, Bk. I, c. ii, 69.

[57] BRADLEY, *Appearance and Reality* (London 1893) 144.

[58] BRADLEY, *Essays on Truth and Reality* (Oxford 1914) 252f.

itself or about reality in general [59]. Still reality can be known only in terms of immediate feeling.

Another English idealist was Edward Caird (1835-1908). For him, the creative movement of the universe is the principal revelation of the nature of the Absolute. John Ellis McTaggart (1866-1925) was an extreme personalistic idealist. According to him, all reality is essentially spiritual. Bernard Bosanquet (1848-1923) was a follower of Green and Bradley.

Philosophic thought took a new trend when Albert Einstein formulated his theory of relativity. A kind of space-time philosophy was evolved by Sir James Jeans (1877-1946), Sir Arthur Eddington (1882-1945), Samuel Alexander (1858-1938) and Alfred North Whitehead (1861-1947). Eddington teaches that the nature of the world is dubious. It has no substance. It is a mere shadow of reality, a world of symbols and formulae. Samuel Alexander conceives space-time as the matrix of all reality [60]. The space-time substitutes the Absolute. Professor Whitehead built up a philosophy of relativity. His *Religion in the Making* [61] and *Process and Reality* (An Essay in Cosmology) [62] are the two books oft quoted by Radhakrishnan.

The basic principle of Whitehead is that the ' process ', the ' becoming ' is the ' being ', the ' existence ' of actual entity [63]. He believes that " there can only be evidence of a world of actual entities, if the immediate actual entity discloses them as essential to its own composition " [64]. Only if the actual entities composing the external world are internally related to the percipient, can there be an evidence of an external world. Therefore the experience of the percipient cannot be an experience of the actual entity external to the percipient [65]. An internality becomes thus the basis of any inference about anything external. From this it is argued that since actuality is ' immanent ' in the experiencing reality they cannot be of utterly different metaphysical natures. Consequently a metaphysical dualism is rejected by Whitehead. Moreover, if the object experienced is immanent in the subject experiencing, the experience itself must be immediate.

---

[59] Cf. Ibid, p. 156f.
[60] SAMUEL ALEXANDER, *Space, Time and Deity* (London 1920) 26.
[61] Cambridge University Press 1926.
[62] Cambridge University Press 1929.
[63] Cf. IVOR LECLERC, *Whitehead's Metaphysics*, (London 1958) 115.
[64] WHITEHEAD, *Process and Reality* (Cambridge 1929) 201.
[65] IVOR LECLERC, *Whitehead's Metaphysics*, p. 117.

Applying this theory to religion, Whitehead defines religion as "what the individual does with his own solitariness"[66]. This is a definition of religion which Radhakrishnan very often repeats.

ii. *Religious Thought among the Intellectuals*

At the time when Radhakrishnan was in England there was a kind of confusion among the intellectuals[67]. They were not sure of their philosophy or of their religion. To escape from this confusion there were two kinds of movements, a rational one and a mystical one.

After separation from Rome, there was a tendency in England to rationalize Christianity and to play down the concept of mystery. Deists acted likewise. Copleston remarks: "Eighteenth century deism meant the desupernaturalizing of religion and the refusal to accept any religious propositions on authority. For the deists reason, and reason alone was the judge of truth in religion as in elsewhere"[68]. There were free thinkers who did not care for tradition or authority, whether of the Scripture or of the Church[69].

Besides this tendency to rationalize religion, there was a feeling of uneasiness about organisation in religion and an insistence on mysticism. These tendencies are perhaps best represented by Baron Friedrich von Hügel and William Ralph Inge. Both have influenced in good measure the intellectuals at Oxford. It seems that they have also influenced to some extent Radhakrishnan's views on organized religion. We shall discuss shortly their religious views.

---

[66] *Religion in the Making* (Cambridge 1926) 6.

[67] T. S. Eliot described the confusion as
    « Shape without form, shade without colour,
    paralysed force, gesture without motion »
                (*The Hollow Man,* 1925)

[68] FREDERICH COPLESTON, *A History of Philosophy,* V. (New York, Image Books 1964) I, 174.

[69] It is interesting to note that Radhakrishnan had carefully read these eighteenth century deists. He brings most of these authors in his criticism on Christianity in ERWTh and makes them speak for him. For example, he quotes John Toland's rational view of the S. Scripture from his *Christianity not Mysterious;* (ERWTh, p. 263). So too he quotes, ANTHONY COLLIN, *A Discourse of Free Thinking, occasioned by the Rise and Growth of a Sect Called Free Thinkers* (ERWTh, p. 263. Radhakrishnan gives the name of the book only as « *A Discourse of Free Thinking* »), to show that only a natural religion is worthy of respect. He quotes also the condemnation of Gospel narratives by Thomas Woolston from *Discourses on the Miracles of Christ* (ERWTh, p. 263).

iii. *The Religious Views of Baron Friedrich von Hügel* (1852-1925)

Von Hügel had a distrust of the scholastic theology that resorted to syllogisms. This distrust was increased by his friendship with Rudolf Eucken, Maurice Blondel, George Tyrell and Alfred Loisy.

According to von Hügel, there is in every man a real eternal life [70] which is not a substitute for God or for man, but "it is the activity, the effect of God or of man or of both" [71]. It consists in the living relation between the human spirit and the Eternal Spirit. This Eternal life is not a matter of speculation. It reveals itself clearly in the course of ages. Only deeper and riper souls will experience it. Therefore, although, God is transcendent to us, He can be experienced by us. Moments of a vivid apprehension of a real experience of Eternity do occur in this life itself because God is immediately present in our lives [72]. This Eternal life present in man is the basis of the brotherhood of humanity.

Hügel gives five reasons to show that the Eternal life abides in every man [73]. 1) There is a keen sense of absolute abidingness or Eternity in God and a relative abidingness in man. Man experiences the Eternity in duration. 2) There is a keen sense of otherness in likeness. We feel that we are genuinely like God. Still there is also a feeling that we are genuinely unlike God. 3) There is a keen sense of other worldliness in contrast with this-worldliness. We look up to heaven as the place of our perfect beatitude. 4) There is a keen sense of Reality, Eternal Spirit, God, over against the realities. 5) There is a keen sense of Unity in Multiplicity and Multiplicity in Unity.

It is religion that awakens this Eternal Life which is in our deepest being. So the insistence of von Hügel is on the "right, privilege, and duty of Religion to experience and conceive Eternity and simultaneity" [74], not merely as an ideal to which we can approach but as already fully extant. Therefore, we have to recognize the value of other religions. "Men who are in the fuller, truer, purer stages and degrees may increasingly learn to recognize

---

[70] Cf. Baron von Hügel, *Eternal Life; a Study of Its Implications and Applications*, 2nd ed. (Edinburg 1913) 383.

[71] Ibid.

[72] Cf. Ibid, pp. 90f.

[73] Cf. Ibid., pp. 365ff.

[74] Ibid., p. 302.

2

in the positive and fruitful constituents and effects of other religions, something good and from God — fragments and preparations for such fuller truth as they themselves possess" [77].

From his study of the importance of the Eternal in man,
von Hügel points out that there are some factors which, once helpful in a way to the Instituted Church, have become causes of dis-
integration [76].

1) Canon law was of a great help to organized Christianity.
But when laws are imposed upon the faithful, von Hügel thinks:

> "They will on the contrary come to feel with Rosmini the
> holy, and with Newman the farsighted, and with many a
> saint down to our own acutely saddening times, that revolu-
> tion and despotism are ever fruitful parents of each other
> and that no fellow mortal, even if he truly represents to the
> fullest degree possible among frail men, the authority and
> power of God, can ever come to be beyond learning and
> receiving from men and through men — those very men to
> whom he has so much to teach and so much to give" [77].

So it is concluded that the presentation of the Canon Law and
the curialist rule in a 'despotic way', which gives a choice between
revolt and self-stultification will not make all the children of God
docile.

2) To insist on religious truth and religious unity is good.
Still our emphasis on unity and truth can make people fanatics.
Such people will easily become intolerant and may even justify
the Inquisition to impose religious truth.

3) To give philosophical explanations of religious truths is
good. But an over-estimated reverence and unconditional adherence
to a particular philosophic system will cause more illumined people
to leave the Church.

4) The same can be said of the insistence on History or
Dogmatic facts. The change of methods and the attitudes towards
History must be taken into account.

5) To have influence in the political sphere is perhaps good.
But when the Church interferes in purely political affairs, she may
be doing more harm to herself than good.

Von Hügel argues that these evils can be cured by a change,
of emphasis from the externals to the Eternal Life in man.

---

[75] Ibid., p. 393.
[76] Cf. Ibid., pp. 336-364.
[77] Ibid., p. 360.

"The experience, conceptions, and habits concerning Eternal Life, which the saints in special teach us, can alone forcibly aid us to avoid, bear, mitigate, abolish or utilize the evils we have found to be closely intertwined with the benefits of Institutionalism" [78].

Consequent upon his belief in the Eternal Life in man, von Hügel sees a cleavage between real interiority and official Authority. He says: "The soul at its deepest is ever profoundly original, isolated, active, daring, interior, penetrative, and super-ficially pessimist; it moves through suffering on to joy" [79]. But the "official Authority is 'as such, ever repetitive of something past and gone'; is the voice of the average thoughts of the many; aims at limiting the action of its subjects to a passive reception and more or less mechanical execution of its commands; is es-sentially timid; cares necessarily more for the outward appearance and material out put, than for the interior disposition and form of the soul's activity; maps out the very phenomenal world into visible, mutually exclusive regions of spiritual light and darkness; and is in so far ever unreal, as it cannot but absolutely disallow, or must at least minimise as much as possible, all even preliminary present sins, pains and perplexities — at least, those of its own creation" [80].

iv. *The Religious Views of William Ralph Inge* (1860-1954).

Inge, Dean of St. Pauls (1911-1934), believes that there is a divine spark in every man, that "there is a mystery in ourselves and in the objects of our knowledge, which the intellect cannot penetrate" [81]. Even the spirit cannot pierce the depths of this mys-tery. This is the basic doctrine of Inge, and his religious views are consequent on this principle. This "spark of the Divine" which never consents to the evil, remains even in the worst of men. Therefore in order to purify ourselves the soul must be cleansed of its external stains and detach itself from the body. When our detachment from body is perfect, and we meditate in solitude, we will be able to have mystical experience. In order to have mystical experience and salvation, "the last metaphysical barrier,

---

[78] Ibid., p. 364.
[79] BARON F. von HÜGEL, *Essays and Addresses on the Philosophy of Religion* (second series) (London 1930) 10.
[80] Ibid., pp. 10-11.
[81] W. R. INGE, *The Philosophy of Plotinus* II (London 1948) 132.

that which prevents subject and object from being wholly one"
must be transcended [82]. Then there is the vision of the One. It
is not something granted to man by an external agent. It is
a gradual growth from sense-perception up to the direct experience
of God. In order to attain this spiritual intuition we have to
retire to meditate in solitude so that we may eliminate all multiplicity, even that arising from discursive thinking.

According to Inge, the essence of religion resides in the immediate intuition of God. So the externals have only secondary
importance. The whole of religion is summed up in the vision
of God in which the subject-object relation is left behind.

A religion founded on the experience of what is the deepest
in man is invulnerable to scientific assault. For it is not contin-
gent on any historical event. "It is dependent on no miracles,
on no unique revelation through any historical person, on no narratives about the beginning of the world, on no prophecies of
its end. No scientific or historical discovery can refute it, and
it requires no apologetics, except the testimony of spiritual experience" [83]. Extraneous support may be of some value for religion at the beginning but will end by strangling it. So religion
must be based on mysticism which must be tested by reason so
that religion be completely free of danger. Such a mystical religion will be superior to all organized religions.

When externals of particular religions are transcended, the
experience of mystics everywhere and at all times is the same.
Inge quotes a number of passages from Plotinus and says that
" The witness of the mystics is wonderfully unanimous" [84]. Therefore there is a unity of all religions.

Inge had visualized some kind of spiritual integration of humanity. " The only final integration is a spiritual one, for spiritual
movements are non-competitive and on this plane is there real
community of interests" [85].

v. *Radhakrishnan's Impressions on the Religious Situation while
   he was at Oxford*

Radhakrishnan observed keenly the contemporary religious
confusion in England. Modern civilization seemed to him to

---

[82] Cf. Ibid., p. 160.
[83] Ibid., p. 228.
[84] Ibid., p. 143.
[85] Ibid., p. 227.

" suffer from the defect of being soulless. Politics and Economics do not take their direction from ethics and religion "[86]. Many who openly profess religious beliefs seemed to him not to take care to translate those beliefs into practice in their lives. The enormous cruelty and evil of the two wars showed how frail religious culture was. Therefore says Radhakrishnan, "Almost all of us are atheists in practice, though we may profess belief in God "[87]. For, " If our actions are opposed to those which are demanded by our religion, we cannot say that we are religious. We are really unbelievers "[88].

Many were using religion as an escape from the troubles of life[89]. Many others were feeling their way from the traditional religions to scientific humanism or to political ideologies or to some other ' isms '[90].

Radhakrishnan observed that there were a number of religious sects. Each one claimed absolute truth and superiority over others. Every one claimed that its views alone were the right ones. Radhakrishnan describes the situation: "A few of us who happened to be in Oxford some years ago felt that the contemporary religious situation was like a house divided against itself "[91]. But in this situation no one can be certain what is revealed and what is not revealed. " We cannot be sure that Christianity is a revealed religion, when no one seems to konw what is revealed or perhaps everybody seems to know that his own version of faith is the true revelation and everything else is a deadly error "[92]. Thus it seems that Radhakrishnan came to the conclusion from his experiences in England that so long as we set forth a doctrine dogmatically, religious rivalries and persecutions were bound to thrive. In his third Beatty Memorial Lecture at McGill University he declares: "We shall have heresies and persecution of heresies so long as we have a sacred doctrine and an authorized body of interpreters. If dogmas are the expression of final and infallible truth we cannot escape from doctrinal controversies and inquisitorial methods. During the early centuries

---

[86] MST, p. 27.
[87] *Fragments,* p. 22. Cf. also EWS, p. 123.
[88] Ibid., p. 23.
[89] Cf. Ibid.
[90] Cf. OSW, February 1956 - February 1957, p. 265.
[91] OSW, October 1952 - January 1956, p. 227.
[92] ERWTh, pp. 263-264.
[93] EWS, p. 112.

of Christianity, seven Councils were held to define the true doctrine and pronounce against heresies " [93]. But so long as the religious rivalries continued, it would be impossible to ward off the growing materialism [94]. A fellowship of religions, discarding the dogmas and authorities, and emphasising only the experiential aspect might have appeared to him as the only way towards religious progress.

---

[94] Cf. OSW, October 1952 - January 1956, p. 227.

II

THE DIVINE IN MAN

A system well founded on sound philosophy will stand the test of time. Radhakrishnan is well aware of this fact. He consciously and laboriously works out a metaphysical basis for his religious views. "Our deepest convictions", says Radhakrishnan, "require to be vindicated by reason. It is the only way by which we can have a sure foundation for our beliefs"[1]. As long as reasoning has an appeal to the mind, philosophy can support religion. "Metaphysics is not the enemy of faith. It alone can restore to men the spiritual wholeness which they seek to attain but fail to do. It is metaphysical effort that gives dignity to the human species. No culture can last unless it supports this effort"[2]. Not everything that man believes can pass for a living faith. For we find that in a man's religious experience there could be absurdities mixed with good elements. Faith must be reasonable if it is to find meaningful acceptance from man. "The faith has to be sustained by metaphysical knowledge. We have to think out the metaphysical presuppositions and attain personal experience of the religious *apriori* from which all living faith starts. We need intellectual effort and spiritual apprehension, metaphysics and religion. Only reasoned faith can give coherence to life and thought"[3].

Therefore it is important for our purpose to see Radhakrishnan's metaphysical basis of religion. We will examine further his concepts of God and man. In this chapter we consider the following points: 1) Radhakrishnan's Metaphysical Basis of Religion; 2) Brahman the Absolute; 3) Man; and 4) God-Men.

---

[1] OSW, July 1959 - May 1962, p. 233.
[2] Ibid., p. 399.
[3] Ibid., 228. (These sentences are repeated in RCW, pp. 71-72); OSW, May 1962 - May 1964, p. 124.

1) Radhakrishnan's Metaphysical Basis of Religion

Metaphysics, of course, is the high-way to the Absolute transcending the world. In St Thomas this starts from the world and sense-data. But in Radhakrishnan it starts from self and spiritual experience [4]. Commenting on Dr Albert Schweitzer's interpretation of Śankara's *māyā* he says: " Religious experience, by its affirmation that the basic fact in the universe is spiritual, implies that the world of sound and sense is not final. All existence finds its source and support in a supreme reality whose nature is spirit. The visible world is the symbol of a more real world. It is the reflection of a spiritual universe which gives to it its life and significance " [5]. And again: " Religious consciousness bears testimony to the reality of some thing behind the visible, a haunting beyond, which both attracts and disturbs, in the light of which the world of change is said to be unreal " [6].

Then, what is the status of this world? Is it a mere phantom or an illusion? Radhakrishnan categorically rejects such a view. He even reinterprets Śankara, " so as to save the world and give it real meaning " [7].

> " Śankara who is rightly credited with the systematic formulation of the doctrine of *māyā,* tells us that the highest reality is unchangeable, and therefore that changing existence such as human history has not ultimate reality (*pāramārthika sattā*). He warns us, however, against the temptation to regard what is not completely real as utterly illusory. The world has empirical being (*vyāvahārika sattā*) which is quite different from illusory existence (*prāthibhāsika sattā*). Human experience is neither ultimately real nor completely illusory. Simply because the world of experience is not the perfect form of reality, it does not follow that it is a delusion without any significance. The world is not a phantom, though it is not real " [8].

A similar interpretation of the mind of Śankara is seen also in *The Hindu View of Life*. " Śankara ", says Radhakrishnan,

---

[4] Indian Philosophy, in general, starts from the ' inner world ' (Cf. *A Source Book*, p. xxii).

[5] ERWTh., pp. 84-85.

[6] Ibid., p. 85.

[7] R. C., p. 800.

[8] ERWTh., p. 86.

"does not assert an identity between God and the world but only denies the independence of the world ... When Śaṅkara denies the reality of effects, he qualifies his denial by some such phrase as 'independent of the cause' or 'independent of God'"[9].

So for Radhakrishnan the empirical world is between being and non-being[10]. It has only a "dependent and derived"[11] or relative reality[12]. In other words Radhakrishnan distinguishes two orders of reality: 1) Order of the spirit or the real in which everything is united to Being as one; and 2) order of *māyā* or empirical order, where we find multiplicity. It has no absolute validity, only empirical[13]. And what is less than that or illusory is absolutely nothing.

Accordingly the problem of the one and the many is thus explained.

> "If our feeble minds are to form any conception of the inconcievable beginning of things, we may think of the cosmos as arising from a selfdivision of the Absolute. In the undivided Absolute, time is not, and there is no history. God negates himself in order that there may be a world. The sundering of the Absolute into the personal God and object is creation's dawn. The object is regarded as the void, the mere framework of space-time"[14].

But if we start from the cosmic end Radhakrishnan admits that it is true to say 'in the beginning was the Logos', the personal

---

[9] HVL, p. 48.

[10] CHARLES A. MOORE, *Metaphysics and Ethics in Radhakrishnan's Philosophy*, in PhSR, p. 302.

[11] MST., pp. 13-14.

[12] Cf. Ind. Ph., II, p. 621 ff; HVL, p. 50; ERWTh, P. 27 ff, 47, 88, 90, 94 f, 100; R. S, p. 104; BG, p. 38; IC, p. 123; MST, p. 14; R. C, 801-802; OSW, October 1952 - January 1956, pp. 261-262; OSW, October 1952 - February 1959, p. 145; Almost all the critics of Radhakrishnan agree that he has departed from Śaṅkara. Cf. SAMARTHA, *Introduction to Radhakrishnan: The Man and His Thought* (New Delhi 1964) 48-49; ROBERT W. BROWNING, *Reason and Types of Intuition in Radhakrishnan's Philosophy*, in PhSR, p. 202; SWAMI AGEHANANDA BHARATI, *Radhakrishnan and the Other Vedanta*, in PhSR, p. 473; LAWRENCE HYDE, *Radhakrishnan's Contribution to Universal Religion*, in PhSR, p. 378; Radhakrishnan seems to echo an Oxford semi-Hegelian, F. H. Bradley, who said: « The positive relation of every appearance as an adjective to Reality and the presence of Reality among its appearances in different degrees and with values — this double truth we have found to be the centre of philosophy » (*Appearance and Reality*, London 1893, 500).

[13] Cf. ERWTh, p. 32.

[14] Cf. Ibid., p. 125.

creator [15]. But this dualism of God and matter, good and evil,
eternity and time, is not ultimate ... It is subordinate to a fundamental monism [16]. Two things may be derived from the above
statement : 1) the self-discrepant character of the multiplicity
shows only that it is an appearance and not ultimately real. The
world has an empirical reality, which is negated when perfect insight or intuition of the oneness of all is attained [17]. 2) The
Absolute is not the creator of the world. God the creator facing
nothingness is the first act and the rest of creation is secondary.
This God and non-being are the two principles that ' interact and
supplement one another '. " Creativeness is out of the freedom
of being; ... not-self is the mother who generates " [18]. So begins
multiplicity which is not final but subordinate to the ultimate oneness of being. Even to man is given such a position so as not
to hurt this fundamental monism. Radhakrishnan readily accepts
the central thesis in Śaṅkara's *Advaita,* which is " the non-difference
between the individual self and Brahman " [19].

Radhakrishnan believes that the natural outcome of a neutral
and unprejudiced philosophy can only be monistic idealism. " The
ultimate oneness of things is what the Hindu is required to remember every moment of his life " [20]. Every other form of philosophy must be subordinated to absolute monism. " Absolute
monism is therefore the completion of dualism with which the devotional consciousness starts " [21]. In his " Introductory Essay " to his
edition of *The Bhagavadgītā,* he holds, against the general trend
of interpretation, that " *The Gītā* does not uphold a metaphysical
dualism; for the principle of non-being is dependent on being " [22].
This monistic belief of Radhakrishnan can be seen in all his
published works.

---

[15] Radhakrishnan's use of *Logos* is a bit confusing. It seems that he
is equating Īśvara of Hinduism and the God of Western absolutists with
the Johannine concept of *Logos.* But the God of whom Radhakrishnan
speaks will be ultimately « dissolved in the Absolute » (PhRT, p. 35), while
the *Logos* of St John is co-eternal with the Father. The concept of *Logos*
is original with John (Cf. JOHN L. McKENZIE, *Dictionary of the Bible,*
London-Dublin, 1966, p. 941). So the comparison is inadmissible.

[16] ERWTh, p. 126.
[17] Ibid., p. 87.
[18] Ibid., pp. 126-127.
[19] Ibid., p. 87.
[20] PhRT, p. 16.
[21] Ind. Ph, I, 565.
[22] BG, p. 39.

One may safely say that in metaphysics Radhakrishnan is an Advaitin [23], although some doubt if he is quite fair to Śaṅkara [24].

It is from this monistic idealism that Radhakrishnan begins his religious quest and arrives at " Religious idealism " [25].

2) BRAHMAN THE ABSOLUTE

The quest for the Ultimate Reality in the Hindu tradition goes back to Vedic times [26]. In the Upanishads the Ultimate Reality is universally accepted to be Brahman or the Absolute [27]. Brahman is *satyasya satyam,* the Real of the real, the source of all existing things [28]. On this Upanishadic notion of Brahman, Śaṅkara built his Absolutism. The really real is one, " the world is illusory while the soul is not distinct from Brahman " [29].

Radhakrishnan's idea of the Absolute or Brahman is essentially Upanishadic and traditional and he belongs to the Advaita School. But he weighs well Śaṅkara's monistic concept of Brahman against modern idealism, and reinterprets Śaṅkara so as to save Śaṅkara's absolutism and world's reality [30], taking into account the criticism made against Śaṅkara, and the counter criticism by his followers.

For Radhakrishnan, the Absolute is the ultimate, the supracosmic, spaceless, timeless Reality, which supports this cosmic manifestation in space and time [31]. It is the impersonal [32] uncaused

---

[23] Cf. W. R. INGE, L. P. JACKS *et al.*, (ed.), *Radhakrihsnan; Comparative Studies in Philosophy, Presented in Honour of His Sixtieth Birthday* (London 1951) Introduction (page numbers are not given).

[24] Cf. EDGAR SHEFFIELD BRIGHTMAN, *Radhakrishnan and Mysticism,* in PhSR, p. 411.

[25] OSW, July 1959 - May 1962, p. 104.

[26] Cf. M. DHAVAMONY, *Indian Philosophy*: New Catholic Encyclopedia VII (New York 1967) 458; *A Source Book*, pp. 4f. 17.

[27] « The religion of the Upanishads centres round the eternal, the immortal, the really real, that goes beyond the individual life which leads to death » (M. DHAVAMONY, *Hinduism and Christianity, The Christian Encounter*: 4, *in Theology* LXX (1967) 157.

[28] Cf. *Bṛhad-āraṇyaka Upanishad,* II.I.20; *Taittirīya Upanishad,* III, I.I.

[29] M. DHAVAMONY, *Hinduism and Christianity,* art. cit. p. 158.

[30] Cf. R. C. p. 800.

[31] Cf. *Fragments,* pp. 39-41.

[32] Ind. Ph. II, p. 536.

cause, the unmoved mover [33]. It is infinitely real, absolutely self sufficient and purely spiritual [34]. It is pure act and prime Being [35].

i) *Nirguna Brahman*

Following the Upanishads and Śaṅkara, Radhakrishnan recognizes two aspects of Brahman: nirguna (without qualities) and saguna (with qualities), which are said to be respectively absolute and relative ways of expressing the same reality [36].

About the nirguna Brahman nothing can be said. He can only be negatively described, because the "self is silence" [37]. "In austerity of silence" we describe the nirguna Brahman at best [38]. Repeated *neti, neti* (not so, not so) is the best description of Brahman without qualities, the Absolute [39]. "To call it being is wrong, because only concrete things are. To call it non-being is equally wrong. It is best to avoid all descriptions of it. Thought is dualistic in its functions, and what is, is non-dual or advaita" [40]. Radhakrishnan points out that even *The Bhagavadgītā* is of this view, which calls the Absolute "unmanifest, unthinkable and unchanging" [41], and "neither existent, nor non-existent" [42]. This does not mean that the Absolute or Brahman is a blank chasm or an abyss of nothingness. "It means only that the Absolute is all-inclusive and nothing exists outside it" [43]. When, for example, "personality is denied to Him, it is only in the interest of super-personality" [44].

---

[33] Cf. BG, 27; IVL, 272.

[34] Ind. Ph. I, 33, 175-176, 184; PhRT, 16; IVL, 41.

[35] Cf. *Fragments*, 22, 39-40.

[36] HVL, 35; OSW, July 1959 - may 1962, p. 232; Cf. *Brhad-āranyaka Upanishad*, II.3. 1f.

[37] Pr. Ups, p. 67; Cf. *Brhad-āranyaka Upanishad*, II.3.6; III, 8.8; III. 9.26; IV.2.4; IV.4.22; IV.5.15; *Kena Upanishad*, I.3; Ind. Ph, I, p. 657.

[38] BG, p. 21.

[39] HVL, 20-21; Ind. Ph., I, p. 663f, EWS, p. 25.

[40] Ibid.

[41] BG, p. 22; Cf. *The Bhagavadgītā*, II, 25; OSW, Oct. 1952 - Jan. 1956, p. 188.

[42] Ibid; Cf. *The Bhagavadgītā*, XIII, 12; Cf. also XIII, 15-17.

[43] Pr. Ups, p. 68; Cf. *The Brahma Sūtra*, p. 126.

[44] ERWTh, 292. Cf. M. DHAVAMONY, *Hinduism and Christianity*, art. cit., p. 159. SAMARTHA, *Introduction to Radhakrishnan: The Man and His Thought*, p. 41

ii) *The Saguna Brahman*

Nirguna Brahman cast through the moulds of logic is saguna Brahman [45]. He is not " the mere self-projection of the yearning spirit or a fleeting air-buble. The gleaming ideal is the way in which the everlasting real appears to our mind " [46]. If Nirguna is " Being-in-repose, Saguna is Being-in-activity. The transition from one to another is through divine freedom " [47]. It is the freedom of Saguna or God that makes it possible for him to actualize multiplicity and create this world. " As to why there is the realization of this possibility " Radhakrishnan's answer is : It is māyā, or a mystery which we have to accept reverently [48].

This nirguna-saguna distinction is ultimately subordinated to the fundamental monism or non-dualism. The personal God (the Saguna) will be " dissolved in the Absolute " [49]. " The two are one " [50] and the distinction is only ' logical ' [51], which comes from our " stand point " [52] and " emphasis " [53]. Therefore the saguna Brahman or God is practically one with the Nirguna or the Absolute. In other words, God is the Absolute from the point of view of one specific possibility which has become actualized [54].

In the discussion on God and the Absolute, Radhakrishnan leaves many perplexities unexplained in many of his books. Sometimes he teaches the twofold distinction of saguna and nirguna, of Isvara and Brahman, of God and Godhead, of God and Absolute in the Ultimate Reality. But in other places he points out that there is a fourfold distinction in the Supreme : 1) Brahman, the transcendental universal being anterior to any concrete reality; 2) *Iśvara*, the causal principle of all differentiation; 3) *Hiranya-garbha*, the innermost essence of the world; and 4) *virat*, the ma-

---

[45] Cf. Ind. Ph, II, p. 540.

[46] Ibid. p. 540.

[47] SAMARTHA, S. J., *Introduction to Radhakrishnan: The Man and His Thought*, p. 38.

[48] Cf. ERWTh, p. 90; BG, p. 38; Ind. Ph, I, pp. 36, 184.

[49] PhRT, p. 35; Cf. IVL, p. 269; MST, p. 33.

[50] IVL, p. 86; Cf. HVL, p. 23.

[51] R. C., p. 796.

[52] IVL, p. 84.

[53] HVL, p. 24.

[54] IVL, p. 272. For more about the distinction between God and the Absolute Cf. RR, 443 f; Ind. Ph., I, 68, 184; SM, 282; RADHAKRISHNAN et al., (ed.), *The Cultural Heritage of India*, 2nd ed. I (Calcutta, 1958) xxix, xxxii; MST, 32-33; ERWTh., 30, 92; *Fragments*, 39-40; R. C, 796-797; RF, 89; Pr. Ups, 63; RCW, 121.

nifest world [55]. These are said to bring about the different aspects of the Supreme and the distinction is maintained logical. Yet at other times Radhakrishnan enunciates a threefold distinction: 1) Brahman, or the transcendent Supreme reality; 2) *Paramātma,* the deepest being of man's self; and 3) *Bhagavan,* the Divine Lord of this universe [56]. With these distinctions Radhakrishnan is not departing from his monistic idealism. Often he reaffirms that the underlying reality is one.

The reconciliation of God and the Absolute is a problem for all idealists. Many like Schelling, Fechner, James and Montague think that the solution is through sheer identity of God and the Absolute. But Radhakrishnan thinks that the problem can be settled only by means of the above explained distinction [57].

From what has been said, two main aspects of Brahman emerge: 1) Brahman the Absolute is transcendent; and 2) Brahman is also immanent. We will treat both these aspects separately, because they have a direct bearing on Radhakrishnan's views on organized religions.

a) *The Transcendent Absolute*

As to why the Absolute is described in negative term, Radhakrishnan answers:

> " The negative account is intended to express the soul's sense
> of transcendence of God, the ' wholly other ', of whom naught
> may be predicated save in negations, and not to deprive God
> of his positive being ... When we call nothing we mean that
> it is nothing which created beings can conceive or name and
> not that it is nothing absolutely " [58].

The utterances of Radhakrishnan on the transcendence of the Absolute remind us of the Barthian concept of the Transcendence of God. Radhakrishnan actually quotes Barth with approval, when he explains the transcendent aspect of the Absolute in *Eastern Religions and Western Thought* [59]. " The negative descriptions of

---

[55] Cf. Pr. Ups, 39-40, 70-72; *The Brahma Sūtra,* 118-135; Ind. Ph., I, pp. 171-172; *Fragments,* 40ff.

[56] Cf. *The Brahma Sūtra,* pp. 49, 460; OSW, May 1962 - May 1964, pp. 157, 161, 162, 178, 211-212; *Great Indians,* p. 80.

[57] *Fragments,* p. 64.

[58] IVL, p. 80; Cf. *The Cultural Heritage of India,* I, *op. cit.,* p. XXIII.

[59] In other places Radhakrishnan is a staunch critic of Barth. Cf. ERWTh., pp. 303, 341-343; *The Brahma Sūtra,* pp. 150, 236; RCW, p. 72; OSW, July 1959 - May 1962, p. 228 etc.

the Supreme ", says Radhakrishnan, " and the doctrine of *maya* ...
are employed to denote the distance between time and eternity,
between appearance and reality. The passionate antithesis between
the real and the unreal, the true and the false, gives the urgency
to the religious effort. God is the unknown, the absolutely different,
the Beyond who cannot be comprehended by our concepts or recognized by our understanding. (Here Radhakrishnan quotes Karl
Barth) ' God is ever transcendent to man, new, remote, foreign,
surpassing, never in man's sphere, never man's possession : who so
says God says miracle " [60]. Because the Absolute is the " wholly
other " [61], the " totally other " [62], it is not perceived by the categories
of reason [63]. " There is an incomprehensible other-ness of God
as the source of all " [64]. Human concepts can in no way be applied
to the Absolute. For, " The Supreme is not an object but the
absolute subject, and we cannot apprehend it by either sense perception or logical inference " [65]; and also because " The Absolute is
neither existent nor non-existent, nor both existent and non-existent, nor different from both non-existence and existence " [66].
Therefore about the Ultimate Reality we can say nothing. Even
the name ' One ' is not apt, " since oneness is an idea derived from
worldly experience ... We can only speak of It as the non-dual,
advaita that which is known when all dualties are resolved in the
Supreme Identity " [67]. That is why the seers indulge in negative
accounts and predicate to It " contradictory attributes " [68] which
only affirms the " positivity of Being " [69].

b) *The Immanent God*

Is the transcendent Absolute utterly transcendent to man's self
also? Is He then like a Sultan in the sky, residing in a remote

---

[60] ERWTh., pp. 298-299; Cf. OSW, July 1959. - May 1962, p. 230.

[61] IVL, p. 80.

[62] ERWTh., p. 299.

[63] *The Cultural Heritage, of India,* p. XXVIII, XXIX; Cf. also *The Brahma Sūtra,* pp. 118, 120.

[64] *The Brahma Sūtra,* p. 121.

[65] *Fragments,* p. 61; The idea is Upanishadic. Cf. *Taittirīya Upanishad,* II, 4; *Kena Upanishad,* I, 3; *Katha Upanishad,* I, 2.7; Cf. also *A Source Book,* p. 38.

[66] Ind. Ph , I, 663 f; Cf. HVL, 20-21; IVL, 84; BG, 21; SM, 285; *The Brahma Sūtra,* p. 122.

[67] BG, p. 21.

[68] Ibid., pp. 21-22.

[69] Pr. Ups, p. 68

home [70]? Radhakrishnan does not consider it so. " If the real
were utterly transcendent to the self of man, it would be impossible for us to apprehend even dimly its presence. We would
not be able to say even that it is ' wholly other ' " [71]. This citation from Radhakrishnan is significant. It contains implicitly an
argument for the immanence of God in man. Radhakrishnan proposes it explicitly in his *Introduction* to *The Principle Upanishads* :
" The wish to know the real implies that we know it to some
extent. If we do not know anything about it, we cannot even
say that it is and that we wish to know it ... The desire for God,
the feeling that we are in a state of exile, implies the reality of
God in us " [72].

Another argument for the divine immanence in man, which
Radhakrishnan believes to be irrefutable and infallible, universally
valid and scientifically provable, is drawn from the ' fact ' of religious experience, which " is not self-sufficient " [73]. " Religious
experience is the evidence for the Divine. In our inspired moments
we have the feeling that there is a greater reality within us, though
we cannot tell what it is. From the movements that stir in us
and the utterances that issue from us, we perceive the power, not
ourselves, that moves us. Religious experience is by no means
subjective ... Prayer is the witness to the spirit of the transcendent
divine immanent in the spirit of man " [74]. The Supreme is at
once transcendent and immanent. " Though unspeakable in its
transcendence, the Supreme is yet the most inward part of our
being " [75].

As to the how of the origin of this double aspect regarding
the Absolute, Radhakrishnan says :

> " The experience of a pure and unitary consciousness in a
> world divided gives rise to the twofold conception of the
> Absolute as pure Transcendent Being lifted above all relati-
> vities, and the Free Active God functioning in the world.
> Some emphasize the transcendent aspect, the fullness of being,
> the sublime presence, the sovereignly subsistent ' other ',

---

[70] Cf. OSW, May 1962 - May 1964, p. 140; HVL, p. 20.

[71] IVL, p. 81.

[72] Pr. Ups, p. 53. Cf. also IVL, p. 137; *The Brahma Sūtra,* p. 176.

[73] RCW, p. 68.

[74] Pr. Ups, p. 53. « If the Spirit were not in us, we would not have
thrilled with joy when face to face with the great works of art, science
or life » (IVL, p. 163).

[75] *The Cultural Heritage of India,* I, pp. xxix-xxx.

above all images and thought; others the immanent aspect, the fullness of life, the living personal God of love who made the world, gave us freedom and wishes us to participate in the riches of life " [76].

About the immanence of God in man one thing is marked out with a particular emphasis. The Supreme is not in there in the heart of man like a swallowed piece of gold, with a nature utterly other than ours.

> " *The consubstantiality* [77] of the spirit in man and God is the conviction *fundamental* [77] to all spiritual wisdom. It is not a matter of inference only. In the spiritual experience itself, the barriers between the self and the ultimate reality drop away. In the moment of its highest insight, the self becomes aware not only of its own existence but of the existence of an omnipresent spirit of which it is, as it were, a focussing ... The great text of the Upanishad affirms it — *Tat tvam asi* (That art Thou) [78]. It is a simple statement of an experienced fact " [79].

Radhakrishnan believes that this doctrine is a universal teaching and adduces in support many texts from various scriptures [80].

What precisely is the meaning of that ' consubstantiality ' and ' *Tat tvam asi* '? They mean that the " Supreme Reality is not out there but is one with our deepest self. Brahman is Atman, the Universal Spirit " [81]; that the " two are co-related " [82]. " He is there dwelling in the innermost depths of each human heart " [83]. " That person who is seen in the eye, He is atman, that is Brahman " [84]. There is a polarity here, a contrast. " Here is the divine in every human being and, at the same time, because we are lost in the glamour of the world, in the pursuit of the finite

---

[76] *Fragments,* pp. 63-64.

[77] Italics mine.

[78] *Chāndogya Upanishad,* VI.8.7.

[79] IVL, p. 81.

[80] Cf. IVL, pp. 81-82; RF, pp. 148-149; RCW, pp. 94-95. The oft adduced texts are *Genesis,* 1:27; *Proverbs,* 20:27; I Cor., 3:16; Rom., 5:5; St AGUSTINE, *Confessions,* III, II; VII, 10 etc.

[81] *The Brahma Sūtra,* p. 122.

[82] RCW, p. 103.

[83] OSW, May 1962 - May 1964, p. 140.

[84] Pr. Ups., p. 77.

goods which can never satisfy the infinite in man, we find that we
are unable to discover what is there " [85].

Therefore the transcendence of God and His immanence are
two co-related, simultaneous aspects of a single reality. Moreover,
" transcendence is, the only means of reaching the soul's deeper
stratum. The power to transcend is the property of the subject
' I '. It always goes beyond the ' me ' " [86].

This immanence of the transcendent, this ' consubstantiality '
of the ' wholly other ' with the inner essence of man is the cornerstone of Radhakrishnan's theology. One may even dare say
that his views on religion are a series of logical derivations from
this first principle, expressed in a masterly, imposing prose. So
far we have explained the consubstantiality between man and God
from the point of view of God, now we proceed to consider the
same from the point of view of man.

3) MAN

When Shakespeare wrote on man, the greatest eulogy flowed
from his gracious pen [87]. When Radhakrishnan speaks about
man his whole person swells with the greatest excitement and
repeats prophetic promises and messianic assurances.

For Radhakrishnan man is not merely a ' rational animal ',
although animality is therein to be found and rationality also.
" The free individual is a child of God as well as the product of
non-being from out of which God creates the world " [88]. The
transcendent and empirical orders are closely related in him [89], and
he belongs to both [90]. Man's body, life and mind, or all that make
him a rational animal, belong to the empirical order. But there
is something more than that, a non-natural element in man [91]. Man

---

[85] OSW, May 1962 - May 1964, p. 140; Cf. Pr. Ups, XI, *Ultimate
Reality: Ātman,* pp. 73-76; XII, *Brahman as Ātman,* pp. 77-78.

[86] *The Brahma Sūtra,* p. 124. « Because the Absolute is not an object
as opposed to a subject, the Upanishads characterize it as ' not this, nor
that ' » (M. DHAVAMONY, *Hinduism and Christianity, op. cit.,* p. 159).

[87] « How noble in reason! How infinite in faculty! In form and
movement how express and admirable! In action how like an angel! In
apprehension how like a God! The beauty of the world! The paragon of
animals! » *Hamlet,* II, ii, 315 ff.

[88] ERWTh, p. 127. Cf. also EWR, p. 82.

[89] BG, p. 13.

[90] ERWTh., p. 97.

[91] OSW, May 1962 - May 1964, p. 136.

is not fully defined merely by reference to body and mind. In the complex of human personality there is an element which uses both and yet is neither " [92]. It is not the ordinary, superficial, empirical self, which is " the problem for psychology " [93]; nor is it an " abstract form of selfhood " [94]. " While the empirical self is always co-related with a not-self, the universal self includes all and has nothing outside to limit it " [95].

In our perverse, pensive mood we may imagine that the universe is chaotic and wicked, loveless and thankless [96]. The day of life sinks inevitably into the night of death [97]. Still something that is in the depths of human soul gives man confidence and a passion for love, justice and righteousness [98], inspires and informs the human soul, animates and enlivens man's mind and life [99].

Radhakrishnan thinks that this third element in man, the most human and essential of all, is often neglected or excluded, as is the supernatural by Westerners. So to reverse the trend of thought, Radhakrishnan is never tired of emphasizing this third element as the basis of life, as the primary element in man. But what is it?

Radhakrishnan calls it sometimes ' *ātman* ', sometimes ' self ', at other times the ' spirit in man ', yet at other times ' the divine in man ' and the ' light in man '.

Are all these identical, or distinct? The definition of *ātman* makes it clear that *ātman* itself is the self. " Ātman is what remains when everything that is not self is eliminated " [100]. Moreover Radhakrishnan sometimes gives the translation of *ātman* as self [101]. Many other times he uses one for the other with an evidently identical sense [102].

---

[92] OSW October 1952 - February 1959, pp. 365-366.

[93] IVL, p. 213.

[94] Ibid., p. 215.

[95] Ibid., p. 215; Cf. also pp. 212, 217-218; ERWTh., 27, 37; *The Cultural Heritage of India*, I, p. xxvii.

[96] GB, p. 51.

[97] *Fragments*, p. 50.

[98] IVL, 38.

[99] OSW, May 1962 - May 1964, p. 158.

[100] Pr. Ups, p. 73.

[101] Cf. *The Brahma Sūtra*, pp. 286, 289, 319, 331; GB, p. 37; *Brhadāranyaka Up*. IV, 5.15 as translated in *A Source Book*.

[102] Cf. *The Brahma Sūtra*, pp. 122, 147, 205, 232; *A Source Book*, p. 507.

The spirit in man for Radhakrishnan is one and the same thing as the true self. He says that " Self " and " self " are better than " Soul " and " soul " " to denote respectively the ultimate spiritual reality and the individual spiritual essence in man " [103]. In his *Religion in a Changing World* Radhakrishnan calls the self " an identity of spiritual being " [104]. Moreover he uses sometimes ' self ' for ' the spirit in man ' and sometimes the other way round.

What is the relation between the " divine in man and the " spirit in man " according to Radhakrishnan? For him what is spiritual is divine [105] — our rational faculties are not spiritual in that sense. He says: " self denotes *Brahman* and not unintelligent matter or individual soul " [106]. And again " there is a vital unity of soul and body in man. The real dualism is between spirit and nature " [107]. So the rational is clearly distinguished from the spiritual. On the other hand the spiritual in man is identified with the divine in man. For Radhakrishnan says that the " spirit in man " is the " spirit of God in him ", " the indwelling light " [108]. Again " the spiritual nature of man " is said to be " the essential divinity of the human soul " [109]. When Radhakrishnan explained what he means by " the Divine ", he makes it sufficiently clear that for him the self, the spirit and the divine are synonyms [110].

Now let us examine what precisely this essential element in man means for Radhakrishnan. He says it should not be confused with our body, life, mind or intellect [111]. It is said to be something immortal [112] and unchangeable [113]. It is the basic element in man [114]. It is the divine element at the rock-bottom of man's outer self [115]. So Radhakrishnan repeats very often that the divine is within us. " Whether we like it or not, whether we

---

[103] *A Source Book,* p. ix f.

[104] RCW, p. 101.

[105] Cf. *The Brahma Sūtra,* pp. 103, 143; OSW, July 1959 - May 1962, p. 199; OSW, May 1962 - May 1964, p. 145.

[106] *The Brahma Sūtra,* p. 286.

[107] BG, p. 46; Cf. also RCW, 97; ERWTh., p. 2, 97; OSW, July 1959 - May 1962, pp. 112, 142; OSW, May 1962 - May 1964, p. 179.

[108] OSW, may 1962 - May 1964, p. 145.

[109] Ibid., p. 375.

[110] OSW, July 1959 - May 1962, pp. 198-199.

[111] Pr. Ups, p. 73.

[112] Ibid., ERWTh., 26. This doctrine is from *Katha Upanishad.* Cf. II, 18-20, 22 f.

[113] ERWTh., p. 26.

[114] Ibid., p. 77; RCW, p. 136.

[115] Ibid., p. 49.

know it or not, the Divine is in us, and the end of man consists
in attaining union with the Divine "[116]. This very same doctrine
is enunciated sometimes in a panentheistic way [117], i. e. by saying
that our true self is a part of God. "The individual self is a
portion of the Lord, a real, not imaginary form of the Supreme,
a limited manifestation of God", says Radhakrishnan in his *Introductory Essay* to his edition of *The Bhagavadgītā* [118]. The
same idea can be seen in several of his other works [119]. And some
times, and this is very important, he reduces the difference between God and the divine element in man practically to nothing.
He says that the divine element in man is the Absolute "imprisoned "[120], or "individualized "[121]. "Man is but the localized expression of God "[122]. Thus Radhakrishnan identifies the true self
of man with Brahman the Absolute in their true reality. He says:
"We always say the *mahavakyas* are there: I am Divine; *tat tvam
asi* — that thou art; the self is divine "[123]. Still more clearly:
"The deepest reality is the inmost being of man. *Brahman is
Atman* "[124].

  Reasons in Favour.

  i) If God is not found in each soul, He is unfindable [125],
just as we cannot squeeze "blood from a stone "[126].

---

[116] OSW, October 1952 - February 1959, p. 285. The same sentence is
repeated n another of his speeches, in the Broadcast Address, Columbia
University in October 1954. Cf. Ibid., p. 290. Radhakrishnan untiringly
repeats that there is divine in man. Cf. HH, 6; HVL, pp. 54-55, 64; ERWTh.,
pp. 102, 196, 301, 303, FF, pp. 6, 17-18, 67, 96, 169; FS, 7; OSW, Oct. 1952
- Jan. 1956, pp. 202-203; OSW, Oct. 1952 - Febr. 1959, pp. 240, 280-81,
410; OSW, July 1959 - May 1962; pp. 129, 286; OSW, May 1962 - May
1964, pp. 73, 74, 121, 123, 130, 131, 136; 139, 140, 142, 145-148, 149; BG,
27; Pr. Ups., 53, 57, 77; EWS, p. 28.
[117] When Pantheism says 'all is God', Panentheism says « all-in-God »
(Cf. ZACHARIAS, *An Outline of Hinduism* (Alwaye 1956) 86-87, n. 1.
[118] BG, p. 45; EWS, pp. 26, 72, 77.
[119] Ind. Ph. II, p. 594; R. C, 805; FF, 111; OSW, October 1952 -
Jan. 1956, pp. 206, 243; OSW, Octo. 1952 - Febr. 1959, p. 98; OSW, May
1962 - May 1964, p. 400.
[120] RF, 139.
[121] *A Source Book*, p. 507.
[122] PhRT, p. 70.
[123] OSW, May 1962 - May 1964, p. 192.
[124] FS, p. 13; Cf. Ind. Ph., I, p. 194; IC, p. 94; GB, 37; RF, 148;
BG, 37, 227; Pr. Ups, p. 73 ff; *A Source Book*, p. 507; *The Brahma Sūtra*,
p. 103; Cf. Also *Mundaka Up.* II, 1.
[125] ERWTh., p. 295.
[126] Ibid., p. 83; Cf. RF, 150.

ii) There is a God-consciousness in man which is " as much an original endowment of human beings as self-consciousness " [127]. Even the " sense of God-forsakenness is itself the witness to the presense of the Divine " [128].

iii) Religious experience and mystical ecstacy are possible because the divine is in man [129].

iv) It is taught by great prophets and various scriptures [130].

v) To deny the divine in man would be to " underrate the humanity of Jesus " [131]. " When Christ says, ' I and my Father are One ', he makes out an *identification between the individual human soul and the Supreme Reality*" [132].

But a question occurs. Why at present do we not see ourselves as ' divines ' moving about? Radhakrishnan's answer to such a question is one with that of absolutistic Hinduism. The answer of Hinduism can be given succinctly as follows:

> " Deluded by *avidyā*, the individual soul (*jiva*) identifies itself with the mind-body composite and considers itself to belong to the world of rebirth, whereas, in reality, it is identical with Brahman. With the removal of *avidyā* through jñāna (intuitive knowledge), the soul gets freed from its individuality and realizes its Brahmanhood " [133].

Radhakrishnan seems to accept this view. He says: " Though the real nature of the selves is *Brahman*, so long as they are surrounded by *avidyā*, they do not realize their real nature " [134]. We may put it in another way. In the order of nature, man keeps up his separate individuality; in the order of spirit, the divine has taken hold of him, remoulding his personality and identifying with it [135]. But Radhakrishnan confesses that " If we ask the reason why there is *avidyā*, or *māyā* bringing about a fall from *vidyā* or from being, the question cannot be answered " [136].

---

[127] RF, p. 103; Cf. IVL, p. 81, 137; FS, pp. 3-4.

[128] RF, p. 99.

[129] RF, 150; Pr. Ups, pp. 53, 57.

[130] Cf. ERWTh., pp. 84, 99; IVL, p. 81; OWS, July 1959 - May 1962, pp. 182, 198, 205, 236; OSW, May 1962 - May 1964, p. 375; RCW, p. 180.

[131] ERWTh., p. 303.

[132] OSW, May 1962 - May 1964, p. 159 (italics mine).

[133] M. DHAVAMONY, *Hinduism and Christianity, art. cit.*, p. 159; Cf. also *Indian Philosophy, art. cit.*, p. 460.

[134] *The Brahma Sūtra*, p. 143. Cf. also pp. 129, 232, 276; ERWTh, pp. 28, 87; Pr. Ups, pp. 88-90; Ind. Ph, I, pp. 36-37.

[135] ERWTh, p. 32.

[136] Ind. Ph, I, 36.

Man is, therefore, essentially spiritual or divine, that is, the most truly human nature is divine. " There is only one ideal for man, to make himself profoundly human, perfectly human ... The whole man, the complete man is the ideal man, the divine man " [137].

Consequently, man is not a mere ' rational animal ', but a ' spiritual (divine) rational animal '. Accordingly, Radhakrishnan defines man constitutively " The body, the mind and the spirit — they constitute the trinity — they constitute the human being " [138]. The three-dimensional concept of man with the divine as the chief constitutive factor is very fundamental and central to Radhakrishnan's views on organized religion. He emphasized, therefore, the divine as the primordial element of these three factors. " For the Hindu, the spiritual is the basic element of human nature " [139]. And again, " If there is one doctrine more than another which is characteristic of Hindu thought, it is the belief that there is an interior depth to the human soul, which, in its essence, is uncreated and deathless and absolutely real " [140]. Therefore " man is one psyche, one whole, of which body, mind and spirit are aspects " [141].

There is, however, one text in Radhakrishnan which reads " Man is essentially an intellectual being, though he shares the vital subpersonal life of animals, and is united with the spirit " [142]. It does not seem that Radhakrishnan has changed his mind in this passage. For in the same context in which the above sentence appears he says also that " if he (man) purifies himself he becomes divine " [143]. Therefore, it is not likely that Radhakrishnan uses the word ' essential ' in the above passage in the sense ' most important ' or ' fundamental ', but in the sense ' that which pertains to the essence '.

---

[137] ERWTh, p. 35. Cf. also p. 81; IVL, p. 93; *The Spirit in Man,* pp. 476-477. Swami Vivekananda said: "He is the atheist who does not believe in himself" (CHIDATMANANDA, ed), *The Complete Works of Swami Vivekananda,* 10th ed. II (Calcutta 1963) 301.

[138] OSW, July 1959 - May1962, p. 90; Cf. also OSW, Oct. 1952 - Jan. 1956, p. 95.

[139] ERWTh, p. 77.

[140] Ibid., p. 83. Cf. also pp. 94, 98, 102, 172.

[141] EWR, p. 81. Cf. also BG, p. 46; FS, p. 3; OSW, May 1962 - May 1964, p. 136. For the three elements in man, Cf. IC, p. 62; OSW, Oct. 1952 - Feb. 1959, p. 365; OSW, July 1959 - May 1962, p. 106, 112. OSW, May 1962 - May 1964, p. 179.

[142] ERWTh, p. 130.

[143] Ibid.

4) GOD-MEN

Radhakrishnan shares the view of classical Hinduism that the " world is not a static mechanism " [144]. It is a perpetual flow of events. The wheel of time goes on turning, the ' ever-rolling stream ' goes on running until it reaches fulfilment [145]. There are no upstart events or broken links in this process. Everything is in continuous movement without sharp cleavages [146]. It is not a blind on-going, in the direction in which the head happens to be, without a guiding hand and still less a purpose. For Radhakrishnan, the world has a purpose to fulfil and God's is the hand working in and behind this world process [147].

The world process is evolutionary and progressive. From materiality, life emerged, and from life animal consciousness. It was from animal consciousness that human intelligence came forth [148]. This rising tide of evolution has brought to the forefront the latest species in the universe — man. But man is not the last word on the cosmic process. He himself is still in the making and has to be surpassed [149].

> " Man, as he is, is not to be regarded as the crowning glory of evolution ... When we look at the steady climb of life in the path of evolution, it is presumptuous to assume that man, the latest product, is the last word or the final crowning glory, and with his arrival the steps of evolution have come to a sudden end. If the past is any clue to the future, we cannot regard mankind anything more than a stage in life's progress and a milestone on the path of evolution toward a greater future " [150].

The next stage is not so much in man's physique as in his psyche [151]. Evolution is headed for the spiritual. From mind,

---

[144] RCW, p. 95. Cf. also IVL, p. 190.

[145] *Fragments,* pp. 47-48; RF, 121; OSW, Octo. 1952 - Feb. 1959, p. 90. Cf. *Taittiriya Upanishad,* III, 1; SAMARTHA, *Introduction to Radhakrishnan: The Man and His Thought,* pp. 70-71.

[146] RCW, p. 83.

[147] Cf. HVL, p. 88; IVL, pp. 268-269; *Fragments,* pp. 35-36, 38; BG, p. 43; Pr. Ups, pp. 58-59; OSW, May 1962 - May 1864, p. 160.

[148] OSW, Octo. 1952 - Feb. 1959, p. 374.

[149] Fs, p. 4; ERWTh., p. 34; RCW, j. 60, 95, 154; OSW, July 1959 - May 1962, p. 258. *On Nehru,* p. 17; Pr. Ups, p. 143.

[150] OSW, Oct. 1952 - February 1959, pp. 84, 304.

[151] Cf. *Fragments,* p. 26; RCW, p. 94; OSW, Oct. 1952 - Feb. 1959, p. 304.

spirit must come forth [152]. Man's self at its best is divine. He
is a " potential candidate for the divine status " [153]. The spiritual
or the divine is the not-yet-developed element in man. The " potential " divinity of man can be made actual [154], which is the end
of evolution [155].

With the advent of the spiritual faculties man will have deep
awareness, profound apprehension and integration of character [156],
where being and knowledge will not be divorced from each other [157],
and intuitive experience will be the rule [158]. Not even the most
sanguine imagination can conjecture the greatness of the coming
stage of evolution. In messianic phrases, with prophetic accent
Radhakrishnan assures us that man will be ascending to divine
perfection, realizing his own divinity [159]. In Nietzschean tone he
declares that the " son of man becomes son of God " [160], and calls
him super-man and master of life [161]. Then man will know
" himself to be the immortal spirit, the son of God and is it ...
When the cosmic process results in the revelation of all the sons
of God, when all the Lord's people become prophets, when this
universal incarnation takes place, the great cosmic rebirth of which
nature strives to be delivered will be consummated " [162].

The " supermen, the masters of life ", whose glory shines
already in the not-too-far distant horizon of humanity, are really
" God-men ", like " Gautama the Buddha, Jesus the Christ " [163].
They " are manifestations of the Spirit through a human medium

---

[152] Cf. RR, p. 419; FS, p. 4; ERWTh., p. 100; RCW, pp. 83, 92 ff,
96, 97; OSW, Oct. 1952 - Feb. 1959, pp. 90, 115, 374, 312f; OSW, May
1962 - May 1964, p. 160; IVL, p. 249; *Fragments*, p. 44; Pr. Ups, p. 59;
The Cultural Heritage of India, p. xxvi; Cf. also *Taittirīya Upanishad*,
III, 1 ff.
[153] OSW, May 1962 - May 1964, p. 132, 140; Cf. RF, pp. 178 ff; RCW,
p. 180; PhRT, p. 70; OSW, Oct. 1952 - Jan. 1956, p. 221. Radhakrishnan
repeatedly affirms that even Karl Marx was of this opinion. He says:
"Marx denied God because he believed in the potential divinity of man"
(OSW, Oct. 1952 - Feb. 1959, p. 67; OSW, July 1959 - May 1962, pp. 48, 309).
[154] RCW, p. 181.
[155] ERWTh., p. 54; RCW, pp. 95-96. 148-149, 153.
[156] OSW, Oct. 1952 - Jan. 1956, p. 84.
[157] IVL, p. 169.
[158] RR, p. 437.
[159] RCW, p. 96.
[160] OSW, Oct. 1952 - Feb. 1959, p. 376.
[161] IVL, p. 240.
[162] Ibid., pp. 98-99; Cf. Ibid., p. 242.
[163] RF, p. 178.

which is a support of this manifestation ... The Buddha like the Christ indicates the universal reality appearing in a human manifestation ... The Absolute is reflected in the relative. Each manifestation is unique, is a relative Absolute, if such a contradiction is permitted. It nevertheless corresponds to a reality. Man perfected acquires the divine status " [164]. The superman is as much divine in character as Christ is, as any incarnation of God would be. " Those who reach perfect union with God will be as much one with God by grace as Jesus *when treated as Christ* is one with God by nature " [165]. The differences between God and the self of man will disappear and " God and man become one " [166]. With God-men the universe reaches its fulfilment and evolution its final stage [167].

Reasons adduced by Radhakrishnan in Favour of This View

i) The past is a real clue to the future. If we just look back and see the " wonders achieved in the course of evolution, the hope is not unreasonable that we may all attain to the greatness that Christ or Buddha reached " [168]. At the same time man is compared to an ape, man's great forefather, living in the long forgotten past and looking forward. " It would have been impossible for the Darwinian ape living its instinctive life in the forest to imagine that one day he would himself grow into an animal using a new power of reasoning " and flying in outer space [169]. " Man today finds it equally difficult to imagine that he might himself grow into the divine status, possessing knowledge without a taint of error, bliss without a shadow of suffering, power without its denial of weakness, purity and plenitude of being without their opposites of defect and limitation " [170].

ii) There are some moments of insight. They " inspire us with the vision of the kingdom of God and the hope that even

---

[164] Ibid., p. 178-179.

[165] Ibid., pp. 179-180. Cf. RCW, p. 109; Pr. Ups, pp. 58-59; *The Brahma Sūtra,* pp. 103-104; OSW, July 1959 - May 1962, p. 174; OSW, May 1962 - May 1964, pp. 117, 127. (italics mine).

[166] RF, p. 139.

[167] Cf. RF, pp. 82, 85, 139; OSW, July 1959 - May 1962, p. 33; OSW, May 1962 - May 1964, p. 117.

[168] IVL, p. 165.

[169] Ibid., p. 165.

[170] Ibid., pp. 165-166; Cf. Ibid., p. 271.

as the anthropoid ape became the human being the human may become the divine " [171].

iii) " God-men are the precursors of the truly human. What is possible for a Gautama or a Jesus is possible for every human being " [172], because man's essential constitutive factor is divine. The saints and sages of all religions are the " first fruits of the new species " [173]. An incarnation is not that God came down as God-man. Then he would be of no use, for nobody can imitate him [174]. He is a man gone up. Therefore anybody can become an incarnation. Radhakrishnan insists on this point. He says : " No Hindu can accept that what has been possible with Christ is impossible with other men. The perfection Christ attained is what all men might if they would " [175]. Jesus himself was a simple man who attained " Christhood " and became the Christ. But this " Christhood " is an " attainment of the soul, a state of inward glorious illumination in which the divine wisdom has become the heritage of the soul ... Mary, the mother of the Christchild, is the soul in her innermost divine nature. Whatever is conceived in the womb of the human soul is always of the Holy Spirit " [176].

iv) Jesus and Christianity teach the possibility of man becoming sons of God [177].

Finally, " the long record of the development of the human race and the great gifts of spiritual men like the Buddha, Socrates, Jesus make out that man has to be transcended by God-men " [178].

The Need of Human Effort for the Evolution of God-Men

Man must make a conscious effort to push the evolution further. In the subhuman species the progress was automatic [179]. But man is God's " fellow worker " [180] and " co-creator " [181]. And there is no such thing as " absolute prescience " on the part of

---

[171] Ibid., p. 166.
[172] RF, p. 179.
[173] OSW, Oct. 1952 - February 1959, p. 376.
[174] RF, p. 181.
[175] PhRT, p. 72.
[176] Fragments, pp. 79-80.
[177] Cf. RF, p. 180; IVL, p. 166; OSW, October 1952 - January 1956, p. 233.
[178] Pr. Ups, p. 58.
[179] OSW, October 1952 - February 1959, p. 374.
[180] HVL, p. 55.
[181] OSW, May 1962 - May 1964, p. 152; Cf. OSW, October 1952 - February 1959, p. 374.

God [182]. So man can mould his future and everything depends on him [183]. His will is the " instrument of evolutionary urge " [184]. Man can by his own effort rise from the stage of intellectuality to that of spirituality [185]. That will be the crowning glory of mankind. Therefore " it should be the endeavour of everyone who calls himself a human being to think that his evolution is not complete; he is not yet a fulfilled human being; he has to grow upward and onward until he is able to realize God in him, until the imprisoned splendour shines through every one of his activities " [186].

[182] HVL, p. 55.

[183] IVL, p. 221, OSW, October 1952 - January 1956, p. 204.

[184] OSW, July 1959 - May 1962, pp. 259, 286.

[185] OSW, October 1952 - February 1959, p. 376.

[186] OSW, May 1962 - May 1964, p. 159; Cf. Ibid., p. 165; IVL, p. 242; RCW, pp. 86-87, 137, 181; OSW, October 1952 - January 1956, p. 233; Fragments, p. 26; The Brahma Sūtra, pp. 103-104; OSW, May 1962 - May 1964, p. 123.

THE FOUNDATIONS OF ORGANIZED RELIGIONS

All religions include belief in the Supreme Reality and many religions explicitly teach the existence and knowability of God, and His intervention in history through revelation. Organized religions, according to Radhakrishnan, on the one hand adduce proofs for the existence of God, which they claim to be absolutely valid[1]; on the other hand they claim to possess supernatural revelations from God which are unattainable by human powers[2]. On these two fundamental and absolute claims, thinks Radhakrishnan, organized religions build their beliefs. How does Radhakrishnan evaluate these two claims? The answer to this question constitutes this chapter which we divide into two parts: 1) The Existence of God and man's way to Him. 2) The Revelation of God and His way to man.

1) EXISTENCE OF GOD AND MAN'S WAY TO HIM

i. *Materialism Rejected*

In his supreme enthusiam for the Hindu religion, Radhakrishnan praises Hindu tolerance because it accepts even atheists into its fold. For, religion and atheism are equally plausible at the superficial intellectual level[3]. He explains ancient Indian ma-

---

[1] Cf. IVL, pp. 159-160; EWR, pp. 48-53; OSW, July 1959 - May 1962, p. 231.

[2] Cf. ERWTh., p. 8. OSW, July 1959 - May 1962, p. 233.

[3] Cf. Ibid., p. 320. Mahatma Gandhi said: "A man may not believe in God and still call himself a Hindu" (*Young India,* 24 April 1924). One is reminded of the main trend of Buddhism which "not merely welcomes atheists but in itself is positively atheistic » (Cf. F. S. C. NORTHROP, *Radhakrishnan's Conception of the Relation between Eastern and Western Cultural Values,* in PhSR, p. 368 f.) But elsewhere Radhakrishnan claims that the Hindu never doubted in the reality of God (Cf. HVL, p. 20).

terialism in milder terms. It " is a return of man's spirit to itself
and a rejection of all that is merely external and foreign " [4], in
Radhakrishnan's words.

But this is not Radhakrishnan's general attitude towards God-
less systems, especially the Western ones [5]. He never comes to
terms with them and avails himself of every opportunity to condemn outright all anti-God attitudes under whatever form. He
feels that the world is passing through an utter demoralization [6].
Life has become without structure, law and rhythm [7]. " The world
has become anonymous and the individual lost in it " [8]. Everything
of worth and value is denied with ' icy cold clarity ' to the human
individual [9]. He is emptied of his own history, of his destiny and
of his inward past [10]. Even fatalism is being accepted by some
who are weary of will.

Radhakrishnan observes that modern humans go about sin-
ning in the name of modernity. Disguised feeling is masquerading
as advanced thought [11]. God is being warded off from life and
adventure of modern man. If Lucretian materialism is antiquated
and crude, modern man prides himself in the thought that he
has become an emancipated, supermodern intellectual by blatantly
asserting that the universe is the product of an unconscious me-
chanistic energy [12] and God a " function of the unconscious ", a
sort of " wet-nurse to humanity " [13]. Intoxicated by the triumph
of science a system of philosophy has come into vogue which says
that nothing is true which is not empirically verifiable [14]. Shocked
by the observation of the Russian cosmonaut, Radhakrishnan sar-
castically remarked in a speech at a banquet at Edinburgh Castle

---

[4] Ind. Ph., I, p. 283.

[5] According to Radhakrishnan materialism is the dominant trait of
Western civilization (Cf. W. R. INGE et al. (ed), *Radhakrishnan: Comparative
Studies in Philosophy presented in Honour of His Sixtieth Birth Day* (London
1951), Introduction (page numbers are not found).

[6] Radakrishnan has announced that the world is passing through a moral
crisis of which the wars — the brutal massacres and mass exterminations —
are only external symptoms. This was heavily stressed in his speeches and
writings of the Hitlerite period.

[7] *The Spirit in Man,* p. 482.

[8] RS, p. 57.

[9] Ibid., p. 56f.

[10] Ibid., p. 56.

[11] HVL, p. 63.

[12] Cf. IVL, p. 40.

[13] Cf., Ibid., p.23.

[14] Cf. OSW, May 1962 - May 1964, p. 164.

on 14th June, 1963 : " Recently the cosmonauts travelled through
space and came back and said, ' we never encountered God; how
can God exist?' Once upon a time we said, we searched the skies
with a telescope and we did not find God there. Others said we
dissected the body of a human being but did not discover any
soul. If sense experience is to be regarded as the only authority
for knowledge then all these gentlemen are correct " [15]. He condemned publicly the denial of God by the cosmonaut at least four
times [16]. Modern humanists like L. A. Feuerbach (1804-1872)
argue that religion is an illusion, and God no more than the attributes man finds in himself, in his own most perfect form. Posi-
tivists, following Auguste Comte (1798-1857) think that human
knowledge passes through three stages : the theological, the metaphysical and the scientific or positive. Only in the last does man
attain truth and certitude. Phenomenologists like R. Otto and
Max Scheler think that the ' holy ' is an *apriori* in our minds.
Pragmatists like William James (1842-1910) view absolute truths
as myths. Psychologists say that man's helplessness here on earth
makes him to look to the beyond. Communism has launched a
relentless war against God. Others like Nietzsche place a superman
in the place of God. All these systems are valued as equal and
considered equally important in the West [17]. Such were the currents of thought that Radhakrishnan found among the intellectuals
of the West.

The main principles held by one or the other of these humanist
schools may be put under four main points : 1) Science is the only
reliable mode of knowing available to man. All human knowledge
derives from experience. 2) There exists a realm of the physical
which is the ultimate matrix of all becoming. 3) Selfhood, consciousness and personality refer to no independent, substantial
spiritual realities but to complex psychological functions. 4) There

---

[15] Ibid., p. 156.

[16] In Delhi on the 5th April 1963 (Cf. OSW, May 1962 - May 1964,
p. 132); at Kabul University, Afganistan on 14th May 1963 (Cf. OSW,
May 1962 - May 1964, p. 135); at Edinburgh Castle on the 14th June 1963
(Cf. OSW, May 1962 - May 1964, p .156); in Madurai on 28th Sept. 1963
(Cf. OSW, May 1962 - May 1964, p. 164). More than three decades earlier
Radhakrishnan had pointed out: "Modern materialism is not so much the
result of rational philosophy as the triumph of modern science » (IVL, 15;
Cf. also IVL, 23; *Fragments,* p. 14).

[17] Cf. BERNARD PHILLIPS, *Radhakrishnan's Critique of Naturalism,* in
PhSR, p. 121.

is no evidence of a transcendent order. So man's goal, salvation and values ought to be this-worldly.

Radhakrishnan rejects every one of these points [18]. He agrees that the principle of verifiability is valid, but to restrict it to sense experience alone is not empiricism but apriorism. He maintains that the claim of naturalism that it can explain the whole process of the universe is not satisfactory [19]. Even if the world is a mechanism, the question remains: what guides this mechanism [20]. The spiritual self of man is defended on the following grounds. i) Our inability to realize consciousness apart from the body does not imply that consciousness is a property of the body. Body can only be an auxiliary to the realization of the consciousness. ii) If consciousness were a property of the body, then, a) there could be no consciousness of the body; for, the subject cannot be reduced to the object or its property and b) it must be capable of being perceived by others than the owner of its body. iii) Even the body which is the nature of a contrivance implies some one who controls it, to whom consciousness belongs [21].

Naturalism under any form is not sufficient for human needs, holds Radhakrishnan. For instance, materialistic humanism has no consolation, " when the foundations of life are shaken, when the ultimate issues force us demanding answer " [22]. The pragmatic view does not satisfy critical intelligence which it must, to be accepted. " If we accept beliefs on the ground that they add to our mental health and happiness, many superstitions will become justified " [23]. Modern science falls short of satisfying human yearnings. Man has made himself master of the universe. "Yet the lord of the earth cannot live in safety. He has to hide under the earth, wear gas masks. He is haunted by fears of wars and lives in the company of uncertainties. This war-haunted, machine-driven civilization cannot be the last word of human striving. Unless we are blind idiots or self-satisfied morons, we will know that scientific organization is not the fulfilment of the spirit of man " [24]. Therefore, naturalism is a kind of self-deception. " There are two ways in which we deceive ourselves: the easy

---

[18] Cf. Ibid., pp. 130-131.
[19] Cf. IVL, 240.
[20] Cf. Ibid., p. 251.
[21] Cf. Ind. Ph. I, p. 284.
[22] IVL., p. 54; Cf. also p. 64.
[23] Ibid., p. 58.
[24] *Fragments,* p. 54.

way of the unlearned who believe that the world we see is all, and the laborious way of the learned who establish the truth of naturalism and are deceived by the definite " [25]. The fact according to Radhakrishnan is this: Though beginners may tend to naturalism, deeper reflection takes them away from it [26].

ii. *Rational Demonstration of the Existence of God as Proposed by Radhakrishnan*

a) *From Man's Despair on Earth*

" The metaphysical quest starts with man's dissatisfaction with the actual world " [27]. When the world appears a futile show, man begins to search for reality beyond the world. " If ultimate nothingness is not all, there should be some meaning behind it all " [28]. Prophets and seers like Buddha and Confucius felt that they were on an estranged earth. The seeker of the Upanishads cries out:

> Lead me from unreal to the real
> Lead me from darkness to light
> Lead me from death to eternal life [29].

Man's sorry plight on earth is at once a blessing also, because it leads him to God [30]. So says Radhakrishnan, " The ability to feel lost is man's tragic destiny and glorious privilege " [31]. God is an absolute need for man [32] and " only a living faith in God will enable man to overcome the paralysing sense of despair " [33].

b) *From the non-self-sufficiency of the World*

When Radhakrishnan argues against materialists, he takes a stand very similar to that of St. Thomas. " We reach the un-

---

[25] ERWTh, p. 23.
[26] Cf. Ind. Ph. I. p. 285.
[27] RCW, p. 61.
[28] Ibid., p. 62; Cf. also p. 63f.
[29] *Bṛhad-āranyaka* Up. I, 3. 28. For Radhakrishnan's use of it as an argument, Cf. FS, p. 3; OSW, October 1952 - February 1959, p. 227.
[30] THOMAS PAUL, *Kanneerinte Katha*: A Study on Human Suffering. (Alwaye 1963) 31f, 61-64.
[31] RCW, 64; « Christianity built its structure of faith on the divine despair » (RCW, 63).
[32] Ibid., p. 64.
[33] OSW, July 1959 - May 1962, p. 215.

mediated by the mediated. The basic fact that there is world at all, that something exists with its qualities and relations calls for enquiry. The world order, beauty, movement and contingency form part of the proof of God and militate against any kind of materialism " [34]. In his inaugural address at the Union for the Study of the Great Religions (India Branch) on 29th May 1955, he admits even that " one of the main arguments for the religious thesis is the objective consideration of the cosmos " [35]. Radhakrishnan rightly emphasizes the primacy of Being as the ground of all existence. " The very existence of this world implies the existence of Being from which the world derives. Being is the foundation of all existence ... If anything exists, Being is " [36]. Because nature is not its own *raison d'être,* no part of it contains its own explanation [37]. The universe is there. It does not exist by itself. It is not self-sufficient. Therefore, there should be another Being, transcendent and self-sufficient, actuating all existents. This is Being without being affected by anything else, Being by itself [38]. We are all finite beings. We do not owe our existence either originally or from moment to moment to ourselves or to beings like ourselves. Therefore, there must be a fundamental cause, a primary Being [39]. There can only be one such Being — the Divine Spirit [40].

c) *From the Cosmic Evolution*

Radhakrishnan holds that of all the logical proofs for the existence of God, the strongest comes from the fact of cosmic evolution or the world process. After repudiating Marx's materialistic position as ' onesided and misleading ' he argues : " That history is an organic or creative process is a proposition which Marx learnt not only from Hegel but from his Jewish ancestors. This meaningful pattern, this creative movement, is not explicable in terms of the development of the productive forces ... To say that history is a meaningful process is to deny the adequacy of the

---

[34] RCW, pp. 79-80.
[35] OSW, October 1952 - February 1959, p. 304.
[36] *Fragments,* p. 38; Cf. Ibid., p. 59; RCW, pp. 87-88; RS, p. 104.
[37] *The Spirit in Man,* p. 445; Cf. IVL, p. 263; RF, pp. 82f; RCW, p. 87; RR, p. 334.
[38] Cf. *Fragments,* p. 58.
[39] IVL, p. 263.
[40] Cf. *Fragments,* p. 38.

materialist view [41]. For, whatever becomes, becomes not by itself but by another [42]. The classic argument, he points out, is that, " it is impossible to evolve a subject from an object, since there is no object without a pre-existing subject " [43]. So if there is the emergence of what is genuinely new in the cosmic process, then the cosmic process is not self-explanatory [44]. For, to interpret matter as auto-dynamic and spontaneous is to read into matter what is non-material, the living and spiritual [45]. It would be to assume a series of miracles [46] which the materialists themselves have rejected. Nor are the evolving universe and the historical effects in it the results of chance [47]. Even science cannot say why they do so. It can only describe them. Therefore, the world process requires an underlying reality — a self-sufficient God — to direct and sustain it [48].

d) *From our Moral Consciousness*

According to Radhakrishnan God is a postulate of man's moral consciousness. The fact that man has moral ideals is incompatible with the theory that he is a product of mere nature [49]. If our moral consciousness means nothing, if there were no Divine corresponding to our moral consciousness, then, argues Radhakrishnan, happiness will be impossible, duality will be eternal and universe will be eternally frustrated. In his words,

"a proper adjustment of happiness to virtue is possible only if we assume a divine being who is able to bring the cosmic into conformity with the moral and regulate the combination of happiness and virtue. Our moral consciousness postulates God, who is adequate to the realization of the *summum bonum* ..... If we do not accept the postulate of God, we shall be faced by a dualism between the moral law which claims our allegiance and a universe which is apparently indifferent if not hostile to the demands of morality " [50].

[41] RS, p. 40; Cf. IVL, p. 23.
[42] Cf. RF, p. 83; RS, p. 103.
[43] Ind. Ph. I, p. 284.
[44] Cf. *Fragments,* p. 38; HVL, p. 288; BG, p. 43; Pr. Ups, p. 58f.
[45] RS, 29.
[46] Cf. *The Spirit in Man,* p. 495; IVL, p. 209f.
[47] Cf. RS, p. 29; Pr. Ups, p. 58.
[48] Cf. OSW, October 1952 - February 1959, p. 313.
[49] Ind. Ph. I, p. 284; HH, p. 29 f.
[50] IVL, p. 55; About the ontological argument Radhakrishnan says that it is valid in as much as it points to the human need of an absolute (Cf. *Fragments,* p. 59).

e) *From the Innate Idea of God*

Man has an inborn idea of God and a desire to be with Him, holds Radhakrishnan. He says, " the search of mind for beauty, goodness and truth is a search for God. The child nursing at the breast of its mother, the illiterate savage gazing at the numberless stars, the scientist in his laboratory studying life under a microscope, the poet meditating in solitude on the beauty and the pathos of the world, the ordinary man standing reverently before a starlit sky, the Himalayan heights or a quiet sea, or before the highest miracle of all, a human being who is both great and good, they all possess dimly the sense of the eternal the feeling for the heaven " [51]. This God-consciousness in man is as much original to man as self-consciousness [52]. Our consciousness of finitude is possible because there is the consciousness of infinitude in us [53]. It gives us an inner urge to seek God [54], an urge to the ideal [55]. To disavow this innate idea of God is like blotting out lights and then cursing the darkness [56]. Without this innate consciousness of God in us even life would have been impossible. " Life is God " says Radhakrishnan, " and the proof of it is life itself. If somewhere in ourselves we did not know with absolute certainty that God is, we could not live " [57]. Our desire to know God is also inexplicable without the reality of God. " The desire for God, the feeling that we are in a state of exile, implies the reality of God in us " [58].

While we may logically argue from this innate God-consciousness to the existence of God, it also indicates that it is not so much a logical demonstration as a felt necessity of thought that compels us to admit an absolute reality [59], that the Supreme is to be experienced in the pulse of our being [60].

---

[51] RS, p. 47; OSW, May 1962 - May 1964, p. 156.
[52] RF, p. 103; Cf. IVL, pp. 81, 137; ERWTh. p. 22; EWR, p. 18; *The Spirit in Man* p. 494.
[53] *Fragments,* p. 57.
[54] FS, pp. 3-4.
[55] ERWTh., p. 22.
[56] Cf. HVL, p. 43.
[57] IVL, p. 124; Cf. ERWTh., p. 22.
[58] PR. Ups., p. 53.
[59] Ind. Ph. II, p. 533; FS, p. 7.
[60] OSW, May 1962 - May 1964, pp. 35, 120.

iii. *Radhakrishnan's Evaluation of the Logical Proofs*

It is true that when Radhakrishnan argues against the materialists and scientists, he makes use of the logical arguments as if they have absolute validity, and demonstrates the existence of God with such certainty as to exclude doubt. He maintains that it is " essential in this age of science that religious belief should be shown to be reasonable " [61]. Still, since he believes in absolute monism and holds that man is a ' spiritual rational animal ', where spiritual is the main element, one might say that he would be illogical if he gave absolute value to rational arguments. In fact he does not do so.

Radhakrishnan believes that to put the main emphasis on logic and rationality is a defect, for which Western systems in the main have fallen. " From the Socratic insistence on the concept to Russell's mathematical logic, the history of Western thought has been a supreme illustration of the primacy of the logical " [62]. He repeats this charge : " The Western mind lays great stress on science, logic and humanism " [63]. " The Western systems are generally characterized by greater adherence to critical intelligence " [64]. This excessive insistence on the logical, which is the " defect of all scholasticism " [65], will cause only unhappiness. " Our anxieties are bound up with our intellectuality, whose emergence at the human level causes a fissure or cleavage in our life " [66]. This cleavage destroys man's oneness with the universe. He is then divided, unhappy and anxious of the future [67].

According to Radhakrishnan the way of the intellect must remain for ever defective because " the objects revealed by logical knowledge are not those which we perceive ... the perceived object is more real than the conceived one ... No amount of conceptual synthesis can restore the original integrity of the perceived object " [68]. So " logical knowledge is a mixture of truth and er-

---

[61] *The Brahma Sūtra,* p. 104.

[62] IVL, p. 105.

[63] Ibid., p. 100.

[64] Ibid., p. 101 ; Cf. Ibid., p. 103f ; EWR, p. 48 ; Later, it seems that Radakrishnan slightly changed this view and recognized that intuition has its place also in the West (Cf. RC, p. 824).

[65] Pr. Ups, 134.

[66] ERWTh., 43.

[67] Cf. ERWTh., p. 43f ; Cf. A. N. MARLOW, *Spiritual Religion and the Philosophy of Radhakrishnan,* in PhSR, p. 338.

[68] IVL, 106.

ror " [69]. Even the ' famous ways of St. Thomas ' do not offer a certain demonstration of the existence of God, unaided by something higher, the experience of the Divine. When the conviction arises otherwise, they will help us to understand its validity [70], showing the inadequacy of the naturalistic explanations [71]. To put it in another way, man's intuitive faculty apprehends God at first. Then only comes the intellect. The rational jutsification of this intuition constitutes the logical proofs and their value is secondary. In Radhakrishnan's words :

> " The *so-called proofs* of the existence of God are the results of critical reflection on the spiritual intuitions of the ultimate fact of spirit. These intuitions inspire the acts of reflection, which only confirm what has been apprehended in another way. The reflections are pure and true to the extent that they refer to the intuited facts ... Reflective accounts are thus *only approximations* " [72].

Therefore the logical proofs are of no use for those who have direct experience of the Divine. They do not seek proofs for the existence of God, but feel immediately certain of what is experienced. But Radhakrishnan agrees that proofs are to be offered for those who do not share this experience, and the reasonableness of the faith requires to be demonstrated [73]. In this context he holds that to the large majority, for whom " religion is a matter of trust and inference " [74], the only way is to show by critical and logical argument what is intuited [75]. This is done by slower and consecutive thinking, whereby discovery becomes proof [76].

So far we have seen that at least a secondary value is given to logical argument by Radhakrishnan. But in some other pas-

---

[69] Ibid., p. 124.

[70] Ibid., p. 63.

[71] *The Spirit in Man*, pp. 494-95.

[72] *Fragments*, p. 63; Italics mine.

[73] Cf. *The Spirit in Man*, p. 494; OSW, May 1962 - May 1964, p. 167.

[74] Radhakrishnan is speaking about those who belong to the organized religions.

[75] Cf. IVL, 174f; Pr. Ups, p. 134. In another context Radhakrishnan argues that dialectic is difficult for the majority and the only way for them is experience. "The reality of the Supreme is not a question to be solved by dialectic which *the vast majority of the human race will be unable to understand* ... Only spiritual experience can provide us with proofs of the existence of Spirit". BG, p. 20. (Italics mine).

[76] Cf. IVL, p. 174.

sages he seems to maintain that God's existence cannot be logically demonstrated, and does not grant any real validity to logical arguments. He says:

"So long as we argue from given data, objective and subjective, it may be said that the Supreme is the necessity of thought, a hypothesis however valid it may be. Articulation in thought of the nature of the Ultimate Reality is quite different from experience of it. An idea remains a stranger in mind, however friendly our reception of it may be, until it receives the stamp of our endorsement by personal experience. Logical arguments by themselves may not be able to demonstrate the existence of God in a way that would satisfy the seeking mind and the devout heart " [77].

The end of ratiocination, it is argued, can only be an idea and not a reality. God is known not as the conclusion of an argument but as something experienced [78].

God is not an object among objects. Therefore our logical categories cannot be applied to Him. So Radhakrishnan says: " All proofs for the existence of God fail because they conceive God as an objective reality ... It is given to us in life and not established by ratiocination " [79]. God is the subject, the basis of thought. Therefore He is not an object of thought and cannot be dealt with in intellectual terms [80], or proved from anything external or accidental [81]. Truth itself is said to be not the reflection of reality in sense and intellect. Radhakrishnan thinks that it is not a question of subject knowing the object. Those who try to show the existence of God from external objects are accused of conceiving the Absolute as something relative and in a naturalistic sense. " The affirmative theology in its anxiety to bring the absolute into relation with the relatives, makes the absolute itself relative ... Arguments for and against the existence

---

[77] Rf, pp. 103-104; Cf. also BG, p. 20.

[78] Cf. *The Spirit in Man,* p. 492 .

[79] Ibid., p. 492.

[80] IVL, p. 51; OSW, October 1952 - January 1956, pp. 202-203, 244; OSW, July 1959 - May 1962, p. 230; OSW, May 1962 - May 1964, p. 119. *Fragments,* p. 22. "No logical knowledge is possible of that which underlies all logical knowledge" (IVL, p. 124).

[81] Cf. IVL, p. 173; Cf. also Ind. Ph. II, 172. Mahatma Gandhi is also of the same opinion. He says: "It is proved not by extraneous evidence but in the transformed conduct and character of those who have felt the real presence of God within" (*Young India,* Oct. 11. 1928).

of God understand the divine in a naturalistic sense, as an object among the objects " [82].

Again it is maintained that from a small fragment of the contemporary world, we cannot argue to the whole. The world and its history as a whole are unique. So we cannot argue from it the existence of something supernatural. Besides, Radhakrishnan points out: " we argue by analogy, from our embodied selves and their operations within the world to a mind which is unembodied and its operations in the world as a whole " [83]. He considers logical knowledge *avidyā* or non-knowledge [84]. For him there are no proofs for the existence of God [85].

So on the one hand the existence of God is shown by logical arguments, and on the other hand it is logically argued that God's existence cannot be shown by rational arguments. The paradox may be solved, it seems, if we apply here also Radhakrishnan's distinction of the two orders of reality: the order of nature or *māyā* and the order of the spiritual or real. Accordingly, the intellect has a real but relative capacity to perceive reality and all the intellectual proofs of the existence of God too have only a relative value. Their value is limited to the order of nature or *māyā*. But the intellectual proofs are unwanted and invalid in the order of spiritual or real where immediate intuition is the way. Without such a distinction one fails to see any logicity in many of the expressions of Radhakrishnan. For example, he calls logic a ' lower form ' [86] not fallacious but insufficient [87] and logical knowledge " non-knowledge " and *avidyā* valid only till intuition arises [88] and trustworthy " within limits " [89]. In these expressions he is clearly applying the above distinction. With this distinction one may understand him when he says that no stable conviction can be built on mere dialectic [90] or that thought is useful but not true, but intuition is true though not useful [91]. Therefore, Radhakrishnan is not denying the validity of logical inference in all orders of reality; he limits it to the order of *māyā*. In his essay, " *Radhakrishnan's Conception of the Relation between Eastern and Western Cultural Values* " [92] F. S. C. Northrop said that the ultimate object of knowledge is not logically inferred. Radhakrishnan criticizes this statement in his " *Reply to the Critics* " [93]:

" Although the great religious teachers of the East tell us that religion is a matter of life, they do not set aside logical

[82] GB, p. 66.
[83] Cf. RCW, p. 88; Cf. also Ind. Ph. I, 355f; IVL, p. 127ff.

inference. There are many for whom the ultimate reality is not an immediately experienced fact [94]; for them the reality of God is conveyed by proofs. The different systems of thought are at great pains to demonstrate the logical necessity of the Ultimate Reality of which we can have direct apprehension also [95] .... God can be known directly or derivatively " [96].

Intellect is valid, but in its own sphere. Above it there is a sphere where the intellect has no sway — the sphere of intuition [97]. Therefore in contemplation of the One, man must leave behind discursive reason [98].

iv. *Radhakrishnan's View of Organized Religion's Approach to God*

From what has been said it is clear that Radhakrishnan fully subscribes to the fundamental thesis of organized religions that there is a God. He is insistent on that point. He says even that not only he but Hindus in general never doubted the existence of the One Supreme Universal Spirit [99]. But he differs from the doctrines of organized religions about the nature of God. This we have seen in the second chapter. Neither does he agree that an assent to the proposition ' God exists ' is the fundamental thing in religion. He says:

"Real religion can exist without a definite conception of the deity but not without a distinction between the spiritual and

---

[84] Cf. IVL, p. 115.

[85] Cf. RCW, p. 67; IVL, pp. 30-31.

[86] IVL, p. 109.

[87] *A Source Book*, p. xxiii.

[88] IVL, p. 115; Cf. also Pr. UPs, pp. 95f, 142.

[89] RC, p. 72. The Upanishads recognized intuition rather than intellect "as the true guide to ultimate truth". Cf. *A Source Book*, p. xvi.

[90] IVL, p. 68.

[91] Ibid., p. 113.

[92] in PhSR, p. 633-658.

[93] in PhSR, pp. 787-842.

[94] ie. Those who are in the order of *māyā*.

[95] ie. Those who are in the order of the spiritual.

[96] RC, p. 823; Cf. also p. 793; *The Brahma Sūtra*, p. 105; *A Source Book*, p. 353; OSW October 1952 - February 1959, p. 284.

[97] *The Brahma Sūtra*, p. 104; Cf. also RF, p. 107; MST, p. 30; IVL, p. 137; *A Source Book*, pp. xxiii, 16f, 355.

[98] Pr. Ups, p. 57.

[99] HVL, p. 20.

the profane, the sacred and the secular. Even in primitive religion with its characteristic phenomena of magic, we have religion, though not a belief in God. In theistic systems the essential thing is not the existence of the deity, but its power to transform man ... There are systems of Hindu thought like the Saṁkhya and the Jaina which do not admit God but affirm the reality of the spiritual consciousness. There are theists like Ramanuja for whom the spiritual consciousness, though not God Himself, is the only way in which God can be known " [100].

Accordingly Radhakrishnan divides the religions of the world into two classes: 1) those which emphasize the object; and 2) those which insist on inner experience. The organized religions belong to the first class. For them religion is an attitude of faith and conduct directed to a power above. The religion of the second class gives supreme value to experience. Radhakrishnan says that for those who belong to this class, religion is a transforming experience which is salvation, while for those who are in the first group religion is more a notion of God [101].

Radhakrishnan differs also as to the way in which the existence of God is reached. The organized religions in the main, especially Catholicism which is the most important of all, teach that with the light of natural reason the existence of God can be reached and demonstrated with certainty. But Radhakrishnan rejects, as we have seen, any ultimate validity to reason and its proofs. He even warns that insistence on reason will result in naturalism or scepticism. He holds that speculative theology cannot consider God as a reality in existence but only as a possibility [102]. Therefore, according to Radhakrishnan all organized religions are to be subordinated to another kind of religion which insists on experience.

v. *Intuition as a Way to God*

a) *Nature of Intuition.* One of the most elusive concepts, and yet most important, in the structure of Radhakrishnan's thought is that of intuition. The difficulty in understanding him comes from the fact that the same term is used in different senses in different contexts. It is unfortunate, admits Radhakrishnan, that

---

[100] ERWTh, p. 21; Cf. also p. 313; IVL, p. 36.
[101] Ibid., p. 21.
[102] Cf. IVL, p. 68. .

a single term 'intuition' should be employed to signify scientific genius, poetic insight, ethical conscience as well as religious faith [103]. Radhakrishnan himself uses the term sometimes to signify the process of knowing a thing or the subject itself absolutely perfectly. At other times the same term refers to the product of such a knowledge, as the registry of the universe in man's mind and its reaction to it. Still at other times 'intuition' means the intuiting faculty in man.

Man is a 'spiritual rational animal', according to Radhakrishnan. Naturally this concept of man should square with his concept of human knowledge. So he is only logical when he says that to limit to intellect all knowledge would be a mistake [104]. Just as sensuous knowledge corresponds to animality, conceptual knowledge to rationality, there would be a superior kind of knowledge which belongs to the spiritual side of man, which we may call intuition [105]. Even as the spiritual is the foundation of man's being, intuition is the basis of all other knowledge [106]. So says Radhakrishnan: "If intuitive knowledge does not supply us with universal major premises, which we can neither question nor establish, our life will come to an end. The ethical soundness, the logical consistency and the aesthetic beauty of the universe are assumptions for science and logic, art and morality, but are not irrational assumptions ... Disbelief in them means complete scepticism" [107]. He claims in this the support of the great thinkers.

Radhakrishnan calls intuition integral insight [108]. It is called 'integral' because it brings into activity not merely a portion of our conscious being, sense or reason, but the whole. It also reveals to us not merely abstractions but the reality in its integrity [109]. In this sense intuition is defined by Radhakrishnan as the

---

[103] Cf. RC, p. 791; Radhakrishnan has tried to elucidate this question in his articles: *Intuition and Intellect: Vidyā (Knowledge) and Avidyā (Ignorance)*. Cf. Pr. Ups, pp. 95-104; *Intellect and Intuition* Cf. IVL, pp. 100-137; Cf. also *The Brahma Sūtra*, pp. 109ff; Ind. Ph. I, 43ff, 173ff. Robert W. Browning's essay, *Reason and Types of Intuition in Radhakrishnan's Philosophy*, is a study of this subject from a philosophical point of view (Cf. PhSR, pp. 173-277).

[104] Cf. IVL, p. 144.

[105] Cf. *The Spirit in Man*, p. 484; IVL, pp. 239f; P. T. Raju, *Idealistic Thought in India* (London 1953) 340f. The source of Radhakrishnan may be traced to *Yoga Sūtra*, II, 35-39.

[106] *Fragments*, p. 61.

[107] IVL, p. 123.

[108] RC, p. 790.

[109] Cf. *Fragments*, p. 60; Cf. also RC, pp. 790-791.

" spiritual apprehension or the kind of awareness of real values which are neither objects in space and time nor universals of thought " [110]. More briefly, it is the " ultimate vision of our profoundest being " [111].

b) *Reaching God Through Intuition.* Man as he is, believes Radhakrishnan, is a prisoner in the world of concepts — of *avidyā.* To cross the barrier of our limited intelligence and see things from the point of view of the supreme identity, to emerge from the insufficiency and ignorance to fullness and wisdom is said to be the fulfilment of man on earth. Man must be liberated into the light and life of superconsciousness [112]. In intuition man acquires a wonderful clarity of mind. He feels that he is filled with light, raised to immediate contact with the eternal reality [113].

The intellect at its best could show God only as a hypothesis — however valid it may be. But in intuition God is experienced as a fact, the mystery of God is known by participation [114]. If the vision of God is misty and dark for the intellect it is bright and clear for intuition [115].

To see God as He is, it is not enough that a part of our being alone namely the intellect, works. " God is the answer which the full being of man utters when it presses against the whole nature of things ", in Radhakrishnan's words [116].

Truth for Radhakrishnan, is something which cannot be proved but only experienced [117] by a personal commitment [118]. Therefore, as long as God has not become the factual content of our personal, spiritual experience, He will remain unknown. All other proofs are called by Radhakrishnan descriptions of God and matters

---

[110] *The Spirit in Man,* p. 485; Cf. also EWS, p. 23.

[111] IVL, p. 114.

[112] Cf. RS, p. 104.

[113] Cf. Ibid., p. 45.

[114] Cf. OSW, October 1952 - February 1959, p. 351; OSW, July 1959 - May 1962, p. 231.

[115] Cf. PhRT, p. 27. This doctrine is from *Katha Up.,* III, 13: "The Self shines not forth, But he is seen by subtle seers with superior subtle intellect" Cf. also IV, 1-4, 10-11.

[116] IVL, p. 134, Cf. also p. 69; RC, p. 793. But in his *Introduction* to Pr. Ups. Radhakrishnan says: « God is revealed only to those who believe that He is ». p. 101. It is difficult to say if this is his opinion. A reference is given to *Katha* Up. II.6.12. and 13. We believe, it should be *Katha* Up. II.3.12-13, where this doctrine is found.

[117] ERWTh, p. 144

[118] RF, p. 105ff.

of definition and language [119]. All that dialectic and philosophy can do is to clarify our intuition [120]. Therefore the only way to reach God and know Him with certainty is intuition.

c) *Reasons in Favour of Intuition.* 1) We cannot have certain ideas without having had the experience of the objects of which they are the ideas. So we should not have had the idea of God if we had never been in immediate cognitive relation with Him [121]. Therefore the causal arguments as ways of inference cannot prove ultimately the existence of God. But if there is an immediate intuition of the essential dependence of all finite things, i. e. an intuition of the priority of the absolute to relative beings, then the reality of God is revealed [122]. So also if the ontological argument is taken as a report of experience, it is valid. But if it is taken as a logical inference it is wrong [123].

2) Man has an inborn yearning for contact with the eternal. If it were impossible to know God by union with Him, which according to Radhakrishnan is the only way of knowing truth with certainty, our life would be meaningless [124].

3) There is an ancient and widespread tradition that we can apprehend God with directness and immediacy. This tradition is found in all lands, ages and creeds [125]. We quote one of the many pronouncements of Radhakrishnan concerning this point:

> " Witnesses to the personal sense of the divine are not confined to the East. Socrates and Plato, Plotinus and Porphyry, Augustine and Dante, Bunyan and Wesley, and numberless others, testify to the felt reality of God. It is as

---

[119] ERWTh, p. 22.

[120] IVL, 137.

[121] Cf. Ibid., p. 174.

[122] Cf. *The Cultural Heritage of India,* I, p. xxiv; ERWTh, pp. 84-85.

[123] Cf. IVL, p. 174, Cf. also pp. 67, 264.

[124] Cf. RS, p. 45 f, 61. Radhakrishnan claims that S. Augustine supports him and cites: "Thou, O Lord, has made us for thyself, and our heart is restless, until it finds rest in thee". *Confessions,* 1, 1. (Cf. RS, p. 46). He refers to psalm xc. 2 in the text and ps. xlii. 1-2 and ps. lxiii. 1 in a foot note (Cf. RS, p. 46). These texts are not unknown to any catholic theologian. They speak of a purely natural desire of intuitive vision of God. But nature cannot give power to realize the intuitive vision of God.

[125] Cf. *Fragments,* p. 60; RF, pp. 104ff; RS, p. 47. Probably Radhakrishnan got this idea from W. R. Inge (Cf. INGE, *The Philosophy of Plotinus,* I (London 1918) 2f; Cf. also BERNARD PHILLIPS, *Radhakrishnan's Critique of Naturalism,* in PhSR, p. 136).

old as humanity and is not confined to any one people. The evidence is too massive to run away from it " [126].

4) If Moses and St Paul could attain to ecstatic union with God, it shows that human nature is capable of attaining immediate intuition of God — *ab esse ad posse valet illatio*. Those who deny it do so because of misapprehension [127].

5) Only this view of the Knowledge of God, i. e. which comes from a steady communion with Him, calls for a change of heart and transformation of life. Then only can it become efficacious.

6) Radhakrishnan refrains from insisting on proofs for everything. Because, citing Theophrastus, he argues, if we ask reason for all things we will utterly overthrow reason. If all knowledge is depending on external criteria for its validity, then no knowledge is valid at all. For one thing depends on another and that on another. Thus it will go on *ad infinitum*. So says Radhakrishnan, " We can escape it only by assuming knowledge which is valid in itself "[128]. Therefore the intuitive principle cannot be proved and need not be proved at all. They are compared by Radhakrishnan to Kant's *apriori* elements. We cannot but admit them. It is impossible to admit their opposites. " They belong to the very structure of our mind. They are native to the soul " [129].

d) *Radhakrishnan's Evaluation of the Way of Intuition.* To make this clear it is sufficient to see what kind of superiority Radhakrishnan gives to intuition over intellect. In the first place it is to be noted that he conceives intuition as needing intellect [130]. So intuition must not ignore intellect, if it does it is useless, because intuition which is not supported by intellect will lapse into self-satisfied obscurantism [131].

But intuition is said to be far above intellect. The position of intuition in relation to intellect is compared to the position of man in relation to ape in the evolutionary process. So intellect cannot be called false. It is inadequate. It fails to reveal the

---

[126] IVL, pp. 71-72.

[127] Cf. RC, p. 793.

[128] *Fragments*, p. 61.

[129] Cf. IVL, p. 123. « Intuitive knowledge is proved on our pulse » (IVL, p. 114).

[130] Cf. *The Spirit in Man*, p. 486.

[131] MST, p. 30.

truth in its fullness. It is, however, an essential stage in the evolution of human consciousness [132]. Even as the sentient is far below the rational, so also the intellectual is far below the intuitive [133].

In moving from intellect to intuition we are moving along the way of perfection. We are said to be, in intuition, delving into the deepest rationality of which human nature is capable: " In it we think more profoundly, feel more deeply, and see more truly " [134]. As the ape perfected is man, so too intellect perfected is intuition. So one is not against the other [135].

Another kind of relationship between the intellect and intuition found in Radhakrishnan is that between part and whole. Intellect stands to intuition as a part to whole [136]. The former is partial and fragmentary and the latter complete and whole [137]. Therefore intellect gives us an analysis of parts while intuition gives us an idea of the whole [138]. One details the relations of the object and tells us the qualities of the object in common with others, and the other gives us the object in itself — what is unique in it [139]. Intellect is roundabout and discursive and therefore superficial. But intuition is direct and deeper [140]. In intuition man sees things by an immediate apprehension. It arises from an intimate fusion of mind with reality. Intuition transcends subject-object distinction and gives us an awareness of the truth of the things by identity [141]. That is why it is self-evident and complete [142]. The knowledge gained in intuition is absolutely certain and compels our assent [143]. The knowledge by identity implies

---

[132] RC, p. 792. Cf. also OSW, October 1952 - January 1956, p. 229.

[133] OSW, October 1952 - January 1956, p. 229. « Intuition stands to intellect in somewhat the same relation as intellect stands to sense » (IVL, p. 115).

[134] IVL, p. 120.

[135] Cf. *The Spirit in Man*, p. 486; IVL, p. 176; GEORGE P. CONGER, *Radhakrishnan's World*, in PhSR, p. 91; P. T. RAJU, *Radhakrishnan's Influence on Indian Thought*, in PhSR, p. 534.

[136] Cf. *The Spirit in Man*, p. 487; RF, p. 107.

[137] Cf. RC, p. 792.

[138] Cf. IVL, p. 107, 166.

[139] Cf. Ibid., pp. 120-121; Cf. also *A Source Book*, 353; RC, p. 794.

[140] Cf. RF, p. 105.

[141] *Fragments*, p. 60f; Cf. also IVL, pp. 108-109; RR, p. 333; RF, p. 130.

[142] Cf. IVL, p. 99; *The Spirit in Man*, p. 485; RC, p. 794; IVL, p. 123; HVL, p. 13.

[143] Cf. Ibid., p. 115; RF, p. 172.

also perfect living. Because "the fully real can be known only by one who is himself fully real" [144].

It is only through intuitive apprehension that we know the deepest realities of life, which the intellect cannot grasp [145]. So it provides man with a higher consciousness, in which duality has no place and therefore defect and error are impossible. It is a kind of knowledge like that of God's [146].

Therefore according to Radhakrishnan, logical validity is not the genuine standard of true knowledge, but personal experience. If our knowledge of nature, soul and God are not rooted in experience it will die [147]. Also Radhakrishnan asks us to "deny the character of knowledge to our ideas of God unless we are traced to the experience of God" [148].

Finally, we may conclude that for Radhakrishnan only intuition can give us metaphysical certainty and therefore it is the final way to God; and since only intuition can cross the barrier of *māyā*, it is the only way to God. In Radhakrishnan's words:

> "In the case of integral insight, the individual does not possess knowledge as an individual but participates in it in his innermost essence, which is not distinct from the divine principle. The metaphysical certitude is absolute because the knower and the known are identical. This is *jñāna,* the most perfect union between God and man" [149].
> "This knowledge does not spring from belief or a process of reasoning. It goes beyond both of them without contradicting them. We can have wordless communion, a transcendental consciousness which exceeds all images and concepts, 'a flight of the alone to the Absolute'" [150].

---

[144] *The Spirit in Man,* p. 487.

[145] Cf. IVL, p. 112.

[146] Cf. Ibid., p. 126, 130-131.

[147] RF, p. 77.

[148] Ibid., p. 104.

[149] Ibid., p. 151. Cf. also OSW, October 1952 - January 1956, p. 256; RCW, p. 100.

[150] Ibid., p. 145. « If it is unknowable and incomprehensible, it is yet realizable by self-discipline and integral insight. We can seize the truth not by logical thinking, but by the energy of our whole inner being » (Pr. Ups. pp. 50-1).

2) REVELATION OF GOD AND HIS WAY TO MAN

In his opening chapter of *Eastern Religions and Western Thought* Radhakrishnan observes that the organised religions' stand on revelation — "insistence on the insufficiency of the intellectual and the importance of the historical" — is very fundamental to them [151]. We are examining here Radhakrishnan's exact views on, and his evaluation of, divine revelation on which he believes the organized religions rest.

As W. R. Inge points out, Radhakrishnan does not argue that there has been no revelation. But does he differ as to its meaning and nature from the established positions of the organised religions? That is an important question.

i. *Revelation in Science and Religion according to Radhakrishnan*

Radhakrishnan often speaks of revelation in science and religion. For the Christian theologian there is a world of difference between the two. But Radhakrishnan seems to recognize no real difference between revelation in science and that in religion. For him whatever be the difference between the two, it is only apparent, not real. He says:

> "If we look deeply, we find that the revelation we are said to have in religion is not distinct in kind from that which we have in science. We assume that scientific knowledge is the result of logical deduction and analysis of accumulated data, whereas religious knowledge is by revelation. Great scientific ideas arise, more or less, like religious revelations. Moses was long troubled by the problem of saving the children of Israel and suddenly had a revelation by the burning bush ... After hard work and intellectual commitment to a problem, the scientists suddenly see the answer by a revelation, as it were ...
> In both religion and science, it is an imaginative leap and not facts that lead to discovery and creation" [152].

In this sense Radhakrishnan suggests that all great art is essentially liturgy. "All great artists who have the subtle, spiritual appeal convey a stillness, a remoteness, a sense of the beyond, the

---

[151] ERWTh, p. 8.
[152] RCW, p. 74. This idea is from *Br. Up.* II, 4. 10.

5

far away " [153].   He calls the artist a priest [154], and says that the
poet is a priest of the invisible world.   An artist or a poet is not
a mere entertainer, but a prophet who inspires and expresses in
varied ways the entire aspirations of his society [155].   So also according to Radhakrishnan, music and literature, dance and drama,
sculpture and painting are intended to purge the soul of its defects
and lead it to the vision of the Eternal.   It is by spiritual intuition that the artist attains the highest power of artistic expression [156].   Therefore the same divine spirit is revealing in scientific
genius, in artistic creation, in moral heroism and in religious experience [157].

Does then Radhakrishnan argue that man is granted supernatural revelations not only in religion and the affairs of religion,
but also in all his endeavours?   Or is he bringing down supernatural revelations to a natural level?   What is the relation between
natural and supernatural according to Radhakrishnan?   What is
the source of revelation — A transcendent God, or a God who is
consubstantial with man?

ii. *The Supernatural according to Radhakrishnan*

When we discussed the nature of God, we saw that according
to Radhakrishnan the wholly other Absolute is also at once the
immanent God who is the real self of man.   The transcendent
Absolute and the immanent God can be distinguished as two
sides of a single thing while they maintain a real identity.   That
implies that for Radhakrishnan the realms of the natural and the
supernatural are not absolutely unrelated or entirely independent.
According to him not only is the eternal manifested in the temporal
but the two are bound together.   To separate them is ruinous [158].
He believes that there is an organic connection between the world
of nature and the world of values or the spiritual.   This organic
relation is said to be salvific concerning man's ultimate goal of
existence.   In order to be delivered from the body of death, from

---

[153] Cf. OWS, October 1952 - February 1959, p. 134.

[154] OSW, October 1952 - February 1959, p. 133; Cf. also IVL, p. 162.

[155] Ibid., p. 128. This idea seems to be a later development in Radhakrishnan. In his EWRTh he classifies spiritual men on the one side and
soldiers, statesmen, scientists, industrialists, poets and philosophers on the
other. (Cf. p. 35 Cf. also *Hibbert Journal,* 35 (1936-7) 26).

[156] Cf. Ibid., p. 133.

[157] Cf. *The Spirit in Man,* p. 492. Cf. also IVL, pp. 138ff, 162, 170.

[158] Cf. IVL, p. 45, 57.

the life of isolation and transience we have to insist on this organic relation between the two orders. Radhakrishnan, in fact, insists on this relation so much that he does not recognize a supernatural order different from the universe. And for him the universe is essentially spiritual [159]. Man at his best is divine. Everyone can perfect himself to become a God-man. Therefore there is no dualism between the world of nature and that of supernatural. The spiritual is said to be an emergent of the natural in which it is rooted [160]. In Radhakrishnan's language " the supernatural is the natural in her true depths and infinity. It is not anything different from nature " [161]. So the temporal and the eternal, the whole belongs to one order — one may call it natural or supernatural. The rest is *māyā* which has no ultimate significance [162]. Still the supernatural can be said to be distinct in a certain way from the natural. The natural is what binds man to the world of *karma* and rebirth, and the supernatural is that which is divine in man; man's spiritual striving consists precisely in making the divine in man emerge free from the fetters of rebirth and phenomenal existence.

iii. *Source of Revelation*

Once the doctrine of man's consubstantiality with the divine nature is admitted, a question arises: do divine revelations come from within or from without? Can man by his own natural powers attain divine revelations or do they depend absolutely on God's will? We are trying here to discover Radhakrishnan's answer to this problem.

Radhakrishnan often says that man can attain to the revelation of God in his human heart. The reward of a life converted into ' one single great continuing prayer ' is said to be not only the ascent of man to God but also " the revelation of God in the heart of man " [163]. The ground of this assertion, as pointed out by Radhakrishnan, is man's divine nature [164]. He explains how the inspirations originate:

---

[159] Cf. Ibid., pp. 86, 248f.

[160] Cf. Ibid., pp. 88, RCW, p. 86.

[161] Ibid., p. 46. Cf. also OSW, July 1959 - May 1962, p. 220, 237; EWRTh, p. 16, 77. Ind. Ph. II, p. 373.

[162] Cf. EWRTh, p. 131.

[163] RCW, p. 127. The same sentence is found in OSW, July 1959 - May 1962, p. 236.

[164] OSW, July 1959 - May 1962, p. 236f.

" There is a mind in man immeasurably superior to the ordinary mind. With the upper surface of the mind we articulate thoughts; deep down is the region where we meditate. We imagine that inspiration comes from above the soul; it comes from within the soul, from above the conceptual reason " [165].

When we are struggling under duality, our intellect stands over against our own real self and feels itself to be not one with the real self, but something external to it. But by developing detachment and objectivity towards one's own needs and sufficient compassion for others' needs and practising renunciation and contemplation one can overcome the duality [166]. Our state of duality is kept up, as it were, by a veil between the real self — the divine in us — and the apparent, superficial self. If ever the veil is pierced or dropped, things divine appear. There we have genuine revelation. So to attain to revelation we are asked " to unveil the deepest layers of man's being and get into enduring contact with them " [167].

The veil is pierced not by anything external but by man's intuitive power. By intuition man comes into immediate touch with the central reality. Following the Upanishads, Radhakrishnan says that man can attain to " direct intercourse with the central reality, intercourse not through any external media such as historical revelations, oracles, answers to prayers, and the like, but by a species of intuitive identification in which the individual becomes in very truth the partaker of the divine nature " [168]. In intuition the subject-object distinction vanishes and the absolute truth is perceived by the individual. When all the distinction vanishes the infinite will naturally reveal at its fullest in the self [169]. So says Radhakrishnan, " integral insight discloses to us eternity, timelessness in which time and history are included. Truth is not the reflection of reality in sense and intellect. It is a creative mystery experienced by soul in its deepest being " [170]. Thus Radhakrishnan believes in the power of the human mind to lead

---

[165] RF, p. 170.
[166] OSW, July 1959 - May 1962, p. 236.
[167] EWRTh, p. 21. Cf. also OSW, October 1952 - February 1959, p. 319.
[168] ERWTh, p. 129.
[169] Cf. A. N. MARLOW, *Spiritual Religion and the Philosophy of Radhakrishnan*, in PhSR, p. 348.
[170] RF, p. 107.

us to all truths, temporal and eternal [171], to let us into the realm of spirit and reality [172]. In those highest moments man feels within himself the spark of the divine and he becomes a ' revealing fragment of the secret plan of the universe ' [173].

Thus Radhakrishnan teaches the revealing power of human intuition and its capacity to substitute for the supernatural revelation of the organized religions. He claims that many philosophers in East and West have reached the conclusion that " religious insights are also genuine revelations of the Ultimate Reality " [174]. No real separation is admitted between God's revelation of a truth and man's intuition of the same truth. It is only a matter of different viewpoints. Radhakrishnan says that the manifestation of a truth may be viewed either as the revelation of God or as the realization of the capacities of man. The two though distinguishable are inseparable. They are two aspects of one process [175]. In one text Radhakrishnan identifies, without mentioning any distinction, revelation with intuition: " There is something transcending the consciousness of self ", says he, " to which many names are given — Intuition, Revelation, Cosmic Consciousness and God-vision " [176].

In short, the real self of man is a genuine source of divine revelation [177]. In Radhakrishnan's language, " whatever is conceived in the womb of the human soul is always of the Holy Spirit " [178]. When integral insight sees it, there is God's revelation.

---

[171] i. e. all truths, natural as well as supernatural.

[172] Cf. Ind. Ph. II, 26; *The Spirit in Man,* p. 484; *The Brahma Sūtra,* p. 107.

[173] Cf. *The Spirit in Man,* p. 489.

[174] OSW, July 1959 - May 1962, p. 230. W. R. Inge also teaches the same doctrine. He says that the « vision of the One » is natural to man and attained by a gradual growth from « sense-perception up to the vision of the One ». It is said to be not a miraculous favour. Cf. *The Philosophy of Plotinus,* II (London 1948) 149. Radhakrishnan has a similar phrase: « Spiritual realization is not a miraculous solution of life's problems but a slow deposit of life's fullness, a fruit which grows on the tree of life when it is mature » (ERWTh, p. 77). At the end of the same article he says that Christians also have such experience but « are more invasions from beyond than developments from within » (Ibid., p. 79f).

[175] IVL, p. 267. Cf. also Ibid., p. 81, 174.

[176] *A Source Book,* p. 353.

[177] Cf. ERWTh, p. 22.

[178] *Fragments,* p. 80.

iv. *External Revelation*

One may ask if Radhakrishnan admits the existence of any external divine revelations which do not originate from the heart of man. If man has the natural capacity to intuit the highest truth and know it perfectly, then an external revelation is unwanted if not useless [179]. The universe is working according to some eternal laws. Its orderly evolution is a revelation in progress. So says Radhakrishnan: " According to the Vedanta philosophy it is not correct to speak of sudden revelation of spirit when we come to life, for even matter is spirit, though in its lowest mode of manifestation " [180]. Therefore, a God who reveals Himself in the exceptional and the miraculous, and to a particular people and " not in the regular course of nature " — a God who intervenes decisively in history — " is a God who breaks in upon a world which would otherwise seem to lack his presence " [181]. Such interventions, if they exist, even if they are for our betterment, will take away man's freedom. " God is no arbitrary despot who denies the freedom of man. His power does not prevent us from being ourselves " [182].

Radhakrishnan holds that an excessive insistence on the importance of external revelation is dangerous to religion itself. He warns us against confusing religion with the acknowledgement of revealed truths. That will cause religion to be dominated by outward machinery [183]. To tie ourselves down to any set of doctrines revealed to a particular person or people is to be static in religious life. In religion it is better to be in perpetual search, to be dynamic [184]. Therefore, if any religion claims to be the depository of revealed truths, that religion is going against the purpose of religion. According to Radhakrishnan this happened in Christianity: " The Roman Empire failed to destroy Christianity by persecution, but the hour of her victory over Rome signalized the defeat of the Gospel of Jesus ... The Church became the depository of sacred wisdom, a sort of reservoir of theological secrets and not a spring " [185]. Thus when the Church became the bearer

---

179 Cf. ERWTh., p. 129.
180 RR, p. 416.
181 RCW, p. 86.
182 Ibid., p. 146.
183 Cf. RS, p. 52.
184 Cf. Ibid., p. 54.
185 EWR, p. 62.

of revelation it ceased to be a religion of growth and freedom and became one of regimentation [186]. " But if we are true to the teachings of Jesus ", says Radhakrishnan, " we shall know that absolute truth goes beyond all forms and creeds, all historic revelations and institutions " [187].

Radhakrishnan does not believe that there are external revelations. The claims of possession of revelation are all inventions of theologians. For example, it was the Apologists who invented revealed doctrines in Christianity. He explains it as follows. The Apologists tried to persuade their world that Christianity was the highest wisdom and absolute truth and used the concepts of Greek thought for this purpose. They accepted the whole tradition, both Old and New, as ultimate revelation, and so their speculations, though not Greek in character, became the foundation of the Church dogma. Human systems of philosophy are said to be not completely true. Christian revelation was shown to be the only complete truth. Thus the teaching of Christianity became with the Apologists revealed doctrine [188].

Radhakrishnan rules out the idea of a final revelation. " There is no such thing as a faith once for all delivered to the saints " [189]. He approvingly quotes Charles E. Raven, who rejects any claim to finality as something that perplexes those who have a proper sense of their limitations:

> " It is precisely this claim to an absolute finality whether in the church or in the Scripture or in Jesus Christ or in anything else, this claim that revelation belongs to a totally different order of reality from discovery ... that perplexes and affronts those of us who have a proper sense of our own limitations " [190].

Hence Radhakrishnan argues that the distinction of revealed and non-revealed religions, which organized religions, especially Christianity, use in their own support is no longer tenable [191]. Religions are said to be the " natural outcome of the human mind " [192].

---

[186] Cf. Ibid., p. 64.

[187] Ibid., p. 65.

[188] ERWTh, pp. 227-229.

[189] *Fragments,* p. 76.

[190] Cf. RF, p. 195, n. 13. Also refered to in OSW, October 1952 - February 1959, p. 309, n. 1.

[191] Cf. EWR, p. 38.

[192] ERWTh, p. 184. Cf. also p. 21, 294. Cf. also OSW, October 1952 - February 1959, p. 377.

They did not come into the world as ready made supernatural systems [193]. That was the conclusion which Radhakrishnan reached after denying the supernatural character of revelation.

There is however one passage in Radhakrishnan, which seems difficult to explain in this way. It appears in his "*Introduction*" to *The Principal Upanishads*. When he explains the meaning of "*śruti* or revealed literature", he says: "The inspired sages proclaim that the knowledge they communicate is not what they discover for themselves. It is revealed to them without their effort. Though the knowledge is an experience of the seer, it is an experience of an independent reality which impinges on his consciousness. There is the impact of the real on the spirit of the experiencer. It is therefore said to be a direct disclosure from the 'wholly other', a revelation of the divine" (pp. 22-23). Does Radhakrishnan here admit an external divine revelation which is not just another aspect of intuition?

Radhakrishnan cannot hold such an opinion without contradicting his own basic theories and a number of his pronouncements on the matter. Therefore we think that here he might be giving the dualistic or theistic understanding of the '*śruti*' as a disclosure from the wholly other God with which he does not agree. Many of his statements which come later in the same "*Introduction*" seem to justify our view. For example he says: "To impress on the people the need for preserving the literature, the Veda was declared to be sacred knowledge or divine revelation" (p. 29). (Veda is admittedly *śruti*). The road by which the Vedic sages travelled was the road of those who seek to inquire and understand" (p. 29. Cf. also p. 44). So the truth is attained by the seers and not "revealed to them without their effort". "The *Upanishads* give in some detail the path of the inner ascent, the inward journey by which the individual souls get at the Ultimate Reality. Truth is within us" (p. 49. Cf. also pp. 95, 96, 97). Once Radhakrishnan clearly says that we have intellectual intuition in *śruti*. "The experience is recorded as a pure and direct intellectual intuition in *śruti*" (p. 103). Therefore, Radhakrishnan does not hold that revelation is a direct disclosure of truth by the 'wholly other', not discovered by man but impinged on him without his effort. This our view is justified also from other writings of Radhakrishnan. For example, in his essay *Reason and Revelation* in *The Brahma Sūtra* (pp. 103-118) he mainly speaks of intuition

---

[193] Cf. OSW, October 1952 - February 1959, p. 381.

which reveals the object perfectly. He agrees that for an educated person it is difficult to rest faith on a miraculous revelation in the past (p. 113). Here also he clearly points out that the Scriptures are the records of human intuition: "The records of the experiences of the great seers who have experienced their sense of the inner meaning of the world through their intense insight and deep imagination are the Scriptures" (p. 113).

v. *Human Element in the Divine Revelation*

Divine inspirations and revelations, according to Radhakrishnan are joint activities of which man's contemplation and God's revelation are two sides [194]. Revelation is said to be 'divine-human' [195]. It is a two-fold act. It issues from God, who cannot be reduced to any catagories of this world. It also depends on man, the recipient, historically conditioned though he be [196]. Every revealed Scripture is therefore, "at once both divine self-manifestation and the way in which human beings have received it. There is reciprocity of inward and outward. Revelation and its reception are inseparably united" [197].

In so far as revelation is considered purely an act of God, it is immemorial, *sanātana,* timeless. It is a "direct disclosure from the 'wholly other', a revelation of the Divine" [198]. But that does not mean that man is in possession of the absolute and the final truth. "Truth is eternal, but there are degrees and varieties in the disclosure of truth and in the way it is received" [199]. So on

---

[194] Cf. Pr. Ups, p. 23.

[195] Cf. *Fragments,* p. 76.

[196] Cf. RC, p. 810.

[197] *The Brahma Sūtra,* p. 112. The phrase 'inward and outward' in relation to revelation is very difficult to fit into the theology of Radhakrishnan. Either he must be here, for argument's sake, assuming the Christian concept of revelation, against whose stand that « Jesus is the final self-manifestation of the Divine » (Ibid.), he is arguing; or 'inward and outward' is parallel to the preceding phrase: « divine self-manifestation and the way in which human beings have received ». Then « divine self-manifestation » stands for « inward » — the real self of man, and « the way in which human beings have received » for the « outward » — the superficial outward self of man, which is the case of one who is in *avidyā* and who feels to have received a revelation from above — the situation of a Christian against whose belief in the finality of the Christian revelation Radhakrishnan is arguing.

[198] Cf. Pr. Ups, pp. 22-23.

[199] RC, p. 810.

the part of God the disclosure is not perfect because God does attune His revelation to the state of the human mind [200]. The recipient, who is imperfect, also receives in his imperfect way. Radhakrishnan observes: " We are the receptacles of the revelation. Our own form of reception cannot be confused with ' an assumedly undiluted and untransformed revelation ', in Professor Paul Tillich's words. ' Wherever the divine is manifest in flesh, it is in a concrete physical and historical reality ' " [201].

Therefore according to Radhakrishnan the Revelation of God in so far as is experienced in the human realm is impossible to be perfect. To put it in his own words:

> " However perfect and final the revelation may be, when once it enters the realm of human apprehension, it is subject to all the imperfections of the human mind. To claim finality or infallibility for human pictures of reality is to claim for man what belongs to God. If anyône tells us that his view of the Supreme is final, it is a human judgement which need not be taken as infallible " [202].

No revelation is to be taken as final or absolute. They are only symbols. When there is an awakening of the mind, the old symbols must be interpreted in a new way [203]. Accordingly Radhakrishnan reinterprets the meaning of the " Revealed Religion ": " Even if religions claim to be the results of divine revelation, the forms and contents are necessarily the products of the human mind " [204]. Thus he puts the emphasis on the human element in revelation, while the accent on the divine is reduced to a minimum. Consequently, he comes to the conclusion that the fundamental error of all organized religions is that they have overlooked the human element in divine revelation and identified the conditioned form of receiving with the divine itself [205], as happened in Christianity with the Apologists [206].

---

[200] Cf. *Fragments*, p. 76.

[201] *The Brahma Sūtra*, p. 113.

[202] RF, p. 154. Cf. also OSW, July 1959 - May 1962, p. 238.

[203] Cf. Pr. Ups, p. 27.

[204] OSW, October 1952 - February 1959, p. 320. Radhakrishnan's source seems to be *Svetasvatara Upanishad*, IV, 17. « That God maker of all things, the great self, ever seated in the heart of creatures is framed by the heart, by the thought, by the mind ... ».

[205] Cf. *The Brahma Sūtra*, p. 112, n. 1.

[206] Cf. ERWTh., pp. 227-229.

vi. *Intuition and Revelation*

On the one hand it is said that truths are breathed out by God and men have received them. On the other, human intuition is presented as real revelation; man's intuitive power reaches the highest reality and apprehends the absolute truth immediately. How are we to reconcile these two views?

The principle that works in the mind of Radhakrishnan, we think, here too is the basic distinction of the two orders: the order of *māyā* and that of the spiritual. Those who are in the order of *māyā* are in duality. In their *avidyā* they think that they are receiving truths from a God who is set over against their own selves, a God who is considered to be absolutely different from themselves. But those who are in the order of the spirit possess *vidyā* and have realized their consubstantiality with the Divine. There is no duality. They intuit immediately the truth which is the real divine revelation, looking at it from an absolute point of view.

All the organized religions belong to the first class. There the revelation is attuned to the nature of the receiver. And he receives it necessarily in an imperfect way. The authority and perfection of revelation in God is admitted. But the revealed truth as expressed by any human agent is necessarily imperfect, relative and unauthoritative. Moreover the truth is revealed to the individual according to his particular nature [207], and so intended only for him. Therefore, the truth given to one is not to be imposed on another [208].

In the second case the seer sees the truth. The truth as immediately seen in intuition is perfect. But as expressed, it is imperfect, because it is conceptualized. Therefore for him, who has immediate intuition of a truth, his own authority, which is absolute, is above any other authority—whether of the Church or of the Scripture. "The authority for revelation", says Radhakrishnan, "is not an infallible book or an infallible church but the witness of an inner light. What is needed is not submission to an external authority but illumination which, of course, is tested by tradition and logic" [209].

This view of Radhakrishnan on divine revelation militates against the most fundamental claims of organized religions. An organized religion, in this view, becomes an organization built on unreal foundations — invalid claims, incorrect assumptions and imperfect beliefs.

---

[207] Cf. RS, p. 60.
[208] Cf. *The Brahma Sūtra*, pp. 112-113, n. 1.
[209] *Fragments*, p. 77.

IV

ORIGIN AND DEVELOPMENT OF ORGANIZED RELIGIONS

Organized religions trace their beginning to a founder-prophet or to God Himself. Whether the founder be a prophet sent by God or God Himself, the act of founding the religion is said to be an intervention by God in the history of man. This divine intervention gives to the religion the superb qualification ' supernatural '.

It has been already hinted that, consequent upon his views on revelation and intuition, Radhakrishnan would not admit the distinction between revealed and non-revealed religions. He maintains that no religion has come into the world as a ' ready-made supernatural system '. In this chapter we are considering how Radhakrishnan views the historical beginning and development of organized religions. This chapter has two parts: 1) Beginning of Religions; and 2) Development of Organized Religions.

1) BEGINNING OF RELIGIONS

i) *Natural Religion*

Even though Radhakrishnan rejects the idea of supernatural religion, it seems that he is not arguing that all religions are natural religions. For, he defines natural religion as " the view of God which we obtain from the employment of reason "[1]. There is a religion which is superior to this natural religion which may be named as intuitive religion. It has been already explained that God is known at best through our intuitive faculties. The religion resulting from the intuitive knowledge is not a ' natural religion ' in the above sense.

---

[1] *The Brahma Sūtra,* p. 104. This is the religion taught by *The Brahma Sūtra* in I, 1. 2. Cf. Ibid., pp. 335 ff.

But reason as well as intuition are natural faculties of man. Intuition is said to be more perfectly human than reason. It is not something bestowed on man by a power living in a world beyond.

Religion is a " personal encounter with the Supreme Reality " [2]. A personal encounter with the Supreme, though it is a ' costly business ' [3], as it is the result of hard effort [4], depends on man. It is he who has to approach God for the encounter, and think out the religion itself [5]. Religion begins to exist when man makes the necessary effort. Hence Radhakrishnan says that " all religions are human attempts to reach the Ultimate Reality " [6]. They are " the natural outcome of the human mind " [7]. God is reached at best through our intuition which is the most perfect human faculty. That means "religion is the perfection of the truly human " [8].

Therefore, if we understand by natural religion that which is not founded directly or indirectly by a supernatural power but which has come into being from the natural working of the human faculties, then all religions are viewed as natural.

ii) *The Truth about the Founding of Religions*

If all religions are the natural outcome of the human mind, native to it [9], what about the claims of organized religions that they are instituted at a definite point of time in history with God-given doctrines, rites and authority? To see the historical accuracy of such a claim we have to return to history itself. A sceptical and critical attitude towards all such claims and a re-scrutinizing of all accepted beliefs are necessary [10].

From his comparative study of religions, Radhakrishnan says that " all religions have had a history and none is final or perfect. Religion is a movement, a growth and in all true growth the new rests on the old " [11]. The geneology of every organized religion is also full of generous borrowings from others. The phe-

---

[2] OSW, July 1959 - May 1962, p. 185. Cf. also RCW, p. 106.

[3] OSW, May 1962 - May 1964, p. 155.

[4] Cf. RCW, p. 125; OSW, May 1962 - May 1964, p. 121.

[5] Cf. *The Brahma Sūtra*, p. 106; IVL, p. 61.

[6] OSW, October 1952 - February 1959, p. 377.

[7] ERWTh, p. 184.

[8] RF, p. 49.

[9] Cf. EWR, p. 18.

[10] Cf. IVL, p. 173.

[11] EWR, p. 19.

nomenology of religion also confirms this [12]. The fundamental
teachings and doctrines, rites and ceremonies of any religion are
found in other religions as well. In this regard much has been
written by Radhakrishnan to show that the basic rites and doctrines
of Christianity are found in other religions. Even St Augustine
is said to have supported this view when he said that Christian
religion existed from the very beginning of the human race, although
it began to be called Christianity only after the coming of Christ [13].

Radhakrishnan's main point is that the doctrines and rites
found in present-day organized religions are neither given by their
so-called founders nor their own making. They have taken them
from other primitive beliefs. Consciously or unconsciously they
have adopted wonder-tales about the ancient heroes and suitably
applied them to their own religious hero. They adapted the
attractive ceremonies from the primitive religions and attributed
their origin to their own founder. Secondly, there is an attempt
to establish that the main sources from which the Western religions have borrowed are the Indian religions, Hinduism and
Buddhism. This theory is applied in a very particular way to
Christianity which is supposed to be adamant on its claim to
divine origin.

The most elaborate exposition of this theory is found in his
Eastern Religions and Western Thought in which Radhakrishnan
often forgets to put into practice his great appeals for tolerance
and goes to the extremes which will certainly offend any devout
Christian reader [14]. Here he maintains that " the accounts of

---

[12] Cf. OSW, July 1959 - May 1962, p. 239 f.

[13] Cf. EWR, pp. 31-32.

[14] Joachim Wach in his essay *Radhakrishnan and Comparative Study
of Religion* (Cf. PhSR, pp. 443-458) had pointed out that there is a notable trace of bitterness in a great number of references to Christianity » in
Radhakrishnan's writings. To this charge Radhakrishnan replied: « If
he finds it so, there must be a basis for his statement and I am sincerely
sorry for it » (RC, p. 807). Still one feels that this attitude towards Christianity persisted in him. A notable change is that criticisms of Christianity
in his later works are often put in the foot notes and as citations from
the bitterest critics of Christianity. e. g. « Professor John Macmurray
maintains that in practice communism is more truly Christian than Christianity itself » (RF, p. 56, n. 21). Even in his *Fellowship of the Spirit* he
quotes Kirsopp Lake's father as saying that the two things that have done
most to relieve human suffering are « Anaesthesia and the decay of Christian
theology » (p. 4, n. 2). He quotes also Soren Kierkegaard's Attack upon
Christendom: « What we have before us is not Christianity but a prodigious
illusion » (Ibid., p. 5).

Jesus transmitted to us by the Evangelists are historically quite untrustworthy "[15]. He tries to prove this position, depending heavily on critics like Lightfoot, Harnack, Loisy etc.[16]. The long discussion in chapter five is mainly intended to establish that " the moral teaching of Jesus with its ascetic and other-worldly emphasis has been anticipated several hundred years by the Upanishads and Buddha "[17], and therefore the " noblest of the moral lessons usually supposed to be characteristic of Christianity are not characteristic of it alone. They are the necessary consequence of the spiritual life "[18]. The same theory is found in many other writings of Radhakrishnan, mainly in *East and West in Religion* and in *East and West Some Reflections*. He seems to have never even doubted the validity of this theory. About forty years after his first noted exposition of this theory in *Eastern Religions and Western Thought*, he expounds the same view in his latest work, *Religion in a Changing World*: " Christianity has much in common with Mithraism. The similarities may be due to direct borrowing or the common Indian background "[19]. We will just indicate the main lines of this theory.

The Essenes of Palestine and Therapeutaes of Alexandria were possibly Buddhist communities. At any rate they were certainly influenced by Buddhist ideas to a great extent[20]. For instance, both have great esteem for continence; both believe in the immortality of the soul[21]. The concept of the Greek Logos which entered the fourth Gospel is " analogous to the Vedic *Vak*, the word as divine power "[22]. The stories about the birth of Christ and of Krishna are similar[23]. Christ's parable of the sower is " evidently from Buddha "[24]. There are temptation stories in the Upanishads and Buddha. The Jews were acquainted with these stories[25]. When pagan polytheism and the Jewish monotheism fused together, the Christian God who is a society — Holy

---

[15] ERWTh, p. 164.
[16] Cf. Ibid., pp. 164 ff.
[17] Ibid., p. 173.
[18] Ibid., p. 174.
[19] RCW, p. 39.
[20] Cf. EWS, p. 63.
[21] Ibid.
[22] Ibid., p. 66.
[23] Ibid., p. 70.
[24] Ibid.
[25] Ibid.

Trinity — came [26]. After a long consideration of the origin of
the Christian doctrines Radhakrishnan concludes with C. F.
Andrews that " it was from India the beauty of Christianity has
sprung " [27].

There are many similarities between Christianity and Mithraism. For example, both believed in baptism and practised
asceticism. Both believed in a mediator between God and man,
who is a saviour-God, who will judge all men in the end of time [28].
Both had consecration of bread and wine, and sacrifice was considered necessary for salvation [29]. Thus Radhakrishnan argues
that " the rites of sacrifice and communion which are the very bases
of Christianity can be traced to such primitive beliefs " [30]. In
short,

> " The concepts of Virgin birth, the death and resurrection
> of the redeemer God, the inspiration of the sacred scripture,
> the efficacy of grace, the use of rosary, the conception of
> Trinity, the Kingdom of God, priesthood, monasticism —
> these are to be found in many religions and are not exclusive
> to any one " [31].

According to Radhakrishnan there are two possible explanations for the striking resemblances among different religions :
Either they are due to a common origin or due to the fact that,
when the same phenomena confront human intelligence, similar
inferences were drawn everywhere and common instincts led to
the building of similar cults [32]. The two solutions may be combined
and we conclude that all religions have like origins. After a de-
tailed exposition of the similarities between Jesus and the Buddha
an evaluation of it is given as follows :

> " Our ignorance of what actually happened need not prevent
> us from noting the resemblances which strikingly make out
> that Buddha and Jesus are men of the same brotherhood.
> Our interest is in the logic of religious experience, and both
> Buddha and Jesus are eminent witnesses to it. There can-
> not be any difference of opinion regarding the view of life

---

[26] Cf. EWR, p. 61.
[27] EWS, p. 79.
[28] Cf. Ibid., p. 69; EWR, p. 17.
[29] Cf. EWR, p. 17.
[30] Ibid.
[31] OSW, July 1959 - May 1962, p. 240.
[32] Cf. EWR, p. 33.

and the world of thought which seem to be common to
Buddhism and Christianity in their early forms. Whether
historically connected or not, they are the twin expressions
of one great spiritual movement. The verbal parallels and
ideal similarities reveal the impressive unity of religious
aspiration. Buddha and Jesus are the earlier and later
Hindu and Jewish representatives of the same upheaval
of the human soul, whose typical expression we have in
the Upanishads. Whether the two met in early times and
one borrowed from the other is of little moment " [33].

Therefore no single religion can have any absolute claim of superiority over another because of its institution. The claim of organized religions that their rites and doctrines are given and fixed
by the very founder himself becomes untenable. This conclusion
brings another important question: How did religions begin?
What is the primary fact which gave rise to the different religions?

iii) *The Historical Beginning of Religions*

We have seen that the intellect, for Radhakrishnan, has no
power in the order of the spiritual [34]. It is religious intuition
from which thought has to start and to which it has to return [35].
All the so-called founders of religions had intuitive knowledge
of religious matters, that is, direct acquaintance with the spiritual
reality [36]. On this direct encounter with the Divine are based
all authentic religions [37]. Thus all religions without exception have
their historical origin from a human experience of the Divine [38].
Radrakrishnan devotes a full chapter in his *Recovery of Faith*
(chapter five: " Spiritual Life and Living Faiths ", pp. 110-143)
to establish that,

> " All religions are founded on the personal experience of
> the seers who became directly aware of an Infinite Spiritual
> Presence beyond and within the range of the world of change
> and succession. The personal experience of union with the

---

[33] ERWTh, p. 186.
[34] Cf. OSW, May 1962 - May 1964, p. 118.
[35] Cf. HVL, p. 14.
[36] Cf. MST, p. 28.
[37] Cf. RCW, pp. 118-119; OSW, July 1959 - May 1962, p. 231; OSW,
May 1962 - May 1964, p. 129.
[38] Cf. *Fragments,* p. 62; RS, p. 42, 44; OSW, July 1959 - May 1962,
pp. 228, 305; *The Brahma Sūtra,* p. 112ff; RCW, p. 72.

Absolute Reality or God has been a common and continuous feature of all the faiths of mankind " [39].

He examines Hinduism, Taoism, Judaism, the Greek religion, Zoroastrianism, Buddhism, Christianity, Islam: Sufism and concludes that in all these spiritual experience is the primary fact. This theory has been constantly upheld and preached by Radhakrishnan. He applies it to every religion. In his Presidential Address at the All India Oriental Conference, Annamalai University, Annamalainagar, on December 26, 1955 he explains the origin of Buddhism in accordance with this theory:

> " The name of Buddha means the Awakened One, from the root ' budh ' to awaken. The Buddha is one who attained spiritual realization. He gives us a way based on clear knowledge, or awakening. Buddhism is a system of spiritual realization. So in Buddhism personal realization is the starting point. The religious experience of the Buddha is the fundamental source of the religious knowledge of the Buddhists " [40].

The Jewish religion has its origin in the spiritual experience of its prophets. Moses had experience of God by the burning bush and Elijah heard the voice of God. Jeremiah also witnesses to his experience of God [41]. In Isaiah and the Psalms we see the same human experience of the Divine [42].

Jesus' experience of God is the basic fact of Christianity [43]. St. Paul's Christianity began with vision and not with an " external revelation " [44]. This is true of Mohammad [45] and the Hindu seers [46]. All religions in their original purity stressed the fact of spiritual experience.

> " When the Upanishads speak of jñāna or gnosis, when the Buddha speaks of bodhi or enlightenment, when Jesus speaks of the truth that will make us free, they refer to the mode of direct spiritual apprehension of the Supreme, in which

---

[39] RF, p. 110.
[40] OSW, October 1952 - February 1959, p. 324. Cf. also GB, p. 31; IVL, p. 71.
[41] Cf. IVL, p. 71; RF, p. 115.
[42] Cf. RF, p. 115.
[43] Cf. IVL, p. 71; RF, p. 124.
[44] ERWTh, p. 221.
[45] Cf. IVL, p. 71.
[46] Cf. Ibid., p. 70; Fragments, p. 62; RF, p. 110ff.

the gap between the truth and Being is closed. Their religion rests on the testimony of the Holy Spirit, on personal experience " [47].

How are we to account for the spiritual experiences, which are essentially similar, of different people in different circumstances? Radhakrishnan's answer is based on the real self of man which according to him is divine. Because of the Divine in man there is an " inner religious consciousness " [48] which is innate to man [49]. Under favourable circumstances this inner religious consciousness reveals itself or unfolds from within [50]. All the founders of religions are such awakened men, whose inner religious consciousness had grown fully and is revealed in an extraordinary way. Accordingly, one may distinguish two things in the religious founders: the person of the founder, and his acquired personality which is different from the original one and may be called " Christhood " or " Buddhahood ". In this way the person of Jesus is said to be a historical fact but Christ is " not a datum of history but a judgment of history " [51], and " Christ is not to be equated with the historic Jesus " [52].

The awakened men, Buddha, Jesus and the seers of Upanishads lived in different circumstances and when they gave voice to their inner experience, it came out in sounds which rang differently [53]. " The Divine reveals itself to men within the framework of their intimate prejudices. Each religious genius spells out the mystery of God according to his own endowment, personal, racial and historical. The variety of pictures of the God is easily intelligible when we realize that religious experience is psychologically mediated " [54]. This means that not only are the differences unimportant but also that no religious account is perfect or infallible. But the followers of each awakened religious genius took every utterance of their leader as immutable and final and therefore every difference as an unbridgeable gulf. The miraculous stories they had heard of the gods of primitive religions began to be retold of their own heroes. Add to this their imagination. " Na-

---

[47] *Fragments,* p. 60.
[48] EWR, p. 32. Cf. also ERWTh, p. 85.
[49] Ibid., p. 18.
[50] RF, p. 143.
[51] RC, p. 802.
[52] RF, p. 159.
[53] Cf. EWR, p. 32.
[54] HVL, pp. 19-20.

turally men made a God of the Buddha who renounced the most precious human ties, of the Jesus who suffered and died " [55]. Based on these differences, stories and tales, theological systems began to be evolved, which marked the beginning of organized religions.

If we consider the same thing the other way round, we get that since the Divine is in every man, everyone is entitled to have spiritual experiences of the same kind and measure as Buddha and Jesus had attained [56]. In the common man the spirit and the inner religious consciousness are latent. In that sense Radhakrishnan says: " We are dead people; we should wake up " [57]. What the great religious teachers tried to do was not to found a new religion but to awaken the sleeping spirit in man. This is said to be the teaching of Jesus and Christianity in their pure form :

> " Christian teaching in its origin, before it became externalized and organized, was about awakening from sleep through the light shed by the inner wisdom. Jesus was one who had awakened and taught others the way of awakening " [58]. " When, according to the Fourth Gospel, Jesus says, ' I am come that they might have life and have it more abundantly ', he means that he opens the eyes of men, quickens their sensitiveness, arouses them from their sleep, discloses to them the reality of the Eternal dwelling in them. This is to be born again " [59].

In the same way Buddha also taught others the way of awakening [60]. It is therefore not by submitting to another's authority or by accepting a dogma that one becomes religious in the real sense [61]. " To be a Christian is not the profession of an outward creed but the living of an inward life " [62]. Organized religions depend on " alleged miracles " [63] or on human authority. " The authority of the Scripture, the tradition of the Church or the

---

[55] EWR, p. 125.

[56] Cf. RF, p. 179.

[57] OSW, October 1952 - February 1959, p. 307.

[58] Ibid. Cf. also EWS, p. 73.

[59] RF, p. 160.

[60] EWS, p. 73.

[61] Cf. RF, p. 143.

[62] Ibid., p. 160.

[63] Radhakrishnan is of opinion that modern man nurtured in the scientific spirit cannot accept the stories about miracles as historically valid (Cf. RC, p. 802).

casuistries of schoolmen who proclaim but do not prove, may not carry conviction to many of us who are the children of science and reason, but we must submit to the fact of spiritual experience, which is primary and positive. We may dispute theologies, but cannot deny facts "[64]. Thus Radhakrishnan subordinates sacred Scripture, tradition and the authoritative teaching of the Church to personal spiritual experience. In other words faith in Jesus as a historic person portrayed in the Gospels and the knowledge of him are not salutary. The inner spirit in every man is the Christ. And for salvation one must have faith in that spirit [65]. Just as with the awakening of the religious consciousness the religion of Jesus and Buddha began, our own personal religion originates when our religious consciousness is awakened and we realize the spirit in us. This view of religion gives the whole importance to experience and life and not to doctrine and dogma. It renders the distinction between true religion and false religion untenable. Radhakrishnan observes:

> " The universal condemnation, pronounced by the Roman Catholic and the Anglican articles on non-Christian faiths as ' all false ' becomes absurd. Generally the distinction between true and false is identical with mine and thine "[66].

The important question, therefore, with regard to religion is " not truth or falsehood but life or death. Is it a dead curiosity or a going concern "?[67]. This view of religion thus deprives every organized religion of any vestige of superiority on account of its doctrinal perfection, which is a fundamental claim of the organized religions.

2) DEVELOPMENT OF ORGANIZED RELIGIONS

i) The Claim to Exclusive Possession of Divine Revelation

Is there a chosen people to whom God has entrusted special revelations? That is evidently an important question with re-

---

[64] ERWTh, pp. 22-23. Cf. also Ibid., p. 61; RF, p. 77.
[65] Cf. RF, p. 159.
[66] EWR, pp. 37-38.
[67] Ibid., p. 38. By ' going concern ' Radhakrishnan seems to mean ' alive ', i. e., the condition when the religion is practised by its followers.

ference to organized religions, as they claim that God has revealed and entrusted to them doctrines with the authority to teach.

In his opening essay in *Eastern Religions and Western Thought* Radhakrishnan discusses how the exclusive claims came to be in Judaism and Christianity. These religions give first importance to historic revelations. God is conceived as a supreme person who intervenes decisively in history, revealing His will to His chosen prophets and law-givers. In addition Christians believe that God assumed human nature and lived a human life on earth [68]. The Jews had an intense expectation of some great event which would be the decisive solution to historical problem. This Messianic idea, which is the determining factor in Jewish history, survived in Christianity [69]. All organized religions have a similar claim to exclusive possession of divinely revealed doctrines.

We have already explained that for Radhakrishnan all men are equally divine at their best and their divine possibilities are also equal. What is possible for one is equally possible for any other [70]. Everything that has come out of the depth of man is holy and every scripture is equally revealed [71]. From this basic stand Radhakrishnan rejects all claims to the possession of special revelations. He thinks that no intelligent man could accept such claims.

> " We are not inclined to take any religious truth as an exclusive divine revelation. A revelation granted to a small group at a particular moment in history, reconstructed by fallible men in narratives which are not always consistent, does not appeal to intelligent men. The case becomes worse when we are unable to agree upon the doctrine or embody it in society " [72].
> " The claim to the possession of a special revelation of the Jews, Christians and Muslims is on the same level. It is not necessary for us to close the door to future revelations " [73].

---

[68] Cf. ERWTh, p. 8.
[69] Cf. ERWTh, pp. 8-9.
[70] Cf. RF, p. 173.
[71] Cf. *The Brahma Sūtra,* p. 117.
[72] OSW, October 1952 - February 1959, pp. 356-357.
[73] *The Brahma Sūtra,* p. 113. Cf. also ERWTh, p. 347; OSW, July 1959 - May 1962, p. 34.

After all God is not the exclusive possession of anybody [74], and nobody has a monopoly of truth [75]. God has not left Himself without a witness anywhere. " The witness has come to men of all races and creeds " [76]. Radhakrishnan claims that this view of revelation was taught by St Peter when he said, " Now of a truth I perceive that God is no respecter of persons, but in every nation, he that feareth Him and worketh righteousness is accepted by Him " [77]. Justin Martyr supported this view when he called those who lived by reason, such as Socrates and Heraclitus, Christians [78]. St Augustine taught the same thing when he said that Christianity existed from the beginning of human race [79]. Hence the conclusion that since God has revealed Himself everywhere there is no necessity for a special revelation and it does not exist. For, God does not make distinction between man and man [80]. The revelation of God in Christ is equal to the revelation through prophets or through the Upanishadic seers or through any great man. " God who has spoken through Christ has spoken through the great men of all ages " [81].

ii) *Reasons against Exclusive Possession of Divine Revelation*

1) It would be unfair to God who is love to say that He has made distinction between man and man. For, that implies that God is partial to a fraction of humanity [82]. Speaking on " Inter-religious Understanding " at Cleveland Council on World Affairs, Ohio [83], Radhakrishnan says:

> " If God is love, it cannot be that mankind lived for thousands of years without the revelation which he gave to the

---

[74] Cf. OSW, October 1952 - February 1959, p. 368.

[75] Cf. ERWTh, p. 346; FS, p. 19.

[76] OSW, July 1959 - May 1962, p. 396.

[77] EWR, pp. 30-31.

[78] Ibid., p. 30.

[79] Cf. Ibid., p. 31. Very often Radhakrishnan quotes the Fathers of the Church, like Origen and St Augustine for example, to prove that there is no special revelation and that all religions are equally good (Cf. ERWTh, p. 343; EWR, pp. 31-32; RF, p. 160; RS, p. 43; RC, p. 809). In all these books the same quotations are repeated. The Fathers were actually speaking of Christianity as prefigured in the Old Testament (Cf. HENRI DE LUBAC, *The Splendour of the Church,* Glen Rock, 1963, pp. 37-40).

[80] Cf. OSW, July 1959 - May 1962, p. 205.

[81] PhSR, p. 72.

[82] Cf. RCW, p. 132.

[83] Newton Baker Lecture on March 27, 1958.

tribe of Israel, and the adherents of other religions were shut away from his love ... The revelation of a God of love must embrace all nations, ages and religions. But if he restricts his revelation to the chosen people of the Old and the New Testaments and allows a large part of humanity to sit in darkness and death he cannot be a God of love. God manifests himself throughout history " [84].

Therefore, the conception of a chosen people and of a unique revelation is contrary to the love and justice of God. It is only a pet fancy of the pious [85].

2) Such a belief makes people intolerant towards other faiths [86]. And intolerance of believers can be a scandal for the unbelievers.

" Belief in the exclusive claims and monopolies of religious truth has been a frequent source of pride, fanaticism and strife. The vehemence with which religions were preached and the savagery with which they were enforced are some of the disgraces of human history. Secularism and paganism point to the rivalries of religions for a proof of the futility of religions " [87].

Even Communism may appear preferable to such intolerant religions [88]. When righteousness is practised because it is the will of God exclusively revealed to His chosen ones, it is then practised with a fervour and fanaticism that are ungodly. When the will of God is believed to be known one feels that it is one's obligation to pass it on and thinks it intolerable that it should be disobeyed.

Moreover such a belief produces a feeling of superiority in the possessors. But when there are different claimants to such absolute truth, they will naturally become impatient of one another If they get power they will use the torture-chamber, the stakes and the executioner, making people conformists rather than seekers [90]. Thus conflict and war become inevitable if we believe

---

84 OSW, October 1952 - February 1959, p. 382. Cf. also RF, p. 192.
85 Cf. MST, pp. 9-10.
86 Cf. RCW, p. 123.
87 *Fragments*, p. 72.
88 Cf. ERWTh, p. 290.
89 Ibid., pp. 9-10. Cf. also Ibid., p. 15; OSW, July 1959 - May 1962, p. 251.
90 OSW, July 1959 - May 1962, pp. 184-185, 247.

in an exclusive possession of divine revelation [91]. The history of religion is a long record of such conflicts [92].

3) If we admit that God has chosen favourites to whom He has communicated absolute truths which are intended also for others, it will give a chance for despots like Hitler. They can also come with the same pretext and justify their totalitarian conduct [93]. For example, the British people ruled for a good while half the people of the earth, claiming that it was the will of God. Hitler was sure that God's blessing was with Germany [94]. He exploited the belief in the chosen people and acted as if he were a chosen one.

4) This claim is a sort of collective selfishness like that of nation States [95]. Down through the history of mankind, we have fought with each other again and again to uphold our distinctive ways of life. Consciously or unconsciously we are inclined to selfrighteousness. This is one of our greatest temptations [96]. But such an attitude makes us arrogant. " We deride what we do not understand; we reject what we do not recognize " [97]. With such arrogance, talking all the time of our own superiority, we will not be able to convert other people to our way [96].

5) A special revelation is against the catholic nature of religion. The prophet-founders of religions declared that the community is world-wide. They made no distinction between Jew and Gentile, Greek and barbarian [99]. Even Jesus challenged the Jewish exclusivism [100]. But the Church became exclusivist. " The damnatory clauses of the Athanasian Creed are in direct opposition

---

[91] Cf. OSW, October 1952 - February 1959, p. 369; OSW, July 1959 - May 1962, pp. 184-185, 252; OSW, May 1962 - May 1964, p. 163; RF, p. 197; ERWTh, pp. 324-325; RC, p. 810.

[92] Cf. IVL, p. 28. Cf. also Ibid., p. 33.

[93] Cf. ERWTh, p. 60. Cf. also Ibid., pp. 17-18; OSW, October 1952 - February 1959, pp. 247-248.

[94] Cf. ERWTh, pp. 289-290. Radhakrishnan does not argue that Hitler believed in God. He is trying to show how a despot can exploit the belief in exclusive divine assistance. His point is that we should leave out such beliefs.

[95] Cf. RCW, p. 20.

[96] Cf. OSW, October 1952 - February 1959, p. 368; OSW, May 1962 - May 1964, p. 155.

[97] RCW, p. 21. Cf. also OSW, October 1952 - February 1959, p. 244.

[98] OSW, October 1952 - February 1959, p. 83.

[99] Cf. ERWTh, p. 39.

[100] Ibid., p. 171.

to the simple determination of discipleship which Jesus laid down " [101], in Radhakrishnan's view.

6) The study of comparative religion also repudiates exclusivism [102]. If the pagan world produces men of sanctity and integrity, no one religion can claim that it alone contains all truth [103]. Therefore God who is active in Christianity is active everywhere [104]. In this connection Radhakrishnan quotes Jacques Maritain who said: "The saints who belong to the invisible Church enable us to recognize their far-off brothers who are ignorant of her and who belong to her invisibly" [105]. Thus judging from the fruits which is the conduct of the adherents and not their theories, we cannot accept any exclusive claim to God's revelation [106].

Further it is argued that even if someone has a special revelation it is proportionate to his particular qualities. It is only for his personal use and not to be imposed on others. Therefore, such a revelation cannot be used to organize a religion. Radhakrishnan quotes with appreciation Paul Tillich:

> " Revelation is never revelation in general, however universal its claim may be. It is always revelation for someone and for a group in a definite environment, under unique circumstances. Therefore he who receives revelation witnesses to it in terms of his individuality and in terms of the social and spiritual conditions in which the revelation has been manifested to him " [107].

So, while one may say that the revelation one had is satisfying for him, he must admit its inadequacy for others. Anything more than that is fanaticism, which is the outcome of a secret and an excessive pride [108].

So Radhakrishnan uncompromisingly rejects the idea of special revelation. ' God has no special favourites ' is an oft-repeated phrase in his writings [109]. He condemns even the idea of a chosen

---

[101] Ibid., p. 320.
[102] Cf. RCW, p. 133.
[103] Cf. ERWTh, p. 320.
[104] Cf. OSW, July 1959 - May 1962, p. 252.
[105] Cf. ERWTh, p. 321. Cf. also Ibid., p. 343f.
[106] Cf. Ibid., p. 320f.
[107] *The Brahma Sūtra*, pp. 112-113, n. 1. Cf. also RC, p. 810f.
[108] Cf. RF, pp. 195, 197.
[109] Cf. ERWTh, p. 60; RC, p. 811; RF, p. 157, 173; IVL, p. 92; OSW, October 1952 - January 1956, p. 124; OSW, October 1952 - February 1959, p. 383; OSW, July 1959 - May 1962, pp. 34, 64, 143; FS, p. 28; OSW, May 1962 - May 1964, p. 118; RCW, pp. 86, 132.

people as a myth [110], as an illusion [111], and as an idea which is out of date, belonging to the barbaric age [112].

iii) *Belief in a Unique Incarnation of God*

a) *The Meaning of Avatāra*. Radhakrishnan admits that an *avatāra* in the popular understanding is a God who limits himself for some purpose on earth, and possesses even in his limited form the fullness of knowledge — a descent of God into man and not an ascent of man into God [113]. In this sense an Incarnation or *avatāra* is considered a special revelation and a unique one [114].

But it seems that Radhakrishnan does not accept this popular understanding of *avatāra*. He suggests that this understanding came when God is looked upon as the saviour of man. For, then, God must manifest Himself, whenever the forces of evil threaten to destroy human values [115]. Further, in the same context Radhakrishnan says that every conscious being is such a descent. The difference is the difference between "self-conscious being of the divine and the same shrouded in ignorance. The human being is as good as an avatar, provided he crosses the *māyā* of the world and transcends his imperfection ... Man comes to full consciousness by actualising his potentiality. It becomes indifferent, then, whether we say God limits Himself in the form of man or man rises to God working through his nature " [116].

b) *Uniqueness of Avatāra*

According to Radhakrishnan there is a continuous incarnation in the world [117]. In this sense the *avatāra* is not an event which happened once upon a time. Everyone has a divine nature which is covered over by the undivine. If we are able to break down this outer covering, the imprisoned splendour reveals itself. Then

---

[110] OSW, October 1952 - February 1959, p. 313. Cf. also ERWTh, p. 10.

[111] ERWTh, p. 40.

[112] OSW, July 1959 - May 1962, pp. 143-144.

[113] Cf. Ind. Ph., I, 545. In his "Introductory Essay" to *The Bhagavadgītā* Radhakrishnan repeats the very same explanation. Some sentences are word by word repeated (Cf. BG, p. 34).

[114] Cf. IVL, p. 267.

[115] Cf. Ind. Ph., 545; BG, p. 34.

[116] Cf. Ibid.

[117] Cf. IVL, p. 267.

" there is the birth of God, the God who is with us " [118]. Thus Radhakrishnan tries to relate Incarnations with the progressively evolving world. The great men who focussed representative ages in their own selves became embodiments of God in a special way. These are the men who could reveal the God within. They teach a lesson that we can also grow into their stature.

> " From them can man take courage and try to grow into their stature. They are the moulds into which the seeking soul tries to cast itself, that it might grow towards God. What has been achieved by one man, a Christ or a Buddha, may be repeated in the lives of other men " [119].

In the same way, of Krishna it is said that his *avatāra* is an illustration of the spirit in us, the Divine hidden in us [120].

Thus Radhakrishnan does not admit the idea of a unique Incarnation. For, that will imply many inconsistencies; " The continuous urge of spiritual life, the growing revelation of ends in which the divine life comes to its own, the immanent law which constitutes the unity of the world and conditions the interactions of its several elements, are not consistent with the conception of unique revelations of complete Godhead on earth " [121]. Therefore, together with Troeltsch Radhakrishnan rejects any idea of a religion centred on any historic Incarnation. He says:

> " In the light of our present knowledge of man's history and the vastness of the cosmos it seems anomalous, if not absurd, to imagine that the earth or the human species or any historic individuals in it form the centre of things ... Geocentrism in cosmology and anthropocentrism in philosophy and Buddhocentrism or Christocentrism in religion are on a par '| [122].

---

[118] OSW, October 1952 - February 1959, p. 313. Cf. also *The Brahma Sūtra*, pp. 174-175; RC, p. 800.

[119] Ind. Ph., I, 546. Cf. also BG, p. 34.

[120] Cf. BG, p. 35. Cf. also Ibid., pp. 28ff, 155. This view is accepted by Gokhale. He says that *nara* can become *narottama* in history and *Narāyana* beyond history (Cf. *Indian Thought Through the Ages*, Asia Publishing House, 1961, p. 13).

[121] IVL, p. 267. Cf. also ERWTh, pp. 222ff.

[122] Ibid., p. 20. Joachim Wach in his essay, " Radhakrishnan and Comparative Study of Religion " (in PhSR, pp. 443-458) criticized Radhakrishnan's rejection of unique revelation and Incarnation. Wach pointed out that nobody can claim to be a Christian if he does not hold Christ's uniqueness to be true. But Radhakrishnan rejected Wach's position saying that there are many scholarly and saintly Christians who will support his view (Cf. RC, p. 808ff).

iv) *Value of Historical Facts in Religion*

The organized religions as they present themselves today, can be said to be centred upon unique historical facts [123]. Organized Christianity, for example, is historically based on the life, works and teachings of Jesus. She often proves her absolute validity for all times from the historical miracles performed by Jesus. This adherence to historical facts is the main source of exclusivism. What value does Radhakrishnan give to such arguments from historical facts? What place does he give to historical facts in religion?

There was no difficulty in accepting the miracle-stories at the time when religions were first formulated. But today in the light of modern discoveries Radhakrishnan is inclined to think with C. G. Jung that " the miraculous tales in the Gospels, which easily convinced people in those days, would be a *petra-scandali* in any modern biography, and would make the very reverse of belief " [124].

Organized religions insist heavily on historical facts, even when they are proved scientifically false and spiritually unreal. For, if they are divested of these beliefs and myths they will become empty and cease to exist [125].

Reasons to Exclude Historical Facts from the Structure of Religious Beliefs

1) The historical validity of the reports about the activities of God on earth may be shaken by scientific and historic discoveries [126]. Ours is a scientific age and a scientific mentality. Therefore, doubtful events, even when they are dogmatically taught, will not be accepted [127]. Sensitiveness in the search for truth makes it difficult to accept " doubtful authority or half-heard traditions " [128]. Therefore miracle-stories such as the report about the resurrection of Jesus do not appeal to the modern mind steeped in science [129].

This argument from scientific discoveries is given with a spe-

---

[123] Cf. HVL, p. 16.
[124] RCW, p. 34, n. 1.
[125] Cf. RF, p. 12.
[126] Cf. OSW, July 1959 - May 1962, p. 231.
[127] Cf. OSW, October 1952 - February 1959, p. 373.
[128] ERWTh, p. 59. Cf. also RCW, p. 34ff.
[129] Cf. RC, p. 802.

cial emphasis in Radhakrishnan's latest work, *Religion in a Changing World*. There are modern criticisms which scrupulously re-examine the historicity of the accepted beliefs. Many are said to hold that we can know almost nothing concerning the life and personality of Jesus. Authors like Lightfoot, Tillich, Rudolf Bultmann, Karl Barth, Emil Brunner and Dietrich Bonhoeffer are referred to in this context [130].

Historical research is said to have revolutionized our understanding of the Old and the New Testaments. The only historical discovery brought forward by Radhakrishnan is that of the Dead Sea Scrolls. He seems to think that the Dead Sea Scrolls will do away with every remnant of belief in the historicity of the Gospels. He does not give us a scientific study of the Scrolls; nor does he give a critical evaluation of the different studies on the Scrolls. Still he affirms that " from the discovery of the Dead Sea Scrolls in 1947, it is clear that Christian doctrine developed from Jewish sectarianism " [131]. Therefore the traditional religion is said to be unacceptable to courageous and upright persons. Their unbelief is a mark of their intellectual integrity, and not of wickedness of heart, because traditional views have lost their authority and psychological justification [132]. Thus the " spirit of free inquiry saps the foundations of supernatural dogmatic religions. It has made faith unnatural to the millions of people to whose ancestors it was once natural " [133]. Although Radhakrishnan wrote in 1955 in his *Recovery of Faith* that men are prone to believe in any dogma, that the distressing feature of " our age " was its readiness to believe in anything taught by the religions [134], in 1967 he writes in his *Religion in a Changing World* that doubt in conventional religion has become " the common property of a whole generation " [135]. The obvious reasons given for this common attitude of scepticism towards the organized religions is the modern scientific discoveries in the field of history [136]. From his discussion

---

130 Cf. RCW, pp. 34-38.
131 Ibid., p. 38.
132 Ibid., p. 39.
133 OSW, July 1959 - May 1962, p. 217. Cf. also Ibid., p. 231.
134 Cf. RF, p. 73.
135 RCW, p. 39.
136 Although Radhakrishnan tries to give a scientific colour to his rejection of the historical facts in religion, it is neither scientific nor critical. He has not made a scientific, personal study of the Dead Sea Scrolls or of the historical facts—at least one can only judge so. For, he does not even give one reference to the Scrolls or analyse any of its

of modern criticisms and scientific researches Radhakrishnan concludes : " Any way at a time of serious questioning, religion cannot be based on an appeal to historical facts " [137]. But if our religious faith is free from historical events, no scientific discovery can shake it [138].

2) To consider the historical events as absolutely valid elements in our religious conviction is to confound eternal truth with temporal facts and theology with history. " For example ", says Radhakrishnan, " in Christendom, theology is busy with such questions as, Are the Scriptures inspired? How shall we explain the divergencies in the accounts of the life of Christ? How shall we reconcile the Biblical account with modern science? Were the Old Testament prophecies fulfilled? Shall we believe in the New Testament miracles? Acute thinkers spend their time and energies in finding modern ideas in ancient texts or reading meaning into them which are not there " [139]. This kind of procedure in religion has made religion a ' phenomenon of the past ' for many. It has made religion a traffic with the past [140].

3) Religion must kindle the flame of the spirit in man, which historical events cannot do [141]. St Paul, says Radhakrishnan, has warned us against over-estimating the historical, instead of viewing it as the symbol of metaphysical truth. For example, the resurrection of Christ must be understood in a symbolic way — as the resurrection of Christ in us from the tomb of our carnal nature. The spiritual self of man is buried in the tomb of mortal self ; but the buried Divine will inevitably rise [142].

4) Religions which insist on a particular kind of event are relevant only for those who can understand it and share that kind of experience. Then those people are tempted to consider other experiences and other religions illusory. Hence comes intolerance.

---

texts. His argument from the modern critics is simply one-sided, because he does not even mention the critics who do not agree with the cited ones. He limits himself to those who rejected the historicity of the Gospel narratives.

[137] RCW, p. 38.

[138] ERWTh, p. 294; Cf. IVL, p. 100; T. R. V. Murti, *Radhakrishnan and Buddhism*, in PhSR, p. 597.

[139] ERWTh, p. 59.

[140] Cf. Ibid.

[141] Cf. OSW, October 1952 - February 1959. p. 376.

[142] If we consider the theory of rebirth and of the attainment of release from it which is salvation, then the argument from resurrection will not have importance for Radhakrishnan.

If the whole of mankind is the offspring of God, we must add the experience of every man into the religion of mankind and should not restrict religious beliefs to the life and activities of one founder alone. Such an attitude alone brings growth in religion [143].

v) *Formation and Development of the Organized Religions*

Our exposition here is likely to take the form of treating Radhakrishnan's views on the development of Christianity. This is so because he considers the Eastern religions as a whole non-dogmatic and spiritual [144] and Western religions as all dogmatic and organized [145], and Christianity as the type of Western religions [146]. Very often instead of treating organized religions in general or each of them in particular, he finishes by speaking about Christianity. This is clearly seen when he traces the formation of organized religions. He begins by saying: " A contemplative spiritual religion becomes a dogmatic secular one, a system of belief and ceremony, which produces sentiments and emotions but fails to change men's lives. Let us briefly trace the process of this transformation " [147]. After this introduction Radhakrishnan traces the formation of organized Christianity alone [148].

Radhakrishnan makes a clear-cut distinction between the religions preached by the so-called founders of organized religions and the present-day organized religions. For him these two are entirely different. It is an unhappy mistake of history that the genuine religions of the great prophet-founders are converted into ruthless organizations. This is treated here under different aspects.

---

[143] Cf. HVL, p. 16f.

[144] EWR, p. 52. Cf. also IC, p. 13.

[145] Cf. Ibid., p. 48f.

[146] Cf. Ibid., p. 47.

[147] ERWTh, p. 272.

[148] Cf. Ibid., pp. 273ff. What is still worse is that at times Christianity itself is identified with that proposed by one or other Christian author. Christianity is at times condemned because a Karl Barth or someone else had said something unacceptable. When this method was applied to Islam, Radhakrishnan could conclude: " Throughout the history of Islam, respect for other faiths has been a persistent tendency " (OSW, July 1959 - May 1962, p. 250). In the same way, some times from one or other action of a person his general character is assessed. Thus even Tipu Sultan (known as the Mysore-Tiger, because of his cruelties and religious intolerance) is shown to be an example of religious tolerance (Cf. Ibid.).

a) *Simplicity of the Religions Preached by the Prophets*

Radhakrishnan strongly holds that the genuine religions preached by the prophet-founders were absolutely simple — non-authoritarian, undogmatic and unorganized. The prophets of Israel such as Amos, Micah, Malachi and Hosea emphasized the simplicity of religion [149]. Buddha did not start [150] or organize a new religion [151]. Jesus' religion was pure and simple [152]. He gave only a simple code to his followers. His institution of the Eucharist as seen from the Gospels was a " simple memorial devoid of any magical significance " [153]. In favour of this position Herbert J. Muller is quoted. For him it is clear from the synoptic Gospels that Jesus did not conceive himself as a revolutionary author of a new world religion. " In a real sense ", it is claimed that " Jesus was not the founder of Christianity " [154]. He did not claim divinity, nor did he offer salvation through the mediation of a redeeming Lord. He rather taught that anyone could earn salvation through his own efforts [155]. Thus on the lines of Jesus' teaching an organized religion is not possible. Faithful to his teaching, early Christianity was a simple unorganized religion [156]. Stress on the distinction between the religion preached by the founders and the present-day organized religions, which claim to be essentially the same as the ones preached by the founders, has its climax in Radhakrishnan's Jowett Lecture on March 18, 1930 at the Mary Ward Settlement, London [157]. It may be well that we conclude this section with a quotation from this lecture. The sixth section of this lecture is on " The Religion of Jesus and Western Christianity " [158]. Here he says:

> " Jesus' religion was one of love and sympathy, tolerance and inwardness. He founded no organization but enjoined only private prayer. He was utterly indifferent to labels

---

[149] Cf. OSW, October 1952 - February 1959, p. 356; OSW, July 1959 - May 1962, p. 243.

[150] Cf. OSW, October 1952 - February 1959, pp. 341, 344.

[151] Cf. GB, p. 31.

[152] Cf. EWR, p. 47; EWS, p. 72f.

[153] OSW, July 1959 - May 1962, p. 244.

[154] Cf. Ibid,, p. 248.

[155] Cf. Ibid.

[156] Cf. Ibid., p. 309.

[157] Published in EWR, pp. 43-70.

[158] EWR, pp. 57-60.

7

and creeds [159]. He made no distinction between Jew and Gentile, Roman and Greek. He did not profess to teach a new religion but only deepened spiritual life. He formulated no doctrine and did not sacrifice thinking to believing. He learnt and taught in the synagogues of the Jews. He observed their ritual so long as it did not blind men to the inner light. He attached no importance to professions and allegiance. There is nothing in common between the simple truths taught by Jesus and the Church militant with its hierarchic constitution and external tests of membership " [160].

b) *The Fact of Organized Religions*

Even though the prophets and founders only called for upright living in the light of their own experiences, at present there are elaborate systems working in the world, claiming their origin from the said prophets and seers. Christianity in its Catholic and Protestant forms, has become a religion of authority. For this it finds support in a tradition believed to be supernaturally revealed. Instead of the pure contemplation of the Supreme who is formless, there is the definitization of the Supreme Absolute or Deity in the personal God or in a concrete individual believed to be the Incarnation of the personal God. Instead of indifference to rites and formulas, dogmas and beliefs, there is great emphasis on them. Though Jesus had not thought of an organization, elaborate ecclesiastical structures have emerged from his teachings. Jesus preached only a Kingdom not of this world. But the most realistic of Church organizations has been built on earth by those who profess to follow him. The teaching of Jesus had the aim of inspiring souls to rise above the creeds and nations. But it is used to make loyal members of an organized Church [161]. In short, the concrete fact before us is that there are highly organized religions.

Therefore, on the one hand the religions as they were preached by the prophet-founders were absolutely simple, and on the other there exist organized religions which claim to be the same as the ones preached by the prophets. The obvious conclusion is that there must have been a transformation from the original pure

---

[159] The suggestion is that Jesus considered all religions equally good.
[160] EWR, p. 58; Cf. also ERWTh, pp. 176, 274; OSW, July 1959 - May 1962, pp. 244f.
[161] Cf. ERWTh, p. 272.

religion to the organized religions. We shall now try to explain this process of transformation.

c) *The Evolution of the Organized Religions*

How was the simple religion of the prophets transformed into our present-day organized religions? One may not find in Radhakrishnan a complete answer to this question regarding every particular organized religion. Still the general principle with which the question should be answered can be found in his Newton Baker Lecture at Cleveland Council on World Affairs, Ohio, on March 27, 1958 [162]. In this famous lecture on " Inter-religious Understanding" he appeals to men to leave the organized religions and come into the spiritual religion. He says that the historic events upheld by the organized religions are of no religious moment and the "findings of priests" have nothing to do with the new religion. All religions are human attempts to reach God. In this context he says that the simple attempts of the prophets were used to build up organizations:

> " It is one of the tragic confusions of religious history that as faith becomes credal, the creed by which man communes with the Divine supplants the Divine. The prophet who announces the message becomes himself an object of worship supplanting the higher truth in which he believes [163]. We become ambitious for our formulas, for our prophets, for our organization " [164].

This principle is evidently applicable to all organized religions. Although he has made some passing reference of this principle to other religions, such as Buddhism [165], he has mainly made use of it to explain how Christianity became an organized religion. As we have earlier noted, even where it is said that the conversion of a simple faith to an organized system is going to be dealt with, the explanation itself is limited to the formation of Organized Christianity [166]. Therefore, we describe here how Radhakrishnan explains the transformation of Jesus' pure and simple religion into an organized religion as the present-day Christianity.

---

[162] Cf. OSW, October 1952 - February 1959, pp. 371-385.
[163] Cf. RCW, p. 45; *The Brahma Sūtra,* p. 112.
[164] OSW, October 1952 - February 1959, p. 377.
[165] Cf. ERWTh, p. 177f.
[166] Cf. Ibid., pp. 272ff.

1) *The Evolution of Christocentrism*

The Jews had a consciousness and an intense expectation of some great decisive event, which will be the definitive solution to their historical problem [167]. This is generally known as their Messianic idea. This idea is the central factor in their history and it survived in the early Christian communities [168].

Christianity soon spread to the non-Jewish parts of the Roman Empire. But the Graeco-Roman religions had also a belief that at some epoch of history there had been a great being, who during his life on earth found a way out of the difficulties of life by his personal experience. This secret divine wisdom was entrusted to his followers who accepted it in faith and performed certain mysterious acts. This united them with the life and purpose of God [169]. Christianity adopted and compromised with this belief. Christ became the Logos. Legends about the death and resurrection of heroes and suffering deities, such as Osiris, Attis and Adonis were utilized to explain the life of Jesus [170]. Thus the supernatural stories in the Gospels are mostly from the legends of primitive religions.

The final perfecting of Christocentralization is attributed to St Paul. This we find clearly in Radhakrishnan's Public Address at Honolulu on July 11, 1959 on " Inter-religious Co-operation " [171]. After a few introductory remarks he spoke of the need to respect other faiths. The fundamental reason for showing respect to other faiths is that " all religions seem to be varied manifestations of the essentials of true religion " [172]. He examines in particular Hiduism, Buddhism, Judaism, Christianity and Islam and ends with an appeal for fellowship of faiths, leaving out the theological discussions and dogmatic controversies [173]. He finds that all these religions throughout their history respected other religions. Speaking about Christianity he says that it was pure and simple as preached by Jesus. There are some Christians who follow this simple spirit. But Christianity in the main has become institutionalized. St Paul is said to have begun this conversion definitely, when he made Jesus the centre of all things. St Paul knew Jesus

---

[167] Ibid., pp. 8-9.
[168] Cf. Ibid.
[169] Cf. Ibid., p. 219.
[170] Cf. Ibid.
[171] OSW, July 1959 - May 1962, pp. 235-253.
[172] Ibid., p. 239.
[173] Ibid., p. 252f.

only by hearsay. On his way to Damascus he had a blinding
vision of the Risen Lord. It is suggested that St Paul might have
understood the Lord whom he saw in vision after the fashion of
the Saviour-God of Mystery religions — one who had died and
risen and through whom man could achieve immortality. This
was a turning point in the life of St Paul:

> " While Jesus proclaimed a Kingdom of God that men earn
> simply by repentance and righteous behaviour, St Paul taught
> that salvation was through Christ and Christ alone. St Paul
> decided to break away from the ritual observances of Judaism
> and to create a new religion. He adopted the ideas of Jewish
> prophets, added to them the teachings of neo-Platonism and
> made Jesus the central figure " [174].

This was the first notable beginning of organization in Christianity. A similar Buddhocentralization has occurred in Buddhism
also. Buddha was also deified [175].

2) *The Evolution of Organization* [176]

The Graeco-Roman Mystery religions were pure and simple —
they were spiritual religions [177]. In the course of time the people
of the Roman Empire accepted Christianity which was very similar
to their own mystery religions.

But " it is a law of life that religions like other things take
on the nature of the organisms which assimilate them " [178]. Jesus'
simple religion travelled from Palestine to the West. But the
Western mind is characterized by its critical intelligence [179]. They
want clearness and definiteness. They formulate, systematize and
organize everything. Naturally a change was inevitable when
Christianity went to Rome and " took over the traditions of
Caesar. When the Greek dialecticians and the Roman lawyers

---

[174] Ibid., pp. 243-244.

[175] Cf. ERWTh, pp. 177ff.

[176] This is treated by Radhakrishnan especially with regard to Christianity in: ERWTh, pp. 10f, 272ff; EWR, pp. 46ff; EWS, pp. 44ff;
Public Address at Honolulu, July 11, 1959 (Cf. OSW, July 1959 - May
1962. pp. 243ff).

[177] Cf. EWS, p. 54; FS, p. 26. It is to be noted that there are two
currents in Greek mystery religion: the Homeric and the mystic (RF.
p. 118. Cf. also EWS, p. 54). The Homeric was exclusive. The reference here should be to the mystic current in Greek religion.

[178] EWR, p. 47.

[179] Cf. Ibid., p. 48.

succeeded to the Jewish divines and the prophets, Christian theology became logical in form and based on law. The spirit was the Jew's but the letter or the dogma was the Greek's, and the polity and the organization were the Roman's " [180]. This was in general the process of transformation. Now we shall see how it happened in concrete historic circumstances.

When the Roman Empire adopted Christianity, Christianity adopted the practices of mystery cults :

> " Adopting the practice of mystery cults, the Church, which was endowed with a personality, claimed due authority to teach and to admit into its membership by specific forms of initiation those who wished to join it and were found worthy. It traced its foundation to a God-man, and its officers claimed to derive their authority through appointments by the founder, who gathered a small group for that specific purpose. In unbroken succession from this group are descended, it is said, the officers who hold sway over the whole body of Christians " [181].

They made Jesus equal to God and began to insist that salvation was possible only through Jesus. Incarnation became the central doctrine which was unknown to Jesus and his followers [182]. They made sacraments necessary for salvation as did the mystery cults. A good deal of formalism got into religion which Jesus condemned in High Priests and Scribes [183]. The Church was a strict corporation and called herself *Ecclesia*. All over the Empire such strict organizations or churches grew up. These were presided over by Episkopoi or bishops. The Church as a whole included all these small churches. The Church developed a body of writings which it preserved for doctrinal instructions and continuity. But this obscured the simplicity of Jesus' personality [184]. In the event of doctrinal controversy the Church claimed authority to decide what was the true tradition. Later it sifted these doctrines and some of them were fixed as authoritative and inspired Scripture [185]. It adopted many pagan beliefs for the sake of proselytizing. The

---

[180] Ibid., pp. 58-59.

[181] ERWTh. p. 273.

[182] Cf. OSW, July 1959 - May 1962, p. 248. Although this idea belongs to a citation from Herbert J. Muller, it is evidently appreciated by Radhakrishnan (Cf. also ERWTh, p. 273).

[183] Cf. Ibid., p. 244.

[184] Cf. Ibid., p. 245. Cf. also ERWTh, p. 273.

[185] ERWTh, p. 273.

fixing of authoritative Scripture was the beginning of dogmatism. But at that time dogmatism helped the spread of Christianity. Radhakrishnan gives the reason :

> " Men had grown weary and disinclined to seek further. Any creed that promised to calm the troubled mind, give certainty in place of doubt, a final solution for a host of perplexing problems, found a ready welcome. Sick with hesitations of thought men turned greedily to a cult which gave them theology instead of philosophy, dogma instead of logic " [186].

Such an adherence to codified dogma and blind obedience to authority made religion a matter of the community, a social phenomenon. It ceased to be a private achievement. This helped the authority to stabilize its position [187]. Thus the hierarchical organization became very strong. The Church supported the supremacy of the state and its divine creation [188]. When Constantine was converted to Christianity, the authorities, both secular and clerical showed systematic intolerance towards all other religions quoting the Scripture : " He that is not with me, is against me, and he that gathereth not with me, scattereth " [189]. Thus the simple teaching of Jesus was converted into a fiercely proselytizing creed [190].

In this new Christianity the Risen Lord took the place of God and the organized Church replaced the Kingdom of God. " Even as the Supreme is identified with an historical individual, the Kingdom of God is identified with a concrete empirical structure with its own specific form and organization " [191].

Whenever the free spirits doubted about anything in the Church, they were condemned to supress the doubt [192]. About such 'ecclesiastical tyranny' Radhakrishnan has this to say :

> " The ecclesiastical tyranny was so ubiquitous that it was perilous to breathe a word against accepted dogmas. Authority was supreme and the Inquisition was actually established at the beginning of the thirteenth century ... The

---

186 Ibid., p. 274.
187 Cf. EWR, p. 54f.
188 Cf. ERWTh, p. 10.
189 Mt. 12 : 30.
190 ERWTh, p. 10.
191 Ibid., p. 176.
192 Cf. Ibid., p. 275f.

Church endeavoured by the stake and the thumbscrew to preserve the faith once delivered to the saints and became alienated from the spirit of Jesus. If He had returned to Europe in the Middle Ages, He would certainly have been burnt alive for denying the dogmas about His own nature " [193].

Still the Church was divided into different independent churches. So arose the different main organized religions of the West, and in the East religions do not give so much importance to organization as to the life of spirit [194].

Therefore, the different elements of organized Christianity came from different religions and peoples. The Jews gave the sense of superiority and the " myth that only one religion could be true " [195], the Greeks gave the logical form and dogmatic setting and the Romans order and organization [196].

---

[193] Ibid.. p. 276.

[194] Cf. EWR, p. 51f. Radhakrishnan seems to believe that Christianity when grown in India is different from that in the West and is "opposed to proselytism" (Cf. ERWTh, p. 345).

[195] ERWTh, p. 10.

[196] Cf. EWS, p. 44; ERWTh, pp. 8, 343.

V

STRUCTURE OF ORGANIZED RELIGIONS

Radhakrishnan distinguishes two main elements in an organized religion: the subjective and the objective. The objective may be distinguished further into doctrinal and ritual [1]. These are enforced by an authority which is the subjective part [2].

In this chapter we shall try to discover Radhakrishnan's views on these main constitutive elements of organized religion. We will first treat the objective elements and then the subjective. This chapter has three parts: 1) Dogma; 2) Cult and Worship; and 3) Authority.

1) DOGMA

i) *Geneology of Dogmas*

Radhakrishnan characterizes the Western mind as rationalistic and ethical, positive and practical [3]. The logical tendency of the Western mind demands clearness in everything and not mystery. It makes distinctions and reduces everything to clear-cut definitions and formulas. Religions of the West also will necessarily contract this characteristic [4]. In religion such a mind will not be satisfied with the concept of the Supreme as a spiritual reality or as an abstract and indefinable power [5]. It admits that men can attain a perfect system of divine knowledge. It refuses to admit a 'superbeing of God' and denies the mystery of religion [6]. It claims that " truth has been found, embodied, standardized and

---

[1] Cf. OSW. July 1959 - May 1962, p. 238.
[2] Cf. ERWTh, p. 273.
[3] EWR, pp. 48, 133; IVL, p. 101f.
[4] Cf. Ibid., p. 47.
[5] Cf. Ibid., pp. 49-50.
[6] Cf. *The Spirit in Man*, p. 503.

nothing remains for us to do except to reproduce feebly some precious features of an immutable perfection " [7].

Such a religion pledges us to rigid definitions. It encourages a hardness of belief which is almost mathematical in its rigidity. It does not recognize anything between truth and falsehood. " In its anxiety to bend all individual wills to the purpose of the group and establish social cohesion, it enforces rites and obligations peculiar to the group and ignores the claims of humanity. It declares that what it affirms is truth, the whole truth and nothing but the truth " [8]. Thus, systems of theology aquire a sacred significance and they appear as absolute and unchangeable [9].

But in doing so the intellectual religions are said to be exaggerating the rôle of intellectual propositions [10]. This exaggeration puts us on the wrong paths in all aspects of human life. To put it in Radhakrishnan's rhetorical way,

> "False intellectualism has led us to prefer in artistic life the supremacy of form to content; in politics, organization to liberty; in morals, authority to personal experience; and in religion, orthodox systems to spiritual life " [11].

There is reflection of God in the mind of man and a mystery behind and beyond it. When the dogmas are said to contain eternal truths and are proposed for man's blind acceptance, the intellectual religion is actually bringing the inexpressible mystery in human formulations [12]. That is why Radhakrishnan accuses the intellectual religions of confusion in forming dogmas. « An intellectual religion confuses pictures with proofs, mysteries with dogmas ... It trades on words and misses their meaning " [13].

ii) *The Meaning of Dogma*

Radhakrishnan, in fact, has never explained what he understands by the term ' dogma'. But from the various contexts,

---

[7] OSW, October 1952 - February 1959, p. 306.

[8] *The Spirit in Man,* p. 503.

[9] Cf. Ibid.

[11] *The Spirit in Man,* p. 504.

[12] Cf. Ibid., p. 503.

[13] EWR, p. 50. Radhakrishnan's authority seems to be *Katha Upanishad*: " This self cannot be attained by instruction nor by intellectual power nor through much hearing " (I, 2.23). We know the meaning of this passage has to do with the transcendental realization (jñāna) proposed by the Upanishads.

where it is employed, one may explain his concept of dogma. It should be noted that we are searching here Radhakrishnan's understanding of the dogmas of the organized religions as they actually are. There is a new interpretation by him of what dogma should mean. This new interpretation will be explained later.

The main trait of dogma which Radhakrishnan's uses of the term reveal is that dogmas of the organized religions, as they present them, are unreasonable — neither experience nor reason can justify the dogmatic statements. Edgar Sheffield Brightman, George P. Conger, Dhirendra Mohan Datta, A. R. Wadia and Clement C. J. Webb had accused Radhakrishnan of using religion in his philosophy, whereas he had condemned the influence of religion in philosophy in his first major work, *The Reign of Religion in Contemporary Philosophy*. To this charge Radhakrishnan replied: " There does not seem to be any inconsistence between the criticism of interference of religious *dogma* with the pursuit of philosophy and the recognition of the value of religious *experience* for philosophical interpretation " [14]. In other words, he believes that dogmas should be kept out in our pursuit of truth. In many other passages he couples dogma with superstition, myth and the like, apparently giving an identical significance to both. For instance we quote some passages to this effect:

> " We cannot cure the affliction caused by ... the myths of religion or the dogmas of politics ... The unscientific dogmas, the crude superstitions tell us more about the mind of man than about the structure of reality, and cannot save man from scepticism " [15].
> " Even as ancient mythologies disappeared, the unscientific dogmas, it is said, will fade out " [16].
> " Religion is not magic or witchcraft, quackery or superstition; it is not to be confused with out-dated dogmas, incredible superstitions " [17].

About abstinence from intoxicants it is said,

> " This advice refers also to the freedom from dogmas and doctrines which are vicious poisons. They fetter our minds and make us ill and unbalanced. Even as we do not feed

---

[14] RC, p. 790.
[15] *Fragments*, p. 54.
[16] RCW, p. 34.
[17] OSW, October 1952 - February 1959, p. 305.

children with opium and alcohol, we should not educate the youth in partisan and provincial creeds " [18].

There are passages which clearly show that Radhakrishnan thinks that a dogmatic statement cannot go with reason. A dogmatic affirmation is said to be as one-sided and unreasonable as a dogmatic negation [19]. Therefore, it is not able to meet the needs of the intellect [20]. When religion is presented in a dogmatic form, we are treating men like machines [21]. Such a religion would be " something foreign to the spirit of reason, intellectual freedom and tolerance " [22].

Finally, a dogma is said to be opposed to truth. When one gives assent to a dogmatic statement one is overlooking the claims of truth [23]. Therefore Radhakrishnan says : " Truth is opposed, not to reason or the Greek spirit, but to dogma and to fossilized tradition " [24]. Consequently the " reverent agnosticism " of a seer is better than the " flippant vulgarity with which some dogmatists speak of divine mysteries " [25].

Therefore a dogma for Radhakrishnan is an assertion by an authority, without considering the demands of reason and truth, which puts the divine mystery in a clear-cut formula and claims our full assent without questioning its reasonableness and searching for its truth [26].

iii) *The Place of Doctrine in Religion*

Before we discuss Radhakrishnan's reasons for the rejection of dogmas in religion, it would be well to see his views on doctrines in religion.

In his opinion even superstitious beliefs will not do real harm to man's spiritual life. The superstitious Indian woman, he ob-

---

[18] Ibid., p. 474.
[19] Cf. IVL, p. 64.
[20] Cf. ERWTh, p. 293.
[21] Cf. IVL, pp. 63-64.
[22] OSW, October 1952 - February 1959, p. 538.
[23] Cf. RF, p. 29.
[24] ERWTh, p. 294. Cf. also EWR. p. 137.
[25] Ibid., p. 318. Cf. also Ibid., p. 338.
[26] *Nyāya* System defines dogma as an ' established tenet resting on the authority of certain school, hypothesis, or implication ' (Bk. I, Ch. I, 26). It is to be noted that Radhakrishnan does not restrict dogma to religion alone. There are dogmas in totalitarian systems also (Cf. RS, pp. 25-26). We are here concerned mainly with the dogmas in religion.

serves, has a noble dignity and magnanimity which many of her more intellectual contemporaries lack [27]. Similarly the village pilgrim who spends all his earnings and undertakes weary marches through toil and suffering to have a bath in the Ganges or a *darsan* of the deity at Puri has an innate spiritual sense [28]. Even if the superstitious beliefs be of the most paralysing kind, they will not make a man devoid of spiritual sense [29]. Every people and clan have their own traditional assimilation of superstitions which is for them the condition for spiritual growth — and spiritual awakening is the purpose of religious life [30]. The savage has his own superstitions. For him his views are live-forces. His way to spiritual perfection is his superstitions. Therefore, Radhakrishnan warns all the preachers of religious doctrines: " To shatter the superstitions of the savage is to destroy his morality, his social code and mental peace " [31].

Religion is transforming experience [32]. It is said to be right living and not correct belief or perfect theology [33]. Belief and conduct, rites and ceremonies are subordinate to conscious self-discovery and contact with the Divine [34]. A man is, therefore, religious or irreligious according to the measure of his self-discovery of his own real self which is divine. This self-realization may be called the fruit of the spirit. And from the fruits we have to judge a man, rather than from his theological affirmations [35]. Even when Communism is considered, it is better to look at the fruits it has produced than to judge the theories of Marx or Lenin [36]. Therefore the primary function of the churches and temples should not be to impart sacred wisdom. If only they can awaken the spirit in man they will become Houses of God [37].

It is maintained also that since beliefs and doctrines are secondary in a man's religious life, he should not be anxious to adopt

---

[27] Cf. MST, p. 7.

[28] Cf. Ibid.

[29] Cf. Ibid.

[30] Cf. *The Spirit in Man,* p. 476.

[31] HVL, p. 31.

[32] Cf. EWS, . 24. Cf. also ERWTh, p. 60. This point will be more elaborately explained in the coming chapter.

[33] Cf. EWS, p. 24; HVL, p. 37; OSW, October 1952 - February 1959, pp. 305 f.

[34] Cf. OSW, October 1952 - February 1959, p: 291; OSW, July 1959 - May 1962, pp. 143. 286; OSW, May 1962 - May 1964, p. 121; RS, p. 43.

[35] Cf. IC, p. 15; RF, p. 192; ERWTh, pp. 320-321.

[36] Cf. OSW, October 1952 - February 1959, p. 20.

[37] Cf. IVL, p. 161.

a particular set of doctrines. The doctrine we adopt and the philosophy we profess do not matter any more than the language we speak or the clothes we wear [38]. It would be unreasonable on our part to worry that a foreigner does not speak our language. Similarly the truly religious man never worries about other people's beliefs [39]. For, doctrine itself is a form of fiction. " Doctrines are useful fictions of a sophisticated culture bound by words as substitutes for realities " [40].

A true seer transcends even this stage of attitudes towards doctrines. He will withhold his assent from all opinions and suspend his judgment [41], because he knows that our deepest experience is inexpressible [42]. He has shaken off all views. Since he has no view to defend and no prejudice to plead, he is free from all doctrinairism [43] and the base delusions of caste and creed [44]. Radhakrishnan points out that the Buddha is the great pioneer of this kind of view of doctrines. The Buddha had declined to tell us whether there is anything positive and real in the universe, in the individual self and in the state of liberation [45]. He did not want to indulge in doctrinal controversies. He discouraged them as prejudicial to inward peace and ethical striving. Thought must not insist on a solution of unfathomably deep mysteries [46]. Therefore he denied dogmatic theology [47] which presumes to give a solution to the ineffable mysteries. He himself proposed no theories. He offered his followers a way of life and not a set of doctrines. He knew that acceptance of a set of doctrines is generally an excuse for the abandonment of the search for truth [48]. A non-stop search for truth is better than possessing it. What expands the powers of man is the search for truth and not the possession of it [49]. Moreover Radhakrishnan feels that " if we adopt definite views

---

[38] Cf. ERWTh, p. 318.
[39] Cf. HVL, p. 37.
[40] EWS, p .75.
[41] Cf. *The Spirit in Man*, p. 479.
[42] Cf. *Fragments*, p. 78.
[43] Cf. RF, p. 191.
[44] Cf. *The Spirit in Man*, p. 476.
[45] Cf. GB, p. 37; IVL, p. 95; FS, p. 16.
[46] Cf. GB, p. 43; OSW, October 1952 - February 1959, p. 348.
[47] Cf. Ibid., p. 37.
[48] Cf. Ibid., pp. 30-31.
[49] Cf. OSW, July 1959 - May 1962, p. 251.

in religion, we get concerned about defending them. This leads to disputations with rival doctrines, resulting in pride " [50].

Therefore we are cautioned most seriously: " I regret to say that the way we are now going about with sharp distinctions of good and evil is the sure road to disaster " [51].

iv) *Reasons against Dogma*

1) *There is no Freedom under Dogma.* Freedom is the supreme law of the spiritual life. Man's search after the Infinite should not be restricted to any given types or ways. There is a many-sided call of the Divine which demands an open and easily flexible religious attitude [52]. The seers were also of this opinion. They have given " absolute freedom to the soul in the faith that a free adaptation of the divine into oneself is the essential condition of spiritual life " [53].

But if we accept a definite creed or a set of dogmas, we are then binding ourselves to it, renouncing our freedom of inquiry. That is like blinding our own eyes [54]. Then we are actually putting our minds in prison [55]. The infinite spirit in man will be submitted to the finite form of a dogma [56]. All our intellectual accounts of God are constructed theories of experience. If they get hardened into articles of faith, then they become real barriers to further insights [57]. If we stop with the finite intellectual dogmas and take them for the infinite truth of God, it is worship of the letter — the greatest idolatry [58].

So dogmas slacken our spiritual seeking and spoils the simplicity of the spiritual life [59]. From this point of view, we will see that there can be no good habits even. All habits are bad, because with habits man's original freedom congeals into bondage [60].

---

[50] RF, p. 191.
[51] RC, p. 836. Cf. also OSW, July 1959 - May 1962, p. 252.
[52] Cf. IVL, p. 95.
[53] Ibid., p. 161. Cf. also Pr. Ups, p. 121.
[54] Cf. *Fragments,* p. 54; FS, p. 4; EWR, pp. 19, 116.
[55] Cf. *The Brahma Sūtra,* p. 170.
[56] Cf. *The Spirit in Man,* p. 503.
[57] Cf. IVL, p. 94; RF. p. 157; FS, p. 6; RS. p. 42; OSW, October 1952 - February 1959, p. 474; OSW, July 1959 - May 1962, p. 120; RCW, p. 122
[58] Cf. IVL, p. 94; RF, p. 190; OSW, October 1952 - February 1959, p. 378.
[59] Cf. OSW. October 1952 - February 1959, p. 305.
[60] Cf. *The Brahma Sūtra,* p. 196.

Hence Radhakrishnan argues that there is no occasion for the free spirit of man to be consigned to dogmas of any character [61].

Where there is no freedom there will be no happiness. If in man's religious life he has to submit to certain rigid dogmas, his spiritual adventure will not be a happy one [62]. The uneasiness of man in accepting a dogma is very much increased in our modern age due to the great advancement of the natural sciences. Once we accept a dogma, we see an "unbridgeable chasm between faith and reason" [63].

2) *Progress is Obstructed*

Dogmas are dead forms [64]. When we submit to a dogmatic religion we are repeating the old formulas mechanically without adding our own personal experience to it [65]. Thus the dogmatists are said to be always conservative, not progressive and prophetic [66]. In their anxiety to be orthodox, they suppress all deviations from the ancient formulations. "Whatever is in conflict with the closed dogma is said to be unscriptural and therefore false. Ancient ignorance is sanctified as revealed truth" [67]. Thus dogmas kill the initiative in religion as well as in politics [68], in religion they deform spiritual growth [69] and in politics hinder the national building up [70]. Radhakrishnan observes that progress is never due to our

---

[61] OSW, May 1962 - May 1964, p. 247.

[62] Cf. *Fragments,* p. 54.

[63] FS, p. 4. In a footnote to this sentence Radhakrishnan says: "When Kirsopp Lake's father who was a physician was asked what had done the most to relieve human suffering he answered: 'Anaesthesia and the decay of Christian theology'" (FS, p. 4, n. 2). The insinuation is clear. It is very interesting to compare this charge against organized religions of not giving freedom with the following pronouncement of Radhakrishnan on taking leave form Peking on 27th of September, Addressing to Mao-Tse-tung and his communist adherents he says: "Your constitution grants freedom of religious belief. Study and research in religions are encouraged and the result is likely to be rejection of obscurantist superstitious beliefs and the acceptance of a reasonable and ethical account of the supreme ends of life" (OSW, October 1952 - February 1959, p. 64).

[64] Cf. FS, p. 6.

[65] Cf. *The Spirit in Man,* p. 491.

[66] Cf. ERWTh, p. 279.

[67] Ibid., pp. 324-325.

[68] Cf. RCW, p. 32.

[69] Cf. IVL, p. 38.

[70] *On Nehru,* p. 17.

conforming to a dogma, but due to non-conformists and heretics [71]. Therefore he cries out in an impatient mood in his Address to the University of Hawaii, Honolulu on 9th July 1959:

> "We must be jolted out of our dogmatic slumbers if the future is to be saved ... The dragon to be slain is the monster of *status quo*. The enemy is in the seat of power: he is the tyrant who uses to his own advantage his power and authority" [72].

3) *Historical Evolution Contradicts Dogma*

Just as the world is in a perpetual process, life and the history of man are also continually evolving [73]. Man by his very nature demands change and growth [74]. There is a perpetual evolution in the notion of God. Each one comes with his own personal experiences and interpretations [75]. He passes by after adding a new element to the traditional treasury of spiritual experiences. Every moment passes by adding something new to the notion of God. Radhakrishnan explains it eloquently:

> "We rise from life to thought and return from thought to life in a progressive enrichment of ever higher levels of reality. Tradition is something which is for ever being worked out anew and recreated by the free activity of its followers. What is built for ever is for ever building. If tradition does not grow, it only means that its followers have become spiritually dead" [76].

Thus man's God-ward endeavour is in continuous development down through the ages. Our notion of God is an accumulated inheritance to which every race and every age has contributed [77]. Unless we add our personal experience to this spiritual treasury, it becomes in effect dead for us. In the changing world we cannot be "mechanical imitators of inherited habits" [78]. Our spiritual ideas, such as the idea of God must be continually evolving. Therefore we cannot say that one idea of God is absolutely true and

---

[71] Cf. EWR, p. 116; OSW, July 1959 - May 1962, p. 170.
[72] OSW, July 1959 - May 1962, p. 214.
[73] Cf. IVL, pp. 119-120, 190.
[74] Cf. Ibid., p. 161.
[75] Crf. *A Source Book*, p. xxii.
[76] HVL, p. 17. Cf. also IVL, p. 70 f.
[77] Cf. ERWTh, p. 306.
[78] IVL, p. 39.

8

that which does not conform to it is false. It is thus impossible to establish inflexible dogmas for the whole human race [79].

4) *Dogmas Are Sources of Intolerance*

When religion becomes dogmatic, intolerance will be inevitable. When man imagines that God's will and nature are known with certainty, he sets them forth in dogmatic assertions. That produces fanaticism and intolerance [80]. Since it is the will of God nobody will be tolerated to change it or deviate from it. "When we insist on right beliefs", says Radhakrishnan, "we are punished not only for the worship of other Gods but for the wrong views about His own unknowable nature" [81]. So originated all strifes and conflicts, crusades and religious wars in the history of man's religion. Radhakrishnan stresses this consequence of dogmas to such a degree that one often feels that he views almost all wars and bloodshed in human history only under this aspect. Rejecting the argument that to coerce a man to accept the right view is as legitimate as to save one by violence from committing suicide in a fit of delirium, he says:

> "The intolerance of narrow monotheism is written in letters of blood across the history of man from the time when first the tribes of Israel burst into the land of Canaan. The worshippers of the one jealous God are egged on to aggressive wars against people of alien cults. They invoke divine sanction for the cruelties inflicted on the conquered. The spirit of old Israel is inherited by Christianity and Islam, and it might not be unreasonable to suggest that it would have been better for Western civilization if Greece had moulded it on this question rather than Palestine" [82].

If there are quarrels among religions it is because we set forth mystery in dogmatic form [83]. Speaking at the All India Oriental Conference, Annamalai University, Annamalainagar on December 26, 1955, after emphasizing the need of a spirit of fellowship among religions, he declared:

---

[79] Cf. HVL, p. 24; RF, p. 59; OSW, July 1959 - May 1962, p. 238.

[80] Cf. RC, pp. 811-812; EWS, p. 40.

[81] OSW, October 1952 - February 1959, p. 356. Cf. also Ibid., p. 309; *The Brahma Sūtra*, p. 172.

[82] HVL, p. 40.

[83] Cf. FS, p. 8; OSW, October 1952 - February 1959, pp. 49-50; OSW, July 1959 - May 1962, pp. 143-251.

"The world has bled and suffered from the disease of dogmatism, of conformity, of intolerance. People conscious of a mission to bring humanity to their own way of life, whether in religion or in politics, have been aggressive towards other ways of life. The crusading spirit has spoiled the records of religions "[84].

In another speech broadcasted on All India Radio on May 19, 1956 he says that "doctrinal orthodoxy has filled the world with unhappiness, injustice, strife, crime, and hatred "[85]. The intolerance of organized religions in the name of dogmatic truth is as bad as the worst political persecutions. "The non-Communists in Russia, the non-Fascists in Italy, the Jews and Socialists in Germany, are treated in the same spirit in which orthodox Churches treated the Dissenters and the Non-conformists "[86]. At present these religions are said to be receiving a retaliation and that for the same reason:

"The modern persecutors who are endeavouring to stamp out all religion, as in Russia, or change its nature, as in Germany, are repeating the old specious arguments which not long ago had wide assent among Christian people ... If the Bolshevists adopt similar measures in the interest of their version of truth, we cannot say that they are impelled by a fanaticism while our conduct is governed by a philosophy. If we defend persecution in the name of the highest truth entrusted to us, there can be no logical objection to the persecution of all religions in the interest of atheism "[87].

In short, if we are not doing away with dogmas, they will do away with all religions [88].

5) *Dogmas Destroy the Unity of Mankind*

Dogmas make closed circles whose narrow limits are determined by their authors [89]. When the believers of inflexible dogmas enclose themselves in different rigidly closed circles, mankind is

---

[84] OSW, October 1952 - February 1959, p. 335. Cf. also OSW, May 1962 - May 1964, p. 122; IVL, p. 28.

[85] OSW, October 1952 - February 1959, p. 342. Cf. also ERWTh, p. 325 f.

[86] ERWTh, p. 325.

[87] Ibid., pp. 325-326.

[88] Cf. OSW, July 1959 - May 1962, p. 152.

[89] Cf. ERWTh, p. 318. Cf. also Ibid., p. 63; FS, pp. 13, 16.

divided into irreconcilable camps [90]. Each group goes on claiming infallibility for their dogmas. And conversely the dogmas destroy the intellectual unity of the people [91] and keep them in different groups [92]. Group-loyalty is always at the risk of loyalty to humanity [93]. Even as we do not feed children with opium, we should not educate them in provincial creeds [94].

When Christianity became dogmatic, opposing doctrines also came up. Soon Christendom became a 'house divided against itself' [95]. Each group adamantly persisted in its views. Spiritual pride and arrogance, intolerance and religious wars were the results [96]. When rival creeds appeal to us we will have to reject both [97]. Radhakrishnan defends his position by quoting Celsus:

> "When rival creeds appeal to us, are we to leave it to chance which we shall adopt? Celsus asks, 'If they introduce this one (Christ) and others another and all have the common formula ready to hand, Believe if you would be saved or go away, what will be done by those who really wish to be saved? Will they cast dice and so get an omen for the path which they are to take and the people whom they are to join'" [98]?

6) Dogma is not Essential for Salvation

A dogma is something imposed from without [99]. It can serve only as a fetter to the spirit of man and therefore cannot liberate man from the fetters of *māyā*. Not only is it not essential for our salvation but it is an obstacle which should be removed in order to be able to reach God [100]. The great body of believers wish to enjoy the consolations of religion without undergoing the necessary labour. They think that a simple global assent to a codified set of dogmas without even examining their truth is sufficient to save them. Such people are not religious with their whole being, but only with their intellect. To be saved, — that

---

[90] Cf. RCW, p. 178; HVL, p. 27.
[91] Cf. ERWTh, p. 33.
[92] Cf. Ibid., p. 40.
[93] Cf. *Fragments*, p. 24 f.
[94] OSW, October 1952 - February 1959, p. 474.
[95] ERWTh, p. 280.
[96] Cf. Ibid., p. 282 f.
[97] Cf. Ibid., p. 294.
[98] Ibid., p. 294.
[99] Cf. IVL, p. 155.
[100] Cf. IC, p. 14.

is, to reach religious experience, — passion and suffering, effort and struggle are needed [101]. " We will be judged not by the creeds we profess or the labels we bear or the slogans we shout but by our sacrificial work and brotherly outlook " [102]. It is not surety of the knowledge of God that is primarily needed but surety of faith in one's own experience [103]. That faith is acquired not by an unscientific dogma but by an inward constraint, following the light of inner enlightenment, even if that be against conventional ways [104].

7) *The Scientific Spirit Rejects Dogma* [105]

Bernard Shaw once said in joking mood that there is nothing which people will not believe if only it be presented to them as science and nothing which they will not disbelieve if presented to them as religion. The modern scientific mind demands empirical proofs for everything. But the truth of dogma, if there is any truth in it, cannot be proved scientifically. In dogmatic systems something is defended not in terms of their reality but according to the correctness of the interpretation of the sacred book on which the dogma depends [106]. Therefore the scientific mind instinctively rejects dogma [107]. So we cannot appeal to the world in the name of dogma. People will simply reject it as superstition [108].

8) *Experience Is Impossible to 'Be Verbalized*

Spiritual experience cannot be doctrinally formulated; it cannot be brought to verbal expression [109]. The reason is that all our intellectual knowledge presupposes a dualism between

---

[101] Cf. IVL, p. 160.

[102] OSW, October 1952 - February 1959, p. 344; Cf. also Ibid., p. 357; ERWTh, p. 24.

[103] Cf. ERWTh, p. 319.

[104] Cf. IVL, pp. 93, 155; OSW, October 1952 - January 1956, p. 277 f.

[105] The incompatibility of dogma with truth and reason, has already been explained, when the meaning of dogma was expounded. Here we are adding only a few lines on the alleged opposition between dogma and science.

[106] Cf. RF, p. 29.

[107]Cf. RWN, pp. 10-11; RCW, pp. 74-75; OSW, July 1959 - May 1962, p. 151.

[108] Cf. OSW, May 1962 - May 1964, p. 161; RS, p. 43.

[109] Cf. *Fragments,* p. 78; RF, pp. 144-145; OSW, October 1952 - February 1959, p. 348.

subject and object. So what is intellectually expressed must be imperfect. Since all intellectual forms contain an element of untruth, any attempt to describe the experience falsifies it to that extent [110]. Religious experience is perfect and infallible by itself. But it becomes necessarily imperfect and fallible when it is expressed in human words. Radhakrishnan has stressed this argument against the possibility of dogma all through his life. Laying the foundation-stone of the Buddha Memorial in Delhi on 23rd May 1956, he said:

> " The inward spirit of truth challenges all forms ... Language is at best an instrument and like all instruments subject to imperfection. The doctrines are rebuked, defeated and swallowed up again in experience " [111].

Again in his Address to the East-West Philosophers' Conference at Honolulu on July 10, 1959, he said:

> " This experience transcends all forms, all images and concepts. ... All religious utterances are vain attempts to deal justly with the meaning of the experience which has been attained " [112].

In other words, no dogma is possible, because truth can never realize an infallible and immutable expression. And conversely we have to transcend and get beyond the dogmas of religions to have the spiritual fulfilment or the experience of the Divine [113].

Because of the inexpressibility of religious experience, the seers shrink from precise statements and clear-cut definitions [114]. Although the seers of religions had attained the experience of God, they did not prescribe definite systems of dogmas [115]. They respect the absolute freedom of the individual and leave him to find out his way by himself [116]. They knew " that the spirit can leap into

---

[110] Cf. IVL, pp. 75-76.

[111] OSW, October 1952 - February 1959, p. 348.

[112] OSW, July 1959 - May 1962, p. 231. Cf. also ERWTh, p. 314: HVL, p. 27; IVL, p. 75 ff; EWR, p. 20; Ind. Ph. I, 174 ff; RS, pp. 43, 45; Pr. Ups, pp. 22 ff, 95 ff, 139; *The Brahma Sūtra,* p. 112 ff; BG, p. 74; RC, p. 811; RCW pp. 118 f.

[113] Cf. EWS, pp. 25-26; FS, p. 8.

[114] Cf. IVL, p. 160; ERWTh, p. 317 f; EWR, p. 116.

[115] Cf. IVL, p. 161; OSW, Ocober 1952 - February 1959, p. 519; *The Cultural Heritage of India,* I, p. xxvii.

[116] Cf. GB, pp. 30-31; IVL, p. 93, 95; OSW, October 1952 - February 1959, p. 348.

life only if the moulds in which it is cast are broken. They are more dissenters than conformists. They are considered to be irreligious and anti-social forces and are often faced with isolation and death, but all progress in religion is due to these persecuted spirits "[117]. Therefore Radhakrishnan contends that it is the half religious and the irreligious and not the truly religious who fight for dogmas[118]. Many examples are brought forward in support of this position: Buddha[119], Confucius[120], prophets of Israel like Amos, Hosea, Micah[121], and Jesus[122]. Instead of rigid dogmas they speak in parables, pictures, allegories and miracles[123].

v) *Reinterpretation of the Meaning of Dogma*

Radhakrishnan's method of effecting religious reform is "to bring about a change not in the name but in the content "[124]. Applying this method, he tries to reinterpret the meaning of dogma.

The experience, as we have seen, is inexpressible in words. But the seer cannot remain completely silent. His creative imagination works and gives us some hints by symbols and suggestions. It is through these symbols and myths that the wisdom of the experience is transmitted. "The profoundest wisdom of the past is transmitted to us in the form of myths and metaphors which do not have any fixed meaning and therefore can be interpreted as life requires "[125]. Radhakrishnan desires that dogma also be treated in this way as a symbol, a mere mode of representation, which does not signify anything definite or bind anyone to anything but points to something profound. Thus dogma must be viewed not as inflexible truth but as an approximation to truth[126] and so as something very relative[127]. When dogma is taken in this sense we will be prepared to modify it continually as we gain more

---

[117] IVL, p. 160.
[118] Cf. HVL, p. 44; RS, p. 47; ERWTh, p. 29 f.
[119] Cf. GB, pp. 30-31; RF, p. 190 f; IVL, pp. 93, 95; OSW, October 1952 - February 1959, p. 348; *Fragments,* p. 78; RCW, p. 69.
[120] Cf. *Fragments,* p. 78.
[121] Cf. OSW, October 1952 - February 1959, p. 356.
[122] IVL, pp. 93, 95; GB, p. 31; ERWTh, p. 272; RF, p. 157; Pr. Ups, p. 143 f.
[123] Cf. IVL, p. 160.
[124] HVL, p. 32.
[125] IVL, p. 76. Cf. also Ibid., p. 161; *The Spirit in Man,* pp. 502-503.
[126] Cf. Pr. Ups, p. 139.
[127] Cf. EWS, p. 42.

and more enlightenment [128]. Moreover this interpretation says also that the different dogmas are only different symbols to signify the same reality which is the religious experience — the same thing is expressed in different colours [129]. This view makes it illogical to say that any particular system is orthodox or final [130]. Thus all religious conflicts will be at an end, contends Radhakrishnan.

When dogma is taken in this sense, Radhakrishnan agrees that it can be a means to the realization of the Divine [131]. The weak mind and the lonely individual wants something external to cling on that he may reach the experience [132]. But once experience is reached all the dogmas can be and must be dispensed with [133]. They are valid only in their proper place, that is, in the realm of *māyā* but not in the realm of realization [134]. But even in this re-interpreted sense a dogma is not better than a myth or a pro-visional hypothesis or a superstition which all can serve as equally good means to realization [135].

2) CULT AND WORSHIP

Radhakrishnan does not treat cult as elaborately as he does dogma and authority. Still we find sufficient passages to enable us make a fair judgment of his mind on the subject of cult and worship. It is certain that he holds that rites and ceremonies are constitutive elements of organized religions. This is clear at least from two passages. The first is found in his *East and West in Religion*. When he deals with " Spiritual Life and Intellectual Formalism " he says that an organized religion is on the " basis of a creed or a ritual " [136]. The second passage is found in *Eastern*

---

[128] Cf. OSW, October 1952 - February 1959, p. 309. This modification, according to Radhakrishnan, is not to be made by an external authority, but by each individual according to the enlightenment he has gained and ac-cording to his necessity.

[129] Cf. RF, p. 155.

[130] Cf. OSW, October 1952 - February 1959, p. 309.

[131] Cf. RC, p. 827; *The Spirit in Man*, p. 503; OSW, July 1959 - May 1962, p. 223.

[132] Cf. RWN, p. 8.

[133] Cf. *The Spirit in Man*, p. 503; ERWTh. p. 301; Ind. Ph., II, 652; RF, pp. 154-189.

[134] EWS, pp. 25-26.

[135] Cf. IVL, p. 76; ERWTh, p. 314; HVL, p. 31; RF, p. 199; FS, p. 7.

[136] EWR, p. 50.

Religions and Western Thought in which he calls organized religion " a system of belief and ceremony " [137]. But what efficacy
have the sacraments, rites and ceremonies got? Does Radhakrishnan admit any causative value for them? What place can
they have in religion? Do they have any social function?

i) *Efficacy of Sacraments*

Speaking about the Hindu sacraments, Radhakrishnan distinguishes four chief ones: 1) *jātākarma,* or birth; 2) *upanayana,*
or initiation into the spiritual life; 3) *vivāha,* or marriage; 4) *an-
tyesti,* or funeral ceremonies. There are other popular sacraments
like *nāmakarana,* giving a name for the child, *annaprāsana,* giving
cooked food to the child for the first time, *vidyarambha,* starting
education for the child etc. [138].

Radhakrishnan agrees that excepting *upanayana* all other sacraments are practised by all Hindus, though in different forms.
Of all these he elaborates the concept of *upanayana* only. It is
said to be " the spiritual birth into union and liberty " [139]. It
means life lived on a deeper interior level. In the Upanishadic
period it was a simple ceremony. The wearing of the sacred
thread with the mantra is the symbol of initiation. It can be
clearly noted that Radrakrishnan places the whole emphasis on
the internal, spiritual transformation. The external ceremonies
are symbols of an internal fact. Here we are not asked to leave
out all external ceremonies. One may even doubt if Radhakrishnan
is admitting that the external ceremonies are essential in religion
when he says, " It is essential that the important sacrament
(samskāra) of upanayana should be permitted for all Hindus, men
and women, for all are capable of the highest goal of spiritual
insight " [140]. Does Radhakrishnan here advocate the necessity of
permitting all to share the external ceremonies? It seems very
unlikely that he was insisting on external ceremonies. For, Radhakrishnan himself says that the essence of upanayana is " in impart-
ing the sacred Gāyatri mantra ", which is a prayer addressed to
the Sun [141]. If we remember that in Hinduism sacred wisdom and
sacred Scripture are in the hands of a few high caste Hindus and

---

[137] ERWTh, p. 272.
[138] Cf. RS, p. 135.
[139] Ibid.
[140] RS, p. 136.
[141] Cf. Ibid., p. 135.

that the essence of upar.ayana is a piece of this sacred wisdom, then what Radhakrishnan asks to be permitted to all is to be understood as the awakening of the spirit. Moreover he was speaking to a Hindu audience at the University of Calcutta [142], which required him to respect their external ceremonies.

But Radhakrishnan's understanding of the liturgical rites and ceremonies of organized religions is not the same. In his sermon at Manchester College Oxford in 1929 he said:

> "Most of us wish to pick up religions as easily as a shell from the sand. We have not the patience or the energy for the laborious quest. As we get books from Blackwell, eggs from the farmer or medicines from the chemist, we expect the parson or the priest to provide us with religion at the cost of a few shillings or an hour a week" [143].

In this passage Radhakrishnan does not seem to admit the internal character of the Christian ceremonies. It may be said that he refers only to superficial Christians, and their participation in the sacraments. But the statement is too general to be interpreted in that way.

Does a man become more religious by receiving a sacrament? This question should be studied in the light of Radhakrishnan's concept of *karma*. *Karma* for him is a spiritual necessity, the embodiment of the word and will of God [144]. This will of God expresses itself in fixed karmic laws. Even God, it is said, is not free to change the working of *karma*.

> "He (God) does not break or suspend his own laws. The liberty to change one's mind is not true liberty. God cannot forgive the criminal even when he repents, for the moral order which is conceived in love and not in hatred requires that wrong doing should have its natural consequences" [145].

Thus *karma* means the working of inexorable justice. The sinner has to atone for himself and there is no escape. "If we fall into error no supernatural deliverer will come to our rescue. There is no forgiveness for a broken law" [146]. Such a theory of *karma* logically rules out vicarious action and the efficacy of the sacraments.

---

[142] *Religion and Society* contains mainly the "Kamala Lectures" delivered by Radhakrishnan at the University of Calcutta in December 1942.
[143] EWR, p. 86.
[144] Cf. HVL, p. 53.
[145] IVL, p. 268.
[146] *Kalki*, p. 58.

" The past guilt cannot be wiped away by the atoning suffering of an outward substitute. Guilt cannot be transferred. It must be atoned for through the sorrow entailed by self-conquest. God cannot be bought over and sin cannot be glossed over " [147].

Evidently, in the light of this theory, to say that sacraments confer grace *ex opere operato* on one who does not place an obstacle [148] is inadmissible. To say that in sacramental confession our sins are forgiven would be like the remark of Lady Macbeth on the murder of Duncan, 'A little water clears us of this deed' [149]. Such a belief comes from the substitution of religion for God, of an infallible Church or book for personal effort [150]. Our sins will be forgiven only by our own atoning suffering, and we improve in our personal spiritual life only by our own personal effort.

ii) *The Place of Rites and Ceremonies in the Structure of Religion* [151]

The ontological basis of all cult is the distinction between the creator and the creature. But this distinction, according to Radhakrishnan, has no ultimate value as the ultimate truth is non-duality. To those who are in the order of *māyā*, non-dual truth appears as dual [152]. The illiterate and the ignorant, the weak and the lowly are not able to contemplate the formless Supreme. They need an easier way, a personal God, to render him cult [153]. Consequently " meditation, worship, ritual are intended for a lower class of aspirants " [154]. In this sense it is said that man is ' incurably religious '. He must have some object or person to fix his attention on [155].

Devotion to a personal God expresses itself in cultual rites and ceremonies. Thus rites and ceremonies are not useless, but

---

[147] HVL, p. 54.

[148] Cf. D851, 849.

[149] Cf. ERWTh, p. 60.

[150] Ibid., pp. 60-61.

[151] Radhakrishnan uses the terms 'rites' and 'ceremonies' as synonyms. The term 'rite' by itself means liturgical rite, canonical discipline, or both together. In Radhakrishnan, only the first sense is implied.

[152] Cf. Ind. Ph, II, 649; BG, p. 61.

[153] Cf. BG, p. 59; Ind. Ph. II, 649; P. T. RAJU, *Radhakrishnan's Influence on Indian Thought*, in PhSR, p. 358.

[154] *The Brahma Sūtra*, p. 36.

[155] Cf. Ibid., p. 167.

lead the ignorant and the weak on by the upward path to pure contemplation, which is the immediate experience of the Divine in us. For their sake it is said, " devotional and ritualistic pieties are *tolerated* " [156].

If one gives absolute values to rites, it will be idolatry [157]. Rites should be treated as symbols which religions use for the sake of the weak, to focus their faith [158]. So all external religious ceremonies and rites have the same value as image worship [159]. Just as we cannot stop with the images, we will have to get beyond rituals [160]. Those who have attained to realization need no rite or ceremonies. Moreover, since the rites are only symbols, we cannot insist on any particular set of rites [161]. The rituals vary according to different religions. Each religion has its own sacraments. All these sacraments and rites of all religions are considered as equally good [162]. All will equally awaken the spiritual sense [163].

Rites are not absolutely necessary for salvation. " Jñāna or wisdom is the path pursued by the higher class of aspirants who have no desire for earthly prosperity or heavenly joy " [164]. As long as we remain with sacraments, rites and ceremonies we will not attain to final perfection. Ceremonial piety can lead us only to new forms of embodied existence [165]. We must cease to be men of external piety and become men of inner realization [166]. Sacraments, rites and ceremonies are secondary, without any ultimate value. " Belief and conduct, rites and ceremonies, dogmas and authorities are subordinate to the art of conscious self-discovery and contact with the divine " [167]. So in the final stage which is the spiritual religion, there will be no rites and ceremonies or prayers or cult to a personal God.

---

[156] Pr. Ups, p. 132.   Italics mine.
[157] Cf. *Great Indians,* p. 83.
[158] Cf. Ibid.
[159] Cf. *The Brahma Sūtra,* p. 173; Pr. Ups, p. 140.
[160] Cf. Ibid.. p. 174.
[161] Cf. Pr. Pps, p. 139.
[162] Cf. OSW, July 1959 - May 1962, p. 238.
[163] Cf. FS, p. 7.
[164] *The Brahma Sūtra,* p. 36.   Cf. also p. 37.
[165] Cf. Ibid., p. 38.
[166] Cf. Ibid., p. 165.
[167] Cf. OSW, October 1952 - February 1959, pp. 291, 379; ERWTh, p. 21; Ind. Ph, II, 649; RS, p. 43.

iii) *Reasons Showing the Unimportance of Rites and Ceremonies in Religion*

1) Since rites and ceremonies are secondary, insistence on them will be harmful to religion. The organized religions use rites to bind themselves within themselves. When they are bound by the rites of a fixed type they will become militant groups and obstacles to the formation of the world community [168]. Each group will try to impose its rite on others which is intolerance [169]. The inner core of all religions is the same, but the externals keep them divided [170]. There is a religion above all rites, ceremonies and dogmas, in which alone the world society can take form [171].

2) Eventhough we have magnificent churches and gorgeous rituals we have not become sufficiently religious [172], because external cult has a tendency to be mechanical [173]. Real spirituality will be thus buried under mechanical practices [174]. When we perform some ritual, we are inclined to believe that we have become religious even without attaining the inner transformation. Thus the rites and ceremonies become an escape from really religious acts which are good thoughts, words and deeds [175]. The real difficulty with the organized religions is that they substitute the external for the internal [176].

3) The great religious seers did not prescribe any rites or ceremonies. The Buddha even rejects all rites and insists on inward discipline [177]. For him religion is not a matter of ceremonies and sacraments [178]. Jesus observed them only so long as they did not blind him to the inner light [179]. He did not prescribe any special ceremonies. All the ceremonies we find in Christianity are said to be later additions. Even the basic rites of communion and sacrifice are borrowed from other primitive religions [180]. " Accidental accretions are not as valid as spiritual truths " [181].

---

[168] Cf. *Great Indians,* p. 84.
[169] RF, p. 123.
[170] Cf. PhRT, p. 108.
[171] Cf. OSW, May 1962 - May 1964, p. 121.
[172] Cf. ERWTh, p. 289.
[173] Cf. Pr. Ups, p. 141; IC, p. 151.
[174] Cf. OSW, October 1952 - February 1959, p. 294.
[175] Cf. RCW, p. 127.
[176] Cf. ERWTh, p. 61.
[177] Cf. RF, p. 123; Ind. Ph, I, 474 f.
[178] *Hibbert Journal,* 32 (1933-1934) 347.
[179] Cf. EWR, p. 58.
[180] Cf. Ibid., p. 17.

iv) *Common Cult*

Everywhere religion has a tendency to degenerate into "mechanical repetition and formal worship without inward piety"[182]. When religion is losing its internal character, the external ceremonies are stressed. Then religion becomes an external conduct and not an inner life. It is then a matter of ecclesia, of the community — a mere social phenomenon. It is then used by the authorities to strengthen social cohesion, and to shield against the innovator. This is what has happened in the organized religions of the West. Even gods are thought to be promoters of social customs. Ceremonies which bind the community are emphasized. The cults however crude they be, provided they favour social harmony, will be tolerated. Thus ceremonial religion loses its real religious character. It becomes an instrument of social salvation[183] or a kind of mystical nationalism[184]. Thus outward piety is a sign of the decline of morality[185].

v) *The Meaning of Worship*

Worship "is the communion of the soul of man with the soul of the universe, a direct and ineffable contact with the light divine"[186]. It is therefore personal and individualistic. In this sense worship is certainly a way to the final spiritual attainment of the individual[187]. This individualistic aspect of worship is so much stressed that apparently the value of the common worship is denied. This also implies that worship must be purely internal. Accordingly Radhakrishnan argues: "We do not worship by mind or body but in spirit and in truth"[188]. The Divine is the innermost in us. Why should we then go to temples or churches to worship Him? In a speech on unveiling a Memorial Tablet for Swami Vivekananda at Madurai on September 28, 1963 Radhakrishnan expresses the same conclusion:

"Many of us go to temples, worship God, practise all sorts of exercises and mutter many *mantras*[189], and yet God is

---

[181] OSW, October 1952 - February 1959, p. 379.
[182] Cf. IC, p. 151.
[183] Cf. IVL, p. 69.
[184] Cf. EWR, pp. 54-56.
[185] Cf. IC, p. 151.
[186] IVL, p. 172.
[187] Cf. Pr. Ups, p. 42.
[188] Cf. IVL, p. 172.
[189] *Mantra* is a Vedic hymn or a sacred text or a mystical verse re-

far away from us. In actual reality, He is not there; He is in our hearts " [190].

To discover the God in us we are asked not to participate in Church functions or do some external rites. We must " get into the house of our innermost self, shut the door on everything outer and pray from the inner self " [191]. Only in solitude and contemplation will one be able to say like Ramakrishna: " I have seen God, I have felt Him in the depths of my being, I have felt Him, I have realized Him " [192]. Solitary contemplation is the final and the only way to realize the God in us immediately [193].

One cannot all of a sudden begin to contemplate. One needs initiation. Radhakrishnan distinguishes three stages in worship [194]. The first stage is *sravana* or hearing. In this stage one learns what the teacher says from his personal experience. The student accepts only what his own experience tells him to be true. The second stage is *manana* or reflection. Here one tries to form clear ideas by the logical process of inference. But the material for this logical thinking should not be taken from the intellect alone. It should be from experience as well. Even this stage is to be transcended to reach perfection. The third stage is *nididhyāsana* or contemplation. " It is the holding of oneself steadily in front of the truth " [195]. This is the final stage of worship. The first and the second stages lead to this final stage. In the final stage one realizes the divine in him. He attains immediate experience. He has no longer any need of external rites and ceremonies. Externally he is not marked as belonging to any religion. Such realized souls proclaim : " We do not belong to the Church of Christ or Buddha, but we belong to the Universal Spirit or God " [196].

---

peatedly saying which the Hindu yogi tries to get an interior illumination (Cf. RENE GUENON, *L'homme et son devenir selon le Vêdânta,* 5th ed., Paris 1966, pp. 164-165, n. 4).

[190] OSW, May 1962 - May 1964, pp. 164-165.
[191] *The Brahma Sūtra,* p. 179. The reference here is to Mt. 6: 6.
[192] OSW, May 1962 - May 1964, p. 164.
[193] Cf. RCW, p. 180 f ERWTh, p. 53.
[194] Cf. Pr. Ups, p. 133.
[195] Ibid., p. 135.
[196] Cf. OSW, May 1962 - May 1964, p. 117.

vi) *Worship and Solitude*

Real worship is pure contemplation. For contemplation one has to retire into solitude [197]. It is in those silent hours that we purify our souls and realize the divine in us.

> " We cannot find ourselves, unless we use our liesure and solitude in contemplation. However difficult it may be, it is still the appointed way. Religion does not consist so much in prayers and rites as in those silent hours of self-communion which will help us to control our character and build up our personality. By it we cleanse our thought, purify our emotions and let the seed of spirit grow " [198].

It is not sufficient that we retire to solitude, but we must there practise yoga or spiritual exercises. This is marked out by Radhakrishnan as the only way to attain perfect realization. In a speech at the University of Tehran on May 17, 1963 he says:

> " How can we overcome this conflict between good and evil? The only way to do it is by the practice of certain spiritual exercises which are given to us. Men are called upon to discipline their natures, to meditate and be solitary. It is not loneliness that they are emphasizing. Most of us are lonely in crowds, but many of us are solitary. We are not lonely since we have the Eternal Companion " [199].

Thus man's salvation is ultimately through intuitive realization. " If man is a part of the Divine, what he needs is not redemption, as an awareness of his true nature ... he requires a technique by which he reminds himself that he is essentially a part of God and any feeling to contrary is illusory " [200]. We have to submit ourselves to disciplines and bind ourselves to certain ways. Salvation is attained only through immense personal effort. This discipline or spiritual exercise is called *yoga* [201]. There are three kinds of yogas: " *jñāna-yoga* or the way of knowledge, *bhakti-yoga* or the way of devotion, *karma yoga* or the way of action " [202]. Of

---

[197] Cf. Pr. Ups, p. 42.

[198] EWR, pp. 96-97.

[199] OSW, May 1962 - May 1964, p. 139.

[200] BG, p. 50.

[201] Cf. Ibid; HVL, p. 57; PhRT, p. 50; *Great Indians*, p. 24, 66. " Derived from the root, *yuj,* to bind together, yoga means binding one's psychic powers, balancing and enhancing them " (BG, p. 50).

[202] BG, p. 50. These are the main three ones. Sometimes Radhakrishnan calls them *Jñāna mārga* (Cf. BG, p. 53; *The Brahma Sūtra,*

these the last two are intended for ordinary people, while the perfect form intended for the sages is the *jñāna yoga*. *Karma yoga* [203] and *bhakti yoga* [204] lead to *jñāna yoga* and finally to the attainment of spiritual illumination.

Thus the common worship is replaced by contemplation in solitude, and the sacramental life with yogic life. In this sense Radhakrishnan repeats the famous dictums of Whitehead: "Religion is what the individual does with his own solitariness" [205]; it is the "art and theory of the internal life of man" [206].

vii) *The Social Side of Religion*

Religion has a double dimension, inward and outward. The inward is God-ward and the outward must reach the neighbour in the service of fellow men. The two are not independent but are related like two sides of a single thing. The love of God expresses itself in the love of the neighbour, in the service of men [207]. For the Divine that is within us is also within the neighbour [208].

The inner feeling of immediate experience of God is bound to issue in the service of humanity [209]. The very life of service is the inevitable outcome of the experience of the Divine and the proof of its validity [210]. So religion is at times said to be not mere contemplation but also active service to men [211]. Thus service to our fellow men is a religious obligation [212]. In this service of fellow men Radhakrishnan finds the social aspect of religion. This is a lesson which Radhakrishnan learned from Mahatma Gandhi, who taught that there is no religion apart from social service [213]. By means of love, service and sacrifice we will convert

---

p. 153), *bhakti mārga* (Cf. *The Brahma Sūtra*, p. 153) and *karma mārga* (Cf. BG, p. 66; *The Brahma Sūtra*, p. 153) respectively. Cf. also HVL, p. 58.

[203] Cf. BG, p. 73.

[204] Cf. Ibid., p. 65.

[205] IVL, p. 69; FS, p. 38; OSW, October 1952 - February 1959, p. 481; OSW, July 1959 - May 1962, p. 19.

[206] OSW. July 1959 - May 1962, p. 220.

[207] Cf. RCW, p. 138; OSW, October 1952 - February 1959, p. 294.

[208] Cf. OSW, May 1962 - May 1964, p. 131.

[209] Cf. IVL, p. 56.

[210] Cf. *Fragments*, p. 66; OSW, July 1959 - May 1962, p. 107; OSW, May 1962 - May 1964, p. 170.

[211] Cf. OSW, July 1959 - May 1962, p. 237.

[212] Cf. HVL, p. 82; OSW, July 1959 - May 1962, pp. 220-221, 345; OSW, May 1962 - May 1962 - May 1964, pp. 48, 139.

[213] Cf. *Great Indians,* p. 20.

our whole life into a long continuing prayer, into one sacrament [215].
At Rishikesh, Radhakrishnan declared on August 12, 1954:

> " We affirm in loud tones that the service of men is the
> worship of God ... No temples should be raised in the country
> which permit social discrimination.   Temples should foster
> social discipline and solidarity " [216].

Thus more importance is given to social service than to religious
rites and ceremonies — than the common cult in the organized
religions.

> " Bead necklaces, rosaries, triple paint on forehead or putting
> on ashes, pilgrimages, baths in holy rivers, meditation, or
> image worship do not purify a man as service to fellow crea-
> tures does " [217].

In this way Radhakrishnan tries to balance the individualistic
character of contemplation in solitude with its social aspect [218].
But here also religion remains purely individualistic and inner,
because social service is only an effect of inner religion.   This
also is an attempt to replace the external cult of organized religions with social service.   Thus he presents his religion in a
way appealing to the humanists [219].

---

[214] Cf. MST, p. 13.

[215] Cf. OSW, July 1959 - May 1962, p. 236.

[216] OSW, October 1952 - February 1959, p. 286.

[217] Ibid., p. 322. Cf. also RCW, pp. 127, 133.

[218] Cf. A. R. WADIA, *The Social Philosophy of Radhakrishnan,* in
PhSR, pp. 484-485.

[219] It is clear that Radhakrishnan's accent on social service is the
continuation of the spirit of service of the Brahmo Samaj, which in turn
was due to Christian missionary activity in this field.   The immediate
inspiration must be from Mahatma Gandhi and Rabindranath Tagore both
of whom were Radhakrishnan's friends.   Gandhi lived a life of service.
But it was Tagore, whom Radhakrishnan esteemed highly, who popularized
this idea.   Here is a famous passage from Tagore's *Gitanjali*:
"Leave this chanting and singing and telling of beads ! Whom does
thou worship in this lonely dark corner of a temple with doors all shut?
Open thine eyes and see thy God is not before thee.
" He is there where the tiller is tilling the hard ground and where the
path maker is breaking stones.   He is with them in sun and shower, and
his garment is covered with dust.   Put off thy holy mantle and even like
him come down on the dusty soil !
" Deliverance? Where is thy deliverance to be found? Our master
himself has joyfully taken upon himself the bounds of creation, he is
bound with us all for ever.

3) AUTHORITY

In Radhakrishnan's view the central element in the structure of an organized religion is authority. It is authority that is exalted, whether of the Pope or of the Council or of the Sacred Scripture or of the Church [220]. When authority is exalted to an absolute and infallible level, it may attract large numbers who are anxious to find a shrine safe and warm where they can kneel and be comforted. The leaders of religions on their part are said to

"enlarge on the beauty and the richness of the worship, the antiquity and the order of tradition, the opportunity for influence and service which the historic Church offers. If we are not to languish as spiritual nomads, we require a shelter, and the Church which is majestically one in creed, ritual, discipline and language, a corporation in which racial and national barriers are obliterated, a kingdom without frontiers, attracts the large majority" [221].

But a spiritual genius who can think out a religion for himself will not come under this authority, in spite of its attractions [222]. For whatever be the comfort the authoritarian Church gives to an individual, Radhakrishnan thinks that in the main it is an obstacle to spiritual attainment. Every authority in matters spiritual must be subordinated to the authority of the individual.

i) *The Individualistic Character of Religion*

Religion springs from the encounter of the human being with Divine. The Divine is not to be sought without, but within. The individual has the natural capacity to commune with God who is within at any time, at any place and in any historical circumstances [223]. Religion is therefore a personal adventure, a personal discovery [224]. Since the Divine is the innermost being of man, his

---

"Come out of thy meditations and leave aside thy flowers and incense! What harm is there if thy clothes become tattered and stained! Meet him and stand by him in toil and sweat of thy brow!" (Gitanjali, 11).

[220] Cf. IVL, p. 60.

[221] Ibid., p. 61.

[222] Cf. Ibid.

[223] Cf. OSW, October 1952 - February 1959, pp. 577-578; OSW, July 1959 - May 1962, p. 185; ERWTh, p. 302; Pr. Ups, p. 139.

[224] Cf. IVL, p. 63; OSW, October 1952 - February 1959, p. 398; OSW, July 1959 - May 1962, p. 185; OSW, May 1962 - May 1964, pp. 124, 145.

real self, the encounter with the Divine is essentially and entirely a personal and private attainment of the individual won by hard effort in solitude and isolation [225]. The real self of man is not an object but subject and is therefore beyond the reach of any external power and organization [226]. It can only be known in an intimately personal experience which is absolutely limited to the individual. " God is to be existentially known and not to be literally described " [227]. Explaining the nature of religious experience in his *An Idealist View of Life,* Radhakrishnan says, " Each individual has to blaze out his own trail into the unknown. And however much others may assist, the achievement is an individual one " [228].

From this personal aspect of religion Radhakrishnan argues that religion is so much inner to the individual that nothing external can interfere in an individual's religious affairs. In these, every individual has got absolute freedom. The only limitation is that he should not interfere with another's religious pursuit [229]. From this he concludes that no external authority is binding, in religious matters and none of its doctrines and dogmas essential. True religion is in the inner soul of man, " not in man-made creeds " [230]. When we are religious by submitting to an authority or by giving an assent to a dogmatic statement, we are acting like one who tries to buy his religion at " second-hand " [231]. Only very little help can be given by an outsider in the matter of religion. " The true form of Reality should be known through one's own clear eye of understanding (bodhacaksu) and not through (the proxy of) a scholar " [232]. We have already seen that Radhakrishnan does not accept the possibility of vicarious suffering. " No tricks of absolution or payment by proxy " [233] can help an individual in his religious pursuit. Each one has to take the whole responsibility on himself [234].

Because the real self of man is divine, it follows that there is an inner light and inner voice in the individual. It is the in-

---

[225] Cf. EWR, p. 56; RS, p. 121; EWS, p. 75; HVL, p. 54.

[226] Cf. EWR, p. 131.

[227] EWS, p. 75.

[228] IVL, p. 96. Cf. also RS, p. 67, 118; *The Brahma Sūtra,* p. 110; *Dhammapada,* p. 21 f.

[229] Cf. IVL, p. 62.

[230] OSW, May 1962 - May 1964, p. 375.

[231] Cf. RS, p. 121.

[232] RCW, p. 100.

[233] IVL, p. 89.

[234] Cf. OSW, May 1962 - May 1964, p. 131.

flexible divine law which is the source of all laws written in the course of ages [235]. This comes immediately from the Divine and therefore has the highest authority [236]. It cannot be subordinated to any other authority. Every man must live his life by the guidance of his inner light [237]. Therefore there can be no master race or master nation [238]. Everything should be accepted only after testing with the inner light [239]. The individual is thus an end in itself and is not to be subordinated to anything external [240]. If only we can follow the inner rhythm, we shall become moral heroes. For the inward constraint is more important than the law imposed from without [241].

Radhakrishnan emphasizes the importance of the inner voice so much that he goes to the extreme of denying the possibility of having an external one. The inner tribunal of conscience is unviolated and inviolable by any intrusion of external powers. It is an inalienable inner sovereignty [242]. Together with Lord Acton he thinks that the external authority is not the true guide [243]. In the organized religions the inner voice is substituted by the infallible Church. Unless this is changed, religion itself will fade away. Many of those who affirm belief in God or in a future life act as if neither existed. We have to change such a situation and its cause. " The centre should shift from reliance on external direction, whose validity is becoming more and more questionable, to a trust in experience, intimate and personal ", argues Radakrishnan [244]. Dogma should be replaced by experience and authority by inner light. He observes that the great religions are realizing this need. Even Christianity is said to be becoming more individualistic than a religion of priests [245].

It is claimed that all seers are of this view. " The seers believe in an individualistic religion and plead for freedom and spontaneity. Science may impose a common standard for all, but

---

[235] Cf. RCW, p. 22.
[236] Cf. GB, p. 16.
[237] Cf. OSW, October 1952 - February 1959, p. 57.
[238] Cf. OSW, May 1962 - May 1964, p. 146.
[239] Cf. Ibid., p. 178.
[240] Cf. OSW, October 1952 - February 1959, p. 87.
[241] IVL, p. 155.
[242] Cf. RF, pp. 17-18.
[243] Cf. RCW, p. 50.
[244] ERWTh, p. 61.
[245] Cf. RC, p. 811.

in art and literature, philosophy and religion, individualism is more true " [246]. The Buddha desires that each one should search for himself, think for himself, and realize for himself [247]. This is so especially because religion is not something supernatural, but a personal attainment by man's natural capacities [248].

Each individual is unique and his relation to God is also unique [249]. The relation to God is developed differently in different individuals. Therefore, in order that each one may attain the fullest development of his religiosity, each one should follow a path according to his own natural lines [250]. In other words, since every individual is a pattern of his own, his religion also is unique [251]. Hence there should be as many ways to God as there are souls on earth [252]. From this basic individualistic view of religion Radhakrishnan rejects the possibility of an organization in religion. On the occasion of laying the foundation stone of the new University Campus and the Gandhi Bhavan at Trivandrum on September 30, 1963, he declared:

> "All great scriptures have affirmed one fact : as there are souls in this world, so are the pathways to God [253]. Infinite is God, infinite the soul of man, and infinite the pathways. There is no need to stereotype them, to bring them down to any particular principle, rigidity or anything like that. We should beware of every kind of dogmatism, religious,

---

[246] Cf. IVL, p. 95.

[247] Cf. RF, p. 76.

[248] Cf. ERWTh, p. 184; OSW, October 1952 - February 1959, p. 377; OSW, October 1952 - January 1956, p. 265.

[249] Cf. OSW, October 1952 - February 1959, p. 378; RS, p. 122. Here Radhakrishnan does not recognize any ultimate value in a relationship between man and God. In fact, because he holds the identity of the real self of man and God, he cannot recognize an ultimately valid man-God relationship. He is arguing against the claim to the uniqueness of organized religions and therefore he is speaking the language of the organized religions. He might recognize a relatively real relationship between the apparent self and God which is valid only so long as man is in the *māyā* order.

[250] Cf. RS, p. 122.

[251] Cf. OSW, October 1952 - February 1959, p. 377; RS, p. 54.

[252] Cf. *The Brahma Sūtra*, p. 153.

[253] "Pathways to God" is the famous Hindu term for religion. Radhakrishnan himself has used it a number of times, as we will see in the next chapter.

philosophical or political. There is no occasion for the free
spirit of man to be consigned to dogmas of any character " [254].

If we follow a common way, which is imposed by an external
authority, instead of the one which is given to us by nature and
verified by the inner light, then we are worshipping not God but
the authority or the group which claims to speak in His name.
Sin becomes disobedience to authority and not violation of integrity.
Therefore it is pointed out together with Simone Weil that faith
in the sense which St Thomas taught, or as a ' global adherence
to all that Church has taught and will teach ' is not faith but social
idolatry. To look for shelter in organized religion is subordination of the supreme freedom of the individual and a disbelief in
the inner light. In that sense organized religion is an obstacle
to true faith and " atheism is purification " [255].

ii) *Place of the Priest in Religion*

Priests are seers who constitute the conscience of society.
They should possess neither property nor executive power [256].
They should not arrogate to themselves any kind of superiority
over others, for that would be against the belief in God. If we
believe in God and if we believe that all human individuals are
similar sparks of the Divine, hierarchical or any other distinctions
are to be considered invalid and unjustifiable [255]. There is equality
of all men before God [258].

Since the divine light is within us and every one possesses it
equally, an intermediary priest between the individual and God is
not needed [259]. What we need is personal experience and not
priests' mediation [260]. Only when religion is confused with the profession and acknowledgment of revealed truths, is the need of an
intermediary priest felt. The priest or the Church then takes the
place of the Divine in us. Then adhesion to a creed and submission to an authority become unavoidable. Religion becomes dominated by an outward machinery. The Church distributes privi-

---

[254] OSW, May 1962 - May 1964, p. 247.
[255] OSW, October 1952 - February 1959, p. 378. Cf. also EWS, p. 41.
[256] Cf. RS, p. 129.
[257] OSW, May 1962 - May 1964, p. 127. Cf. also Ibid., pp. 145-147.
[258] Cf. IVL, p. 63.
[259] Cf. OSW, October 1952 - February 1959, p. 57.
[260] OSW, July 1959 - May 1962, p. 396.

leges and immunities [261]. It is like attaining salvation by proxy in herds [262]. But we have seen that an external agent cannot in any way work salvation or remission of sins for us [263]. Therefore the spirit of man and his critical intelligence ask, "every priest and dictator, are they necessary" [264]? A thinking man, therefore, can only be restive under external authority [265].

iii) *Reasons for a Priestless Religion*

1) In olden times, when the Scriptures were in languages other than the spoken one and when the people were mostly illiterate, there was some use for priests. They could explain the Scripture to the people in their language and thus awaken their spirit to realize the truth by themselves. But today,

> "the authoritairians show somewhat imperfect acquaintance with reality. When John Wycliff and his followers translated the Bible into English about 1382, the study of the Scriptures was no longer confined to the priests who knew Latin, but was extended to those who could read English. Every subsequent event emphasized the equality of all men in the sight of God and their right to serve God in their own way without dictation from Popes and priests" [266].

2) Religious leaders do not rise to the occasion when great injustice occurs. They do not stand above national politics and urge people to change their immoral ways. They either divorce religion from politics or even compromise with worldly politics [267]. As an example Radhakrishnan says that after the Lateran Treaty in 1929 the Pope blessed Mussolini and in 1936 the armies of General Franco were also blessed [268].

This accusation against religious leaders is especially brought forward in *Religion in a Changing World*. A full part of the second chapter is dedicated to this theme. He begins by saying: "The moral abdication of religious leadership has also contributed

---

[261] Cf. RS, pp. 52 f.

[262] Cf. ERWTh, p. 354.

[263] Where the doctrine of *karma* is explained.

[264] RF, p. 68.

[265] Cf. IVL, p. 63.

[266] Ibid., p. 63.

[267] Cf. OSW, October 1952 - February 1959, p. 373; IVL, pp. 36-37; RF, pp. 126-127; RCW, p. 45.

[268] Cf. RF, pp. 27-28, n. 17; Cf. also EWR, p. 107.

to the waning influence of religion " [269]. Then he goes on to charge
that " when the world is threatened by atomic destruction when
we are piling up nuclear armaments, which is a sure way to annihilation, many religious leaders are silent " [270]. He observes that
we live in a crumbling world without any hope, refuge or light.
But our leaders still speak in such a way that their authority may
not be lost. They do not give good example when they are using
such methods [271].

But this is not Radhakrishnan's attitude when he discusses
Krishna's advice to Arjuna to fight. He says :

> " When Krishna advises Arjuna to fight, it does not follow
> that he is supporting the validity of warfare. War happens
> to be the occasion which the teacher uses to indicate the
> spirit in which all work including warfare will have to be
> performed " [272].

3) Priests are said to be feeding on the weakness of human
nature. They tell the people that it is necessary to believe in
order to be saved. Thus they enforce their mechanical theology
and dull formalism [273] and try to bring about complete conformity [274]. They exploit the baser passions of fear and greed [275].
They do not teach their followers the equality of all religions,
that none is very bad and none perfect [276]. By declaring the greatness of their own religion they are dividing mankind [277]. Thus

---

[269] RCW, p. 46. Cf. also Chapter II, part iv: " The Religious Predicament ".

[270] RCW, p. 47.

[271] Cf. Ibid., p. 48. Radhakrishnan says that " Lenin is reported to
have said that if we would show him a dozen Christians who lived their
faith as fully as St Paul lived his, then he would become a Christian "
(RCW, p.. 48). In FS, p. 5 Lenin is said to have needed only one Christian.
But the difference will not effect the validity of the argument. It seems
that Radhakrishnan also accepts this view of Lenin. But one wonders
what would have been Radhakrishnan's position if he found not only one
dozen but, say, a dozen million Christians who live their faith " as fully as
St Paul lived his "! It is very probable that his oft repeated quotation from
A. N. Whitehead will show the position: " ... the first interpreter of the
New Testament was the worst, Paul " (Cf. OSW, July 1959 - May 1962,
p. 238; OSW, October 1952 - February 1959, p. 201).

[272] BG, p. 68

[273] Cf. IVL, p. 160.

[274] Ibid., p.. 60.

[275] Cf. ERWTh, p. 40.

[276] Cf. RCW, p. 52.

[277] Cf. ERWTh, p. 40.

they develop group-loyalties, perpetuate divisions and foment intolerance [278]. By doing so they are defeating the cause of religion
itself [279]. Thus they are said to be offenders of truth [280]. In impatient mood Radhakrishnan cites even Diderot's cry of anger:
" Men will never be free, until the last king is strangled with the
entrails of the last priest " [281].

4) Radhakrishnan appeals to the authority of the great seers
to do away with priests. He points out that the Buddha had condemned priests for not having openness [282]. In his Newton Baker
Lecture in Ohio on 27th March 1958 [283] he says that " Jesus asks
us to free ourselves from priestly control and undergo spiritual
growth " [284]. Therefore it is prophesied that the destiny of true
religion does not depend on ' priest-minds ' but on ' prophet-
souls ' [285].

In short, the priests have lost their priestly qualities, that is,
they have not the qualities of a seer, while they have gained no
other good qualities in the secular line. In spite of their public
profession they are said to be against the very religion they preach.
" The dignitaries of the Church are alarmed if any of its followers
take the Gospel of Jesus seriously and put into practice " [286]. In
a bitter attack on priests in his essay *The Spirit in Man* Radhakrishnan puts together almost all the afore-said accusations. After
stating that men with the qualities of a seer are not to be found
among priests, he continues:

> " The present class of priests, with rare exceptions, have lost
> their good breeding, kindliness and polish and have not gained
> in sureness of intellect, learning or adaptability. They know
> only that the discipline of tradition erects a barrier against
> radicalism and excessive individualism. They think that they
> are safeguarding the community against revolutionary change
> but are only fomenting it. If we pull off their masks,
> doubters stand revealed in many cases. They are not sure
> of what they preach and are mere opportunists by reason
> of a dumb growing despair whose nature they themselves

---

278 Cf. Ibid., p. 39.
279 Cf. IVL, p. 63.
280 Cf. RCW, p. 52.
281 Ibid., p. 50.
282 Cf. GB, p. 16.
283 Cf. OSW, October 1952 - February 1959, pp. 371-385.
284 Cf. Ibid., p. 376.
285 IVL, p. 39. Cf. also OSW, October 1952 - February 1959, p. 377.
286 EWR, p. 67.

do not understand. They are to some extent responsible
for the prevalent spiritual sluggishness. They thrust formulas into our heads, which we repeat mechanically, without
any real knowledge of what they mean " [287].

iv) *The Nature of Authority in Organized Religions*

Dogma and authority in organized religions are intimately
inter-related. Once we are convinced of the absolute truth of the
revelation that we possess and of the falsity of that which others
have, it will be impossible for us to tolerate other views and we
will feel compelled to convert all those who hold other views to
our own view — And we overlook the important fact that they are
also equally convinced of the necessity to convert us to their views,
for the same reasons [288]. Those who are convinced of such a
mission, do also feel and claim that their authority for such conduct is from God. Thus they arrogate to themselves the place
of God in relation to the individual and regard as sin whatever
is against this self-assumed authority [289]. Such a stand will make
authority even morally insensitive. Radhakrishnan is also inclined
to think with Baron von Hügel that " the more orthodox the
Christian Catholic became doctrinally, the less sensitive he became
morally " [290]. Orthodoxy will be insisted at all costs; tradition
as transmitted by a holy book or Church will be universally
imposed; critical enquiry and sceptical questioning will be dismissed
as pernicious [291]. Thus Radhakrishnan conceives of authority in
organized religions as a hard, despotic power.

> " An organized religion or Church is hostile to every belief
> which is opposed to its own creed. If our knowledge threa-
> tens the old creeds, it is the knowledge that suffers. A
> Church cannot allow liberty of thought within its borders
> or, for that matter, even without. It is obliged to enforce
> beliefs and persecute unbelief on principle. If the fair name
> of Greece is not stained by any religious wars, it was due
> to its polytheism " [292].

---

[287] *The Spirit in Man,* pp. 477-478.
[288] Cf. *The Brahma Sūtra,* p. 172.
[289] Cf. EWS, p. 41.
[290] RCW, p. 50.
[291] Cf. RF, p. 70.
[292] EWR, pp. 50-51.

So the despots in politics and authority in organized religions are equally totalitarian [293]; both overlook the values of individual freedom and personal integrity [294]. Eventually organized religion with authority will serve as a useful ally to a despotic State [295].

Some passages show authority in organized religion as a ruthless, blind power which take no heed of reason and common sense.

> " Political dictatorships and religious dogmatisms have no understanding of the profound identity of human beings, their passion and reactions, their ideals and aspirations in all ages and in all places " [296].

Authority dictates definite creeds for belief and codes for conduct, which all have to accept [297]. It desires the people to go by beaten tracks, looking neither to the right nor to the left. It asks the people to repeat the sayings of the illustrious dead [298]. If the free spirits of the community object, they will be answered with inquisition and the stake. " Rome made Galileo recant, Calvin's Geneva might have burned him. Tennessee would have put him in prison " [299]. " Three hundred thousand persons were put to death for their religious opinions in Madrid alone ... Since they thought these were permitted by divine justice, they did not shrink from adopting refinements of cruelty in human affairs " [300]. Thus Christianity which was originally a simple faith, when organized under an authority, became one of the worst of totalitarianisms. " As a matter of fact there is hardly any phase in the history of Communism that has not its parallel in the history of Christianity " [301]. It is also suggested that perhaps Communism is better than Christianity and other authoritarian organized religions [302].

If dogma is considered a superstition, then authority in religion is a victim of that superstition.

---

[293] Cf. RCW, p. 45.
[294] Cf. RF, p. 71.
[295] Cf. ERWTh, p. 283.
[296] Ibid., p. 40.
[297] Cf. RF, p. 71.
[298] RWN, p. 8.
[299] IVL, p. 60.   Cf. also ERWTh, p. 283.
[300] Cf. ERWTh, pp. 276-277.
[301] RF, p. 54.
[302] Cf. Ibid., p. 56, n. 21.

" The authoritarian faiths and atheism which stands at the opposite extreme are both victims of superstition. They deny the free man, the responsible actor. They eliminate initiative and tend to dehumanize man. In extreme forms of totalitarianism, religious and political, there is a tendency to reduce human beings into mechanisms responding to stimuli, puppets twitched into sacrifice and suffering by the dictates of the leaders " [303].

A foot-note to the cited passage reveals the authoritarian faith that Radhakrishnan has in mind. It reads: " In 1870 when an announcement of a new dogma was made, Lord Acton said that he did not see why he should change his religion because the Pope changed his " [304].

Regarding the subjects who submit themselves to authority, it is said, that by accepting an authority over them in religious matters which should be entirely personal, they are abdicating the moral obligation of thinking for themselves [305], abandoning the search for truth [306] and destroying the ' integrity of the self ' [307].

Therefore it is clear that Radhakrishnan conceives of authority in organized religion after the fashion of a blind, totalitarian, despotic power in politics.

v) *Who Needs an External Religious Authority?*

From the individualistic theory of religion it follows that no external authority in religion is essentially necessary. It cannot have a binding force on the individual.

Still an external authority may be useful for people who are incapable of thinking out a religion for themselves [308]. " For them it is a question of either accepting an authority or going without religion altogether " [309]. Something is always better than nothing. There are others who are tired of the effort of thinking, frightened by the difficulties of doubt, fall back on authority [310]. This is what happens in a period of social slackness. The victimized individual feels that,

---

[303] Ibid., p. 72.
[304] RF, p. 72, n. 30.
[305] Cf. RCW, pp. 43-44.
[306] Cf. GB, p. 16.
[307] Cf. BG, p. 44.
[308] Cf. RCW, p. 43; IVL, p. 61.
[309] IVL, p. 61.
[310] Cf. Ibid., p. 60.

" The old has vanished, the new is nebulous. Nothing in human life holds good. Where can we discover peace of mind except in the Word of God, which will stand fast when all the host of heaven is dissolved and when the skies are rolled like a scroll " [311]?

Then the individual turns to an authority which claims to possess the Word of God and give definite solutions for any problem. In this case it is not important that the authority be of any particular kind. It is sufficient that it gives them a refuge from scepticism. Burdened and tired to death by his loneliness, man is ready to lean on any kind of authority, if it only saves him from hopeless isolation and the wild search for peace [312].

But Radhakrishnan thinks that it is better to avoid such consolation which is bought at the price of the integrity of the individual [313]. Arjuna, for example, could have overcome anxiety by submitting to social authority. But then he would not have been acting out of personal conviction [314].

vi) *Reasons against Authority in Religion*

1) *Authority Takes away the Freedom of the Seeker of Truth*

Every man has got a moral obligation to engage in a perpetual search for truth, because the realization of the eternal truth is his final goal. The essential characteristic of this search is freedom. Everyone has the fundamental right to choose that form of belief and worship which appeals to him most [315]. This freedom of the individual is absolute. It is inviolable by any external authority. Therefore, no one should impose his religious views on others. Even when our advice is sought, it should be given without any intention of converting the seeker to our religious views. We should enquire what the religion of the seeker is and help him to perfect it [316].

But the authority in organized religion does not respect the religious freedom of the individual. It desires that men should " go by beaten track, like horses in blinkers, looking neither to

---

[311] RF, p. 70.
[312] *The Spirit in Man,* p. 483.
[313] Cf. BG, p. 44; IVL, p. 41.
[314] Cf. Ibid., RF, pp. 71-72.
[315] Cf. HVL, p. 34.
[316] Cf. Ibid.

the right, nor to the left " [317].   In his recent work, *Religion in a Changing World,* Radhakrishnan gives a concrete example of denying the religious freedom to the individual :

> " The Vatican newspaper, *L'Osservatore Romano,* in warning Italian Christian democrats against allying themselves with Marxist groups said :
> " The Church has full powers of true jurisdiction over all the faithful and hence has the duty and the right to guide, direct and correct them on the plane of ideas and the plane of action. A Catholic can never prescind the teachings and the directives of the Church. In every sector of his activities we must inspire his private and public conduct by the laws, orientation and instructions of the hierarchy " [318].

Such a view according to Radhakrishnan is inconsistent with freedom of conscience and religious liberty [319].

When freedom is denied and people are educated in absolutist faiths they will become men of fanatical fervour and not free spirits who enquire deep into Reality [320]. Under pressure of authority there can be no independent thought and spiritual search. By compulsion it is not spirituality that is formed but herd minds and a mechanical society [321]. Thus authority becomes an obstacle or even an hostile power to spiritual growth.

The imperative command of life is to obey one's own inner light. An obedience to ' ecclesiastical pundits or social rules is a form of self-indulgence ' [322]. When we are accepting another's judgment as final, we are surrendering our freedom of spirit. That depersonalizes the human being [323]. When authority is most powerful, it acts like a blind mechanism and becomes " an almost organized opposition to the values of life and spirit " [324]. The result will be dull obedience, unthinking custom which is a sort of death [325].

Therefore, whenever there is belief in an external authority, the spiritual values of the individual suffers most. The purpose

---

[317] RWN. p. 8.
[318] RCW, p. 44. No reference is given.
[319] Cf. Ibid., p. 45.
[320] Cf. RF, p. 70.
[321] Cf. RCW, p. 45. Cf. also Ibid., p. 33; IVL, p. 38; BG, p. 44.
[322] EWR, p. 142.
[323] Cf. Ibid., p. 116.
[324] Cf. ERWTh, p. 279.
[325] Cf. *The Spirit in Man,* p. 503.

of religion is to help man to attain to spiritual freedom. But when religion upholds authority, it acts adversely.

> " Religions by upholding the authority of their organizations, tend to crush the individuality of the people, debase their sense of moral responsibility, and corrupt the conscience of the community " [326].

2) *Authority Does Not Trust Reason*

Authoritarianism has a mistrust of reason [327]. That is why it does not encourage free inquiry. It dictates beliefs for people and asks them to accept these beliefs as life-principles. The fundamentalists, who are " not confined to America or to Christianity " ask the people to shut their eyes to the facts of modern thought and inquiry [328]. They call upon the people to repeat blindly the sayings of the illustrious dead. " It does not matter whether they are illustrious or not, ... what matters is that they should be dead " [329]. However for them there is a great calamity — education [330].

Considering those who are under authority Radhakrishnan thinks that their blind belief is not salutary. It is faith and not blind belief that can work our salvation. At present there is said to be a confusion between faith and belief. " It is an unfortunate legacy of the course which Christian theology has followed in Europe that faith has come to connote a mechanical adherence to authority " [331]. But the faith which is saving, is an act of surrender to the creative intuition which transcends the limited awareness of the intellectual self [332]. Therefore, to have faith is to have the awareness of the direct encounter with the Supreme [333].

When, however, reason is distrusted and intellectual subordination is asked for, two kinds of results are said to follow : superstition and rebellion.

Sometimes it is argued that when reason is distrusted superstition will grow stronger. Man will then hold all sorts of irrational ideas born of fear and ignorance as fashionable. " In some

---

[326] RCW, p. 45.
[327] Cf. IVL, p. 62.
[328] RWN, p. 8.
[329] Ibid.
[330] Ibid.
[331] HVL, p. 14.
[332] Cf. *The Brahma Sūtra*, p. 116.
[333] Cf. Ibid.; HVL, p. 14.

quarters ", says Radhakrishnan, " religion itself is being transformed into a superstition " [334]. He does not say which religions are being converted to superstitions and what these superstitions are. But a foot-note to the cited sentence may give us a clue to the mind of Radhakrishnan. It reads :

" Even the liberal schools are unwilling to shake off the materialism associated with theology in the way of supernatural revelations, interferences, miracles and such other superstitions " [335].

When the vital energies of religion are paralysed by superstitions, honest and upright people will leave that religion [336]. In India, for example, points out Radhakrishnan :

" When we find men of undoubted piety range themselves against common sense and scientific knowledge, against the dictates of humanity and the demands of justice, all in blind obedience to laws whose infallibility is a myth, our leaders are getting tired of religion and think it is time we part with it " [337].

Another result of subordination of reason to authority is open rebellion. In affirming that reason should not be trusted, that God should be approached " with eyes coloured by faith, that its systems should not be regarded too closely, authoritarianism seems to harbour a secret scepticism " [338]. That is why authority cannot have any appeal to the intellectuals of an age remarkable for its criticism of creeds. The free spirits have an intellectual curiosity by their very nature. They will go on questioning the value and the validity of every authority. When authority on its part attempts to smother intellectual curiosity " the mind of man rebels against it, and the inevitable reaction shows itself in an impatience of all formal authority and a wild outbreak of the emotional life long repressed by the discipline of the ceremonial religion " [339].

---

[334] IVL. p. 62.
[335] Ibid., p. 62, n. 2.
[336] Cf. Ibid.
[337] Ibid., p. 38.
[338] Ibid., p. 63.
[339] Ind. Ph, I, 273.

3) *The Unscientific Nature of Authority*

Radhakrishnan sees an absolute incompatibility between science and authority in organized religions. He opens his *Recovery of Faith,* after a short introduction, with this problem. The unscientific character of organized religions is said to be one of the major causes of the decline of religion itself [340].

Ours is a scientific age. The scientific age is reluctant to accept anything on trust [341]. It scrutinizes and criticizes everything. Its method is empirical while that of authority in the organized religions is dogmatic [342]. To accept statements on authority is " to be satisfied with second-hand evidence " [343], which is not the way of science. To show the incompatibility of scientific research with authority, Tertullian is referred to, as he asks, " Where is there any likeness between the Christian and the philosopher ... " [344]? Further in a foot-note it is pointed out that Luther and Calvin did not agree with the Copernican idea of the universe and that a priest rejected the invitation of Kircher to look through his telescope to see the Sun's spots saying that there cannot be such spots since Aristotle has not spoken of it [345]. Immediately Radhakrishnan goes on to give a strong warning to all established religions :

> " If established religions become rigid, closed and confined narrowly to a world whose boundaries are marked out in the scriptures written centuries ago, those attracted by scientific method, which has demonstrated its validity, not only theoretically but practically, through the spectacular technological results, are inclined to prefer the laboratory to the altar " [346].

If only we know the meaning of doubt, we cannot accept authority. For even if the authoritarian dogmas undergo violent

---

[340] Cf. RF, p. 10.

[341] Cf. Ibid.

[342] Cf. OSW, October 1952 - February 1959, p. 347; RF, p. 10 f.

[343] Cf. Ibid.

[344] RF, p. 11.

[345] Cf. Ibid., p. 11, n. 1. For the alleged answer of the priest no reference to any document is given. It should be marked also that the said priest did not say so quoting sacred Scripture, but one of the greatest intellectuals of all times. So it is very difficult to present it as an argument against authority in religion. Moreover, Radhakrishnan is arguing from one or two isolated examples. He seems to forget that these ' authoritarian religions ' have produced the greatest scientists.

[346] Ibid., pp. 11-12.

distortion, they cannot go with reason [347]. So the spirit which revolted against divine right and sanctified tyrannies in politics, which protested against social abuses and established conventions, is 'today expressing itself in a demand for the sway of science and social idealism [348].

Radhakrishnan considers that intellectual authority is superior to inherited authority [349]. Therefore external authority in religion should be subjected to our critical study. But on a critical analysis authority breaks down. For, the ground for the claim to the acceptance of authority is that the author possessed superior opportunities of knowing the truth which the others did not have. This ground is said to be unacceptable, because, when

> " the New Testament and the Qu'ran conflict, we cannot assume that the author of the one had better opportunities of knowing the truth than the other. We must turn to some other criterion, e. g. the rationality of their contents. The supernatural nature of religious authority will have to be given up " [350].

Authority will then cease to be an authority. That is why religious authorities condemn all attempts which result in undermining belief in their sacred Scripture [351].

The anti-scientific attitude of authority has made it difficult for the honest men to accept religion. For the modern scientific mind will dismiss as superstition authoritarian statements if they are not clear by reason [352]. Nothing can be true by faith if it is not true by reason. But authoritarian religions impose incredible beliefs [353]. " People nurtured in the spirit of science and ethical humanism are unwilling to accept anything on authority " [354].

Therefore a scientific method should be adopted in religion. The Hindu way, for example, is said to be non-authoritarian. Nothing is accepted on authority. Everything is tested by experience [355]. Experience can be empirically repeated. But miracles, marvels and so-called supernatural interventions which are

---

[347] Cf. IVL, p. 63.
[348] Cf. Ibid., p. 37.
[349] OSW, October 1952 - February 1959, p. 377.
[350] IVL, p. 13.   D
[351] Cf. RF, p. 12.
[352] Cf. OSW, May 1962 - May 1964, pp. 161, 173; ERWTh, p. 14.
[353] Cf. *Fragments,* p. 19.
[354] OSW, May 1962 - May 1964, p. 178.
[355] Cf. Ibid.

the crutches of authority are not empirically observable. They cannot be repeated on an empirical level. Hence religion is not to be based on supernatural or natural authority which is external to the individual [356].

4) *Belief in Authority Generates Despots*

In the third chapter of his *Recovery of Faith,* Radhakrishnan cautions us that the result of exalting authority in religion will be the rise of despotic rulers:

> "When we repudiate reason and demand faith, we play into the hands of dictators who profess to supply us with definite creeds for belief and codes for conduct. As a totalitarian faith is neither liberal nor democratic, it becomes easily an ally of political totalitarianism. Those authoritarian creeds overlook the value of individual freedom, of personal integrity" [357].

This is said to be confirmed by Karl Barth's statement: "Antisemetism is right ... Israel is an evil people" and the fact that it was "a Christian minister in the U.S.A. who revived the Ku Klux Klan in 1915 with the slogan 'Protestant Christianity and White supremacy'" [358]. If people are taught that religious leaders have divine authority and therefore our reason should be submitted to their authority, they will be prone to accept like claims by totalitarian rulers in politics. If political rulers were themselves once educated in blind subservience to authority, it is no wonder, if they in their turn demand blind obedience to themselves.

> "If the Roman Catholics accept the Pope's Encyclical on Marriage, the National Socialists accept the decrees of Hitler as Holy Writ. Those who question the true faith are thrown into concentration camps ..." [359].

It is therefore no accident, contends Radhakrishnan, "that Hitler and Mussolini have been brought up in Roman Catholic societies, where it is blasphemous to criticize infallible authority" [360].

---

[356] Cf. OSW, October 1952 - February 1959, p. 347.
[357] RF, p. 71.
[358] Ibid.. p. 71, n. 27.
[359] ERWTh, p. 60.
[360] Ibid., p. 60, n. 1.

5) *Authority Fosters Intolerance*

Reason should teach us to doubt our own infallibility. Unless we learn that we are fallible beings, there is no chance for tolerance in this world [361]. Instead of such a humble outlook, authorities in the organized religions cultivate a sort of 'sacred egoism' or 'spiritual pride' [362]. In their anxiety to enforce their own views, they become very intolerant and condemn all those who do not accept their dictates. Religious persecution such as the Inquisition has darkened many pages of the history of religions. Organized religions are like Nation States — Bad citizens belong to it, good neighbours are aliens [363].

Radhakrishnan gives an anecdote to show how hard submission to an absolute authority is:

> "It is said of Confucius: Once he heard the mourning wail of a woman on the lonely side of Mount Ta'i. When she was asked the reason she said: 'My husband's father was killed here by a tiger, my husband also, and now my son has met the same fate'. 'Then why', asked Confucius, 'do you dwell in this dangerous place'? She replied: 'Here there is no oppressive ruler'" [364].

It is also true that organized religions have done "great services" to humanity. But these are said to be "inconsiderable compared with their claim to absolute authority and the attempt to enforce that claim, by punishment, by torture and even death" [365].

6) *Authority Causes Division*

Instead of strengthening the invisible bonds that bind together humanity into one, authority keeps people in separate camps hostile to one another. In any particular camp, the adherents are taught a kind of mystic worship of their group. Radhakrishnan bitterly attacks religions for dividing humanity:

> "By force and fraud, by politics and pseudo-religions [366], diplomats and priests exploit the baser passions of fear and

---

[361] Cf. *The Brahma Sūtra,* p. 172.

[362] Cf. Ibid.

[363] Cf. RCW, pp. 51-52; ERWTh, p. 314.

[364] IC, p. 68.

[365] RCW, p. 44.

[366] The allusion is to the established religions. They are said to be 'pseudo-religions' because they have deviated from their original purity.

greed and impose on us the deadly restrictions of blood, race, and nation [367] and thus accentuate the division in man's soul ... Religions by propagating illusions such as the fear of hell, damnation [358] and arrogant assumptions of inviolable authority and exclusive monopolies of the divine word ... destroy the sense of oneness with the world and divide humanity into narrow groups which are vain and ambitious, bitter and intolerant " [369].

7) *The 'Founders' of Religions Rejected Authority*

Radhakrishnan continually brings forward the authority of the seers and religious founders as an argument against authority. This is the final argument which Radhakrishnan adduces in the concluding paragraph of the eighth chapter of *Eastern Religions and Western Thought* against authority in organized religions [370]. This chapter begins by showing how Hinduism has been tolerant down through the centuries. Then he condemns authority in organized religions as intolerant and cruel as Bolshevists [371]. He predicts that the future hope of religion and of mankind is with

---

[367] Radhakrishnan carefully avoids any mention of caste-divisions.

[358] From the theory that man's real self is one with the Divine, it follows that man, however wicked he be, cannot be eternally damned. Radhakrishnan himself has often argued in this way (Cf. OSW, October 1952 - February 1959, p. 290; RC, p. 798; RF, p. 173; EWS, p. 27; HVL, pp. 51 f; OSW, May 1962 - May 1964, p. 158). Hell is said to be inconsistent with a God of love (Cf. IVL, p. 233), with the omnipotence of God (Cf. IVL, p. 227) and with the perfect sanctity of God (Cf. EWS, p. 77). In many other places also the idea of an eternal Hell is rejected and salvation for all is said to be certain (Cf. MST, p. 44; HVL, pp. 46 f, 88; GB, pp. 23 f; *The Brahma Sūtra,* pp. 219 ff; IVL, pp. 164, 226, 233, 244, 246).   D

[369] Cf. ERWTh, p. 40; Cf. Ibid., p. 280 f.

[370] The eighth chapter, "The Meeting of Religions", comes after long discussions on the religions of the East and the West. Therefore, this chapter may be considered as the concluding one, although we have another chapter on "The Individual and the Social Order in Hinduism". This last chapter is not a fitting conclusion to the general theme, and therefore it may be considered an appendix to the book. At any rate the fitting conclusion is the eighth chapter. If this is so, then evidently the argument from the seers against authority in religion is certainly considered by Radhakrishnan as the final and the strongest. For it appears in the concluding paragraph as a prelude and a support to his life's great ideal—a world community on a spiritual basis, not on a particular authority or doctrine.

[371] Cf. ERWTh, pp. 325-326.

the " leftwing liberals " who do not submit to the claims of absolute authority and admit that no religion in its present form is final [372]. So he appeals to stop the practice of " killing one another theologically " [373], and warns that if the religions persist in fratricidal war " the swift advance of secular humanism and moral materialism is assured " [374].

After showing the grave consequences of authoritarian methods of religion, Radhakrishnan introduces his great ideal " of a world society with a universal religion of which the historical faiths are but branches " [375]. The great obstacle to this final goal is the unbending authority in different organized religions. In this context Radhakrishnan puts forward his final argument against the position of the authorities : " Each religion has sat at the feet of teachers that never bowed to its authority " [376]. Today mankind has to imitate these great religious teachers on a large scale. The pioneers and pathfinders believed more in their inner light than in an external authority and they declared what their deepest being found true [377]. They ask us also to discover the truth for ourselves and not to trust on authority [378]. For the evidence of truth is not in the declaration of authorities but in man's experience of it [379]. When the inward and the outward become one, " religion is lived truth " [380].

Almost every time that Radhakrishnan speaks or writes about the Buddha, he brings out the above characteristic of the Buddha's religious views. The Buddha refused to accept views on the authority of others [381]. For truths accepted on authority and not ascertained and realized by personal experience are of no avail [382]. Therefore he asks us not to believe any sacred book because of its antiquity or respect for its author [383]. He does not wish us

---

[372] Cf. Ibid., p. 347.
[373] Ibid.
[374] Ibid.
[375] Ibid.
[376] Ibid., p. 348.
[377] Cf. IVL, p. 63.
[378] Cf. OSW, October 1952 - February 1959, p. 313.
[379] Cf. Ibid., p. 308.
[380] RCW, p. 50.
[381] Cf. OSW, October 1952 - February 1959, p. 347.
[382] Cf. RF, p. 124; *The Brahma Sūtra*, p. 113.
[383] Cf. GB, p. 15; RF, p. 75. " ... not because it is a report, not because it is a tradition, not because it is so said in the past, ... but if you yourself understand that this is so meritorious and blameless, and when

to recognize his authority either. We are asked not to accept his words out of regard for him [384]. He advised his followers not to abandon the search for truth by accepting an authority [385]. Each one must search for himself and realize for himself [386].

The *Bhagavad Gītā* opens with Arjuna's refusal to conform to the social codes [387]. Lao Tzu in China wanted abolition of all forms of governmental control over the individual [388].

A similar attitude towards authority is found also in the conduct of Jesus. He did not seek power for himself [389]. He never submitted to the authority of the High Priests and Pharisees [390]. "He sets aside all authorities. Whatever they may say, 'I say unto you'" [391]. For, Jesus valued the freedom of the inner spirit more than anything external [392]. Hence "authoritarianism is based on the principle of anti-Christ", concludes Radhakrishnan [393].

vii) *A Re-evaluation of Authority*

We have seen that Radhakrishnan presents the authorities of "Pope or of Council or of Book" [394], which the organized religions uphold, after the fashion of Bolshevists and Nazists and that he calls for a universal disobedience to such authorities in the cause of world religion and world society.

But, certainly, this is not his manner and tone when he treats of the authority of Hindu Scriptures. Many passages put the reader into serious doubt as to whether he is admitting the absolute authority of the *Vedas* and the *Upanishads*. Innumerable citations from the sacred books in favour of his views can also in-

---

accepted is for benefit and happiness, then you may accept it" (*Anguttara*, III, 653).

[384] Cf. OSW, October 1952 - February 1959, pp. 279, 308, 347; OSW, May 1962 - May 1964, p. 173.

[385] Cf. GB, p. 16, 65 f.

[386] Cf. RF, p. 75; OSW, October 1952 - February 1959, p. 279; OSW, May 1962 - May 1964, p. 173; "Be ye as those who have the self as their light. Be ye as those who have the self as their refuge. Betake yourselves to no external refuge" (*Mahāparanibhana Sutta*, 33).

[387] Cf. BG, p. 44; RF, pp. 71-72.

[388] IC, p. 70.

[389] Cf. RF, pp. 67 f.

[390] Cf. ERWTh, p. 272.

[391] EWS, p. 72.

[392] Cf. RF, pp. 68, 75.

[393] Ibid., p. 72. Cf. also EWR, p. 58.

[394] IVL, p. 60. Cf. also Ibid., n. 2.

dicate the acceptance of their authority. Radhakrishnan opens his
Introduction to *The Brahma Sūtra* with the sentance : " The *Vedas*
have remained for centuries the highest religious authority for
all sections of the Hindus " [395]. He admits that all the orthodox
systems — *Sāṁkhya, Yoga, Vedānta, Mīmāṁsa, Nyāya* and *Vai-
śeṣika* — accept the authority of the *Vedas* as infallible [396]. Several passages in *A Source Book in Indian Philosophy* of which
Radhakrishnan is a joint editor show also acceptance of the authority of the sacred Books [397]. He begins his " Introduction "
to *The Principal Upanishads,* acknowledging that their authority
was admitted down through the centuries. " Every subsequent religious movement has had to show itself to be in accord with
their philosophical statements " [398]. This pro-authority attitude of
Radhakrishnan is indubiously clear in his " Preface " to the *Upanishads* (in Hindi) by Professor Satyavrata :

> " Human progress is built on acts of faith. The acts of
> faith on which our civilization is based are to be found in
> the Principal Upanishads. When we are now setting out
> on a new era in the life of our country, we must go to the
> Upanishads for inspiration. They contain the principles
> which have moulded our history from its earliest dawn.
> Where we have failed, our defeat is due to our infidelity
> to the teachings of the Upanishads. It is therefore essential
> for our generation to grasp the significance of the Upanishads
> and understand their relevance to our problems " [399].

So on the one hand we have an uncompromising condemnation of trust in authority, and a call to revolt against it, and on
the other great reverence for authority and a call to remould our
lives according to the doctrines of the sacred Scriptures. Is there
a contradiction here? If so, is it real or apparent?

A closer understanding of the meaning of faith in the mouth
of Radhakrishnan may help us to solve the problem. Blind belief
in dogma or a mechanical adherence to authority is not the saving
faith. In the proper sense faith is said to be ' spiritual conviction '.
It is called faith " because spiritual perception, like other kinds of
perception, is liable to error and requires the testing process of

---

[395] *The Brahma Sūtra,* p. 19.
[396] Cf. Ibid., p. 20.
[397] Cf. *A Source Book,* pp. xxiv-xxv, 37, 99, 350.
[398] Pr. Ups, p. 17. Cf. also pp. 25, 133.
[399] OSW, October 1952 - February 1959, p. 531.

logical thought " [400]. Radhakrishnan sees a real distinction between faith and belief. An act of faith involves a surrender to the creative intuition which transcends the limited awareness of the intellectual self. Faith is the spiritual conviction born out of personal encounter with the Supreme. Therefore, in order that a belief may become an ' organic expression of faith ' it must be reborn and continually renewed in personal experience [401], which in turn is checked by sound reason [402]. When we understand faith in this sense, it will be easier to understand those texts in which Radhakrishnan seemingly endorses the authority of the sacred Scriptures.

We shall re-examine in what sense the *Vedas* are said to be authoritative. The *Vedas* are the registers of the spiritual experiences of the experts in religion [403]. They are the accumulated treasure of spiritual discoveries of different persons at different times. They are ever growing [404]. Everyone can test by his spiritual experience the truths of the *Vedas* and the *Upanishads* and other sacred books. In the light of his personal experience and under his personal criticism anyone can re-interpret them and thus add a new fibre to the variegated tissue of the *Vedas* [405]. When a new awakening comes old symbols are interpreted in a new way [406]. These new interpretations may be different, but the truth of the *Vedas* stand. " Astronomies change but the stars abide " [407]. Each one needs to accept only what appeals to him in his personal experiments with them by means of logic and also through life [408]. Historically the *Vedas* and the *Upanishads* have inspired generations of Indians with vision and strength by their inexhaustible significance and spiritual power. In this way the *Vedas* and *Upanishads* are accepted and not because they are " *śruti* or revealed literature " [409].

Therefore Radhakrishnan does not insist on conformity with or bondage to the sacred Scriptures. He explicitly says that they

---

[400] HVL, p. 14. Cf. also OSW, July 1959 - May 1962, p. 262.
[401] Cf. *The Brahma Sūtra*, p. 116.
[402] Cf. Ibid.
[403] Cf. HVL, p. 14; *The Brahma Sūtra*, p. 19.
[404] Cf. OSW, October 1952 - February 1959, p. 284.
[405] Cf. HVL, p. 15; Pr. Ups, pp. 133 f.
[407] *The Brahma Sūtra*, p. 114.
[408] HVL, p. 15. Cf. also GB, p. 65.
[409] Cf. Pr. Ups, p. 18.

are " not infallible " [410]. He insists only on a loyalty to the accumulated wisdom of the past in order that we may not " lapse into
individualistic rationalism and ultimate negation " and that we
may not be " led astray by our wandering whims " [411]. And
loyalty means " not only concord with the past but also freedom
from the past " [412].

So we can conclude that the apparent contradictions dissolve
once we appreciate the viewpoint of Radhakrishnan. And he
himself affirms this [413]. Personal authority is the primary authority. An authority is accepted in so far as it accords with the
personal spiritual experience and judgment [414]. The realized men
may discard any statement of sacred Scripture or of another authority if it is in conflict with the experienced truth. Summing
up these two aspects of authority Radhakrishnan says : " When
the awakening takes place scripture ceases to be authoritative " [415].

---

[410] OSW, October 1952 - February 1959, p. 319; *The Brahma Sūtra*,
p. 115.
[411] IVL, p. 61. Cf. also HVL, p. 15.
[412] Pr. Ups, p. 145.
[413] Cf. *The Brahma Sūtra*, p. 117; RC, pp. 789-790.
[414] Cf. GB, p. 65.
[415] Pr. Ups, p. 137.

VI

BEYOND ORGANIZED RELIGIONS

We have seen a number of charges levelled against doctrines and dogmas, rites and ceremonies, leaders and authorities in organized religions. These charges are directly against certain element of the organized religion, but in many other passages Radhakrishnan has found fault not merely with authority or dogma or rite but with organized religion as a whole. These accusations are often the same as those against the separate elements of organized religion. In this chapter we will first discuss how and why Radhakrishnan insists that the present organized religions are to be left behind in the ultimate stage of religious experience; then, we shall define his concept of religion as pure experience of Reality; and finally describe his call for a universal religion. This chapter therefore will have four parts: 1) Present Organized Religions Are to Be Surpassed; 2) The Experiential Nature of Religion; 3) Consequences of Considering Religion as an Experience of Reality; and 4) The Universal Religion.

1) Present Organized Religions Are to Be Surpassed

i) *Reasons for Leaving behind Organized Religions*

1) *Failure in Social Obligations.* Radhakrishnan gives one of his general tests of the authenticity of a true religion in the first chapter of his *An Idealist View of Life*: " That religion is worth little, if the conscience of its followers is not disturbed when war clouds are hanging over us all and industrial conflicts are threatening social peace " [1]. Organized religions, he continually says, have failed in their social obligations, and they have supported oppressors by lending authority to them and sanctifying their pretences [2]. They " bless our arms and comfort us with the

---

[1] IVL, p. 35.
[2] Cf. Ibid.

belief that our policies are just and inevitable. In every age, religion adjusted itself to the follies and cruelties of men " [3]. Religion supported the use of force even in the interest of trade and empire [4]. Instead of opposing and condemning social injustices they have sanctioned them. In this respect Radhakrishnan points the finger especially at Christianity. " A soulless system of economics and building of empires involving the subjection of vast populations received the blessing of the Church " [5]. Every social movement received a condemnation from the " official spokesmen of religion " [6]. As if to prove this Radhakrishnan gives two instances : " In 1864 Pope Pius IX issued the encyclical *Quanta cura* in which he condemned as ' pests, socialism, communism, Bible Societies, and Clerico-Liberal Societies ' " and " In 1891 Pope Leo XIII, in his encyclical *Rerum Novarum* denounced socialism as robbery and demanded that its tenets be ' utterly rejected by all Catholics ' " [7]. The official attitude of the Roman Catholic Church is said to be the same towards socialism and communism even now [8]. The main defect of organized religions is the setting up a barrier between the sacred and the secular [9]. Thus they withdraw from the scene of mankind's agony, " proclaiming that justice can be found only beyond the grave " [10]. Because organized religions uphold such principles they have failed utterly in this field in spite of their enormous resources [11]. When opportunities came, as they were afraid of losing their sanity and peace, they carefully passed by on the other side, like the Levite of the parable [12]. There is not even the possibility of a social regeneration under these religions [13]. And a religion which has failed in social responsibilities has no claim to our allegiance [14].

All religions are trying to appease those who hold power in

---

[3] ERWTh, p. 111.

[4] Cf. Ibid., pp. 282-283.

[5] Ibid., p. 282. Radhakrishnan is probably alluding to colonization by some of the Christian countries.

[6] RF, p. 26.

[7] Ibid., p. 26, n. 14.

[8] Cf. Ibid.

[9] Cf. Ibid., p. 23.

[10] Ibid.

[11] Cf. IVL, p. 37; *Fragments,* pp. 25, 67; OSW, October 1952 - January 1956, p. 259; RCW, p. 45.

[12] Cf. IVL, p. 110.

[13] Cf. RF, p. 23.

[14] Cf. Ibid., p. 30.

the world [15]. This tendency has made them a useful ally of despotic States [16]. Even those who profess to be religious are worshippers of the nation-states. Their religion is nothing more than a "saluting of flags and a singing of national anthems" [17]. In some weak countries nationalism itself has become the religion [18]. Thus organized religions by supporting material values have become the arch enemy of spiritual ideals [19].

2) *Intolerance*

Organized religions claim absolute authority over their adherents and insist that the doctrines that they teach are final [20], that they are superior to all others [21]. In this way they have become "intolerant absolutisms, condemning all those who do not accept them to eternal perdition. Religious persecution, inquisition, tortures have darkened many pages of the history of religions" [22]. Because they impose limits of dogmas and rites, they have become closed totalitarian systems. Each religion teaches that it is the only means to salvation [23]. Thus when religion becomes organized, bigotry will be increased. "The spirit of bigotry increased in the West only after Christianity became organized by the Catholic Church" [24]. Such closed final sects are formidable obstacles to the unity of mankind [25]. These obstacles are to be removed if we are to realize the world community.

3) *Opposition to Reason*

Organized religions do not respect reason and science. "The anti-rational attitude is common to all established institutions and organizations" [26]. This indeed affects the freedom of ideas which

---

[15] Cf. Ibid., p. 24. Radhakrishnan admits that this is true to some extent with regard to Hinduism also. But in Hinduism this defect is vanishing (Cf. RF, p. 24).

[16] Cf. ERWTh, p. 283.

[17] RF, p. 50.

[18] Ibid.

[19] Cf. ERWTh, p. 114.

[20] Cf. RCW, p. 44, 53; RF, pp. 32 ff.

[21] Cf. RF, p. 36.

[22] RCW, p. 51. Cf. also *Fragments,* p. 24.

[23] Cf. RF, pp. 21-22.

[24] ERWTh, p. 149.

[25] Cf. FS, p. 5; IVL, pp. 33, 65; RF, pp. 30 f; OSW, October 1952 - February 1959, p. 294; *The Cultural Heritage of India,* I, *op. cit.,* p. xxxif.

[26] RCW, p. 32. Cf. also RF, p. 23.

is essential to religion and inner life [27]. In imposing unscientific dogmas and repulsive rites they are actually confusing the temporal and the eternal [28], worship and mystical experience [29]. After all, religion is more than the worship of a personal God [30]. With their insistence on external forms, they have forgotten the inner experience. Thus although they may keep the external forms, they have become internally empty [31]. In order that religion be acceptable today, it must be based on a scientific and a reasonable basis. Outward forms are to be left out for the sake of the inward.

4) *Organized Religions Make for a Mechanical Society*

Every organized religion is said to violate two fundamental principles: one objective and the other subjective. Objectively, " truth is a pathless land and cannot be organized. When organized, it cripples the individual mind and prevents it from growing " [32]. Subjectively, humanity is a living organism and it should not be reduced to an organization [33]. " When our minds get incarcerated within the narrow confines of dogma, the spirit of free adventure is checked " [34]. Consequently when religion becomes organized (for Radhakrishnan every religion in its original purity is unorganized), man ceases to be free [35]. In an organization we are losing ourselves in the anonymity of the human mass. We become mere tools of an organization. As the organization becomes more and more elaborate and complex, it crushes more and more whatever is creative, spiritual and human in man [36]. Modern civilization is a mass-civilization. In a mass-civilization it is the individual who suffers most.

> " A mass-civilization has the tendency to crush the individual, reduce him to the average and produce a level of mediocrity. Education becomes an instrument for training docile, passive, obedient, servants of a bureaucracy ready to accept whatever is handed out, from philosophy to asprin tablets. This tyr-

---

[27] Cf. FS, p. 4.
[28] Cf. Ibid., p. 5; ERWTh, p. 59.
[29] Cf. ERWTh, p. 139.
[30] Cf. Ibid.
[31] Cf. OSW, October 1952 - February 1959, p. 42; RF, p. 21 f.
[32] *The Brahma Sūtra*, p. 170.
[33] Cf. RCW, p. 27.
[34] The *Brahma Sūtra*, p. 170.
[35] OSW, October 1952 - February 1959, p. 378.
[36] Cf. *The Brahma Sūtra*, p. 111.

anny is more crushing and demoralizing than any political
or religious despotism. It destroys the root of all aspiration
and freedom " [37].

Thus like every strict organization, organized religions are making
not the free individual but " an organizational man in a technological
society " [38]. In his inaugural address at the exhibition of Canadian
paintings in Delhi on January 13, 1955 Radhakrishnan clearly
pinpoints the above mentioned effect of the organization on the
individual : " The individual today is beaten by organization. He
is dwarfed, imposed upon, brushed aside by his group or party,
business or propaganda " [39]. This is the effect of any organization.
It is seen also in organized religions.

> " When religion becomes organized, man ceases to be free.
> It is not God that is worshipped but the group or the
> authority that claims to speak in his name. Sin becomes
> disobedience to authority and not violation of integrity " [40].

But the highest work of genius is individual, free and uncontrolled.
Therefore the " art of living should be entirely free " [41] from the
forces of organized religions.

5) *Nothing Sacred about Organization in Religion*

The organized religions may trace their beginnings to God.
But historically it is said to be not true that their first beginning is
God. " Every people, Jew and Gentile, Greek and barbarian,
attribute the first institution of their laws to the gods. We know
now that they all originated in the discordant passions and groping
reasons of human beings " [42]. The great seers of religions were
opposed to organization. But their followers have built up big
organizations around them [43]. As the organization became stronger,
the religions became ' outward allegiance and inward betrayal ' [44].
They have departed from their original purity, lost their dynamic

---

[37] OSW, October 1952 - February 1959, p. 60.
[38] RCW, p. 141. Cf. also p. 45.
[39] OSW, October 1952 - February 1959, p. 155.
[40] EWS, p. 41.
[41] Ibid.
[42] IVL, p. 29.
[43] Cf. ERWTh, p. 272.
[44] Cf. RF, p. 21.

vigour and degenerated into arrogant sects [45].   Thus Radhakrishnan refuses to admit any sacredness in organization or in its elements.

"A welter of superstitions and taboos, primitive myths and unhistorical traditions, unscientific dogmatisms and national idolatries, constitutes the practising religion of the vast majority of mankind today" [46].

ii) *The Present Religious Situation*

At present all organized religions are said to be undergoing a process of decay.   They may be keeping the external forms, but, as we have seen, internally they are empty.   "Most of us who profess to be religious, do so by habit, sentiment, or inertia.   We accept our religion as we do the Bank of England or the illusion of progress.   We profess faith in God and are not inclined to act on it" [47].   We give great emphasis to the external, with the consequence of the loss of the internal [48].   People have lost their old faith and have not yet gained a new one.   In such a situation superstition grows [49].   There is uncertainty, a fundamental agnosticism and a sense of uneasiness.   Men are aware of the "emptiness and profaneness of life" but not a way of escape from it [50].   They may make use of the outer framework of religions but lack a real belief in the teachings of their religion [51].   The old religions are thus losing their hold on man and influence in his life [52].   About thirty years ago Radhakrishnan diagnosed our present sickly situation as a tendency to irreligion.   "A general tendency to irreligion", said he, "is in the air. Unbelief is aggressive and ubiquitous" [53].   Thereafter, he affirmed this in many of his major works.   In *Recovery of Faith* he says, "Religion is being slowly edged out of existence" [54].   In his latest work, *Religion in a Changing World,* he repeats the same thing: "We seem to be moving towards a state of no religion.   We may sing the old hymns, recite the familiar

---

[45] Cf. OSW, October 1952 - February 1959, p, 294.
[46] ERWTh, p. 290. Cf. also OSW, July 1959 - May 1962, p. 327.
[47] Ibid., p. 16.
[48] Cf. Ibid., p. 107 f.
[49] Cf. RF, p. 73.
[50] Cf. Ibid., p. 18. Cf. also IVL, p. 64.
[51] Cf. RF, p. 36.
[52] Cf. ERWTh, p. 270.
[53] Ibid., p. 267.
[54] RF, p. 21.

11

creeds, pray earnestly for peace on earth, but deep down there
is a state of doubt, a mood of uncertainty " [55]. The present confusion
is compared to that at the fall of Rome and of the Athenian
Empire [56].

What are the causes that have contributed to the modern confusion? Radhakrishnan points mainly to three. The most important, according to him, is organized religion itself.

> " For the spread of religious scepticism, historical religions
> have to bear a heavy measure of responsibility. In spite of
> the great contributions religions, through the ages, have made
> for the promotion of art, culture and spiritual life, they
> have been vitiated by dogmatism and fanaticism, by cruelty
> and intolerance and by the intellectual dishonesty of their
> adherents " [57].

The other reasons are : 1) the spirit of science and criticism which
shows the unscientific character of beliefs and dogmas, rites and
ceremonies ; and 2) the awakened social conscience which protests
against the inequities practised in the world and which the religions
approve or at least have not opposed [58]. In *Fragments* the development of technological civilization also is said to be one of the major
influences which foster a spirit of scepticism in regard to religious
truth [59].

iii) *The Meaning of Modern Religious Confusion*

Radhakrishnan is not a pessimist. He interprets the modern
religious confusion as a sign of hope. The opening passage of
Recovery of Faith reads :

> " Great movements of spirit arise when despair at the break
> down of civilization makes the mind susceptible to the re-
> cognition of the insufficiency of the existing order and the
> need for rethinking its foundations and shifting its bases " [60].

When the process of shifting the foundations of the old order
and religion has begun and the new ones are not yet fully de-

---

[55] RCW, p. 53.
[56] Cf. RF, pp. 1 f.
[57] RF, p. 29.
[58] Cf. OSW, October 1952 - February 1959, p. 373.
[59] *Fragments.* p. 14.
[60] RF, p. 1.

veloped, there must be some kind of confusion. Therefore it is argued, " If the world is today passing through a mood of atheism, it is because a higher religion is in process of emergence " [61].

The confusion comes mainly from a cleavage between the changed or awakened spirit of man and the unchaged old forms. " The present organization of the world is inconsistent with the *Zeitgeist* shining on the distant horizon as well as the true spirit of religion " [62]. This is a period of change and every period of conversion is a period confusion [63]. Mankind is today in a situation which can be the end or a beginning of an era [64]. If we cling still to the old forms which are dead, we will pass out [65]. But there is already a tendency towards change. In spite of the utter confusion there is ' deep mystical yearning ' in the contemporary mind [66]. If people are leaving the conventional religions, it may mean that their inner spirituality is stressed and deepened. " The indifference to organized religions is the product not so much of growing secularism as of deepening spirituality " [67]. After a long discussion on ' The Religious Predicament ' [68] Radhakrishnan concludes in his *Religion in a Changing World* :

> " Scepticism, which is said to be the chastity of the intellect, riddles the faith of yesterday and prepares us for the faith of tomorrow. In spite of the total secularization of the world, man will again be able to recapture an understanding of the sacred. We need to find a way back to the living spirit which combines opposites. If the world is to be saved, we must recover the spirit of religion. We are persuaded that we are advancing toward the light; when the darkness is deep, the stars begin to shine. There have been prophetic revolts on behalf of spiritual values in all religions. The seers of the *Upanishads,* Amos, Micah and Isaiah, the Buddha and Jesus leap to our mind. They reformed traditional faiths and made new beginnings. A similar movement is taking place today in men's minds and hearts. We are on the threshold of a new age of spirit " [69].

---

[61] *Fragments,* p. 26.
[62] ERWTh, p. vii.
[63] Cf. RCW, p. 138.
[64] Cf. RF, p. 3.
[65] Cf. RCW, p. 8.
[66] Cf. RF, p. 3.
[67] ERWTh, pp. 58-59. Cf. also RCW, p. 39.
[68] RCW, pp. 34-56.
[69] Ibid., p. 56. Cf. also RF, p. 8; ERWTh, p. vii; P. T. RAJU, *Radhakrishnan's Influence on Indian Thought,* in PhSR, p. 520.

Thus an age of spiritual awakening is the meaning of today's spiritual confusion. Radhakrishnan gives often dire descriptions of the present confusion. But he never leaves the reader go away with a pessimistic view. Immediately after the description of the unhappy situation of today he will remind us that if we are ready to change the old forms, the old organized religions, we will escape from the confusion, and a new era of spirit and peace will come.

iv) *We Must Leave the Old Religions for the New*

Those who are born and reared in a religion may have the feeling that their religion is perfect. Even the savage believes that his superstitions are divine truths. But " self-righteousness is our deepest spiritual malady " [70]. In our scientific age, when everything is critically re-examined, religion alone cannot claim exemption from critical inquiry [71]. We have already seen the results of Radhakrishnan's ' critical ' study of the the existing organized religions. They have failed in their duties; they have become intolerant and closed sects; they cannot go with reason; and they make only for a mechanical society. At present there is religious confusion. But the organized religions are unable to remedy this spiritual sickness. " There is a void ", observes Radhakrishnan, " today in men's minds which dogmatic religions are unable to fill " [72]. From all his studies he concludes :

> " The days of external ceremonial religion which can co-exist with a deceitful paganism are over. Men are asking for reality in religion. They want to penetrate to the depths of life, tear away the veils that hide the primordial reality and learn what is essential for life, for truth, and righteousness " [73].

Radhakrishnan often declares that ' the old gods, the old verities, the old values are fading ' [74], that the old religions are already in process of changing and that we are in the dawn of new era of spirit [75]. At other times he appeals to humanity to be ready

[70] OSW, October 1952 - January 1956, p. 7.
[71] Cf. OSW, October 1952 - February 1959, p. 347.
[72] Ibid., p. 293.
[73] MST, p. 27.
[74] OSW, October 1952 - February 1959, p. 293.
[75] Cf. IVL, p. 161; ERWTh, pp. viii, 19, 33; OSW, October 1952 -

to question the old faiths and leave them for the sake of spiritual one [76].

2) THE EXPERIENTIAL NATURE OF RELIGION

i) *Evolution in Religion*

We have seen in the second chapter that the world is never static, but ever in process. This cosmic evolution affects man and all his endeavours. Naturally, it follows that religion also must be ever evolutionary, never static. " In a moving world we must not cling to frozen attitudes ... Orthodoxy is not necessarily a test of integrity " [77]. " For religion as for many other things there is no such thing as standing still " [78].

The *Rig Vēda* is said to contain the first indication of the different stages of religious evolution. The first stage is a naturalistic polytheism; the second is monotheism and the third monism. Monism is said to be the final stage [79].

The *Upanishads* also speak of the three stages of development of religion in man. The first stage is *sravana,* or hearing by which we hear and obey. The second is *manana* or reflection by which we argue and criticise. The third is *nididhyāsana,* or disciplined meditation. It is the stage of the spirit [80].

From these it seems, Radhakrishnan adopts a general theory of religious evolution. Religion according to him begins in a primitive or sensuous form. Then it takes a reflective form corresponding to the rational faculties of man. The last stage is said to be a mystic form. Here religion is not a mere speculation of reason or a feeling of dependence or a mode of behaviour [81].

All the primitive, polytheistic and naturalistic religions belong to the first stage of evolution. These religions are practically left behind by mankind. The gods of these religions are forgotten

---

February 1959, p. 372; OSW, July 1959 - May 1962, p. 344; OSW, May 1962 - May 1964, p. 49; RCW, pp. 7, 8, 15, 138, 155.

[76] Cf. ERWTh, pp. 11, 16; OSW, October 1952 - February 1959, pp. 365, 372 f, 520; OSW, July 1959 - May 1962, pp. 152, 207, 214; OSW, May 1962 - May 1964, p. 32 f; IC, p. 53; RF, pp. 8, 76, 197, 204 f; RCW, 7 f, 29, 31, 32, 46, 56, 152.

[77] OSW, October 1952 - January 1956, pp. 7-8.

[78] Ibid., p. 219.

[79] Cf. *A Source Book,* p. 4.

[80] Cf. *Fragments,* p. 69.

[81] Cf. ERWTh, p. 63; RCW, pp. 140-141.

and their altars smoke no more. Then begin the reflective religions which are the organized religions. These religions give
primary importance to forms.

But the organized religions, which are usually monotheisms,
are not the highest kind of religion. They correspond to the
intellect of man, which is not his highest faculty. The highest
faculty of man is spiritual. Therefore the highest form of religion is a spiritual religion. In the age of the spirit, organization in religion is not needed. Everyone will be taught directly
by the spirit [82]. " The individual can attain an intuitive knowledge
of God which is unmediated by institutions or theologies " [83].
Moreover for those who have attained realization the external
forms have no importance [84].

> " Image worship is the first, doing *japa* and chanting *mantras*
> is the middle; meditation or mental worship is superior; re-
> flection on one's own true nature is the highest of all. Image
> worship is a means to realization. When we gain our ends,
> the means fall away " [85].

Therefore, religion in the age of the spirit will be " independent
of all ecclesiastical organizations " [86]. It will be an " open unorganized community " [87]. All religions are evolving to this final
stage. Therefore every organized religion is to be evolved further.
None of them is final. We must also consciously help this religious
evolution by transforming our own religion. This is the conclusion
of *Recovery of Faith*:

> " We can transform the religion to which we belong as to
> make it approximate to the religion of spirit. I am persuaded
> that every religion has possibilities of such a transforma-
> tion. We must look upon Hinduism or Christianity as part
> of an evolving revelation that might in time be taken over
> into the larger religion of the spirit " [88].

---

[82] Cf. RCW, p. 140.
[83] FS, p. 35.
[84] Cf. HVL, p. 27.
[85] *The Brahma Sūtra*, p. 174.
[86] RF, p. 203. Cf. also OSW, October 1952 - February 1959, p. 285.
[87] RF, p. 143.
[88] Ibid., pp. 204-205.

ii) *The Future Religion*

The future religion will be the purest and the highest form of religion. It is often called the spiritual religion. Let us examine its nature.

Radhakrishnan in innumerable contexts has used the term ' religion '. When we compare these usages we can see that the term is not employed univocally.

Sometimes he makes a distinction between the singular and plural forms of religion. For example, " Cling to religion, let religions go " [89]. ' Religions ' (in plural) signifies, it seems, organized religions, while ' religion ' (in singular)stands for the true, purely spiritual religion which is universal.

At other times he speaks of ceremonial religion, external religion, dogmatic religion, authoritarianism, organized religion, church etc. From our discussions it can be seen that all these belong to the class of organized religion. When any one aspect of it is emphasized or especially criticized, it is called after the proper name of that aspect. The basic argument that is employed everywhere is the same. Radhakrishnan himself says, " The religions of the world can be distinguished into those which emphasize the object and those which insist on experience " [90]. All those which emphasize the object of religion will have to be external in some way or other, while the experiential religion is essentially internal. All the organized religions belong to the first class. But whenever Radhakrishnan tries to explain or define religion without qualifying it, he means religion of pure, internal, spiritual experience. This alone is for him the true religion or *the* religion, while the organized religions are externalisms or formalisms or dogmatic, ritualistic, ceremonial religions. We have already seen the nature of organized religions. Now we shall explain how Radhakrishnan conceives the true nature of religion. This, we hope, will help to deepen our understanding of Radhakrishnan's concept of organized religions.

iii) *Religion as Experience of Reality*

Religion should begin from within and is directed inward. It has been amply explained that man's innermost self is divine. Religion should be directed towards the God who is within man.

---

[89] PhRT, pp. 108-109.
[90] Cf. ERWTh, p. 21.

The very Divine who is our real self and known only through experience is the ultimate ground of religion. The ineffable, existential, spiritual experience, " the revishment of the soul when it meets in its own depths the ground of its life and reality " [91], is the ultimate religious evidence. All religions are based on a personal encounter with the Divine [92]. They begin when we realize the truth of our own divine self. The truth is never preached; but one has to experience it within oneself [93]. Therefore the primary fact in all religions is the direct experience of the Divine [94].

Very often Radhakrishnan defines religion as the direct experience itself of the Divine. In his recent book, *Religion in a Changing World,* he devotes a full chapter to explain " Religion as Experience of Reality " [95]. In the first part of this chapter he establishes that God can be really known only through personal experience of God and not by proxy. The second part begins with a definition of religion and an explanation of it:

> " Religion is the direct apprehension of the Supreme. It is the attaining of a state of illumination. While the reality is omnipresent, the human being is able to apprehend it directly in his own inmost being. The principle is enunciated in the Upanishadic maxim, *tat tvam asi.* That art Thou. The fish in the water are thirsting and people in the world are roaming all over the world to seek the Divine, while they are all in the Divine, fragments of it " [96].

Radhakrishnan claims that the essence of all religions is the experience of the Divine which is the same everywhere, whatever be the differences in the thematic and categorical expression of it. " Religion, in essence, is experience of or living contact with the ultimate reality " [97]. Even organized religions, in their original purity, if not in their present condition, are experiential religions. " While the experiential character is emphasized in the Hindu faith, every religion at its best falls back on it " [98]. Radhakrishnan examines the truth of this statement with regard to the major

---

[91] Cf. OSW, October 1952 - February 1959, p. 377.
[92] Cf. RCW, pp. 106, 118-119; OSW, July 1959 - May 1962, pp. 185, 204.
[93] RCW, p. 122.
[94] Cf. RF, p. 110 ff. We have already explained this more elaborately.
[95] Chapter V, pp. 98-116.
[96] RCW, pp. 102-103. Cf. also *Fragments,* pp. 69-70.
[97] *The Spirit in Man,* p. 492. Cf. also IVL, p. 70.
[98] IVL, p. 71.

religions briefly in his *An Idealist View of Life* [99] and more elaborately in the fifth chapter of *Recovery of Faith* [100]. In the Hindu tradition religion is the " direct experience of the Divine " [101]. In Taoism virtue is the spontaneous expression of the Tao within [102]. For the Hebrews the voice of God is said to be heard in the prophetic consciousness. Moses' communing with God in the mountain and Elijah in a cave are examples of pure internal experience. Isaiah and the Psalmist are also brought in as examples of this type [103]. In the Greek religion the " initiate does not learn anything but undergoes an experience " [104]. Plato and Plotinus had spiritual experiences. Zarathustra declares that the union with the Divine is the highest ideal [105]. Buddhism is the champion of enlightenment which is the immediate union with the Absolute truth [106]. In Christianity, Jesus' personal experience of the Divine is the supreme example of direct knowledge [107]. Clement of Alexandria and Origen describe Christianity as a " mystery religion " [108]. The core of Augustine's religion is derived from his personal experience [109]. In the Middle Ages also Christian theologians viewed religion as experience of the Supreme [110]. St Thomas of Aquinas, Meister Eckhart, George Fox, William Law, Nicholas of Cusa, St Theresa, St John of the Cross and a number of others are said to support the view of religion as experience [111]. The same is true in Islam also [112]. The life of every great religious teacher proves that religion is the experience of God.

> " The life of Jesus, the witness of St Paul, of the three apostles on the Mount of Transfiguration, of Ezekiel, and of scores of others are impressive testimony to the fact of religion as experience " [113].

---

[99] Ibid. p. 70-72.
[100] RF, pp. 110-143.
[101] Ibid., p. 110.
[102] Ibid., p. 114.
[103] Ibid., p. 115. Cf. also IVL, p. 71.
[104] Cf. Ibid., p. 118.
[105] Cf. Ibid., p. 121.
[106] Cf. Ibid., p. 122; IVL, p. 71.
[107] Cf. Ibid., p. 124.
[108] Ibid., p. 128.
[109] Cf. Ibid., p. 129.
[110] Cf. Ibid., p. 130 f.
[111] Cf. Ibid., pp. 132 ff.
[112] Cf. Ibid., p. 138.
[113] *Fragments*, p. 69.

Whenever Radhakrishnan speaks of religion he brings out the experiential character of religion. And he speaks with such epigrammatic charm that one is beguiled into overlooking the fact that it has been said many times before [114].

There are a lot of passages in which Radhakrishnan clearly says that religion is the direct experience of God or that experience of God is the highest kind of religion or essence of religion. [115]. Here are some of his expressions:

" It is not true religion unless it ceases to be a traditional view and becomes personal experience " [116].

" Religion means conscious union with the Divine in the universe, with love as its chief means " [117].

" Religion is not science nor is church an academy. It is the perception of the eternal in the finite " [118].

" It is the truth of our complete being, the consciousness of our personal relationship with the Infinite. It is the true centre of gravity of our life " [119].

Religion is a " state of mind, a relationship with reality, a way of life " [120].

" Religion is an *isness* and not an oughtness as Baron von Hügel loved to repeat " [121].

" Religion is experience of reality " [122].

" ... you have to aim at the highest goal of living in the consciousness of the Divine ... looking upon Him as the eternal Presence in your heart. That is the highest kind of religion " [123].

" Those who are religious at second-hand, that is, those who have not had an insight into Reality ... " [124].

---

[114] Cf. A. N. MARLOW, *Spiritual Religion and the Philosophy of Radhakrishnan.* in PhSR, p. 345.

[115] Cf. HVL, pp. 13 f, 19; IVL, pp. 56 f, 64, 99, 136; *Great Indians,* p. 71; OSW, October 1952 - February 1959, pp. 197, 213-214, 408; OSW, July 1959 - May 1962, p. 204.

[116] IVL, p. 69.

[117] Ibid., p. 161.

[118] Ibid., p. 167.

[119] OSW, July 1959 - May 1962, p. 129.

[120] Ibid., p. 204. Cf. also OSW, October 1952 - January 1956, p. 255.

[121] IVL, p. 31.

[122] EWS, p. 24.

[123] OSW, May 1962 - May 1964, pp. 167-168.

[124] Ibid., p. 163. Cf. also Ibid., pp. 146, 174; RF, p. 129, 199; MST, pp. 12. 28; RF, p. 275; *Fragments.* pp. 69, 72; FS, pp. 6, 7, 38; OSW, October 1952 - February 1959. pp. 185, 187, 205, 230 f, 385; RCW, p. 102.

Our ordinary intellectual faculties cannot attain to spiritual experience. No amount of training of the senses will enable them to perceive thought. So also no amount of intellectual skill can lead us to spiritual experience [125]. So long as we are at the intellectual level, we are said to be outside the realm of the spirit [126]. Therefore we must reach a new level of being and consciousness to which the spiritual truths are revealed even as colours are given to the senses [127]. Emphasizing this aspect he conceives of religion as the "uplifting power" [128]. In this sense religion is said to be the 'force which can bring about the inward renewal' [129], and the 'cleaning of the inward life' [130]. Only spiritual discipline can bring about this inward transformation. Therefore spiritual discipline is of high importance in religion.

> "Salvation is attained not so much by placating God as by transforming our being, by achieving certain quality and harmony of the passions through severe self discipline. The effort is costly. No tricks of absolution or payment by proxy no greased paths of smooth organs and stained-glass windows can help us much. The spirit has to be stripped bare if it is to attain its goal" [131].

The discipline that is required is not something external, but meditation and self discovery. By them we turn our mind homeward and establish contact with the deepest centre of our self. For, in order to know the truth we have to look deep into our own self. Silence and solitude are necessary for spiritual discipline and they are not easy in our age [132].

Sometimes the discipline which effects the change in us is also called religion. "The discipline which helps us to change ourselves is religion" [133]. In this sense religion is said to be a stre-

---

[125] Cf. IVL, p. 167.

[126] Cf. OSW, May 1962 - May 1964, p. 118.

[127] Cf. IVL, p. 167.

[128] Cf. Ibid.

[129] Cf. OSW, October 1952 - February 1959, p. 296.

[130] OSW, July 1959 - May 1962, pp. 182, 233.

[131] IVL, p. 89. Radhakrishnan here clearly maintains that salvation can be attained by our natural powers and that no Redeemer or Mediator is needed. Cf. also GB, p. 53; OSW, October 1952 - February 1959, p. 295; OSW, July 1959 - May 1962, p. 165.

[132] Cf. IVL, p. 89.

[133] OSW, July 1959 - May 1962, p. 215. Cf. also Ibid., pp. 75, 219, 395; RCW, p. 106; OSW, October 1952 - February 1959, p. 90.

nuous endeavour to apprehend the truth and not the apprehending of truth itself [134], and the purpose of religion is said to be spiritual conversion [135].

The very transformation of our being into the higher plane is also called religion. Speaking at Guru Nanak's birthday celebrations in New Delhi on November 10, 1962, Radhakrishnan says that religion is a " transformation of one's soul. It is the lifting up of one's consciousness to a higher level " [136]. In this sense he calls religion ' rebirth '. " Religion is essentially rebirth, *dvitiyam janma* " [137].

So, religion is said to be the discipline which effects an internal transformation of our being, the very transformation itself and the spiritual experience that is enjoyed in the transformed state. Radhakrishnan does not seem to be changing his concept of religion. For him all these three are very intimately connected with one another and form a single whole. Even if one of these be distinguished from another, they cannot be separated from one another. " Religion is an endless adventure of man's entire being towards a truth which is revealed in this very quest " [138]. So where there is quest of truth, there is also a realization of truth. Similarly the very transformation or the rebirth means attaining a higher consciousness in which " the distinctions of subject and object are fused into an undivided state. In the state of ecstacy, or transcendental consciousness, the individual soul feels itself invaded by and merged with an enfolding presence, exalted with a sense of having found what it always has sought " [139]. The transformation itself is a spiritual experience or conversely, spiritual experience is a " transforming experience ". " Religion is essentially a transforming experience, an illumined life. It is essentially a rebornness " [140]. This identification of the experience of the Divine with the transformation of our being is clearly seen in his essay on Sri Ramakrishna in his *Great Indians* [141].

---

[134] FS, p. 7.

[135] Cf. RF, p. 158; OSW, October 1952 - February 1959, p. 295.

[136] OSW, May 1962 - May 1964, p. 118. Cf. also OSW, October 1952 - February 1959, pp. 60, 374, 376; *The Brahma Sûtra*, p. 181.

[137] RF, p. 112. Cf. also Ibid., pp. 126, 158; *Fragments,* p. 69; OSW, October 1959 - February 1959, pp. 340, 376.

[138] OSW, July 1959 - May 1962, p. 143.

[139] RF, p. 113.

[140] OSW, October 1952 - February 1959, p. 348. Cf. also p. 291.

[141] Originally Introduction to *The Cultural Heritage of India,* I (Calcutta 1937).

" Religion is matter of experience. It is not an awakening from swoon, but a transformation of one's being. It is not an addition to one's intellectual furniture, but an exaltation of one's personality into the plane of the universal spirit. It is *Brahmadarsana* — insight into reality, a direct awareness of the world of values " [142].

The transformation is effected when we undergo spiritual discipline. So the spiritual discipline also is intimately related to the experience of the Divine.

In short, the change that is to be effected is the expelling of the distinction between the self and the Self. The higher consciousness that has to be attained is the realization of our divine nature. In other words, an existential experience of the Upanishadic principle *tat tvam asi* (That thou art) [143] is what religion means for Radhakrishnan [144]. This " experiential religion ", prophesies Radhakrishnan, " is the religion of the future " [145].

" To regain that integrity, to attain to life where knowledge and being are not divorced from each other is the essence of human evolution. To recover the lost unity is to be reborn. It is the secret of spiritual life, the mystery of the Kingdom of God " [146].

iv) *Nature of Religious Experience*

In our ordinary conditions we look upon the Divine as an other to us. We are conscious of a division of the self from the Divine and the universe. There is a separation of object and subject.

But in the spiritual experience every aspect of man's being is raised to the highest point, " ... all the senses gather, the whole mind leaps forward and realizes in one quivering instant such thing as cannot be expressed " [147]. In such supreme moments,

---

[142] *Great Indians,* p. 71. (*The Cultural Heritage of India,* p. xxiv) Cf. also OSW, October 1952 - February 1959, p. 49.

[143] *Chāndogya Upanishad,* VI, 8. 7.

[144] Cf. RCW, p. 102 f.

[145] Ibid., p. 134.

[146] IVL, p. 169. This is the traditional Hindu concept of religion. " Religion is God-realization; but God-realization, for the Hindus, is the same as self-realization, for every man in the depth of his being is divine " (M. DHAVAMONY, *Hinduism and Christianity, art. cit.,* p. 163).

[147] OSW, October 1952 - February 1959, p. 292.

man and his faculties are transfused with the highest spirit [148]. A flash of Absolute Reality breaks through the normal barriers of conscious mind. "A lightening flash, a sudden flame of incandescence, throws a momentary but eternal gleam on life in time " [149]. The division of our self from the Divine vanishes. Man is then raised to a divine status [150]. In a beautiful passage in *An Idealist View of Life* Radhakrishnan explains this divine status of man:

> "It is a condition of consciousness in which feelings are fused, ideas melt into one another, boundaries broken and ordinary distinctions transcended. Past and present fade away in a sense of timeless being. Thought and reality coalesce and a creative merging of subject and object results. Life grows conscious of its incredible depths. In this fullness of felt life and freedom, the distinction of the knower and the known disappears. The privacy of the individual self is broken into and invaded by a universal self which the individual feels as his own " [151].

This is the nature of religious experience. Elsewhere he puts it more briefly: It is the "direct and active participation in the truth, the affirmation of the supreme identity of man in the depth of his being with the Transcendent Reality " [152]. Still more briefly, "The experience is a pure and direct intellectual intuition " [153].

Characteristics of Spiritual Experience

The direct apprehension of God has some characteristic notes. Because the experience is by the realization of the identity of our self with the divine self, there is the immediate presence of Reality. So there must be necessarily complete awareness. The awareness of the Divine in us gives us complete freedom. It frees us from the dominion of passion and ignorance and shows our identity with the Divine [154]. "In the divine status (which is the status of the individual in religious experience) reality is its own immediate witness, its own self awareness, its own freedom of complete

---

[148] Cf. Ibid., RS, p. 44.
[149] ERWTh, p. 50.
[150] Cf. IVL, p. 80.
[151] Ibid., p. 72.
[152] RF, p. 110. Cf. also *The Spirit in Man*, p. 501.
[153] *The Brahma Sūtra*, p. 103.
[154] Cf. Ind. Ph., II, 26; IVL, p. 80; RF, p. 111.

being ... It is a perfect being, perfect consciousness and perfect freedom, *sat, cit, ānanda* " [155].

In the fifth chapter of *Religion in a Changing World* the characteristics of spiritual experience are explained in a slightly different way.

1) " The experience is given. It cannot be induced by will or prolonged by effort ". It comes like a lightning when we least expect it. The capacity of any individual to receive the experience is dependent on age, psychological make-up and cultural milieu [156].

It is difficult to understand what Radhakrishnan means by saying that ' experience is given ', and that it occurs when least expected. There are many passages in which he says that by hard effort we can attain to spiritual experience. Once he even says that it is not given but a task. In his public Address at the Buddha Jayanti Celebrations in Delhi on May 24, 1956 he says: " Enlightenment is *not something given but a task*. Man is the architect of his own future. Man has to mould himself " [157]. Similarly in his Address to the East-West Philosophers' Conference in Honolulu on July 10, 1959, he says: " The experience may be gained by any one who is willing to undergo a certain discipline and put forth effort " [158]. On the next day he said, " The way to attain the experience is by meditation and prayer " [159]. In *Gautama the Buddha* even the process of achieving experience is explained: " When we purify our heart by ethical training, when we focus the total energy of our consciousness on the deepest in us, we awaken the inherent divine possibilities, and suddenly a

---

[155] IVL, p. 80. Cf. also *The Cultural Heritage of India*, p. xxiv. There are two kinds of freedom in Hindu thought: freedom of man and freedom of will. " Man is free when he is liberated from the bondage of senses. But then he loses what is usually meant by freedom of the will, that is to say, freedom to do good as well as evil; because evil doing is the result of the domination of the senses, and therefore it is not possible for a man who is completely free from this domination to do evil" (S. K. MAITRA, *The Gītā's Conception of Freedom as Compared with that of Kant*, in W. R. INGE *et al.* (Eds.), *Radhakrishnan: Comparative Studies in Philosophy, Presented in Honour of His Sixtieth Birthday* (London 1951) 348-349. Cf. also pp. 349 ff).

[156] Cf. RCW, p. 104.

[157] OSW, October 1952 - February 1959, p. 351. (Italics mine).

[158] OSW, July 1959 - May 1962, p. 231. Cf. also *The Spirit in Man*, p. 493.

[159] Ibid., p. 238.

new experience occurs with clarity of insight and freedom and joy " [160].

Can it be that Radhakrishnan has changed his mind in his last work? Seemingly not. Even in some of his first works we find similar assertions. In *An Idealist View of Life* he says: " the intuitive experiences are not always given but occur at rare intervals ... We cannot command or continue them at our will. We do not know how or why they occur. They sometimes occur even against our will " [161]. In *Religion in a Changing World* itself we can find a number of passages in which spiritual experience is said to be attained by hard effort. We shall quote some of them.

> " Though all men are capable of it, few put forth the effort needed for it " [162].
> " Each one has to realize for himself, unveil the God in Him " [163].
> " This experience is through the cultivation of man's inward life ... Until the human individual explores the contents of his consciousness and *with deliberation and effort* makes himself one with the Divine and affirms with conviction ' I and my Father are one ', the Divine is transcendent " [164].
> " Each individual should mature into a seeing human being " [165].
> " It is up to each individual to attain harmony, awakening to spiritual truth " [166].

Therefore, since Radhakrishnan has maintained both views together in his earlier as well as later works, we cannot say that he has changed his mind of late. There must be some other explanation.

Probably he is making a distinction between ' given ' and ' granted ' of which the former signifies a state of being by the eternal ordination of things and the latter means that another agent is its source. There is one passage in which Radhakrishnan seems to approve of this explanation: " The general impression that the mystic experience is granted and not achieved is far from correct, except in the sense that all great moments of experience

---

[160] GB, p. 53. Cf. also IC, p. 14.
[161] IVL, pp. 73-74.
[162] RCW, p. 104.
[163] Ibid., p. 107.
[164] Ibid., p. 181. (Italics mine).
[165] Ibid., p. 102.
[166] Ibid., p. 104.

are in a measure given " [167].   By its very nature our real self is divine.   So by our own effort we can attain a direct experience of it.   It is not something which an external agent granted us, but given in our nature.   Still one passage, which we quoted above, remains.   " Enlightenment is not something given but a task " [168]. In this case one must admit inconsistency in Radhakrishnan, or at least a confusion. He might be speaking about our ordinary external self only, which is in *māyā* order. It is not divine. Before our two selves are integrated, enlightenment is not a given state of the external self.

2) The subject of experience gets an absolute conviction of its spiritual reality.   " Whatever the contents of the experience the subject is absolutely convinced that it is a revelation of reality. It bears an authority within itself, an authority of unquestionable and immeasurable power " [169].   Such an authority comes from its self-sufficient and complete nature.   It does not appeal to anything external to it for a proof of its validity.   " It is its own cause and explanation ... It is self-established (*svatassiddha*) self-evidencing (*svasamveda*) self luminous (*svayam prakāśa*) [170].   It is pure comprehension and self-authenticating [171] and complete validity [172]. It constrains our assent [173].   The experienced man has absolute certainty of it and nothing can disturb his conviction [174].

3) The spiritual experience is inexpressible and incommunicable.   Human language is inadequate to express the direct apprehension of the Reality which is wholly other [175].   Spiritual knowledge is superlogical.   So our ordinary concepts cannot express it [176].   We have explained this characteristic as the eighth objection to dogma.

4) With whatever the experience is concerned, it is experienced

---

[167] GB, p. 28.

[168] OSW, October 1952 - February 1959, p. 351.   Enlightenment for Radhakrishnan is a synonym of spiritual experience (Cf. *Fragments,* p. 60).

[169] RCW, p. 104.

[170] IVL, p. 73.

[171] RF, p. 110. Cf. also OSW, October 1952 - February 1959, p. 519.

[172] Cf. IVL, p. 73 .

[174] Cf. Ibid., p. 75; *The Cultural Heritage of India,* p. xxiv; RCW, p. 100.

[175] Cf. RCW, pp. 104-105, 119; IVL, p. 75 f; RF, p. 144 f; OSW, October 1952 - February 1959, p. 378.

[176] Cf. MST, p. 28.

as in great light and glory. " God is deep within us, around us, below us, above us, and beyond us " [177].

5) The experience completely absorbs the attention of the subject. While this vision lasts the subject forgets his own self [178].

In various other writings Radhakrishnan gives some other qualities of religious experience such as its universality and scientific character. Our explanation of the universality of intuition in chapter III [179] holds good here also. The scientific character of experience is explained later in this chapter.

Mysticism

Sometimes Radhakrishnan says that the new religion is mysticism or mystical religion [180]. This is not anything different from the experiential religion which we have just explained. Mysticism is only another name for it. This can be clearly seen from the identical descriptions of mysticism and experiential religion. In mystical experience we are said to be in direct communication with the Infinitude [181]. Just as experiential religion, mystic religion lays stress on the personal experience of God, direct contact with the creative spirit. The highest goal of the mystics is said to be " union with Reality in which distinction between subject and object fades away " [182]. The mystics declare that there is " union of the knower and the known " [183]. In some passages Radhakrishnan speaks in a way which clearly indicates that for him mysticism is identical with religion as experience. For example, he speaks about the mystical trend of the Hebrews: " Among the Hebrews there are evident indications of a mystical faith such as the experiences of the great prophets, the visions they saw and the voices they heard " [184].

The explanation of mysticism in his *The Brahma Sūtra* [185] makes perfectly clear what we have been saying. He says that

---

[177] RCW, p. 105.

[178] Cf. Ibid., pp. 105-106.

[179] Ch. III, v, c. 3.

[180] Cf. ERWTh, p. 293.

[181] OSW, October 1952 - February 1959, p. 367.

[182] *The Brahma Sūtra*, p. 129. Cf. also p. 171; FS, p. 33.

[183] RC, p. 799. Cf. also HH, p. 135; BERNARD PHILLIPS, *Radhakrishnan's Critique of Naturalism*, in PhSR, p. 148; E. S. BRIGHTMAN, *Radhakrishnan and Mysticism*, in PhSR, p. 396.

[184] *The Brahma Sūtra*, p. 112. Cf. also p. 249.

[185] Cf. Ibid., pp. 109-111.

the term 'mysticism' is sometimes used "to define spiritual apprehension"[186]. The other use is in its etymological sense, which is "I close". This suggests "shutting of the ears, eyes, and lips. This shutting of the senses is the pre-requisite of the spiritual perception"[187]. So in all cases it indicates spiritual apprehension.

v) Science and Spiritual Religion

a) *Spiritual Religion is Scientific.* Radhakrishnan rejected all organized religions as they are not scientific enough. They impose unscientific dogmas, and their claim to authority is unscientific. At the same time if religion is not given a scientific basis it will perish[188]. "We require a religion which is both scientific and humanistic", says Radhakrishnan[189]. Religion, science and humanism "must combine today if we are to attract all those who are equally indifferent to organized religion and atheism, supernaturalism and nihilism"[190].

If religion is considered as the experience of reality it will be scientific. Science is reasoning from observed data. Generally, only the experiences of the external world are considered by science. But experience is not limited to the outward world. There are mental facts, psychological experiences and spiritual experiences[191]. "Psychologically the experience we have of the world before us ... is on the same level as St Paul's vision on the road to Damascus or Augustine's in the Italian garden"[192]. In the spiritual experience not one faculty alone is involved, but all work together[193]. So we cannot say that while our sense perception corresponds to reality, our spiritual intuition does not[194]. There is no reason to exclude any of the observable facts from science. The method of study that is adopted with regard to one should be equally applied to the other[195]. Moreover the interpretation of the religious experience must be in conformity with the

---

[186] *The Brahma Sūtra,* p. 109.
[187] Ibid., p. 110.
[188] Cf. IVL, p. 100.
[189] ERWTh, p. 294.
[190] Ibid.
[191] Cf. OSW, May 1962 - May 1964, pp. 129 f.
[192] IVL, p. 66.
[193] Cf. Ibid., p. 159.
[194] Cf. Ibid., p. 66.
[195] Cf. Ibid., p. 67; Cf. also Ibid., p. 179; OSW, October 1952 - February 1959, p. 305; E. S. BRIGHTMAN, *Radhakrishnan and Mysticism,* in PhSR, p. 291.

findings of science and reason. Thus the experiential religion is shown to be fully scientific [196].

b) *No Scientific Discovery Can Refute the Religion of the Spirit.* If religion is depending on historical events, scientific discoveries may prove them to be unacceptable, as is the case with the organized religions. But the experiential religion or the religion of spirit takes its stand on verifiable truth and not on dogmas. As it is not dependent on any event of the past or future, no scientific criticism or historical discovery can refute it. " It is not committed to the authenticity of any documents or the truth of any stories about the beginning of the world or prophecies of its end " [197]. At the same time, since it is observable, it remains fully scientific. Anyone who respects science must accept religion of the spirit also. So to base religion on spiritual experience, thinks Radhakrishnan, is the only way to make religion scientific. Experience is as wide as the human race itself. Therefore a religion based on spiritual experience will be acceptable to all humanity [198].

3) Consequences of considering Religion as Experience of Reality

i) *The Unity of Religions*

Indian thought is generally characterized by a synthetic approach to the various aspects of experience and reality. In religion, as well as in other things, it tries to find unity [199]. Even in *Rig Veda* the seers realized that " true religion comprehends all religions ", so that " God is one but men call him by many names " [200].

Nurtured in traditional Hindu thought, Radhakrishnan is inclined to find unity wherever division appears [201]. As a youth he was troubled to see the " bewildering variety of faith and creeds " in India. He believed that unless unity in religion is

---

[196] Cf. HVL, p. 16: ERWTh. pp. 25, 107; OSW, July 1959 - May 1962. pp. 233 f; OSW, May 1962 - May 1964, pp. 129 f; RCW, p. 108.
[197] ERWTh, p. 295.
[198] Cf. HVL, p. 16.
[199] Cf. *A Source Book*, p. xxv f.
[200] Ibid.
[201] Cf. Charles A. Moore, *Metaphysics and Ethics in Radhakrishnan's Philosophy,* in PhSR, p. 282.

established the religious future of India would be dark [202]. Soon he found that there is unity in Hinduism. For every Hindu recognizes one Supreme Spirit, though different names are given to it. Under the multitudinous forms there is unity of purpose [203]. But when he resolved the problem of religious diversity in Hinduism, the different religions of the world and the sharp divisions among them troubled him.

The basic principle with which Radhakrishnan tries to solve the problem of religious diversity is found in his preface to Prafulla Chandra Das' *Impact of Tagore's Life and Work on the Western World* [204]. Here he says that "Unity is truth, division is falsehood" [205]. Even where the diversity seems to be final, if there is truth there is also unity. "The principle of unity in variety is not only a profound spiritual truth but the most obvious common sense" [206]. We shall see how Radhakrishnan applies this principle to the different religions of the world.

Religion, as we have seen, is the experience of the Absolute. This experience is expressed by psychological mediation. Thus all expressions of religion are temporal, while experience itself is divine and eternal. Now the unity of all religions, according to Radhakrishnan, is to be sought "in that which is divine or universal in them and not in what is temporary and local. Where there is spirit of truth there is unity" [207]. The formulations of doctrines, rites and authority in religion, he maintains, are man-made, temporal and changeable. So we need not seek unity in them.

Radhakrishnan says that his studies on the origin and growth of the chief religions of the world showed him that in the mystic traditions of the different religions there is remarkable unity of spirit. "A study of the classic types of the mystical experience discloses an astonishing agreement which is almost entirely independent of race, clime, or age" [208]. This is clear from the fact

---

[202] Cf. PhRT, p. 108.

[203] Cf. HVL, p. 88.

[204] Written on April 27, 1961 (Cf. OSW, July 1959 - May 1962, pp. 390-391.

[205] Cf. Ibid., p. 391.

[206] *Fragments,* p. 72.

[207] Ibid., p. 76.

[208] ERWTh, p. 64. But this does not mean that all mystical experiences are identical. "There are the individual variations within the large framework. In the East, for example, the mysticisms of the *Upanishads,* of the *Bhagavadgītā,* of Śaṁkara, of Ramanuja, of Ramakrishna, of Zen Buddhism, of Jalāludin, Rūmi are different from one another. Similarly

that the descriptions of the seers of their experiences reveal an impressive unity. They are said to be " near to one another on mountains apart " [209]. We may not find clear similarities in the dogmas and rites of different religions and we need not find exact parallels [210]. But " when we enter the world of ideals the diffe- rences among religions become negligible and the agreement striking " [211]. Whatever be the religion, there is only one ideal for man — to make himself the perfect man, the divine man [212].

> " When the Upanishads proclaim the great truth ' That art Thou ', when the Buddha teaches that each human individual has in him the power to grow into a Buddha or a Boddhi- sattva, when the Jews say that the ' spirit of man is the candle of the Lord ', when Jesus tells his hearers that the Kingdom of Heaven is within them and when Mohammad affirms that God is nearer to us than the very artery of our neck, they all mean that the most important thing in life is not to be found in anything external to men but is to be found in the hidden strata of his thought and feeling " [213].

Thus in the most important thing all religions agree. The basic moral principles are also similar in all religions. For they are the necessary consequences of spiritual experience which is essen- tially the same in all religions [214].

Radhakrishnan discerns some other trends which are common to all religions [215]. The divine origin of the soul, its pre-existence and fall, its final redemption and return to God, are common to ancient Eastern and Western religions [216]. Comparing Jesus and the Buddha he says : " The verbal parallels and ideal similarities reveal the impressive unity of religious aspiration " [217]. Since religion is viewed as the natural outcome of the human mind, the various accounts of religious experience should be similar [218].

---

in the West, the mysticisms of Plato and Paul, of Proclus and Tauler, Plotinus and Eckhart differ from one another. The variations are not determined by race, climate, or geographical situation " (ERWTh, p. 64).

[209] *Fragments,* p. 62, Cf. also RF, p. 144, 155.
[210] Cf. ERWTh, p. 149.
[211] Ibid., p. 35.
[212] Cf. Ibid.
[213] RF, pp. 148-149.
[214] Cf. ERWTh, p. 176.
[215] Cf. FS, p. 9 f.
[216] Cf. ERWTh, p. 149.
[217] Ibid., p. 186.
[218] Cf. Ibid., p. 184.

For not only is the kernel of every human soul the same, but the "hopes and fears of men, their desires and aspirations are the same on the banks of Ganges as on the shores of the Lake of Galilee" [219]. Human nature reacts in the same way before the indefinable mysteries of life and the outcome is similar religons [220].

There is a transcendental union of all religions. All religions have the same goal, to attain the experience of God [221]. We should not remain at the superficial level and take the diversity as final. In his Public Address at Honolulu on July 11, 1959 [222] Radhakrishnan explains this transcendental unity:

> "The empirical fact of the plurality of religions, each with its own peculiar character and structure, should not hide from us the transcendent unity of religions. The vital differences among the living faiths of mankind are overarched by a fundamental unity of vision and purpose which embraces all mankind. If we can discern a common basis underlying the different modes of Christian thought from the Roman Catholic to the Quaker faith, from the Unitarian Church to the Salvation Army, students of comparative religion may find a common substractum of religions. The unredeemed situation of man, the longing for liberation, the recognition of the Divine Reality and the many ways to reach the Real are found in all religions" [223].

Therefore if we look deeper into the nature of religions, we will perceive that there is unity of aspiration and endeavour underlying the different religions. As we become more and more spiritual we will be able to see the unity clearer. "The diversity in the traditional formulations tends to diminish as we climb up the scale of spiritual perfection. All paths of ascent lead to the mountaintop" [224]. All those who have reached the mountain-top of spiritual perfection witness to the convergent tendency of different religions. Hence when we attain realization we also will perceive the fundamental unity of all religions and will not be worried by the apparent differences [25]. Therefore all religions have like be-

---

[219] Ibid.

[220] Cf. OSW, October 1952 - January 1956, p. 282.

[221] Cf. RF, p. 188; FS, p. 36; OSW, October 1952 - February 1959, pp. 48, 356.

[222] Given in OSW, July 1959 - May 1962, pp 235-253.

[223] Ibid., p. 235.

[224] *Fragments,* p. 77. Cf. also HVL. p. 27; RF, p. 155, 197.

[225] Cf. OSW, October 1952 - February 1959, p. 366.

ginning and like end. " All religions are intertwined at the roots
and meet at the summit " [226].

Radhakrishnan agrees that there are ' important ' differences
among religions [227]. These differences come because of the psychological mediation of spiritual experience [228]. When the experience
ceases, we begin to reflect on it. But when we reflect, we lose the
immediacy and begin to discriminate. The act of reflection itself
contains within itself the principle of duality. So by philosophical
reflection we will not be able to regain the lost unity [229]. Therefore
the seers make use of symbols. But the nature of symbolic expression depends on the prevailing theological or metaphysical conceptions of the time and place [230]. In this sense Radhakrishnan
says that it is misleading even to speak of " different religions ".
We have only " different religious traditions " [231], like different
buildings on a common foundation [232].

But dogmatic religions mistake the symbolic character of tradition for reality and neglect the underlying unity. This attitude of
organized religions is condemned in strong terms : " To neglect the
spiritual unity of the world and underline the religious diversity
would be philosophically unjustifiable, morally indefensible, and
socially dangerous " [233]. If we overlook the unity of religions, we
are told that " we will not be able to overcome nihilism, lack of
faith, and irreligion " [234].

Therefore in reality there is only one religion and we should
not consider the limits of organized religions which are only superficial. We shall conclude this part with a famous passage which
Radhakrishnan uttered in his Newton Baker Lecture on Inter-
religious Understanding at Cleveland Council on World Affairs [235].

---

[226] Ibid., p. 90. Cf. also Ibid., p. 292; OSW. July 1959 - May 1962,
p. 198; W. R. INGE, et al (Ed.), Radhakrishnan: Comparative Studies in
Philosophy, Presented in Honour of His Sixtieth Birthday (London 1951)
Introduction (no page number is given).

[227] Cf. OSW, October 1952 - February 1959, p. 365.

[228] Cf. IVL, p. 77 f; HVL, pp. 19-20, 22.

[229] Cf. RF, p. 144 f.

[230] Cf. RF, p. 154; Fragments, p. 64.

[231] Fragments, p. 77.

[232] Cf. RF, p. 118.

[233] Fragments, p. 73. This sentence is word by word repeated in
Recovery of Faith (Cf. pp. 197-198).

[234] OSW, October 1952 - February 1959, p. 336.

[235] On March 27, 1958, in Ohio. Given in OSW, October 1952 -
February 1959, pp. 371-385.

" One Godhead alone is at work in the Universe, *one* religion alone prevails in it, *one* worship, *one* fundamental natural order, *one* law, *one* Bible in all. All prophets are *one* Prophet, they have spoken on *one* common ground in *one* language, though in different dialects " [236].

ii) *All Religions Are Equally Good Means*

Two or more religions can be equally good, either because they are at bottom identical and the differences are negligible, or because they all are true though basically different [237].

We have already seen that Radhakrishnan upholds the unity of all religions. From this basic stand he reduces all religions to one fundamental truth, which is the fact of spiritual experience [238]. This single truth is communicated through myth, symbol and history [239]. The different religions appear to us as really different only because we do not know the basic truth of our own religion [240]. In fact they are all varied expressions of a single truth [241]. In other words, all religions are equally good means of salvation.

Radhakrishnan teaches this point in many ways. Sometimes he calls the different religions different facets of a single truth. " Our intellectual representations differ simply because they bring out different facets of the one central reality [242]. At other times he says that different religions are like one truth said in different languages [243], or like one language spoken through different tongues [244]. Truth wears many vestures and speak in diverse tongues [245]. Yet again he calls them ' dialects ' of the ' same language of the spirit ' [246]. The same universal religion appears under dif-

[236] Cf. Ibid., p. 382.
[237] Cf. F. S. C. NORTHROP, *The Relation between Eastern and Western Philosophy*, in W. R. INGE *et al.* (ed), *Radhakrishnan: Comparative Studies in Philosophy, Presented in Honour of His Sixtieth Birthday*, pp. 362 ff.
[238] Cf. GB, p. 28 ff; Ind. Ph, I, 360 ff; K, p. 45.
[239] Cf. OSW, July 1959 - May 1962, p. 75.
[240] Cf. RF, p. 188.
[241] Cf. ERWTh, p. 306 ff; OSW, July 1959 - May 1962, pp. 239, 251; *Fragments,* p. 78; RS, p. 43.
[242] HVL, p. 27. Cf. also OSW, July 1959 - May 1962, pp. 143, 239.
[243] Cf. RF, p. 157; Pr. Ups, p. 144.
[244] Cf. OSW, July 1959 - May 1962, p. 75.
[245] Cf. RC, p. 811; HVL, p. 27.
[246] OSW, October 1952 - February 1959, p. 366.

ferent colours in different circumstances, like the colour of the water is the colour of the vessel containing it [247], and the same experience with different labels [248]. In these similes it is the unity that is mainly emphasized. But the consequent equality also is implied.

In a number of other passages the equality of all religions as means to salvation is stressed more than their unity. In these cases the religions are apparently taken as they appear. And all of them are shown to serve the purpose equally well. Whatever be our religion, we are sure to reach God. One famous simile that is employed to illustrate how all religions serve equally well to reach God, is that of many paths to the hill-top. Whatever be the way we take we are sure to reach the hill-top. So also all religions lead ultimately to God. "In heaven there are not only many mansions but also many vehicles to reach them" [249]. Radhakrishnan agrees that this doctrine is the traditional Hindu view. The *Rig Veda, Upanishads* and the *Bhagavadgītā* teach the same doctrine. "As men approach me so do I accept them. Men on all sides follow my path" [250]. It is God Himself who leads the people of the world on to the fullness of life by different paths [251]. Radhakrishnan has borrowed a number of Hindu and Buddhist similes to explain and illustrate the equality of all religions. "The cows may be of different colours but the milk they give us is of one colour, white. The lamps may be different but the light, the flame, the illumination they generate is the same. The story of the elephant and the six blind men is well known. When our eyes are opened we see that the different parts we stressed are parts of the whole, different sides of one truth" [252]. The story of the blind men comes from Buddha. Once upon a time a king gathered together six men all blind from birth. He offered a prize to the one who could give the best description of an elephant. The first blind man felt one leg of the elephant and declared that the elephant was the trunk of a tree; the second felt the tail and said that the elephant was rope-like; another touched the ear and

---

[247] Cf. *Fragments*, p. 74.

[248] Cf. RS, p. 53.

[249] EWR, p. 52. Cf. also ERWTh, pp. 310, 331; OSW, October 1952 - February 1959, pp. 321, 356, 384; OSW, May 1962 - May 1964, pp. 121, 143, 145, 166, 167, 170, 178, 387; EWS, p. 40 f; *Great Indians*, p. 83.

[250] BG, iv, 11.

[251] Cf. RF, p. 156 f.

[252] OSW, October 1952 - February 1959, p. 356. Cf. also p. 320 f.

argued that the elephant was like a palm leaf; and so on [253]. Even so each religion stresses one or another aspect of the same eternal religion. None of them is wrong; all descriptions are equally good. But none of them contains the whole truth [254].

The equality of all religions is also shown by an *a posteriori* argument. Sanctity is the mark of authentic religion. But saintliness is not an exclusive prerogative of any one religion. Every religion has it. All religions have produced saintly people [255]. So all religions must be considered equal.

iii) *Tolerance*

The above view puts on the same level all religions [256]. Every form of religion, even image worship, is worthy of adherence [257]. " In the name of toleration we have carefully protected superstitious rites and customs " [258]. The individual has complete freedom to select that form of religion which is most suited to his nature. All religions are capable of serving him equally.

> "Any name, any form, any symbol may set the whole being astir, and the divine in the heart of the seeker lifts him up and accepts the offering. God is sometimes viewed as personal friend and lover. Many feel the need for human intermediary, example or incarnation. Some want to feel the divine in something entirely close to humanity, an *avatār* like Krishna, Buddha or Jesus. Some find that even this is not quite sufficient and seek for a prophet like Mohammad, and still others are restless without a living teacher, a *guru* ... " [259].

All these different people need different forms of religion; they cannot be brought under any one single dogma or creed. Therefore the different religions should be tolerated.

Hence toleration is not the result of scepticism or ignorance [260] or a mere concession to human imperfection and weakness or a sympathy with error [261]. It is based on a definite view of re-

---

[253] Cf. ERWTh, p. 308 f; OSW, October 1952 - January 1956, pp. 225, 258 f.

[254] Cf. OSW, October 1952 - February 1959, p. 366.

[255] Cf. HVL, p. 43; RF, p. 176.

[256] Cf. Ibid., p. 32.

[257] Cf. OSW, May 1962 - May 1964, p. 126.

[258] HVL, p. 25. Cf. also pp. 16 f, 31.

[259] IVL, p. 96.

[260] Cf. ERWTh, p. 314.

[261] Cf. Ibid., p. 316.

ligion, a philosophy of religion that teaches the unity of all religions and their equality as well [262], that no religion is absolutely perfect, but only symbolical and partial [263]. Once we attain to realization we will see that the external forms which the organized religions uphold as final, have no ultimate validity and that no single religion contains the whole truth about the Supreme. All attempts to submit the transcendent Infinite to finite forms are wrong [264]. The Absolute can never be fully known [265]. Therefore Radhakrishnan says : " Toleration is the homage which the finite mind pays to the inexhaustibility of the Infinite " [266].

This is active toleration. It calls for a positive appreciation of all other faiths and also for a fellowship of different faiths [267]. Respect for other men's belief must be absolute. Tolerance must be ideological, not a mere concession to the believer [268]. " Even if the ideas are erroneous it is good for truth to struggle with error. Nothing is more fatal to truth than suppression of error by force " [269]. Freedom is the supreme law of the spiritual life. Our intellect should be free even to deny God [270].

We are all engaged in the same quest and are spiritual brothers [271]. We are pilgrims moving towards the same shrine. Therefore there is no point in quarrelling on the way because of the differences of names given to the ultimate goal [272].

If we quarrel about words or dogmas or names which are given to the Supreme, it only shows that we have not understood our own religion well. The authentically religious will not quarrel about shadows. They penetrate to the substance. Only those who are religious ' at second-hand ', that is, those who have no insight into Reality, quarrel about the names they give to the inexpressible Reality of God [273]. Had we realized the unity of all religions, there would have been no reason for strife among

---

[262] Cf. Ibid., RF, p. 197.
[263] Cf. Ibid., p. 317 ff.
[264] Cf. OSW, July 1959 - May 1962, p. 223.
[265] Cf. Ibid., p. 250.
[266] ERWTh, p. 317.
[267] Cf. OSW, July 1959 - May 1962, p. 223; OSW, February 1956 - February 1957, p. 365 f; ERWTh, p. 335.
[268] Cf. OSW, October 1952 - February 1959, p. 520.
[269] RF, p. 199. Cf. also HVL, pp. 36, 38.
[270] Cf. RC. p. 803.
[271] Cf. OSW, October 1952 - February 1959, p. 384.
[272] Cf. Ibid., p. 296; OSW. July 1959 - May 1962, p. 185.
[273] Cf. OSW, May 1962 - May 1964, pp. 163, 174.

those who are in the same universal religion [274]. Moreover we would have admitted that the mystery of the Godhead is inexpressible [275].

In the past many religions practised intolerance. But it did not help the cause of religion. When our own ideas of God are defended uncompromisingly, it can only help atheism [276]. Burning a human being for his beliefs is not faith or religion but a crime of murder [277]. A defeated enemy remains an enemy, while a reconciled foe becomes a friend [278]. Intolerance has caused only suffering and defeat [279]. These past sufferings should be good lessons for us. "If we do not learn from the past, we have to live the past over again" [280]. Our world is already torn by conflicts and is stricken by fear. Therefore tolerance is an urgent need [281].

The prophets of all religions were tolerant towards other faiths [282]. The Buddha recognized many ways to reach the goal [283]. He condemned religious intolerance as the greatest enemy of religion [284]. Jesus counted other religious practices as worthy of our adherence [285]. Asoka's twelfth Rock Edict shows that he conceived tolerance as something necessary for the growth of our religion [286].

---

[274] Cf. OSW, July 1959 - May 1962, p. 241.
[275] Cf. OSW, May 1962 - May 1964, pp. 119, 143.
[276] Cf. RC, p. 810.
[277] Cf. OSW, July 1959 - May 1962, p. 212 f.
[278] Cf. Ibid., p. 289.
[279] Cf. Ibid., p. 83.
[280] OSW, May 1962 - May 1964, p. 128.
[281] Cf. OSW, February 1956 - February 1957, p. 263.
[282] Cf. ERWTh. p. 39 f.
[283] Cf. OSW, October 1952 - January 1956, p. 260.
[284] Cf. GB, p. 17.
[285] Cf. EWS, p. 78.
[286] Cf. OSW, October 1952 - January 1956, pp. 240, 393 f; OSW, February 1956 - February 1957, pp. 247, 261. The source of Radhakrishnan is certainly the *Bhagavadgītā*. He makes it clear when he says: "The famous Hindu Scripture, *Bhagavadgītā,* declares that if one has faith and devotion to other gods, it is the faith and devotion to the Supreme One, though not in the prescribed way" (MST, p. 8). The Allusion is to *Bhagavadgītā*, VII, 21-22. The verses read: "Whatever form any devotee with faith wishes to worship, I make that faith of his steady. Endowed with that faith, he seeks the propitiation of such a one and from him he obtains his desires, the benefits being decreed by Me alone".

iv) *Missionary Activity*

Once the unity and equality of all religions are admitted and absolute tolerance and positive co-operation among all religions are advocated, there can be no missionary activity whose purpose is to convert others to our point of view or religion [287]. Even the crudest superstition has a place in the general religious scheme, " for gorgeous flowers justify the muddy roots from which they spring " [288].

Our missionary fervour originates from an ignorance of the true nature of our own religion as well as that of other's [289]. Ignorance of the true nature of our religion gives the conviction that ours is the only true religion, while ignorance of the other's faith makes us think that all other faiths are absolutely false and lead to damnation [290].

Gandhi wrote in 1938 : " It would be the height of intolerance — and intolerance is a species of violence — to believe that your religion is superior to other religions and that you would be justified in wanting others to change to your faith [291]. Radhakrishnan takes up this view and says that if we want to live together peacefully in this world, evangelism in politics, in business and in religion will have to be restrained [292]. For missionary activity has an element of intolerance in it. " Advocates of religion sometimes become missionaries of hatred towards other religions " [293].

There are other reasons also against religious conversions. When an individual is converted to another religion he is torn up from his traditional roots. Hence, psychological comfort will be destroyed [294]. The original religion, therefore, has " absolute advantage over any imported religion, for a convert to a new religion feels an utter stranger to himself. He feels like an illegitimate child with no heritage, no link with the men who preceded him ... there is no inner development or natural progress to the new religion. It does not arise out of the old, but falls from one knows not where " [295].

---

[287] Cf. *Fragments,* p. 74.

[288] HVL, p. 43.

[289] Cf. *Fragments,* p. 74; RCW, p. 117.

[290] Cf. Ibid.

[291] *Harijan,* May 14, 1938.

[292] Cf. OSW, October 1952 - January 1956, p. 139.

[293] RCW, p. 117. Cf. also OSW, July 1959 - May 1962, p. 185; *Fragments,* p. 72.

[294] Cf. ERWTh, p. 328.

[295] Ibid., p. 329.

The missionaries try to bring all men under one common creed. That implies the suppression of different religious creeds, which will be a great loss to humanity at large. We have no right to destroy what we have not learnt to appreciate. " To drag into the dust what is precious to the soul of a people, what has been laboriously built up by the wisdom of ages, is spiritual vandalism " [296]. A religion which fosters such attitudes towards other religions is not worth the name.

Conversion work by the missionaries is said to be like changing labels without changing the content. The convert lives under imported forms. He may use the same words and forms, yet may give different meanings and have different experiences. For example, even though the West took over Christianity, the essentials of it never became the inward property of the West. It accepted what suited to it, dropped out or refashioned others [297]. Therefore mass-conversions are said to be Hinduizing Christianity rather than Christianizing Hinduism [298].

Missionary activity motivated by the desire to convert other people to our religion discards divine revelations in other religions. It is an offense against God the revealer and adversely affects the individual's spiritual growth. " If missionary activities such as are now, are persisted in, they will become a prime factor in the spiritual impoverishment of the world. They are treason against Him who ' never left himself without a witness ' " [299].

Therefore Radhakrishnan takes up Swami Vivekananda's interpretation of the meaning of missionary work. We should not aim to make converts, Christians to Buddhists or Buddhists to Christians. We must help both Christians and Buddhists to rediscover the basic principles of their own religions and to live their own religions more fully [300]. What the missionaries must do is to awaken the spirit in their clients. That will help them to attain personal experience of the truth. When the inward is changed the outward also will be changed [301]. Conversion consists

---

[296] Ibid., p. 330.

[297] Cf. Ibid., p. 333.

[298] Cf. Ibid., p. 333, n. 1.

[299] *Fragments*, p. 74.

[300] Cf. Ibid., HVL, p. 34. This was the main theme of Swami Vivekananda's speech in the Parliament of Religions in Chicago in 1893 (Cf. SWAMI NIKHILANANDA, *Vivekananda: A Biography* (Calcutta 1953) 121).

[301] Cf. ERWTh, p. 336.

in the awakening of the spirit, and not in imposing beliefs or in bringing all under a single authority.

4) THE UNIVERSAL SPIRITUAL RELIGION

i) *The World Community*

All the great prophets had visualized a world community. They all preached one God in Heaven and one family on earth [302]. The unconditional demand : thou shalt love thy neighbour as thyself, asks for the establishment of a universal community [303]. With the prophets and seers the world community remained a dream and an ideal. Alexander the Great was the first to implement to some extent the great ideal. Of late in India Rabindranath Tagore took up the idea and popularized it. By establishing Visvabhārati, as an international university he gave an institutionalized expression of his great hope in the world community [304].

Radhakrishnan loved the idea of the world community even from his youth. His close friendship with Radindranath Tagore, membership in the International Committee of Intellectual Co-operation of League of Nations and membership and presidentship in UNESCO offered him favourable opportunities to evolve the idea of a world community and work for its speediest realization.

The world community is a necessary stage in the cosmic evolution. The world is meant to be a partnership. We are born to love not to hate; to help one another, not to destroy one another [305]. History is marching towards a " moral community, a single commonwealth in which the human race will find order and peace, settled government, material prosperity, the reign of law and freedom for all " [306]. In a famous speech on " World Community " at the United Nations General Assembly, on June

---

[302] Cf. Ibid., pp. viii, 39; OSW, October 1952 - February 1959, p. 365; OSW, July 1959 - May 1962, pp. 223, 266; OSW. May 1962 - May 1964, (pp. 49. 219; RCW, p. 130.

[303] Cf. GB, p. 19.

[304] Cf. OSW, July 1959 - May 1962, p. 135. Tagore's universal view is clear in the poem *Pravasi* (The Emigrant). Here is a stanza from it:
" My home is everywhere;
I am in search of it;
My country is in all countries;
I will struggle to attain it ".

[305] Cf. OSW, May 1962 - May 1964, p. 4.

[306] EPW, p. 32. Cf. also MG, p. 19.

10, 1963 declares Radhakrishnan : " I have no doubt that the world will become one ... it is in the mind of events, it is the will of the universe, it is the purpose of Providence. We are being led from state to state to the concept of one family on earth " [307].

There is only one race, the human race [308]; and there is only one community, the world community [309]. At present there are many divisions and there are many groups in the world. The present-day order of the world is that of nation states. We are victims of the past and not builders of the future. Our loyalty hitherto was to nation states and not to the human race. We must get out of this rut and subordinate our group loyalty to that of the world community [310]. For " nationalism is not the highest concept. The highest concept is world community " [311]. Our personality can grow to the fullest only in the world community [312]. Therefore as long as the world community is not an accomplished fact, we are not fully human [313].

Consequently, man must work " for a world in which all races can blend and mingle, each retaining its special characteristics and developing whatever is best in it " [314]. Radhakrishnan missed no opportunity to exhort us to work for this great goal. He ends his *Eastern Religions and Western Thought* with an appeal to " develop in place of an angular national spirit a rounded world view " [315]. His latest work, *Religion in a Changing World* concludes with a similar call: " In man and his future we must have confidence. The ideal of a world community, our obvious destiny and duty, is at once a summons to creative endeavour, and a call to co-operative action " [316]. Education and culture must be orientated to the development of the world community [317]. With the world community mankind will enter upon a great era [318].

---

[307] OSW, May 1962 - May 1964, p. 33.
[308] Cf. RCW, p. 165.
[309] Cf. OSW, May 1962 - May 1964, p. 74; ERWTh, p. 40.
[310] Cf. OSW, October 1952 - February 1959, p. 245; OSW, May 1962 - May 1964, p. 32 f.
[311] OSW, May 1962 - May 1964, p. 33.
[312] Cf. OSW, July 1959 - May 1962, p. 108.
[313] Cf. OSW, October 1952 - February 1959, p. 270.
[314] HVL, p. 76.
[315] Cf. ERWTh, p. 385.
[316] RCW, p. 182.
[317] Cf. OSW, July 1959 - May 1962, p. 58; RCW, p. 158.
[318] Cf. RCW, p. 161 f.

13

ii) *Fellowship of Faiths*

a) *Nature of the Fellowship*

Radhakrishnan very often calls for a fellowship of all religions. We shall examine his concept of religious fellowship and his arguments for it.

The fellowship is not a fusion of all religions [319]. It is not mere "passive co-existence" either [320]. In his Inaugural Address at the International Congress of World Fellowship of Faiths in Tokyo on October 3, 1956 he points out that he is not proposing an eclectic religion, or encouraging the merging together of different faiths into a vague synthetic creed [321]. Five years later in his Address on receiving the Peace Prize of the West German Book Traders in Frankfurt, Radhakrishnan rejects the accusation that he is preaching an eclectic religion and says that his vision of the fellowship of religions is based on the transcendental unity of religions.

> "Let me make it clear that I do not believe in the emergence of a 'world faith', of an eclectic or syncretistic character which will take in the valuable elements of all religions. Any attempt to have a religion which will be no religion in particular is as untenable as an attempt to speak without speaking any particular language. We recognize the different religions but discern the unity underlying them. We do not wish to flatten our diversity or impose uniformity. Difference does not mean division, nor does diversity mean discord. Each religion while maintaining its individuality will learn to appreciate the values of others ... The different faiths are like different fingers of the loving hand of the Supreme extended to all, offering completeness of being to all" [322].

So the different religions can develop their individual characters, their distinctive doctrines and piety within the fellowship [323]. And each religion will have scope for the full expression [324]. Con-

---

[319] Cf. OSW, October 1952 - February 1959, p. 383; *Fragments,* p. 75.
[320] Cf. OSW, July 1959 - May 1962, p. 223.
[321] Cf. OSW, October 1952 - February 1959, p. 354. A complete text of this speech is given in OSW, October 1952 - February 1959, pp. 353-358.
[322] OSW, July 1959 - May 1962, pp. 33-34. Cf. also RC, p. 812.
[323] Cf. *Fragments,* p. 76; OSW, October 1952 - February 1959, p. 383; OSW, July 1959 - May 1962, p. 224; RCW, p. 134.
[324] Cf. OSW, October 1952 - February 1959, p. 336.

sequently, those who enter into the fellowship of religions need not give up their own religion [325]. The only limitation is that the doctrine or rite of any one religion should not impair the sense of spiritual fellowship [326].

The theory of fellowship of religions is based on the *Bhagavadgītā*, IV, 11. "As men approach me, so do I accept them: men on all sides follow my path, O Pārtha (Arjuna)". This teaches that God accepts all religions as equally good means to reach him [327]. Radhakrishnan points out that this equality of all religions is the basis of fellowship in religions [328]. No religion is absolutely perfect or final. All religions are relative and all possess some truth but not the whole truth [329]. Therefore different religions, in their essence, are not incompatible but complementary. So all of them are necessary and indispensable to each one for the realization of the common end [330]. Hence they need not go on quarrelling but can enter into a fellowship.

In some passages the fellowship of faiths appears as the religious counterpart of the Commonwealth of nations in politics. In *The Hindu View of Life* the political ideal is said to be a Commonwealth of nations. After describing its structure he argues that this ideal must be extended to the religious sphere also [331]. In a Commonwealth all enjoy freedom and equality. "In the spiritual Commonwealth every one has a definite place by reason of his specific mode of being. No man, whatever be his qualities, has any claim to precedence over others ... We are called upon to love our enemies even as ourselves, a rule more honoured with our lips than observed in our lives" [332]. In his famous Inaugural Address at the International Congress of World Fellowship of Faiths in Tokyo Radhakrishnan compares the fellowship of religions with the United Nations Organization. "If we can have a United Nations Organization, cannot we have a United Religions Organization" [333].

The first step to the fellowship of religions is the study of

---

[325] Cf. Ibid., p. 383.

[326] Cf. *Fragments,* p. 76.

[327] Cf. RCW, p. 173; DHIRENDRA MOHAN DATTA, *Radhakrishnan and Comparative Philosophy,* in PhSR, p. 669.

[328] Cf. OSW, October 1952 - January 1956, 236 f.

[329] Cf. EWR, p. 52.

[330] Cf. HVL, p. 43; IC, p. 16.

[331] Cf. Ibid., p. 42; RCW, p. 157.

[332] IVL, p. 92.

[333] OSW, October 1952 - February 1959, p. 354.

other religions [334]. A new and enlarged study of the old religions will show the " fundamental unity with a free differentiation " [335]. This will help every religion to extend hands of friendship to each other [336]. Thus mutual respect will be fostered among religions. " Mutual respect helps us to interpret other religions at their best and learn from them. We cannot have respect for another religion, when all the time our attempt is to obliterate it " [337]. Thus we can develop active co-operation, which is a close inter-relation among religions [338].

b) *Reasons for Developing a Fellowship of Religions*

1) Scientific and technological development has effected a physical unity. Geographical barriers have no more their old meaning [339]. " Nations are no more islands; frontiers are losing their significance " [340]. Thus physically the world is getting to be one [341]. This physical unity is not sufficient; the world must have a psychological oneness, a soul [342]. Radhakrishnan constantly argues that in order to support and sustain the physical unity which is emerging, a spiritual unity is essential. " The City of God has for its counterpart the City of men and the latter can only be a universal human society founded on a belief in the same fundamental vision of the common good and indeed upon a certain communion in things of the spirit " [343]. God Himself must be the common bond that unites the fellowship of religions [344]. But no organized religion, which only divide mankind, can give this spiritual unity. Only a spiritual fellowship of religions can serve the purpose.

2) If religions do not come into a fellowship, there will be grave dangers. Science and technology have made division of mankind and war suicidal to humanity. The only way to redeem the future from fear and danger is fellowship. This is the final

---

334 Cf. *Fragments,* p. 13; RC, p. 814.
335 RF, p. 199.
336 Cf. HVL, p. 43.
337 OSW, October 1952 - February 1959, p. 357.
338 Cf. Ibid., p. 223, 357, 396.
339 Cf. Ibid., p. 77, 270; FS, p. 39.
340 RCW, p. 22.
341 Cf. Ibid., p. 18 f.
342 Cf. *Fragments,* pp. 7, 24 f.
343 RF, p. 168.
344 Cf. OSW, October 1952 - February 1959, p. 599.

argument which Radhakrishnan proposes at the International Congress of World Fellowship of Faiths in Tokyo. He concludes his Inaugural Address with this argument:

> "At a time like this when we live in fear of the future on account of the great advances of science and technology, it is essential for all those who have faith in the wisdom and love of God, whatever may be their religious denominations, to get together, form a sacramental brotherhood and work for fellowship in which alone lies the redemption of man " [345].

The need for fellowship is said to have become very urgent with the rise of nuclear weapons [346]. Very often Radhakrishnan forecasts grave dangers, even total annihilation, if dogmatic barriers are not broken down and fellowship is not established [347].

3) The world must be united on a religious basis. But it cannot be united on the basis of this or that religion [348]. If one particular religion is to be accepted for the whole world, the spiritual tradition and the wealth of all other religions will be lost to the world [349]. Mankind is the spiritual heir not merely of Palestine or Greece or Rome but of India, China and the Middle East also [350]. All the spiritual traditions must have a place in the world religion. For all of them are growing under the inspiration of the Holy Spirit [351]. And since men are of varied natures and aptitudes, there are bound to be differences among religions [352]. Therefore we cannot adopt a policy of " either or " with regard to the different religions, but of " this and that " — an active coexistence or fellowship of all religions [353].

4) All religions are engaged in a common quest. They are fellow seekers [354]. Each religion represents a special quality of its own. Hinduism is said to be marked by its spiritual radiance,

---

[345] OSW, October 1952 - February 1959, pp. 357-358.
[346] Cf. RCW, p. 132, 155; OSW, July 1959 - May 1962, pp. 97 f, 114.
[347] Cf. RCW, pp. 19 f, 132, 155; OSW, October 1952 - February 1959, pp. 385, 587; OSW, July 1959 - May 1962, pp. 22, 30, 87, 97, 211, 235; OSW, May 1962 - May 1964, p. 47.
[348] Cf. OSW, October 1952 - February 1959, pp. 335.
[349] Cf. K, 45.
[350] Cf. OSW, October 1952 - February 1959, p. 385; OSW, May 1962 - May 1964, p. 156.
[351] Cf. *Fragments,* pp. 75, 77.
[352] Cf. OSW, October 1952 - February 1959, p. 385.
[353] Cf. Ibid., p. 50 f.
[354] Cf. FS, p. 39.

Judaism by its faithful obedience, Greek religion by the life of beauty, Buddhism by noble compassion and Christianity by a vision of the divine love [355]. If all religions come together into a fellowship, each can gain from the others, and humanity will be more enriched [356]. Our understanding of religion will be deepened and widened from the friendship and knowledge of different religions [357]. Then each one will be able to seek the truth in a better way and reach the goal more easily. Therefore fellow seekers should come into a fellowship and co-operation.

iii) *The Underlying Religion*

Radhakrishnan distinguishes between superficial religious forms and religion itself. There are a number of forms of religion, while there is only one universal religion underlying all these forms. The rites and beliefs of different religions vary apparently. But there is coherence with respect to certain essential features [358]. The different organized religions are merely apparent forms of a single universal religion on which all the religions are founded.

> " We recognize the common ground on which the different religious traditions rest. This common ground belongs of right to all of us, as it has its source in the Eternal. The universality of fundamental ideas which historical studies and comparative religion demonstrate is the hope of the future. It makes for religious unity and understanding " [359].

The different religions at best may serve as means to this universal religion [360]. Comparing different religions to different paths Radhakrishnan says, " After a divergence of few yards or a few miles, they may well unite to form a single concrete highway to perfection " [361]. All great seers and scriptures teach only this universal religion. This is the religion which the *Upanishads,* Buddhism, Jainism, Greek mysteries, Zoroastrianism, Platonism and the Gospels teach mankind [362]. This is the religion which

---

[355] Cf. *Fragments,* p. 76.
[356] Cf. OSW, October 1952 - February 1959, p. 365.
[357] Cf. Ibid., p. 336; RC, pp. 813-814.
[358] Cf. EWR, p. 18; *Fragments,* p. 25.
[359] OSW, October 1952 - February 1959, p. 537.
[360] Cf. MG, p. 16.
[361] EWS, p. 40.
[362] *Fragments,* p. 80; Cf. also OSW, October 1952 - February 1959, pp. 326-331.

according to St Agustine existed from the beginning. " Those who overlook this perennial wisdom, the eternal religion behind all religions, this *sanātana dharma,* this timeless tradition ... and cling to outward forms and quarrel among themselves, are responsible for the civilized chaos in which we live " [363]. The forms are man-made and are accidental.

This universal religion is said to be hampered by ' man-made ' formulas' and ' church-ordinances ' [364]. Therefore, Radhakrishnan summarizing the whole religious message of Tagore, says, " Cling to religion, let religions go " [365]. This in fact is the religious message of Radhakrishnan too. Only when the external barriers are broken down, will religion be a congenial home to the spirit of man. Then religion will attract all men and will serve as the basis of the new order [366]. Therefore, it is " our duty to get back to this central core of religion, this fundamental wisdom which has been obscured and distorted in the course of history by dogmatic and sectarian developments " [367].

iv) *The Spiritual Fraternity*

The fellowship of religions is only the first step towards the final goal of human society, which is a spiritual fraternity. The fellowship is based on the Divine in man [368], which is the root of all religions [369]. When man attains the direct experience of the Divine in him, his religion is said to be evolved to the fullest. All those who have attained this direct experience, though they may belong historically and geographically to different circumstances, share the same experience [370], and therefore they all together form the one great invisible community of God, a spiritual fraternity. " Those who have this experience, whatever religion they may adopt, belong to a single spiritual fraternity. These are the saints who live their life in God and form a spiritual nobility " [371]. This is the ' Household of God ' [372], the ' Church of God

---

[363] Cf. Ibid., p. 80.

[364] Cf. PhRT, p. 109.

[365] Ibid.. pp. 108-109.

[366] Ibid., p. 109. Cf. also *Fragments,* p. 81.

[367] *Fragments,* p. 81.

[368] The Divine in us is also called "indwelling Logos" (Cf. EWR, p. 30).

[369] Cf. OSW, July 1959 - May 1962, p. 338; EWR, p. 30.

[370] Cf. Ibid., p. 238 f.

[371] OSW, October 1952 - February 1959, p. 367.

[372] Cf. OSW, May 1962 - May 1964, p. 163.

Universal ' [373] to which persons like Socrates and Plato, Rama-krishna and Gandhi belong. This is said to be a religion above all other religions, based on the Divine in us. It supersedes all our religiosities, all our pieties, rituals, dogmas and doctrines. So this may well be the religion on the basis of which the whole world can unite [374].

From the theory that man's self is divine, it also follows that to whatever religions we may belong at present, even if we do not have attained the spiritual realization, we are at least poten-tially members of the spiritual fraternity.

> " Whatever point of view we start from, Hindu or Muslim, Buddhist or Christian, if we are sincere in our intention and earnest in our effort, we get to the Supreme. We are members of the one Invisible Church of God or one fellow-ship of the Spirit, though we may belong to this or that visible Church " [375].

In this sense it is said that there are no outcastes in the House-hold of God [376].

But when the common man discovers what is uncommon in him, when he attains the immediate experience of the Divine in him, he becomes a full member of the spiritual fraternity [377]. As long as the seekers of truth are on the way, and have not attained realization, they may feel the differences of their ways and make quarrel. But " when the pilgrims reach the end of their quest, they will feel that they belong to one supreme family, they form kindred spirits, whether they come from Islam, Christianity, Hinduism or Buddhism, they all belong to one Church of God Universal " [378].

The spiritual fraternity, therefore, does not recognize the limits put by authoritarian dogmas or religious differences.

> " The pathways we tread, the names we give, fade away into insignificance when we stand face to face in the glowing light of the Divine. When we touch the flame of the Divine, a generous hospitality to different creeds and forms arises ...

---

[373] Cf. Ibid., p. 248.
[374] Cf. Ibid., p. 121.
[375] OSW, October 1952 - February 1959, p. 310. Cf. also OSW, May 1962 - May 1964, pp. 145, 248.
[376] Cf. OSW, May 1962 - May 1964, p. 174.
[377] Cf. OSW, October 1952 - February 1959, p. 521.
[378] OSW, May 1962 - May 1964, pp. 145-146.

Naturally such a religion requires us to recognize the potential spiritual possibilities of the human being and to discard the artificial distinctions which man-made institutions have inflicted on human beings as also the shackles of serfdom and helotry " [379].

Therefore, all those who have experienced God immediately " believe and proclaim, ' We do not belong to the Church of Christ or Buddha, but we belong to the Universal Spirit of God ' " [380]. Because of their supra-organizational view, they look upon all believers as belonging to the Household of God [381]. Hitherto only a few individuals have attained the full membership in the spiritual fraternity. These are the mystics, the God-men of all religions. They appeal to us to cross the barriers and enter into the spiritual fraternity, the ideal society " where there is neither Jew nor Gentile, neither Greek nor barbarian, where all men *qua* men are of equal worth " [382]. They are all bound together intimately into one spiritual fraternity, not by an external authority, creed or ritual, but by God Himself whom they have experienced in their own selves [383]. Since there is no authority or creed and since it is an invisible Church of Spirit, science and criticism will have nothing to say against it [384].

Radhakrishnan applies the theory of evolution also to the concept of spiritual fraternity. " The purpose of the cosmic process is the city of God in time. Earth is the seed-ground of the new life of spirit " [385]. The long labour of the cosmic process will receive a crowning justification only if man grows as to be able to participate in divine action, life and essence [386]. Since the " humanity of Christ is representative of all humanity ", contends Radhakrishnan, " not only the historic Jesus but the whole race will have the gifts of Incarnation. The end of the world is the transubstantiation of the whole creation " [387]. Men will become

---

[379] Ibid., pp. 178-179.

[380] Ibid., p. 117. Cf. also p. 146.

[381] Cf. Ibid.

[382] *The Spirit in Man*, p. 494.

[383] Cf. OSW, October 1952 - February 1959, p. 599; OSW, July 1959 - May 1962, p. 396; OSW, May 1962 - May 1964, p. 167.

[384] Cf. IVL, p. 172.

[385] OSW, October 1952 - February 1959, p. 304. Cf. also Ibid., p. 386.

[386] Cf. IVL, p. 97.

[387] EWS, pp. 77-78. Radhakrishnan is not arguing that we will receive the benefits of Incarnation, but we ourselves will become God-men.

God-men and humanity a spiritual fraternity. In an eloquent passage in *Fragments* Radhakrishnan describes the last stage of evolution as follows:

> "Then will come a time when the world will be inhabited by a race of men, with no flaw of flesh or error of mind, free from the yoke not only of disease and privation but of lying words and of love turned into hate. When human beings grow into completeness, into the invisible world which is the Kingdom of Heaven, then will they manifest in the outer world the Kingdom which is within them. That day we shall cease to set forth God dogmatically or dispute about his nature but leave each man to the worship of God in the sanctuary of his heart, to feel after him and to possess him" [388].

This is the universal religion, the eternal religion which is underlying all religions, evolved to the fullest; this is the perfection of the spiritual religion which will unify the whole world; this is the final perfection of the fellowship of religions; and this is the final stage of our spiritual evolution in which there will be a "universal incarnation" [389].

---

[388] *Fragments*, p. 81.
[309] RC, p. 800.

VII

CRITICAL EVALUATION

It is hard to criticize the opinions and actions of those whom we love and esteem. But "it is", says Radhakrishnan, "what one expects and longs for from true friendship"[1]. In a research work, loyalty to ourselves — to our intellect and conscience — and to truth requires us to withhold our assent to propositions which do not seem to us reasonable. In that event we are duty-bound to give our personal judgments, however unpleasant they may be to the other[2]. It is with this conviction that we state our personal evaluation of Radhakrishnan's views on organized religion.

Radhakrishnan is a versatile genius and commands world wide respect. After going through the critical essays which different thinkers contributed to the volume *The Philosophy of Sarvepalli Radhakrishnan*, its editor, Paul Arthur Schilpp remarked that 'owing to the high esteem in which Radhakrishnan is held everywhere' those essays have become more eulogic in character than critical[3].

He is one of the great sages of India who dedicated their lives to the pursuit of wisdom. In his Presidential Address to the Indian Nation on the eve of the Republic day of 1967[4], he revealed the secret of his noble life: "The pursuit of wisdom has attracted me for many years. Whatever my other preoccupation may have been, this search has been my main inspiration"[5]. In his article "The Religion of the Spirit and the World's Need: Fragments of a Confession" he declares that his "one supreme interest has been to try to restore a sense of spiritual values to

---

[1] MST, p. 46. Cf. also *Fragments,* p. 8; Ind. Ph., I, 9.
[2] Cf. Ind. Ph., I, 9.
[3] Cf. PhSR, p. xii.
[4] Republic day in India falls on January 26.
[5] *India News,* London, January 28, 1967.

the millions of religiously displaced persons " [6]. He deserves our admiration especially because he had the courage to give utterance to the religious truth in which he believed even in communist capitals like Moscow [7] and Peking [8].

Radhakrishnan presents his themes in such brilliant style that as Naravane said, "frozen fossils of long forgotten ideas burst forth into new life " [9]. He loves to repeat the same doctrine in new phrases over again, like the Taoists of the ancient East. The primacy of spiritual values, the lack of spirituality in our time and its necessity, the inevitability of spiritual absolutism, the unity and equality of all religions and the immense harm that is done to the religious life of man by dogmas and authority in religion are the ever recurring themes of almost all of his writings and addresses. His pages are replete with brilliant phrases and telling quotations. Thus he compels a hearing whenever he speaks. Where his logic wins his calm reason reigns; where his reason fails his stormy eloquence breaks out.

1) Radhakrishnan's Basic Doctrine on Religion and his General Preparations for its Presentation

i) The Basis of Religion

Radhakrishnan's idea of organized religion and his approach to it are certainly dependent on his concept of the basis and the nature of religion. Therefore, these we have to evaluate first.

We have seen that Radhakrishnan is a monistic idealist, an advaitin of the Sankarite School. The Absolute (Brahman) is the Self (Atman) and every subject and object are ultimately identical. This, he believes, is a necessary implication of all relevant thinking, feeling and willing [10], so that any other position would be illogical [11].

Because of this monistic belief, Radhakrishnan maintains that man's being is entirely derived from that of God by some sort of emanation [12]. Consequently both should be univocally of the

---

[6] *Fragments,* p. 14.
[7] Cf. OSW, October 1952 - February 1959, pp. 39 ff.
[8] Cf. Ibid., p. 64.
[9] Naravane, *Modern Indian Thought* (Bombay 1964) 259.
[10] Cf. Ind. Ph., I, 170, 194.
[11] Cf. Ibid., p. 195.
[12] Cf. BG, p. 39.

same nature even as the water in a bucket drawn from a well
is of the same kind as that in the well. Therefore it is only logical
for him to think that man and the world around him are consubstantial with God, who in turn is the Absolute looked at from the
point of view of the actuality of this world [13].

The identity of the Absolute and the real self of man is not
evident to the intellect. But man is endowed with intuitive faculties to which even the mysteries are transparent [14]. Man can have
an intuition of his own self which is the Divine in him. He then
realizes that the Divine in him is the very Absolute — Brahman
is Atman. This identity of man's self with the Absolute, argues
Radhakrishnan, is witnessed by innumerable seers of various religions who lived in different circumstances [15].

The basis of religion according to Radhakrishnan is this consubstantiality of man's self with the Absolute. All his doctrines
of religion are logical derivations from this fundamental doctrine
of the substantial immanence of God in man [16]. If man's real
self is identical with the Supreme Reality, then the one goal of
human existence must be to realize his identity with the Supreme.
Since the human intellect is affected by *avidyā* or nescience, man
can never have a true intellectual grasp of his oneness with the
Supreme. But he can have a spiritual experience of it. The experiential realization of this identity is said to be the true religion.
Whatever is not purely experiential in religion is considered secondary or even an obstacle to the attaining of the goal. It is in
this sense that Radhakrishnan says that religion is a " fact of
experience " [17]. Since the Divine in man is not an exclusive gift
to any one chosen individual, but something constitutionally given
to every man, every one can and must realize his identity with
the Absolute. Therefore religion is necessarily mystical and individualistic in character. Man is not so much in need of a Redeemer as a discipline by which he can attain realization. No
mediator can come between man and God. All the great religious
leaders of all time are said to be men like every other man, who
have realized their consubstantiality with the Absolute. In this
sense Radhakrishnan says : " Buddha and Jesus are men of the

---

[13] Cf. Ind. Ph., I, 195.
[14] Cf. MST, p. 35.
[15] Cf. IVL, p. 83.
[16] Cf. P. D. DEVANANDAN, *The Gospel and the Renascent Hinduism*
(London 1959) 37.
[17] BG, p. 203.

same brotherhood " [18]; and " the illuminations of the Hindu and
the Buddhist seers, of Socrates and Plato, of Philo and Plotinus,
of Christian and Muslim mystics, belong to the same family " [19].
In other words, the truth which is the kernel of every religion
is one and the same. The great religious leaders like Jesus and
the Buddha, according to Radhakrishnan did not found any religion. We are called upon to imitate them and become God-men
like them by realizing our identity with the Absolute.

This preconceived idea of religion regulates Radhakrishnan's
approach to organized religion and forms his concept of it. He
claims that the so-called founders of religions did not found any
religion or organization. They had given expression to their
inner spiritual realization of their identity with the Supreme. This
external expression of their internal experience is not infallible and
conveys therefore no definite infallible doctrine. They had asked
others to strive after this realization. But great organizations were
formed around them claiming direct, special revelation from the
Supreme as their authority. This claim is said to be invalid.
(Chapter III). Since religion is considered the mystical experience
of one's own identity with the Supreme, an organization in between
God and man is thought to be not only unnecessary but injurious
to man's spiritual life, an obstacle to real religion. Organization
in religion is said to be an obstacle to real religious life especially
because its dogmas and authority always tend to restrict man's
religious freedom, which is the supreme law in religion. Since
organized religions assume infallible authority and claim that their
doctrines are absolute truths, they keep people in uncompromisingly
closed sects. This causes intolerance and hatred among religions.
Thus organized religions have become the greatest obstacles to the
realization of a world community and a world religion. Therefore
religion should be open and unorganized. The organized religions
are said to be in an inferior stage of religious evolution. They
must evolve themselves to perfection by giving up their organizational claims and thus coming into a fellowship of religions.

In support of this new vision of religion Radhakrishnan had
to re-interpret Hinduism and show support from great religious
leaders like Jesus and the Buddha. Such a spade-work was necessary to introduce his own new religious conception and to inaugu-
rate it as a world religion. Before we explain this re-interpreta-

---

[18] ERWTh, p. 186.
[19] BG, p. 203.

tion of Hinduism and re-picturing of Christ and Christianity we shall see briefly the geneology of his religious conception.

ii) *The Geneology of Radhakrishnan's Conception of Religion*

a) Radhakrishnan, following Hindu Philosophy, considers materiality a result of the introduction of the element of negation into the Absolute. The world is a consequent emanation from It. Therefore the more we use material and external means the more we are alienating ourselves from the Supreme Being. So the religion which can lead us to the Absolute must be totally free from externals.

b) Because Radhakrishnan conceives person in the manner of a human person, as limited and imperfect, he denies personality to God. He says, " Personality is a limitation ... Personality implies the distinction of self and not-self, and hence is inapplicable to the Being who includes and embraces all that is " [20]. Consequently, he says that the Supreme must be utterly impersonal and inexpressible by any positive term. Therefore he argues that man's religion, in order to be able to lead him to the absolutely impersonal Supreme, must surpass all relations so that the self can no longer think of its own self as distinct from the Supreme. Otherwise we will be in an imperfect state. Therefore he thinks that religion must be able to make us realize our identity with the Supreme. It is the very experience of that identity.

c) In the time old traditions of Hinduism the world is considered to be in a state of continuous change. Time is not rectilinear with a beginning and an end, but a movement in recurring cycles. Man is inexorably caught up in this cycle and is condemned to move on eternally in ever recurring births, unless he finds a way out. But what is transient is necessarily painful, since the transient thing must come to an end. Even life, considered in this perspective, is an evil from which escape must be sought. This precisely is the belief in transmigration which is the " unchallenged premise from which all Indian religion ... starts and the prospect of eternal life in *this* sense seemed too appalling to be borne. Hence Indian religion concerned itself not with the existence of God or with any service we might owe Him, but

---

[20] Ind. Ph., I, 97. This is the common Hindu concept of personality. The first Vedic seers thought of God as having intelligence and free will (*Rig Veda,* VII, 86. 88). The emphasis on the personal aspect of the Supreme is highest in *Bhagavad Gītā.*

with the practical ways and means of escaping from this eternal round of ever recurring birth and death, rebirth and redeath " [21]. R. C. Zaehner points out that " given this pessimistic view of human life, Indian religion was bound to develop on mystical lines " [22]. An attempt to identify oneself with the unchangeable Absolute was conceived by the non-dualists to be the only way to escape from the painful transient aspect of life.

iii) *Re-interpretation of Hinduism*

Is Radhakrishnan a modern seer in the line of the ancient rishis? Critics differ in their answer. A few like A. M. K. Coomaraswamy think that he is " thoroughly unindian ". There are others who go to the other extreme and praise him as the " greatest religious philosopher of modern times " in the traditional line of Hindu seers who save Hinduism from time to time from the onslaughts of secularism and materialism [23]. Some others like T. M. P. Mahadevan consider him as the defender not only of Hinduism but of the religious faith of mankind [24]. Swami Agehananda Bharati contends that Radhakrishnan is a theologian of Hinduism [25]. P. T. Raju and D. M. Datta study more critically his exposition of Hinduism. They maintain that he has not deviated from the main lines of classical Hinduism; but that influences of Western idealism are obvious in his writings.

However the critics may differ, it can be fairly maintained that Radhakrishnan is a defender of Hinduism [26], an apologist of Hinduism [27]. In his early days he defended whatever was Hindu and Indian. This is clearly seen in *Hindu View of Life*. He begins by proudly declaring that " half the world moves on independent foundations which Hinduism supplied " [28], and at the

---

[21] R. C. ZAEHNER, *The Catholic Church and World Religions* (London 1964) 17.

[22] Ibid.

[23] Cf. D. S. SARMA, *The Renaissance of Hinduism* (Benares 1944) 585.

[24] T. M. P. MAHADEVAN, *Outlines of Hinduism* (Bombay 1956) 286.

[25] Cf. PhSR, p. 465.

[26] Cf. H. BÜRKLE, *Dialog mit dem Osten, Radhakrishnans neuhinduistische Botschaft im Lichte christlichen Weltanschauung* (Stuttgart 1965) 96, 103.

[27] Cf. H. KRAEMER, *Religion and the Christian Faith* (London 1961) 120.

[28] HVL, p. 11.

end he reminds us that " in the great days of Hindu civilization, it was quick with life, crossing the seas, planting colonies, teaching the world and also learning from it " [29]. There is also an attempt to justify the caste system, although later it is condemned as an evil. There is a tendency to identify Hinduism with an ideal religion which he later calls the spiritual religion [30]. In his earlier writings this identification and his idea of the spiritual religion are not clear. But in his later works the spirit of Hinduism is shown to be very similar to the ideal spiritual religion. It is always claimed that Indian wisdom is essential for the re-education of the human race [31].

Even as a student Radhakrishnan was convinced that the ' classical culture of India ' " is at the root of much that we know and almost all that we practise " [32]. The criticism of Christianity which he encountered only strengthened his conviction. But as his understanding of Hinduism was deepened a " cold sense of reality " and a " depressing feeling of defeat " crept over him because he noticed a " causal relation between the anaemic Hindu religion and our political failure " [33]. This made him to resolve to make Hinduism relevant to the intellectual climate of the modern world [34].

Radhakrishnan knew that the Hinduism that is practised by the huge majority of the people of India cannot be defended as such but must be re-interpreted. All his critics agree that some of the fundamental concepts like *Karma, Māyā* and *Samsāra* have undergone considerable change in his thought [35]. He interpreted the monistic core of the Upanishads and identified it with Hinduism. ' Brahman is Atman ' became his most basic principle and the mystic realization of this identity was said to be salvation. This mystical experience is considered to be the true religion.

We may summarize Radhakrishnan's basic doctrines on Hindu religion as follows:

1) The spiritual experience of the identity of our real self

---

[29] Ibid., p. 90. Cf. also ERWTh, p. 313.
[30] Cf. ERWTh, p. 338.
[31] Cf. *Fragments,* p. 11; ERWTh, p. 115.
[32] MST, p. 14.
[33] *The Spirit in Man,* pp. 475-476.
[34] Cf. Ibid.
[35] Cf. P. T. RAJU, *Contemporary Indian Thought,* in *History of Philosophy Eastern and Western* I (London 1952) 535.

with the Absolute (Brahman) is not merely consciousness of such
an identity, but a real fact.

2) This mystic experience is the highest possible human experience. It is set on the same level as Christ's vision of the
Eternal Father.

3) Those who have come to this realisation cannot be subordinated to any external authority.

4) In the past some have reached this lofty religious experience. Jesus and the Buddha are the oft-cited examples. The
fact that some have attained to realization shows that everyone
has the natural capacity to attain to the same experience.

5) Pure mystical experience is the highest and most perfect
form of religion. All other religions are still imperfect and should
evolve further to attain to perfection.

6) Spiritual experience is the core of every religion. So
no one religion is false, though no one religion is absolutely perfect.

This re-interpreted and idealized Hinduism, believes Radhakrishnan, could well be the future world religion. This idea is
first expressed in his *Eastern Religions and Western Thought* and
is found in all his later works. In the first chapter of *Eastern
Religions and Western Thought* Radhakrishnan shows Hinduism
as a mystical religion distinct from the theistic religions [36], and in
the seventh chapter he declares: "The fate of the human race
hangs on a rapid assimilation of the qualities associated with the
mystic religions of the East" [37]. In his *Religion and Society*
there is a similar declaration: "The mystic religion of India ... is
likely to be the religion of the new world, which will draw men
to a common centre even across national frontiers" [38]. Radhakrishnan has never changed this conviction which is found in all
his later works [39].

iv) *Criticism of Christianity*

Whenever Radhakrishnan writes on religion, he has a word
of criticism for Christianity. Stephen Neill observes that "much
of what he writes is the expression of a dislike, amounting at
times to a passionate hatred, of Christianity. Christianity must

---

[36] Cf. ERWTh, p. 21.
[37] Ibid., 259.
[38] RS, p. 49. Cf. also Ibid., p. 244.
[39] Cf. RF, pp. 204-205, n. 1; FS, p. 40; RCW, p. 134.

not be allowed to score a single point " [40].   The third chapter in
Eastern Religions and Western Thought is " Mysticism and Ethics
in Hindu Thought ".   But in reality it is more a condemnation of
Christianity than an exposition of Hindu thought.   Even where
one would least expect anything to be said against Christianity,
one notes that there is a preoccupation to criticize and condemn it.
When, for example, the transformation of a spiritual religion into
a dogmatic one is explained, his main interest rests on enumera-
ting the evils of Christianity.   He is like a Renan, a Loisy or a
Strauss.   Hendrik Kraemer sums up: " He (Radhakrishnan) mi-
sunderstands Christianity completely ... he makes subtle invective
remarks, timely and untimely, which manifests not only misunderstanding but a very strong dislike and aversion " [41].   He has
systematically ignored all traditional Christian writers and depicted
Christianity from the pages of her determined enemies.   If he
shows some respect for Christian mystics, it is to argue against
organized Christianity.   In 1952 Joachim Wach had pointed out
that a " notable trace of bitterness " can be seen in Radhakrishnan's
references to Christianity.   The latter did not deny the charge, but
replied " if he finds it so, there must be basis for his statement
and I am sincerely sorry for it " [42].   He added that he had treated
the personality of Jesus with high respect [43].   But when a choice
between Jesus and Celsus came he preferred Celsus [44].   Even in his
latest work he is inclined to think with Mr. Young that " Christianity
must be squarely qualified as anti-life " [45].   He believes that a
critical and scientific study of the foundations of Christianity and
other organised religions will do away with their organizational
claims.   Yet Radhakrishnan himself, for all his learning, has never
given us a critical study of Christianity [46].   For example, he affirms
that there is nothing in common between the teachings of Jesus
and the hierarchical Church [47].   Such assertions by themselves
have no value, unless they are unquestionably proved by critical

---

[40] STEPHEN NEILL, *The Christian Faith and Other Faiths* (London
1961) 82.
[41] H. KRAEMER, *Religion and the Christian Faith*, p. 121.   Cf. also
Ibid., pp. 129-130.
[42] RC, p. 807.
[43] Cf. Ibid.
[44] Cf. ERWTh, p. 294.
[45] RCW, p. 114.   Radhakrishnan is quoting from Young's *Eros Denied*.
[46] Cf. STEPHEN NEILL, *The Christian Faith and Other Faiths*, p. 227,
n. 16.
[47] Cf. EWR, p. 58.

expositions of the doctrines of Jesus and of Christianity which show the contrast. But Radhakrishnan is content to refer just to two enemies of Christianity, Hatch and Harnack, without examining how far these authors are right. Adopting such a method, anybody could claim anything. Even in his latest work there is an attempt to show that the historical facts which Christianity upholds can no longer be believed. He tries to show it simply by citing some one-sided critics, all of whom reject the historicity of the Gospels. But he does not examine any one critic who argues for their historicity. Instead he argues that since some doubt their validity, Christianity should not appeal to them [48]. If this argument were valid, then it would equally count against Radhakrishnan himself.

The method of relying on some authors who all hold the same opinion without for a moment examining the validity of their opinions and of ignoring all those who differ from them or of branding them as " authors already commited to certain definite views " [49], without examining the value of their arguments, can be anything but critical. When in this way it is concluded that " traditional views have lost their authority and their psychological justification " [50], critical readers ask if the author of this statement is not already committed to certain definite views.

When we carefully examine Radhakrishnan's criticisms of Christianity we can discern that he had some important motives behind these criticisms.

1) Radhakrishnan wanted to show that Christianity is a natural religion grown up in the course of history just as any other religion. Therefore he argues that Jesus was not its founder.

2) He applied his own theory of religion to Jesus. According to Radhakrishnan Jesus is not God incarnate but a mystic who realized his inner divinity [51]. Thus Jesus is included in the universal mystical religion.

3) Jesus is not to be worshipped [52] but imitated. Imitating

---

[48] Cf. RCW, p. 38 f.

[49] RCW, p. 39.

[50] Ibid.

[51] Cf. A. KRÄMER, *Christus und das Christentum in Denken des modernen Hinduismus: Untersuchungen zur allgemeinen Religionsgeschichte*, ed. by von G. Mensching, No. 2 (Bonn 1958) 140; H. BÜRKLE, *Dialog mit dem Osten, Radhakrishnans neuhinduistische Botschaft im Lichte christlichen Weltanschuung*, p. 122.

[52] Stephen Neill, it seems, did not discern this motive of Radhakrishnan. He thinks that Radhakrishnan would admit that " Christians

Jesus, we ourselves should develop the 'Christhood' in us and become 'incarnations'. "Jesus", thinks Radhakrishnan, "was one who had awakened and taught others the way of awakening " [53]. So we are not saved by beliefs and creeds but by spiritual experience [54].

4) So there is said to be a cleavage between Jesus and Christianity. The understanding of the person of Jesus in Christianity is a later interpretation and it does not correspond to truth. Jesus was against authority, dogma and organization in religion.

So according to Radhakrishnan, the history of organized Christianity is a history of a betrayal of the mystic Jesus [55]. In short, the main purpose of Radhakrishnan's criticisms of Christianity is to show Jesus as a mystic like any Hindu seer. He severely criticized whatever element he found in Christianity which was incompatible with this idea. Radhakrishnan had to bring the words of Jesus and the Apostles as evidence in support of his view on Christ and Christianity. But in doing so, it seems to us, he has misquoted many passages.

v) *Misquotations*

The pages of Radhakrishnan are replete with quotations. He seems to be extremely well read. Often he brings together the keywords from a number of authors in support of the view which he is presenting. For everyone of his arguments he brings support from the Upanishads and the Buddha, Jesus and St Paul, Greek thinkers and Church Fathers, from ancient and modern scholars. Thus, his ideas often come to us through the greatest of the scholars and saints whom he uses as vehicles of his ideas. As such there is a grandeur about them. Radhakrishnan's capacity in this respect is indeed amazing.

But a careful reader, perhaps after a second reading, could doubt whether his citations correspond to and convey their original

---

are not wrong in worshipping Christ " (Cf. Christian Faith and Other Faiths, London 1961, pp. 83-84). But Radhakrishnan clearly says that it is a " tragic confusion " of religious history that " the prophet who announces the message becomes himself an object of worship supplanting the higher truth in which he believes " (OSW, October 1952 - February 1959, p. 377. Cf. also RCW, p. 45; The Brahma Sūtra, p. 112).

[53] OSW, October 1952 - February 1959, p. 307. Cf. also EWS, p. 73.
[54] Cf. The Brahma Sūtra, p. 107 f.
[55] Cf. H. BÜRKLE, Dialog mit dem Osten, Radhakrishnans neuhinduistische Botschaft im Lichte christlichen Weltanschauung, p. 136.

and real meaning in the context in which they were first written.
One hesitates to imagine such a defect in an author of Radhakrishnan's standing.   But on closer examinations of the sense
in which he has employed the sayings of great religious leaders
and comparing it with the original sense in which the authors of
these passages have expressed them, one finds it honestly impossible to agree that their original sense is carefully preserved by
Radhakrishnan.   T. R. V. Murti, an admirer of Radhakrishnan,
has also reached the same conclusion after studying some of the
Buddhist texts cited by Radhakrishnan.

Radhakrishnan argues that the Buddha and the Upanishads
have the same doctrine on the Self (*Ātman*).   In support of this
view he brings many texts from *Mahaparanibbāna*.   After a long
and critical study of the cited texts and their contexts Murti criticizes Radhakrishnan for using texts out of their contexts.   Murti
shows critically that the Buddha did not teach anything about
Ātman, while the Upanishads " blazen forth the reality of *Ātman*
in almost every line ".   He then cautions that " passages must not
be counted but weighed " [56].   He also observes that Radhakrishnan
" evaluates every system of philosophy, including the schools of
Buddhism in terms of Advaita Vedanta of Sankara " [57].

We shall now examine Radhakrishnan's use of some of the
Biblical texts in important contexts.   One of his basic criticisms
of Christianity is that it is a natural religion and not founded by
Jesus.   For this he claims support from St Paul.   In his Newton
Baker Lecture, at Cleveland Council on World Affairs, Ohio, on
March 27, 1958, he argues:

> " It is now generally admitted that in the course of its de-
> velopment, Christianity has drawn upon Greek metaphysi-
> cians and mystery religions.   Even the religion of the New
> Testament, in the words of St Paul, is ' debtor both to
> Greeks and to barbarians '.   It is obvious that Christianity
> is an organic part of world religious development.   It has
> grown like any other religion, in a long, historical process " [58].

Radhakrishnan repeats the same argument almost word for word
in his commentary on *Brahma Sūtra,* I, 1. 4 [59].

Mere phrases like ' it is now admitted ', ' it is obvious '

---

[56] Cf. PhSR, p. 574.
[57] Ibid., p. 580.
[58] OSW, October 1952 - February 1959, p. 381.
[59] Cf. *The Brahma Sūtra,* pp. 250-251.

unaccompanied by evidence may have some kind of appeal for the ignorant, but not for the critically minded. But what we are concerned with is the original sense of the text from St Paul which Radhakrishnan has brought as a support of his opinion that the religion of the New Testament is a natural religion.

The passage in question is Rom. 1, 14: "I owe a duty to Greeks just as much as to barbarians, to the educated just as much as to the uneducated" [60].

The first seven verses of St Paul's Epistle to the Romans consist of the customary 'salutations'. The following eight constitute the introduction to the Epistle. Towards the end of the introduction St Paul expresses his desire to visit Rome and the hope that his visit will be for their mutual benefit and will help the cause of the Gospel. The cited passage appears in the last part of the introduction. The name Greek was applied at the time of St Paul to any one who by knowledge and use of the Greek language was a sharer in the Hellenistic culture. A barbarian was originally one who spoke an unintelligible language [61]. But its conventional meaning was 'uncultured'. Thus Greeks and barbarians in the language of St Paul means "cultured and uncultured" [62]. The phrase that immediately follows, "educated and uneducated", is in apposition to 'Greeks and barbarians" [63]. Therefore what St Paul meant, as shown by Fr. S. Lyonnet, is this: "The obligation towards them presses me as anyone who is obliged by a debt to another (Cf. I Cor. 9, 16. The necessity compels me); and indeed not only towards those uncultured whom so far he evangelized, but also towards those cultured men whom he meets in Rome" [64]. The antithesis of Greeks and barbarians echoes the conviction expressed in Gal. 3, 28; and Col. 3, 11, that Christianity transcends distinctions of race, sex, class and culture, and St Paul's conviction of having an obligation to preach the

---

[60] Unless otherwise stated our Biblical citations are from *The Jerusalem Bible*, ed. by Alexander Jones, *et al.* (London 1966).

[61] In this original sense St Paul used in I Cor. 14, 11.

[62] Cf. C. H. DODD, *The Epistle of Paul to the Romans* (London 1960) 7-8.

[63] Cf. STANISLAUS LYONNET, *Exegesis Epistulae ad Romanos Cap. I-IV* (Rome 1963) 60.

[64] "Obligatio mihi incumbit erga eos, sicuti is qui aere alieno premitur (Cf. I Cor. 9, 16: 'necessitas mihi incumbit'): et quidem non tantum erga istos incultos quos hucusque evangelizavit, sed etiam erga illos viros doctos quales Romae inveniuntur" (STANISLAUS LYONNET, *Exegesis Epistulae ad Romanos*, p. 60).

Good News to the whole world [65].   This is the only interpretation
of this passage that has come down to us from antiquity. Great
Scripture commentators like Origen [66] and St John Chrysostom [67]
understood the passage in this sense. This is also the interpretation which most modern critics such as Lyonnet, Hauck and Dodd
give. It is therefore clear that the original sense of Rom. 1, 14
is not preserved in Radhakrishnan. Stephen Neill who calls the
above cited argument of Radhakrishnan " a curious and elementary
misunderstanding of Romans 1, 14 " [68] clearly supports our view.

What Radhakrishnan has done is this. He took the whole
sentence out of its context. Then he changed the subject of the
sentence, which was ' I ' (St Paul) and conveniently put a new
subject, ' the religion of the New Testament '. Further, the Biblical
sense of the word ' debtor ' is changed and a modern sense is
given to it; the same happens also with ' Greeks and barbarians '.
Thus St Paul is adduced as admitting the natural origin and evolution of Christianity.

We shall now examine another important Biblical citation in
Radhakrishnan. According to Radhakrishnan Jesus did not teach
new doctrines or insist on beliefs. He insisted only on spiritual
experience. He did not even care what others believed. In support of this view he quotes the Bible. Here is his argument:

> " The truly religious never worry about other people's beliefs.
> Look at the great saying of Jesus: ' Other sheep I have
> which are not of this fold '. Jesus was born a Jew and
> died a Jew. He did not tell the Jewish people among whom
> he found himself, ' It is wicked to be Jews. Become Chris-
> tians '. He did his best to rid the Jewish religion of its
> impurities. He would have done the same with Hinduism
> had he been born a Hindu " [69].

---

[65] Cf. C. H. DODD, *The Epistle of Paul to the Romans,* p. 8.   " So
weiss sich Paulus, der einstige Verfolger des Evangeliums, seit seiner
Begnadigung und Berufung durch Christus zum Botschafter an der ganzen
Menschheit verflichtet " (HAUCK, in *Theologisches Wörterbuch zum Neuen
Testament* V (Stuttgart 1954) 565).

[66] Cf. *Commentarium in Epist. ad Rom.* Liber I, 469: PG 14, 858.

[67] Cf. *Commentarium in Epist. ad Rom.* Homi. II, 5: PG 60, 407.
St Paul speaks of his conviction of having the obligation to preach the
Gospel in his first letter to the Corinthians also (Cf. I Cor. 1, 17; 9, 16 f.).

[68] Cf. STEPHEN NEILL, *Christian Faith and Other Faiths,* p. 82, n. 15.

[69] HVL, p. 37.

The Biblical Context

The cited passage [70] is from the parable of the Good Shep-hed [71]. The shepherd and the sheep is a well known Biblical figure [77]. The leader of the people is the shepherd and the people are the sheep. Here Jesus says that He is the good shepherd (vv. 11, 14), because He gives salvation to His sheep (Jo. 10, 28) and because He is the model or noble shepherd who is willing to die for the sheep (Jo. 10, 15) [73]. There is a close relationship between the good shepherd and his sheep (vv. 3b-5). He knows his sheep intimately and they him. "To know' in this precise context (v. 14) means "knowledge of love which provokes obedience and following which is to be expressed in communication of life" [74].

The sheep follow the good shepherd and he leads them out to pasture. In the evangelical tradition 'to follow' is a technical term specifically used to signify the following of Christ by His disciples [75]. The good shepherd goes ahead, leading. By the figure of leading the sheep, Jesus is hinting at the constitution of a new community [76].

The Text

It is in this precise context that Jesus said, "And there are other sheep I have that are not of this fold". The phrase 'other

---

[70] Jo. 10, 16.

[71] Jo. 10, 1-18.

[72] Because of the Patriarchal civilization and pastoral life, the imagery of the shepherd was very telling to the Jews. Jahweh is said to be the Shepherd of the people (Cf. Pss. 23, 1-2; 78, 52-53), impious kings were wicked shepherds (I Kings, 22, 17; Jer. 10, 21; 23, 1-2). The crowds that thronged round Jesus to hear Him are compared to sheep without a shepherd (Cf. Mk 6, 34). The parable of the lost sheep is an attack on the pharisees who did not care for the out-casts (Cf. Lk 15, 3-7). For further use of this figure Cf. Ez. 34, 5-6; Num. 27, 16-17; Mic. 2, 12-13; Mt. 26, 31; Lk 12, 32; 15, 3-7.

[73] Cf. also Mk 14, 27; Jo. 21, 15-19.

[74] IGNATIUS DE LA POTTERIE, Exegesis quarti Evangelii, capita IX-X (typed notes), (Rome 1966) 136.

[75] Cf. Jo. 1, 37.38.41; 8, 12.

[76] Cf. IGNATIUS DE LA POTTERIE, Exegesis quarti Evangelii, capita IX-X, p. 103. The remote context also confirms the existence of a new community. One of the sheep, namely the man born blind and miraculously cured by Jesus was expelled from the old community, the Jewish Synagogue, by the false shepherds. But he was received by the good shepherd in the new community (Cf. Jo. 9, 1-41).

sheep' clearly shows that Jesus distinguishes different categories
of sheep.   But all belong to Him [77].

In what sense did Jesus say "other sheep I have"?   Maldo-
natus and Lagrange think that Jesus was speaking of the sheep
of the future by anticipation.   But modern exegetes think that
it is more correct to understand the whole sense in the present.
So the other sheep, that is, the gentiles, are also His own sheep
not only in the future but at the present, because they are given
by the Father to Him.   They are His possession by reason of
the will of the Father [78].   So the new 'flock' is positively consti-
tuted according to a mandate from the Father.

Jesus' Duty towards the 'Other Sheep'

The other sheep are not yet within the fold.   So Jesus has
a special duty towards them.   He says: "And these I have to
lead as well" [79].   The term "have to" ($\delta\epsilon\acute{\iota}$) is very significant.
In all four Gospels it expresses the necessity which follows from
the divine counsel for realizing salvation [80].   In the Synoptics it
is used to show the divine necessity of the Passion and Resurrection.   In Jo. 3, 14 and Jo. 12, 34 it indicates the necessity of the
exaltation of Christ.   In Jo. 9, 4 it is used to indicate the necessity to do the work of Him who has sent Jesus. Thus the "have
to" indicates clearly the aspect of a divine mission to be fulfilled,
namely to lead the other sheep, the Gentiles to the flock of Christ [81].
But this leading will be realized only in the future, by the exaltation of Jesus [82]. Jesus clearly affirms: "they too will listen to
my voice" [83].   "Listen to my voice" is parallel to "follow me"
and expresses the same meaning — full obedience and perfect doc-
ility [84].   When this is fulfilled "there will be only one flock and

---

[77] 'his own' in v. 3 and 'I have' in v. 16 have the same meaning.

[78] Cf. IGNATIUS DE LA POTTERIE, Exegesis quarti Evangelii, capita
IX-X, p. 140.

[79] Cf. Jo. 10, 16.

[80] Cf. E. FASCHER, Theologische Betrachtungen zu $\delta\epsilon\acute{\iota}$, in "Theologische Literaturzeitung" 21 (1954) 222-254; GRUNDMANN, in ThWN,
II, 21, 25.

[81] Cf. IGNATIUS DE LA POTTERIE, Exegesis quarti Evangelii, capita
IX-X, p. 141. All commentators agree that by saying "other sheep"
Christ meant the Gentiles.

[82] Cf. Jo. 12, 32.

[83] Cf. Jo. 10, 16.

[84] In this sense St Peter has also used this term (Cf. I Pet. 2, 25).

one shepherd [85]. The fundamental principle of unity and cohesion in this flock is unity with the shepherd [86]. Commentators see here the unity of Jews and Gentiles in the Church as the only meaningful interpretation. " Church is here as a community of believers, who live under one pastor in communion with him and who are led by him " [87].

Therefore the text in its original context shows that Christ was instituting a new community which was meant to substitute the old Judaic community. The man born blind who was expelled from the ancient community is received by Christ into the new community. This event confirms our interpretation [88]. Both together make one community under one head. The constitution of the new community is realized in two stages; the faithful are led into this new community. This is what we understand when we read the text fully in its context.

Radhakrishnan deserves our praise for singling out one of the most important clauses in the Gospels which deals with the non-Christian peoples of the world. The religious insight which he has shown in pointing out that in spite of the diversity of beliefs every non-Christian regardless of his religion is a possession of Christ is to be appreciated.

But it is unfortunate that he has limited himself to a single clause, picked it out of its context and left out the words of Christ which did not please him. It is true that every human being regardless of his creed and culture belongs to Christ — and it is a great fact. But it is not true that Jesus did not wish that these others also follow Him, believing in His words and join the community which He has instituted. The words that immediately follow the clause which Radhakrishnan quoted argue conclusively just the opposite to what he has argued from the words of Jesus. Jesus does not leave the " other sheep " to live in the same way they lived hitherto. He has to lead them also to the new community. Jesus who said " other sheep I have which are not of this fold ", has also said and in the same breath, " and these I have to lead as well. They too will listen to my voice, and there will be only

---

[85] The Vulgate has 'one fold'. But it is more correct to say 'one flock' (Cf. RAYMOND E. BROWN, *The Anchor Bible. The Gospel according to John, I-XII* (New York 1966) 387.

[86] Cf. Jo. 17, 21.23.

[87] Cf. IGNATIUS DE LA POTTERIE, *Exegesis quarti Evangelii, capita IX-X*, p. 145.

[88] Jo. 9, 1-41.

one flock and one shepherd " [89]. A little later Jesus makes it absolutely clear that those who are not listening and following Him are not His sheep [90].

Therefore our study of the words of Jesus in their original context compels us to conclude that Radhakrishnan is not faithful to the original sense of the words of Jesus. To our surprise we find that the evident missionary intention of Jesus is so much distorted that Jesus is shown as anti-missionary. We do not presume that it was intentional or conscious on the part of Radhakrishnan. If it is unscientific to read our own ideas into ancient authors, it is unfortunate to cite Biblical texts in a way as to express a sense out of harmony with the truth of the Bible and the spirit of its author [91].

vi) *Use of Double Standard*

We have seen that Radhakrishnan has a basic interest in defending a re-interpreted and idealized Hinduism and a preoccupation to criticize Christianity wherever possible. These were necessary to exalt the experiential religion which he believes is the future religion of the world. But in doing so at times he has gone to the extreme of being inconsistent on some minor points. This, we agree, cannot be considered as a serious defect, because he has never altered his general principles and fundamental convictions. We shall point out just a few.

1) Radhakrishnan appears as a prophet of tolerance. Everywhere he preaches the necessity of tolerance and condemns every form of intolerance. Yet scarcely anywhere in his writings does one find a tolerant attitude towards Christianity. He calls belief in the most holy Trinity — one of the most sacred beliefs of Christianity — a " jugglery of words " [92]. " His description of Christian Faith ", observes P. Fallon, " amounts to a caricature, and his presentation of the history of Christian Religion, based as it

---

[89] Jo. 10, 16.

[90] Jo. 10, 26-27. Jo. 11, 52 offers further confirmation for Jesus' intention to convert the ' other sheep' to His flock (Cf. RAYMOND E. BROWN, *In Gospel according to John I-XII*, p. 442.

[91] Radhakrishnan has claimed support from the Old and the New Testaments for his basic principle which says that the self of man is identical with the Absolute. We will examine later a representative passage of this kind.

[92] ERWTh, p. 343.

is on the works of Gibbon, Lecky, Couchoud, Loisy and other determined enemies of the Christian Church, is nothing but a bitter and unfair indictment " [93]. Even though he tells us that " the truly religious never worry about other people's beliefs " [94], a good deal of his writings deal with what others believe. He even admits that he is ill at ease because still many believe in dogmas [95] and accuses the adherents of organized religions of " intellectual dishonesty " [96]. " In fact ", says Fallon, " his very tolerance is passionately intolerant of all dogmas and creeds, of all religious institutions and also of all metaphysical systems that lay claim to any absolute intellectual truth " [97].

2) Radhakrishnan's views on missionary activity and conversion from one religion to another religion are also not very consistent. He accuses the Christian missionary activity of destroying other religions, and of hardheartedness. He attributes Christian missionary enthusiasm to the " desire of world dominion " [98]. But when he saw that Hinduism and Buddhism had also engaged in similar activities he praises them [99]. Hindu missionary activity is described as ' religious reform ', 'growth' and ' positive fellowship ' [100]. Again, arguing against religious conversions, he says that " a convert to a new religion feels an utter stranger to himself. He feels like an illegitimate child with no heritage, no link with the men who preceded him " [101].

Still in order to induce all the adherents of historical religions to leave their religions and enter a religion of the spirit which he favours, he says, " It is said that to be born in a Church is good but one should not die in it. The easy course for men is to follow established usage, conform to general forms of human existence " [102].

---

[93] P. FALLON, *Ramakrishna, Vivekananda and Radhakrishnan,* in *Religious Hinduism: A Presentation and Appraisal,* 2nd ed., (Allahabad 1964) 290.

[94] HVL, p. 37.

[95] Cf. RCW, p. 34.

[96] RF, p. 29.

[97] P. FALLON, *Ramakrishna, Vivekananda and Radhakrishnan,* in *Religious Hinduism,* p. 290.

[98] Cf. ERWTh, p. 10.

[99] Cf. HVL, p. 90; ERWTh, p. 335 f; OSW, October 1952 - February 1959, p. 326.

[100] Cf. ERWTh, p. 335.

[101] Ibid., p. 329.

[102] RF, p. 191.

3) Sometimes Radhakrishnan picks out isolated examples of bad Christians like Hitler and Mussolini, who did not live their religion well, and condemns Christianity for having failed, to make her followers really religious [103], although millions and millions of other Christians live intensely religious lives.

Regarding Hinduism his attitude is different. He does not condemn Hinduism, because of a handful of bad Hindus. Not only does he not condemn Hinduism but he praises it, because of finding some saints in it or because thousands of years ago there was no child marriage in it and caste was not determined by birth. All this, despite the fact that for hundreds of years Hinduism practised widow-burning, and child marriage and the caste system were, in fact, determined by birth. Thus to take the exceptions for a general rule is illogical.

4) We shall refer to one more example of inconsistency. When a certain bishop of London excused killing of enemies " not for the sake of killing, but to save the world ", Radhakrishnan called him irreligious [104]. He also found fault with the Pope who blessed General Franco and Mussolini [105]. But when he saw that Krishna, who according to the Hindus is the incarnation of God, did the same thing, he says, " When Krishna advises Arjuna to fight, it does not follow that he is supporting the validity of warfare. War happens to be the occasion which the teacher uses to indicate the spirit in which all work including warfare will have to be performed " [106]. So he admits a spirit of action in which war is justified. We do not readily understand why this principle is not applied to the said bishop and to the Pope.

2) A CRITIQUE OF RADHAKRISHNAN'S
BASIC PRINCIPLES ON RELIGION

i) *Difficulties in the Advaitist Position.*

1) One of the most difficult problems faced by all forms of monism is to give a universally acceptable explanation of the relation of the One and the many. Śaṅkara applying his rigid logic concluded that only the One exists, and the many are illusions.

---

[103] Cf. ERWTh, p. 60. Cf. also IVL, p. 34, n. 2.
[104] ERWTh, p. 46. Cf. also Ibid., p. 46, n. 1.
[105] Cf. RF, pp. 27-28, n. 17; ERWTh, p. 290.
[106] BG, p. 68.

Rāmānuja represents the reaction to this extreme monistic theory. He argues that God is real. But the souls are also real and are related to God as attribute to a substance or as body to the soul. For him the pluralistic universe is real in precisely the same sense as God is real [107].

As a monist Radhakrishnan also confronts the same problem. But his monism is not as unyielding as that of Śankara. Critics like P. T. Raju and R. C. Zaehner think that he is taking a middle course between Śankara and Rāmānuja [108]. With Śankara Radhakrishnan holds that only Brahman is absolutely real and with Rāmānuja that the souls and the universe are not mere illusions [109]. He believes that God is not a mere appearance as in Śankara but is the very Absolute looked at from the " cosmic end " [110]. This explanation also does not show us clearly the first beginnnig and the ultimate meaning of multiplicity. God and many do not get any ultimate significance. So Radhakrishnan's view does not give us a reasonable explanation of the fact of multiplicity. P. T. Raju tries to solve the problem by saying that Radhakrishnan meant the distinction between the Absolute and God to be of the same kind as that between gold and a golden ring [111]. Raju's explanation has, of course, considerable weight. Still the problem remains. For then the world and God do not differ from the Absolute in any real way. And if they do, the origin of their difference is unexplained. Radhakrishnan himself is aware of this unsolved problem. Once he attempted to solve it by saying " when the element of negation is introduced into the Absolute, its inwardness is unfolded in the process of becoming. The original unity becomes pregnant with the whole course of the world " [112]. But it still can be asked, who did introduce the element of negation into the Absolute and why? His final answer was that it was " māyā, or a mystery which we have to accept reverently " [113]. Such an answer is obviously no answer at all. It can be taken

---

[107] Cf. Ind. Ph., II, 682 ff.

[108] Cf. P. T. RAJU, *Idealistic Thought of India* (London 1953) 336; R. C. ZAEHNER, "Forward" to *Radhakrishnan and Integral Experience* (London 1966) p. v.; J. G. ARAPURA, *Radhakrishnan and Integral Experience* (London 1966) 185.

[109] Cf. BG, p. 214.

[110] Cf. BG, p. 38 f; IVL, p. 273.

[111] P. T. RAJU, *Idealistic Thought of India*, p. 348.

[112] BG, p. 39.

[113] IVL, p. 272. Cf. also ERWTh, p. 90; Ind. Ph., I, 184; BG, p. 38; NARAVANE, *Modern Indian Thought* (Bombay 1964) 249.

only as an admission of the insolubility of the problem. M. N.
Roy has stated the fact plainly : " No orthodox Hindu speculative
thinker has been able to prove how the diversities of nature could
arise from a common cause. The sheer impossibility of this task
ultimately draws Indian speculation to the monumental absurdity
of the Maya vada " [114].

Radhakrishnan's disapproval of Śaṅkara's extreme monism
and his firm stand for a relative reality of the world are to be
commended. But it is strange that to explain the nature and the
origin of relative reality Radhakrishnan has gone back to Śaṅkara
and the Hindu Scriptures [115], though he himself had blamed the
Western thinkers for being under the ' reign of religion '. His
explanation of the relative reality shows that he is not really defending the reality of the world but of the Brahman underlying
it. The world is ultimately unreal. Thus in spite of his strenuous
attempts, he fails to escape from the defects of Śaṅkara's Advaita
theory. He falls back on absolute monism and believes that the
world and God will be ultimately dissolved in the Absolute [116].
Thus Radhakrishnan fails to give a reasonable explanation of the
relation between the Absolute and God as also between the Absolute and the world.

2) According to Radhakrishnan the Supreme Reality is inac-
cessible to the human intellect. All our knowledge regarding the
Supreme Reality is relative. At the same time he maintains that
the mystic has an absolute and self-evident knowledge of the
identity of his self with the Supreme Reality. Hendrik Kraemer
and J. G. Arapura see an incompatibility between these two stands.
Kraemer says, " it is impossible to see (and even against Indian
epistemological principles) why the " highest " symbol, reached by
the great seers, is the adequate vision of the Truth. Is it suddenly
beyond imperfection and relativity because the " highest " in the
scale of possible symbols is the absolute, on the undemonstrable
and questionable assumption that the more abstract the human formulations about ultimate reality, about God, the more adequate
they are " [117]? Relative knowledge and absolute knowledge are

---

[114] PhSR, p. 558.

[115] Cf. HORST BÜRKLE, *Dialog mit dem Osten: Radhakrishnans neuhinduistische Botschaft im Lichte christlichen Weltanschauung* (Stuttgart
1965) 85.

[116] Cf. PhRT, p. 35; Cf. IVL, p. 269; MST, p. 33.

[117] HENDRIK KRAEMER, *Religion and the Christian Faith* (London
1961) 109.

absolutely different from each other. Therefore the assertion that the relative crossed from its relative state to an absolute state is inadmissible [118]. Radhakrishnan explains the difficulty by saying that the absolute knowledge of Reality is reached by the seers and can be reached by any one by a mystical discipline [119]. But if the absolute knowledge is reached by a special discipline, is it not then the result of a special technique? How can we assert that a technique can lead us from relative knowledge to self-evident and absolute knowledge of Reality? Besides, if we consider the discipline itself which Radhakrishnan proposes, it makes such vast phenomenological changes in us which is " akin to what takes place in brain washing" that " the sense of reality that we now entertain and what constitute knowledge for us now may have no connection with the corresponding factors that will be present in the changed condition. So it would be senseless to regard the resultant experience as constituting knowledge of reality" [120].

Therefore to assert that what the mystic has experienced is the Absolute Reality as such is not an act of knowledge but an act of faith. This act of faith is very fundamental to Radhakrishnan's system. But only God can demand an act of faith, or else it will open a possibility to agnosticism of the mind, persisting in denying such an identity [121].

3) Radhakrishnan proposes the doctrine of the Divine in man, that is, the identity of the Absolute with man's real self, as the basis of religion, in order to save the world from materialism. But it is very doubtful whether this doctrine will serve the purpose. For, if man's real self were really divine, in the fullest sense of the word, then whatever is really human is necessarily divine. Materialism will be necessarily as divine as Radhakrishnan's experiential religion. For, materialism, according to the materialists comes from one's inborn tendencies and inner impulses. Radhakrishnan was logically forced to explain Marx's denial of God as a religious act [122]. He should also accept Marxian materialism as a good form of religion. Logically enough, he had to see a saint in the Nietzchean superman [123]. In fine, when we teach the con-

---

[118] Cf. J. G. ARAPURA, *Radhakrishnan and Integral Experience*, (London 1966) 192.

[119] *The Brahma Sūtra*, p. 103.

[120] J. G. ARAPURA, *Radhakrishnan and Integral Experience*, p. 194.

[121] Cf. Ibid., p. 198.

[122] Cf. OSW, October 1952 - February 1959, p. 67.

[123] Cf. BG, p. 129. Nietzche is one of the most decided atheists of

15

substantiality of man and God, we are sanctifying mere materialism. Commenting on Radhakrishnan's religious system Hendrik Kraemer observes: " Religiously speaking, it (Radhakrishnan's theory of the Divine in man) amounts to obliterating ' God ' and putting man in his place. *Ātman* swallows *Brahman*. This radical anthropocentrism bereaves ' God ' of all real significance, so that not only from the angle of logical thinking, but also from that of ... ' religious cleanliness ', atheism must be considered the most appropriate position " [124].

4) The doctrine of identity of man's self with God is panentheistic and contradicts God's simplicity and immutability.

ii) *Radhakrishnan's Arguments for the Identity of Man's Self and the Absolute.*

Let us examine the most fundamental and oft repeated arguments of Radhakrishnan in favour of his theory of the identity of man's real self with the Absolute.

a) *Argument from the Testimony of the Seers*

Radhakrishnan's strongest argument for the identity of man's self with the Supreme Reality is from the testimony of the seers. Certainly we cannot deny the fact of mystical experience in non-Christian religions. The second Vatican Council teaches that in Hinduism men contemplate the divine mystery and that there is in it " deep meditation, or a loving, trusting flight toward God " [125]. Spiritual inspiration and mystical experience are granted by God to non-Christians also for their own and their community's spiritual uplift. The Christian position can be summed up as follows:

"... in the present historical order of salvation we cannot consider non-Christian religions as purely natural or manmade. Every non-Christian people have been called to a supernatural end ... The incarnational presence of Christ in

---

all times, of whom G. K. Chesterton said that he lived only to blaspheme. His superman is the very opposite of a spiritual man, an utterly inhuman power-monger who would pass ' columns of fire ' over humanity to attain his end. There are many critics of Nietzche who see the first born of his superman in Hitler.

[124] HENDRIK KRAEMER, *Religion and Christian Faith* (London 1961) 111.

[125] *Declaration on the Relationship of the Church to Non-Christian Religions,* art. 2.

the heart of humanity has already consecrated the whole world; what is wanting is an individual's, a nation's, a culture's wilful acceptance of and submission to the sovereignty of Christ. In the course of history non-Christian people with God's help have developed their own religion and have been unawares tending to Christ ... Great many mystics of Hinduism are no doubt God-filled souls ... Even doctrinally there have been valuable insights into religious truths in those religions. Their deeply spiritual experience and religious truth cannot be explained except on the supposition that God has helped them in a special way " [126].

But while we admit the fact of spiritual experience, we differ from Radhakrishnan regarding the nature of the thing experienced and of the experience itself on the following grounds.

1) Radhakrishnan's most basic claim is that in mystical experience the seer realizes immediately the simple identity of his self with the Absolute. The way which Radhakrishnan proposes to attain this mystical experience is the same old way of the Hindu seer. It is a way of negation that by-passes all interrelations of things. Because of this special technique, the seer of Hinduism is not and cannot be aware of the limitation of the absolute he is experiencing. The absolute experienced is in reality the spiritual act of existing (*esse*) of the self. The seer thinks that by his experience he has reached the ontological Absolute itself [127] while in fact he realized the spiritual, timeless and spaceless essence of the self [128]. Therefore the assertion that the reality thus reached is the Absolute Brahman is unwarranted. For, from the negative, psychological unawareness of limitation is made a transition to a positive, ontological exclusion of the limitation in the absolute experienced.

2) The experience of the seer can be explained by a natural, 'finite absolute'. The substantial act of existence of one's own soul, though limited and finite in itself, can be called a true ab-

---

[126] M. DHAVAMONY, *Christian Experience and Hindu Spirituality,* in " Gregorianum." 48 (1967) 782.

[127] L. GARDET, *Recherches sur la mystique naturelle*: *Revue thomiste* XLVIII, 94.

[128] " Mystical theory is often in danger of explaining such experience in terms of monism, pantheism or 'theopanism', for the mystic experiences the influence from the Absolute as that which is most inward in his soul, while losing consciousness of time and external things " (Cf. KARL RAHNER and HERBERT VORGRIMLER, *Theological Dictionary,* ed. by Cornelius Ernst, trans. by Richard Strachen, New York 1968, p. 302).

solute, because of its likeness to the Supreme Absolute. It is
indisputable that the experience which Radhakrishnan speaks of
is primarily the intuition of one's own self — penetration of the
soul into its own ground and depth [129]. But human intuition even
at its highest, can only be of the creaturely absolute, not of the
Supreme Absolute. God so transcends the human powers that for
direct experience of God, He must choose us, elevate our faculties
and communicate Himself to us. " One of the things we need
to stress most about God is that He is transcendent in a way
that precedes any direct contact with God " [130].

3) Radhakrishnan admits that the self does not know what
it is when it reaches the mystic identification. It is rather lost in
contemplation and enjoyment [131]. The knowledge that it was a
moment of realization of the simple identity of the self and the
Absolute is only a conclusion drawn from later logical reflection.
Against the infallibility of the Christian Scriptures and dogmas
Radhakrishnan argues that they have only relative value and therefore are fallible. According to him, whatever be the nature of
direct experience, the moment it is conceptually expressed, there
is duality which means that there is an element of error in it.
Therefore the expressed form of spiritual experience is not absolutely valid. We do not understand how he can maintain then
the absolute validity of the reports of the Hindu mystics about
the realization of the identity with the Absolute; how he can
dogmatize the doctrine of the oneness of man and God. Is it
not more logical on the part of Radhakrishnan himself to regard
such reports as symbolical, as a way of expression to show the
inexpressibly intimate nature of the spiritual experience? If no
knowledge is entirely true [132], how can he believe the reports of
the mystics as entirely true? We cannot take the assertion of
seers about their experience of perfect identity with the Absolute
as infallibily true, though the seers themselves may be absolutely
sincere. These reports are also conceptual expressions, and, of
necessity, contain an element of untruth.

4) We would further assert that with Radhakrishnan the
Ātman-Brahman equation seems to be neither his own experience
nor a conclusion from his theological speculations, but a heritage
from the Upanishadic past, a basic assumption on the authority

---

[129] Cf. Pr. Ups, p. 104.
[130] Cf. H. D. LEWIS, *Philosophy of Religion* (London 1965) 204.
[131] Cf. Ind. Ph., I, 177.
[132] Ibid., p. 175.

of the monistic Upanishads. We would state these assertions on the following grounds : a) Radhakrishnan himself has never claimed to have experienced the simple identity with the Absolute. b) We know that this is the monistic tradition of Hinduism [133]. c) His commentary on the Upanishadic dictum *tat tvam asi* confirms our claim : " *tat tvam asi* : that art thou. This famous text emphasises the divine nature of the human soul " [134]. He is simply accepting the authority of the Upanishad. d) He has never shown it as a logical conclusion. e) He aprioristically declares that the endeavour of speculation is to discover this unity. " The ideal of intellect is to discover the unity which comprehends both subject and object " [135]. Therefore that there is such a unity is an assumption, not a conclusion.

b) *A Search into the Truth about the Reports of the Identity of Man's Self with the Absolute*

We cannot question the sincerity of the seers who report that they have realized their identity with the Absolute. It is certain that they had experiences of a remarkable kind. If their description of their experience of identity with the Supreme is only a form of expression designed to show the intimate character of their experience, we can understand it. But if they mean ontological oneness with the Absolute, we find it aprioristic. After a long critical study on the mystics, H. D. Lewis says, " I would not agree that they have described them correctly when they claim to have known God directly, to have ' touched ' and ' tasted ' the Divine nature in this sense " [136]. In their enthusiasm and concern they have described their experience as unmediated contact with God. But if the distinction between man's self and God disappears, if he is dissolved into the Absolute — this could be true only on the monistic presupposition — the mystic is not saved, but just ceases to be, which is the worst for a personal being and therefore least desirable and incompatible with the idea of personal salvation [137].

---

[133] This is seen in the monistic tendencies of *Rig Veda* (Cf. *Rig Veda*, I, 164; VIII, 36; X, 31, 72.81.90.129) and of Upanishads (Cf. *Chāndogya Upanishad*, VI, 8, 7; VI, 9 ff).

[134] Pr. Ups, p. 458.

[135] Ind. Ph., I, 173.

[136] H. D. Lewis, *Philosophy of Religion* (London 1965) 205.

[137] Cf. Horst Bürkle, *Dialog mit dem Osten, Radhakrishnans neuhinduistische Botschaft im Lichte christlichen Weltanschauung*, p. 91.

Bede Griffiths, a student of Hindu mysticism, has a very reasonable explanation of the reports of Hindu mystics about the realization of their identity with the Brahman. He thinks that some mystics, by special privilege of God, participate in God's own knowledge. God knows the world in His knowledge of Himself. But God's Being is identical with His Knowledge of Himself. Therefore the mystic participating in the knowledge of God sees God and himself in a simple mode of knowledge, 'without duality'. Here is his argument:

> "If therefore the soul by grace should participate in God's own mode of knowledge, it would know all things, itself included, in this simple mode of knowledge; 'without duality'... Yet it remains true, that though 'identified' with God by knowledge the soul yet remains distinct by nature. Though the mode of knowledge is different and distinctions, *as we conceive* them, cease to exist, yet the distinctions remain in reality. Man and the world are not lost in God, nor are the persons absorbed in the unity of the Godhead. It is these distinctions which Christian orthodoxy is concerned to maintain, since they allow (room) for relationship both between man and man in the Mystical body of Christ, and between man and God"[138].

This, indeed, is an ingenious explanation of the reports of the mystics. There is non-duality in knowledge and experience and yet duality in reality. The sincerity of the mystics and the real distinction between man and God are both upheld.

But this explanation runs into some dificulties. If ever the mystic is given a special privilege to look at God, himself and the world through God's eye, then either he knows things as they really are, with their distinctions or he knows them as identified with God. In the first case, the mystic must be aware of his reality as distinct from God. In the second case we will have to admit that God also does not see the distinctions of things, which is not admissible. Moreover such a view makes it impossible for the mystic to find out his distinctness from God.

Our View

When we consider the reports of the Hindu mystics about their experience of simple identity with the Supreme Absolute,

---

[138] BEDE GRIFFITHS, *Experience of God—Hindu and Christian*, in "The Clergy Monthly Supplement" VI (1962-1963) 141.

we must bear in mind two important things: 1) the special technique adopted by these mystics to attain the experience of the Absolute; and 2) the psychological background of the Hindu mystics.

The discipline which Radhakrishnan asks us to undergo to attain to realization is taken from the Hindu yoga. It has got eight degrees. The first five are preparatory. The last three degrees constitute the state of reintegration of the self. They are, 1) concentration (*dhāranā*) which is the application of the mind's attention to a particular thing or idea without wandering away from it; 2) meditation (*dhyāna*), the continued fixing of the mind to the particular thing or idea; and 3) contemplation (*samādhi*), an ecstatic state in which there are pure objectless consciousness and integration of the self. The mystic in this stage feels that the distinction between object and subject has totally disappeared. The object of attention of the Hindu mystic is his own self. When all the experiences of senses and reason are transcended, and there is perfect detachment from everything, the soul penetrates into itself, and experiences itself in its own deepest substantial being — in its own act of existing (*esse*). The human soul in its essence is an image of God. Further, since the actual historical order is not the natural, but the supernatural, we cannot deny the presence of supernatural grace in these "God-filled" souls. Thus the experience of the soul of itself is something ineffable and divine. But the mystic has sought only the existential depths of his own self.

In this context we have to take into account the psychological background of the Hindu mystic. The Hindu monistic tradition is that man's real self is one with the Brahman and all his religious endeavours must be directed to realize that identity which is his salvation [139]. It is with this life-long conviction that the Hindu monistic mystic undergoes hard discipline with the sole intention of realizing his identity with the Brahman. Therefore, it is quite natural for him to think that he is experiencing his identity with the Brahman when he experiences something transcending space and time, spiritual, eternal and changeless which in reality is his own self in its own depths. Radhakrishnan has argued that the mystical experience is conceived according to our

---

[139] Cf. *Brhad-āranyaka Upanishad,* I, 4, 10; *Chāndogya Upanishad,* VI, 8,7; VI, 9 ff. The first monistic tendencies are seen in the Vedas (Cf. *Rig Veda,* VIII, 36; X, 129).

psychological background [140]. The divine image of the mystic's soul, though faint and analogical is incomparable with anything in the world around him and immeasurably higher than them. In the experience itself, however, he does not know what it is [141]. When the mystic later reflects on what happened, he can merely argue that he has sought only the depths of his own soul, but has experienced something ineffable, something divine — *aham brahmasmi* [142], *tat tvam asi* [143], he concludes.

It may be asked, what about the first seers who declared for the first time the identity of self with Brahman? They were not influenced by any tradition.

Those first seers were searching for the Real which they believed to be underlying all that existed around them. As they were not satisfied with the things around, they searched for it in themselves. There they found something indescribable, which was immeasurably superior to anything they had seen before. Naturally they believed and declared that they had found God in their own self. This seems to us the only reasonable interpretation of the words of the Upanishadic seer: "*Brahman*, indeed, was this in the beginning. It knew itself only as 'I am Brahman', therefore it became all. Who ever among the Gods became awakened to this, he, indeed, became that. It is the same in the case of seers, same in the case of men" [144]. This explanation is in the line of Radhakrishnan's own explanation of the reports of the mystics [145]. Therefore it must be acceptable to him.

Further, it is important to note that the seers of other religions do not claim realization of their identity with the Supreme Reality. For example, we do not find such a claim in Judaism, even though all her prophets enjoyed spiritual experience. They were also seers in the fullest sense of the word. They usually declare that the God they have come to know is a God who hides Himself. They clearly say that they were called by God and appointed by Him as His messengers and that their doctrine is

---

[140] Cf. HVL, pp. 19-20. A great mystic, St Teresa of Avila, writes: "I know by experience that there are souls which ... so absorbed in their own idea as to feel *certain* they see whatever their fancy imagines" (*Castle*, VI M., ch. IX).

[141] Cf. Ind. Ph., I, 177.

[142] Cf. *Brhd-āranyaka Up.*, I, 4, 10.

[143] *Chāndogia Up.*, VI, 8, 7.

[144] *Brhad-āranyaka Up.*, I, 4, 10.

[145] Cf. HVL, pp. 19-20.

not their own but received from God who revealed it to them. St Peter puts it succinctly: " No prophecy ever came from man's initiative. When man spoke for God it was the Holy Spirit that moved them " [146].

c) *Argument from the Bible* [147]

As we have said earlier, Radhakrishnan quotes a number of passages from the Bible to prove his thesis of the Brahman-Ātman equation. He argues thus :

> " The consubstantiality of the spirit in man and God is the conviction fundamental to all wisdom ... The great text of the Upanishad affirms it — Tat tvam asi (That art thou) ... the Biblical text, ' So God created man in his own image; in the image of God created he him ' [148], asserts that in the soul of man is contained the true revelation of God ... ' I and my Father are one ', ' All that the Father hath are mine ', is the way in which Jesus expressed the same profound truth. It is not a peculiar relation between any one chosen individual and God but an ultimate one binding every self to God ... Recognizing us all as children of God and made in his image, Jesus shows us by his own example that the difference between God and man is only one of degree ... The phrase in I Peter of a birth ' of the incorruptible seed by the word of God ' [149] refers to the divine in man " [150].

Elsewhere he argues :

> " When Christ says ' I and my Father are One ', he makes out an identification between the individual human soul and the Supreme Reality " [151].

The texts from the Old and the New Testaments flow from Radhakrishnan with an ease that is rarely seen in a non-Christian. Still, in the wake of our former study of some of the Biblical texts

---

[146] II Peter, 1, 21. Cf. also Amos, 7, 15; Is. 6, 1-9; Jer. 1, 7; Ez, 22, 2. 5; Zach. 2, 9. Cf. also THOMAS PAUL, *Pravachakanmar Kanda Kristu* (A Study on Messianic Prophecies), (Alwaye 1964) 9 ff.

[147] This is another example of misquotation in Radhakrishnan. Confer our foot-note 91 on page 282.

[148] Gn, 1, 27.

[149] I Peter, 1, 23. Cf. also Col., 1, 15. 18.

[150] IVL, pp. 81-82.

[151] OSW, May 1962 - May 1964, p. 159.

used by Radhakrishnan, we hesitate to accept his argument. A critical study of the texts is necessary.

1) *The Text from the Old Testament*

In the creation account [152] man is said to be created after the image of God Himself [153]. Sacred Scripture does not tell precisely in what this likeness consists. Therefore we have to interpret it and the only reasonable way to understand it is to interpret it in harmony with the general teachings of the Bible.

Modern Biblical scholars like Eichrodt and John L. McKenzie place the " likeness in the spiritual qualities of man, his capacity of self consciousness and self determination — in a word his personality " [154]. But since in the Old Testament Yahweh is especially distinguished from other gods as " the living God ", it would be more proper to see the resemblance of man to God in His "living" quality [155]. But it is difficult to determine what exactly this likeness is.

One of the best commentaries on this passage comes from Gerhard von Rad. He asks us to read the passage in the light of the fundamental doctrines of the Bible. He says:

> " The distinctive meaning of the divine likeness in the Old Testament can be understood only when we see it in strict connection with a faith which is basically orientated by the sense of the greatest possible distance from God. The central point in Old Testament anthropology is that man is dust and ashes before God and that he cannot stand before His holiness. Thus the witness to man's divine likeness plays no predominant role in the O. T. It stands as it were on the margin of the whole complex " [156].

Another leading scholar, Jean Mouroux, observes:

> " Man, it is true, is made in God's image, and is his son, but even more profoundly he is a creature — dust and ashes ... All that we say or feel about our resemblance to God, our

---

[152] Gn. I.

[153] Ibid., 1, 27. St Paul often refers to this image of God in man (Cf. I Cor., 11, 7; Eph. 4, 24; Col., 3, 10).

[154] JOHN L. McKENZIE, *Dictionary of the Bible* (London-Dublin 1966) 385.

[155] Ibid.

[156] KITTEL, *Theological Dictionary of the New Testament II* (Michigan 1966) 390.

family likeness to him, our nearness to him needs to be
understood in the light of an infinite difference, an infinite
otherness, an infinite distance.   We cannot connect them
positively from within; we can only affirm their existence
in a context in which the absolute distance between them
will never be done away with " [157].

It is important to note that man's divine likeness is revealed in
the context of the creation account.   God has created the world,
and everything within it, from absolute nothingness by an act of
His will.   Such a doctrine without doubt places an infinite distance
between the creator and the creature.   That is why Biblical scholars
who comment on the divine image in man, emphatically separate
man from God and show him as dust and ashes before God.

We do not defend an utterly absolute separation of God from
man.   Neither can we stress the Biblical doctrine of the divine
image in man, so as to make it a consubstantiality between God
and man — a *tat tvam asi.*   To see the doctrine of identity between God and man in this passage is to ignore the context of
creation in which the passage of likeness is set.   Such an idea
was unthinkable for the Jews.   When Jesus declared, " The Father
and I are one " [158], " the Jews fetched stones to stone him " [159] for
his ' blasphemy '.   " You are only a man and you claim to be
God " [160], said the Jews.   Therefore we have to conclude that the
likeness lies somewhere in between these two extremes of identity
and total separation.

This interpretation is only confirmed when we remember that
in Old Testament Yahweh is always considered as the revealing
God.   On the one hand, man by his effort alone, however hard
it be, can never attain to divine revelation; on the other hand,
man is never so absolutely separated from Yahweh as to be absolutely unable to receive the divine revelation from Yahweh.

2) *Texts from the Gospels*

There are two important questions regarding Jesus: 1) Is
he the promised Messiah? and 2) is he the son of God?   On the

---

[157] JEAN MOUROUX, *The Christian Experience,* trans. by George Lamp
(New York 1954) 17-18.

[158] Jo. 10, 30

[159] Jo. 10, 31.

[160] Jo. 10, 34.

feast of Dedication, Jesus was asked at Jerusalem: "If you are the Christ, tell us plainly"[161]. Jesus had already spoken of himself as the good shepherd, which in the Biblical tradition meant the true Messiah. Here he simply points to his works, the miracles, and tells the people that they speak for themselves[162]. Then, regarding his relationship with God the Father, he says, "The Father and I are one"[163] — an affirmative answer to the second question though not in the traditional terminology.

Radhakrishnan claims that this declaration of Jesus is only just another expression of the famous Upanishadic saying *tat tvam asi* and that Jesus' relation to God is the same as that of every self to God[164].

Did Christ actually mean this? All the Biblical evidence seems to affirm the contrary. In all the four Gospels and in the Epistles the uniqueness of Jesus' relation to God is emphatically affirmed. St John begins by saying that the "Word was God"[165]. St John the Baptist calls Jesus "the Chosen One of God"[166]. Jesus distinguishes himself from his hearers: "You are from below; I am from above"[167]. He comes from God as God's special envoy to men[168]. His relationship to God is so intimate and so transcendental to our reason that we need a special revelation from the Father to understand it[169]. The distinction that Jesus makes between 'my Father' and 'your Father'[170] referring to God in relation to himself and to men, is clearly based on the different relationships of Jesus himself to God and of other men to God. All theologians agree that by this distinction Jesus appropriates to himself, in a unique and singular way, the full divine sonship[171].

Whenever Jesus associated himself with God, the Jews did

---

[161] Jo. 10, 25.

[162] Cf. Mt. 11, 2-6.

[163] J. 10, 30.

[164] In his Presidential Address to the Indian Nation on January 25, 1967 Radhakrishnan translated the dictum "*aham Brahmasmi*" into "I and my Father are one" (Cf. *India News* (London) January 28, 1967, p. 1).

[165] Jo. 1, 1.

[166] Jo. 1, 34.

[167] Jo. 8, 23.

[168] Cf. Jo. 8, 17. 28. 42.

[169] Cf. Mt. 11, 27; 16, 17. Cf. also Lk, 10, 21-22; Mt, 7, 21; 18, 35; Jo, 20, 17.

[170] Mk, 11, 25; Cf. also Mt, 5, 48 = Lk, 6, 36.

[171] Cf. EDUARDUS DHANIS, *De Testimonio Jesu circa seipsum*, 6th ed. (Rome 1968) 131.

actually sense a claim to uniqueness in his relation to God as distinct from theirs and were naturally provoked to anger [172]. When Jesus said " the Father and I are one " [173], he was hinting at a more comprehensive and profounder unity. The Jews did not miss the implication. They felt keenly the claim of Jesus to Godhead as their reaction to this utterance of Jesus shows [174].

Hence it is clear that Radhakrishnan's attempt to interpret the words of Jesus, " The Father and I are one " in the Upanishadic meaning of *tat tvam asi* fails completely and does not carry conviction.

3) *The Text from St Peter*

The argument that St Peter's teaching " of a birth " ' of the incorruptible seed by the word of God ' refers to the divine in man " is just another example of interpreting a Biblical passage in the Upanishadic meaning. A critical study of the text in its context makes it absolutely clear that St Peter never for a moment believed in the consubstantiality of the self of man and God. The term ' seed ' has a specific meaning in the Bible. Jesus himself explained it in the parable of the sower. The seed is the word of God [175]. " What is the word of God "? St Peter answers: " It is the Good News that has been brought to you " [176], that is, the Gospel. This word of God or incorruptible seed is certainly not considered an inner constitutional part of man. For, there is opposition between the mortal seed and the incorruptible. What by nature belongs to man comes from the mortal seed; what is eternal takes its origin not from himself but from the revelation of God which is Christ. The salvation of man through Christ is the theme of the Epistle. Christians are asked to put their trust in nothing but the grace that will be given them when Jesus Christ is revealed [177]. Salvation by our natural endowments alone is certainly not thought of in St Peter's Epistles. It comes only through Christ and in union with Him. For, as St John explains, re-

---

[172] Cf. Jo. 5, 17-18; 8, 58-59.

[173] Jo. 10, 30.

[174] Cf. Jo. 10, 33. Cf. also Jo. 8, 28. 29; 10, 38; 14, 9-10; 17, 11. 21.

[175] Mt, 13, 18 ff.

[176] I Peter, 1, 25. Cf. also I Cor. 4, 15; Eph. 1, 13; Col. 1, 5; I Thess. 2, 13; GEORGE ARTHUR BUTTRICK (general editor), *The Interpreter's Dictionary of the Bible*, IV, 26.

[177] Cf. I Peter, 1, 13.

generation means union with Christ.   "To all who received him,
who believed in his name, he gave power to become children of
God " [178] ; " He who believes in the Son has eternal life " [179]. Here
again Radhakrishnan's interpretation of the Biblical passage is
unacceptable.

Therefore, we see that the arguments of Radhakrishnan fail
to prove in any meaningful way his fundamental conviction that
the real self of man is identical with the Supreme Being.

iii) *A Positive Appraisal of the Doctrine of the Divine in Man*

We have found that Radhakrishnan's most basic doctrine on
religion, namely the oneness of man with the Absolute, is unacceptable.   But while we do not accept the doctrine of the Divine
in man, as Radhakrishnan has expressed it, we do not reject the
idea wholly and absolutely.   It is now up to us to point out in
what sense we can accept the doctrine of the divine in man.   This
is important because we are living in an ecumenical period of religious history, and therefore it should help to a more fruitful
dialogue with other religions.   But we shall discuss this point
here precisely because a discussion of how far Radhakrishnan's
doctrine of the divine in man can be received in Christian theology
will complement our evaluation of Radhakrishnan's concept of the
basis of religion.

a) *The Causal Presence of God*

Radhakrishnan, depending on the Vedic and the Upanishadic
doctrines concerning the beginning of the world [180] maintains that
somehow or other the world flows from the Absolute [181].   Such
a view, as we have seen, necessarily implies the consubstantiality
of the world and the self with the Supreme Reality, and involves
many difficulties.

Christian theology teaches creation out of nothing as the only
explanation which can at the same time save the simplicity and
immutability of God and the fact of the real existence of the

---

[178] Jo. 1, 12.

[179] Jo. 3, 36. Cf. also GEORGE ARTHUR BUTTRICK (general editor),
The Interpreter's Dictionary of the Bible, IV, 26.

[180] " All these creatures even though they have come forth from
Being, do not know that we have come forth from Being" (Cf. *Chāndogya Upanishad,* VI, 10, 2).

[181] Cf. BG, p. 39.

many. God created the world out of nothing, from no pre-existing subject-matter, by a simple act of the will. God created the world absolutely freely, out of His goodness [182]. When we say that creation was out of nothing, we are not denying efficient, exemplary or final causes. What we deny is that the world is made out of the divine substance or out of any other pre-existent being. Therefore the world is entirely dependent on God and must be preserved in existence by God every moment of its existence, that it may not fall back to nothingness [183]. So creatures cannot be consubstantial with the Creator; nor are they utterly unrelated. God's causal act and therefore His causal presence, reaches the deepest part of every atom in the world. " It is in Him that we live, move, and exist ", says St Paul [184]. The Psalmist declares that there can be no escape from the presence of God:

> " Where could I go to escape from your Spirit?
> Where could I flee from your presence?
> If I climb the heavens, you are there,
> there too, if I lie in Sheol " [185].

This causal presence of God is the first kind of divine presence which Christian theology discerns in everything. But it teaches a more intimate and supernatural presence of God in the human soul. This also we have to see in order to find how far Radhakrishnan's idea of the Divine in man can be accepted in Christian theology.

b) *The Supernatural Presence of God in the Human Soul by Divine Grace*

By nature man belongs to an order entirely other and infinitely lower than that of God's. Man's sins keep him at an infinite distance from God. But by an utterly free and mysterious decree of His wisdom and goodness, God willed to endow man with a participation in His own divine life [186]. For this it was

---

[182] This is the constant teaching of the Catholic Church (God created the world out of nothing, (Cf. D 19, D21, D29, D54, D86, D235, D343, D421 ,D428, D461, D706, D994, D1782 f, D1801, D1805). God created freely, (Cf. D374, D706), out of His goodness (Cf. D374, D607, D706, D1655, D1783, D1805, D1908, D2317).

[183] D1784.

[184] Acts, 17, 28.

[185] Ps. 139, 7-8. Cf. also Ibid., vv. 9-11.

[186] Cf. The Second Vatican Council, *Dogmatic Constitution on the Church,* Ch. I, art. 2.

necessary that man who offended God by his sin be reconciled to God and be redeemed. Out of His unfathomable wisdom and goodness, the second Person of the Blessed Trinity assumed human nature and became the unique mediator between man and God. Christ through His passion, death and resurrection has reconciled us to the Father. God in view of the merits of Christ, sanctifies us and elevates us to participate in His life by means of His grace [187]. This grace is described in Sacred Scripture as that by which we are born again to 'live eternal life in Jesus Christ' [188]. But the life of Christ is the life of God. So when we receive divine grace we become participants in the divine life. St Peter observes: "In making these gifts, he has given us the guarantee of something very great and wonderful to come: through them you will be able to share the divine nature and to escape corruption in a world that is sunk in vice" [189]. This new life begins with baptism [190]. Christ is the son of God. So when we participate in His life we also become sons of God, sons in the Son — Christ naturally and perfectly and we by participation and adoption. This makes us co-heirs with Christ, heirs of the divine good which is eternal life [191].

c) *The Divine Indwelling in the Human Soul*

Together with the created grace we receive in us God Himself who comes and dwells in us. "If anyone loves me, he will keep my word, and my Father will love him, and we shall come to him and make our home with him" [192]. St Paul writes: "The love of God has been poured into our hearts by the Holy Spirit which has been given us" [193]. "The Spirit of God has made His home in you" [194]. "He who raised Jesus from the dead will give life to your own mortal bodies through His Spirit living in you" [195].

The Divine Indwelling is the common doctrine of the Fathers of the Church, especially the Greek Fathers. St Basil observes that the supernatural life comes from God, through Jesus Christ

---

[187] Cf. Eph. 2-8.
[188] Cf. Col. 3, 4; II Cor. 5, 17; Rom. 6, 23; Tit. 3, 5.
[189] II Peter, 1, 4.
[190] Cf. Rom. 6, 3-4; Jo. 3, 5.
[191] Cf. Rom. 8, 15; Gal. 4, 5.
[192] Jo. 14, 23.
[193] Rom. 5, 5.
[194] Rom. 8, 9.
[195] Rom. 8, 11. Cf. also Ibid., 8, 16. 26; I Cor. 3, 16; 6, 19; II Cor. 6, 16; Eph. 1, 14.

in the Holy Spirit. In fact, it is God Himself who vivifies us, Christ gives us life and thus we become vivified by the Holy Spirit [196]. In other words, God abides in us and vivifies us. A similar doctrine is seen in St Cyril of Alexandria [197] and in St Augustine [198]. St Cyprian teaches that through baptism the Holy Spirit is received by us [199].

The Fathers generally explain the nature of the Divine Indwelling by the comparison of a seal set on wax. The Holy Spirit sets His 'image' on the soul and thus produces created grace [200]. In this way we become sharers in the divine nature.

The Second Vatican Council puts this teaching very succinctly. All believers have "access to the Father through Christ in the one Spirit [201]... Through Him the Father gives life to men who are dead from sin, still at last He receives in Christ even their mortal bodies [202]. The Spirit dwells in the Church and in the hearts of the faithful as in a temple [203]. In them He prays and bears witness to the fact that they are adopted sons " [204]. In this sense St Paul calls the Christians 'temple of God' [205].

Therefore we are far from denying the doctrine of the Divine in man. We are emphatically supporting the idea of the divine presence in the human soul. But we do differ from Radhakrishnan as to the nature of this divine presence. We hold that this divine presence is causal and supernatural and cannot be understood in the monistic or pantheistic or panentheistic sense.

---

[196] Cf. *Adv. Eunomium*, III, n. 4: PG 29, 664-665.

[197] Cf. *In Isaiam*, IV, 2: PG 70, 936; *In Iohannem*, XI, 8: PG 74, 509.

[198] S. Augustinus, *Epist.* 187: PL 33, 837.

[199] S. Cyprianus, *Epist.* 63, 8: PL 4, 380.

[200] S. Cyril, *Thesaurus*, 34: PG 75, 609-611; S. Athanasius, *Ad Serapionem*, I, 23: PG 26, 585.

[201] Eph. 2, 18.

[202] Cf. Rom. 8, 10-12.

[203] Cf. I Cor. 3, 16; 6, 19.

[204] *Dogmatic Constitution on the Church*, Ch. I,, art. 4.

[205] Radhakrishnan attempts to interpet the words of St Paul addressed to the Christians regarding the supernatural presence of God in them through divine grace (Cf. I Cor. 3, 16; 6, 19; II Cor. 6, 16 etc) as being addressed to every human being, because of the substantial immanence of God in them (OSW, October 1952 - February 1959, p. 332; OSW, July 1959 - May 1962, p. 236). Such an interpretation is definitely contrary to the obvious intention and to the whole doctrine of St Paul. He is speaking of the believers who make up the body of Christi which is the Church, as the contexts show (Cf. I Cor. 6, 15).

3) A critique of Radhakrishnan's rejection of organization
   in religion

After having made this value-judgment of Radhakrishnan's
concept of the basis of religion, we shall now see if his rejection
of organization in religion can be accepted. Religion, according
to Radhakrishnan, as we have seen, is the spiritual experience of
the Supreme Reality. It is this concept of religion that primarily
determines Radhakrishnan's approach to organized religions. This
idea of the nature of religion is, in fact, his criterion for a value-
judgment on organized religions. Elements in organized religions
which are in conflict with this idea of religion are judged to be
unnecessary and unwanted or even injurious to man's spiritual
life. Therefore it is important at first to evaluate his idea of
religion itself. Then we shall inquire into the nature of religion.
We shall examine if some kind of organization, cult, authority
and dogmas are necessary in religion. We shall consider also
whether Radhakrishnan is right in his accusations against authority
and dogmas in religion. This, we hope, will put us in a position
to see clearly if Radhakrishnan's idea of organized religion is
acceptable or not.

i) *Radhakrishnan's Idea of Religion — Its Merits and Demerits*

The idea that religion is a pure spiritual experience of Reality
has certainly some merits. But it is not without its defects.

a) *Merits of Radhakrishnan's Idea of Religion*

Certainly religion is primarily internal and experiential in
character. A religion which has nothing to do with the internal
aspects of human life is not worth the name; that is, a religion
which is mere formalism or externalism can never redeem man
from his fallen state or serve him as a means to eternal life. In
recent years there is in fact a greater emphasis on the internal
aspects of religion [206].
Radhakrishnan's firm stand against the modern tide of materialism and his emphasis on the spiritual nature of man and the
inner aspect of religion are certainly praiseworthy. In a spiritually
out-of-focus world in which brute force and material welfare are

---

[206] Cf. KARL RAHNER, *Wie sieht die Frömmigkeit von morgan aus*,
in *Neue Züricher Nachrichten*, February 11, 1967.

eulogized, Radhakrishnan upholds the inner religious experience and calls for a spiritual view of life and existence. In this respect he carries to the world the religious message of India which is the homeland of great religious movements.

Radhakrishnan has constantly appealed for greater understanding and co-operation among the great religions of the world. He sees a world civilization slowly taking shape. But he feels that this world civilization and a world community need a spiritual force to sustain them. Therefore religions should not go on as closed sects but must work together for one world religion. This insistence on an understanding among religions is to be commended. The ideal of one world civilization and one world community with one world religion is high and noble.

Radhakrishnan deserves our praise also for his life long endeavour to find a common ground on which every religion can safely stand and enter into dialogue with other religions. The merit of Radhakrishnan lies in the fact that he has shown the world that such a dialogue and understanding among religions are of great importance in the modern world.

However, his concept of a world religion and his approach to other religions are not wholly faultless.

b) Defects of Radhakrishnan's View

The most fundamental defect of Radhakrishnan's view of religion is that it is directly derived from a principle which, as we have seen, is untenable. Hence even apriori we can say that his view of religion is unacceptable. Apart from this we find some other defects in his idea of religion.

1) The spirituality that Radhakrishnan offers, which he borrowed from monistic Hinduism, is a solitary interiority. Each self realizes all by itself its identity with the Absolute. The Absolute itself is absolutely without qualities and is described as an infinitude of negations. Relation and personality are considered limitations and imperfections and therefore are denied in God. God is said to be absolutely impersonal. This is perhaps a fundamental point where we disagree with Radhakrishnan.

Even though Radhakrishnan denies personality in the Absolute, he maintains that the Absolute is " pure being, awareness, and bliss " [207]. Such expressions seem to imply personality in

---

[207] The Brahma Sūtra, p. 31. Cf. also Ibid, p. 89; Pr. Ups, p. 57; ERWTh, pp. 28, 125.

some sense. Radhakrishnan sees this difficulty and says, " such is the way in which we formulate in intellectual terms the truth " [208]. But even these intellectual formulations correspond at least in some sense to the absolute truth; otherwise they would be mere illusions.

2) The spirituality of solitary interiority " does not phenomenologically explain the urge in the depth of the soul to commune with other persons, to live in interpersonal relationship with other persons in the exact measure in which they remain as other; a reciprocal relation is established at the level of the most profound consciousness. The relation to the other is constitutive of personality. The recognition of the neighbour and God as persons follows my own awakening to myself as person " [209]. Therefore the recognition of God's personality and my relationship to Him are not destructive but most helpful to the growth of my own personality, and to my religious perfection. And that religion is most suited for man which helps develop his personality.

3) By holding that all religions in their original purity are purely experiential, Radhakrishnan is led to accept religious syncretism, like most modern Hindu theologians. He confuses what is general with the supreme, and what is common with what is proper to each, and effaces the essential difference between different religions under the pretext that all religions are different expressions of a single religious truth [210].

It is true that at times Radhakrishnan declares that he is not syncretic. On March 27, 1958, he said at Ohio, " No one need give up one's own religion and engage in a syncretism " [211].

Here he seems to be using the term ' syncretism ' in the sense of a mixing of religious elements of different origin. He says that he is not preaching syncretism in the sense that he is not advocating ' a fusion of different divinities and doctrines of different religions '. But this is not the only form of syncretism. It is also the effacing of essential differences between the different religions, and the mingling of different religions by bringing them to a general, primitive religiosity. Here the general element in all religions is taken for the supreme element of every religion

---

[208] ERWTh, p. 28; Cf. also Pr. Ups, p. 57.

[209] M. DHAVAMONY, *Christian Experience and Hindu Spirituality*, in " *Gregorianum* " 48 (1967) 786.

[210] Cf. N. BANERJEE, *et al., Religious Forces Shaping India Today*: Orientation Paper E of the All India Seminar on The Church in India Today (New Delhi) 1968) 13-14.

[211] OSW, October 1952 - February 1959, p. 383.

and the common for that which is proper to each religion[212], and an attempt is made to establish unity claiming that all religions are relatively true expressions of a single underlying religion. In this sense Radhakrishnan is certainly syncretic, as Hendrik Kraemer points out[213]. For, in the aforesaid speech immediately after claiming that he is not a syncretist, Radhakrishnan adds: "We give up notions of chosen peoples, chosen nations and chosen creeds ... All religions will express themselves as forms of the universal religion "[214].

ii) *An Investigation into the Nature of Religion*

To the question 'what is religion' a host of answers have been suggested, though none is universally accepted. But all agree that men of every religion, no matter how primitive, distinguish between the sacred and the profane. The sacred is something awe inspiring and attracting, 'fascinans' and 'tremendum', and hence demands our veneration and love. Religion, therefore, in general, without any value-judgment, can be described as man's relations with the holy; subjective religion is veneration and adoration, which become objective religion when embodied in creed, word, actions and law. These relations are possible only in so far as the holy appears to man[215].

There is no agreement among the various religions regarding the nature of the holy. But it is always considered a reality superior to man and beyond his control. If we consider the higher religions, the holy is said to be a personal God or an impersonal Absolute. In our discussion on Brahman (chapter II) we have shown that Radhakrishnan conceives the holy as impersonal Absolute. Man in the empirical order feels and acknowledges a dependence on the Absolute, while he experiences his own identity with the Absolute in the spiritual order. Therefore Radhakrishnan does not deny categorically a relationship between God and man. But he denies any absolute value to this God-man relationship.

---

[212] For further details about syncretism Cf. W. A. VISSERT HOOFT, *Kein anderer Name: Syncretismus oder christlicher Universalismus* (Basel 1965) 11 ff; HENDRIK KRAEMER, *Religion and the Christian Faith* (London 1961) 392 ff.

[213] Cf. HENDRIK KRAEMER, Religion and the Christian Faith, p. 401.

[214] OSW, October 1952 - February 1959, pp. 383-384.

[215] K. RAHNER and H. VORGRIMLER, *Theological Dictionary* (New York 1968) 399.

This position is consequent upon his basic principle of the identity of man's self and the Supreme Reality, and the emanation theory of the world. We have already seen that such a position involves many difficulties.

The other great trend of religious thought teaches that man as a creature depends entirely on God and therefore there is a real intrinsic and transcendental relation of dependence on God on the part of man. Religion is founded on this ontological relation of dependence on God. Since man is an intelligent being, endowed with free will, he must consciously acknowledge this dependence and live accordingly. Metaphysically, man as a creature is at an infinite distance from the creator. Yet wider is the moral gap between them; God is the Holy One and man is a sinner. The sinner must be pardoned and elevated so that he may commune with God and partake of the divine life. Only God can take the initiative in this pardoning and elevation, which He does by means of His grace. If this act of God's loving initiative is answered by man with an acceptance of grace, adoration and love, a supernatural relation is established between man and God. Thus religion fundamentally consists in a conscious, personal relationship with God. If the relation to God and the doctrines and rites are deduced from mere consideration of human nature and its ontological dependence on God we have a natural religion. But if on the other hand God freely reveals Himself supernaturally to man and determines the ways and means to reach Him, that relation established by God is a supernatural, revealed religion.

In monistic systems the being of man and the world are considered to be due to some sort of emanation from the Supreme Being. Explaining the meaning of creation, Radhakrishnan says, " *sṛṣṭi* (the sanskrit word for creation) means literally emanation, letting loose " [216]. So man is said to have univocally the same nature as that of the Supreme. According to the Hindu theologians man at present does not see his divine nature due to *avidyā*. Therefore man does not require to be elevated by God. He needs only to find a way to get rid of the *avidyā*. But even in this emanationist view of man, he is dependent on God. Radhakrishnan agrees that " the world is dependent on *Brahman* " [217]

---

[216] Cf. *The Brahma Sūtra*, p. 140.
[217] Cf. Ibid., p. 140; RC, p. 800.

and that there is a "distance between" the world and God [218], although he does not give any ultimate value to this dependence and to the distance between God and man.

The theory of emanation and the belief in the identity of man's self with the Supreme involve, as we have seen, many unsolved problems. Moreover, the moment that dependence on God and the distance from Him vanish, there is only God, and we can no longer speak of a religion of man.

Religion therefore is a confrontation with God. It involves necessarily a personal relationship. If this personal relationship between God and man is to bear supernatural fruit, to enable man to enjoy supernaturally intimate union with God, it is to be determined by God Himself. This, we believe, is the only way for man to enjoy an intimate supernatural union with God. Only God the Supreme, the All Powerful, can take the initiative in a personal encounter between Himself and man the powerless creature. Even as the part cannot grow into the whole, the creature cannot grow into the creator or determine the mode and the way of his approach to the creator and oblige the creator to subscribe to his decision. As long as religion remains a purely human attempt to reach God, as Radhakrishnan says [219], it remains on the human level and cannot lead man to participation in the divine nature. Only that religion which originates from God, which is God's love and wisdom reaching out to man, can elevate him and lead him to an intimate personal union with God.

This divine love reaching out for man, this God-man relationship finds its supreme realization in the incarnation of God; a higher degree of God-man relationship is absolutely inconceivable. When God assumes human nature, He is effectively consecrating the whole of humanity itself; hence such a Divine Incarnation and the consequent God-man relationship are absolutely unique. Therefore the God Incarnate is The Way to God for man. All other men can find their way to God and a supernatural union with Him only through the God Incarnate. Every other God-man relationship is subordinated to this paramount God-man relationship brought about by the God Incarnate.

---

[218] Cf. *The Brahma Sūtra*, p. 141; RC, p. 800.
[219] Cf. OSW, October 1952 - February 1959, p. 377; ERWTh, p. 184.

The Christian Stand

The Christian believes that Jesus Christ is the true Divine Incarnation. Therefore for him religion is the experience of a God who is made known objectively in the person of Christ, the only God-man. In him the God-man relationship is perfectly established. No other religious relationship can be equal to that which is brought about by and in Christ in whose Person human nature and the living God are united. Christ *is* the religious relationship. Not only were His words and deeds divine revelations, but He Himself is the Divine Revelation — the revelation of the Supreme Person, and the revelation of the supreme God-man relationship established by God. Greater spirituality, deeper interiority and a more certain assurance of the experience of intimate union with God are impossible to find in any other religion except in the religion established by Christ. No other religion can be compared with the one Christ instituted, and every other religion has value only through Him [220].

iii) *Necessity of External Expression of Religion*

The Second Vatican Council observes that " of its very nature the exercise of religion consists before all else in those internal voluntary and free acts whereby man sets the course of his life directly toward God " [221]. That does not mean that the Council advocated a merely internal religion. For, it immediately adds, " However, the social nature of man itself requires that he should give external expression to his internal acts of religion " [222]. Man's religion must be suited to his nature. He has an interior spiritual principle and an external body, both of which are created by God and both depend on Him. Therefore it is necessary that man acknowledge not only internally but also externally his dependence on God. This he does by external acts of worship.

2) History and experience show that if our interior acts have no external expression, they will die out; likewise, external acts utterly unrelated to the interior are of little worth. The spiritual soul of man necessarily seeks expression in all of his external actions. Therefore a religion which is merely internal is defective,

---

[220] Cf. M. DHAVAMONY, *Hinduism and Christianity: The Christian Encounter*: 4, in " Theology " LXX (London 1967) 163 f.

[221] *Declaration on Religious Freedom*, ch. I, art. 3.

[222] Ibid.

just like that which is only external. Whatever the Hindu theologians may say, religion has always had its external expression.
The millions that crowd the banks of Ganges and the hundreds
of beautiful temples that decorate India and a thousand other
such things support our view.

3) Religion is the first sacrament of salvation. A sacrament
that is purely internal is inconceivable and ineffective just as that
which is merely external. In a sacrament the external is intimately related to the internal. External is the essential symbol of
the internal, the very expression of the internal. The external
expression is not merely a mode of representation of the internal
religious facts (which may imply that there is something arbitrary
in the choice of sign and therefore can be substituted by another),
but rather the most direct manifestation of the internal facts, com-
municating the reality itself [223]. For example the visible Catholic
Church is a sacramental sign of something divine. The visibility,
the exteriority of the Church is essential to her identity. She is
the visible sign of the mystery of God's plan of salvation. The
visibility of the Church in its sacramental role is the instrument
through which God acts and saves us and dwells with us. If to
save us is the task of religion, then its external form is an indispensable necessity to our human condition. Real religion is both
external and internal. Both aspects are intrinsically interlocked [224].
If a merely external religion would have no spiritual value, an
utterly invisible religion would have no sacramental value. The
internal is to be perfected and manifested by the external, while
the external is animated and spiritualized by the internal.

4) Radhakrishnan's claim that Jesus' religion was one of pure
inwardness and of private prayer is not true [225]. He was very
careful to fulfil the external acts of religion. He received baptism [226], observed the Sabbath, though not in a blind way [227], at-
tended the temple service [228], and normally the synagogue service [229].
He prayed aloud, taught us a communal prayer [230] and asked us

[223] Cf. HERVE CARRIER, The Sociology of Religious Belonging (London 1965) 224.
[224] Cf. Y. CONGAR, The Mystery of the Church (London 1965) 66 f.
[225] Cf. EWR, p. 58.
[226] Cf. Mt. 3, 13.
[227] Cf. Mt. 12, 9 ff.
[228] Cf. Lk. 2,, 41 ff; Jo. 7. 10 ff; 10, 23 f.
[229] Cf. Lk. 4, 16 ff.
[230] Cf. Mt. 6, 9 ff.

to pray in groups [231]. He enjoined some external signs (which we call sacraments) as the ordinary means of obtaining divine grace. The Holy Spirit came on the Apostles with clear external signs [232]. When Christ asked his followers to be the light of the world [233], He was certainly insisting on the external which is the manfestation of the internal.

It is true that Jesus has also asked us to worship God in spirit and in truth [234], and to pray behind closed doors [235]. Here Jesus was not condemning external cult but a merely external cult which has no inner life at all.

iv) *The Social Nature of Religious Experience*

1) In noble accents that are at once persuasive and dignified, Radhakrishnan invites divided humanity to come into a world religion where each human being belongs to the household of God, where truth alone is the only abiding reality and experience of the inner divinity the only rule of life. The doctrine of Fellowship of the Spirit also seems to point to the social aspect of religion. But this spiritual fellowship is not for realizing spiritual perfection. Every member of this fraternity is supposed to have already individually and all alone attained to perfection. It is precisely because one has realized one's inner divinity one is said to belong to the Spiritual Fraternity. Radhakrishnan coined the phrases " Spiritual Fraternity " and " Fellowship of the Spirit " to stress the point that the realized men no longer belong to their original religion but transcend them. By these phrases Radhakrishnan does not seem to be emphasizing the social aspect of religion. He even points out that this Fellowship of the Spirit is an " open community " and an " Invisible Church " [236].

But, for him, only a totally interior religion can assume all other religions and thus become the world religion. But because he refuses to recognize the inter-personal relationship between God and man and upholds the solitary interiority, no other religion except his own can be integrated into the universal religion without being essentially mutilated and its identity being destroyed.

---

[231] Cf. Mt. 18, 19-20.
[232] Cf. Acts, 2, 2-4.
[233] Cf. Mt. 5,14.
[234] Cf. Jo. 4, 24.
[235] Cf. Mt. 6, 5-6.
[236] Cf. OSW, October 1952 - February 1959, p. 310.

For example, Christianity without Christ's personality and His unique mediation between God and man would be no longer Christianity.

Only that religion which is founded on the inter-personal relationship between God and man as revealed by God can assume whatever is true, good and beautiful in other religions without sacrificing its own essential character or destroying their true identity but by elevating and perfecting them, yet remaining at the same time more true to itself. Therefore, if there exists between man and God who is the Absolute Person a distance across which man is confronted with God who reveals Himself to him, then the totally interior religious experience can be assumed into the Christian experience. This Biblical confrontation is the only metaphysical 'locus' for the meeting of religions [237]. That is to say to promote the movement towards a world religion, the experiential religion of Radhakrishnan must be radically altered as to include the proper notion of creation and consequently of supernatural elevation and inter-personal relationship between God and man.

2) Man is not a solitary wanderer in the wilderness, but a social being born to lead a social life [238]. Because of his social nature he requires to evolve and perfect himself in and with society under all aspects of his being [239]. Not only in temporal aspects but also in spiritual, is he to be perfected in society [240].

Since man is a social being, his relationship with God has not only an individual aspect; it is of necessity bound to involve a social or communal dimension. A person even in solitude has relationships with other persons. Man can approach God only as he is, that is " bound up with all other persons — and therefore by integrating himself with others, by uniting himself with them, by deliberately immersing himself in the human community which he must serve, because from it he draws his life and because its essential bond is its relationship with God, ' Source and End of all human being ' " [241]. Therefore it is the most natural tendency

---

[237] Cf. M. DHAVAMONY, *Christian Experience and Hindu Spirituality*, in " Gregorianum " 48 (1967) 778.

[238] Cf. LEO XIII, *Ency. Diuturnum illud* 29, June 1881: ASS 14 (1881-1882) 4 f.

[239] PIUS XI, *Quadragesimo anno*, 15, May 1931: AAS 23 (1931) 215 f.

[240] Cf. Rom. 13, 1.

[241] JEAN MOUROUX, *The Christian Experience*, p. 8.

of man to give social expression to his religion. The Second Vatican Council puts beautifully what we have been trying to explain :

> "God did not create man for life in isolation, but for the formation of social unity. So also ' it has pleased God to make men holy and save them not merely as individuals, without any mutual bonds, but by making them into a single people, a people which acknowledges Him in truth and serves Him in holiness '[242]. So from the beginning of salvation history He has chosen men not just as individuals but as members of a certain community "[243].
> This " social nature of man itself requires that he should give external expression to his internal acts of religion ; that he should participate with others in matters religious ; that he should profess his religion in community "[244].

Believers naturally and inevitably tend to commune with one another in their common concern to worship God ; aware of God's Fatherhood of all men, they join together to pay Him homage socially. If sharing creates community, shared religious beliefs and spiritual thoughts create religious communities, which speedily express themselves as structural and visible parts of history[245]. Therefore, we have an obligation to enquire whether God has revealed a supernatural society such as the Church for us.

3) Radhakrishnan does not see the momentous sacramental function of an externally established spiritual society. A sacramental sign by its very nature signifies something far greater than what is merely externally apparent. An essential sign is the immediate manifestation of the internal reality, as we have explained earlier. Therefore our visible coming together as a community in the power of the spirit makes religion not only a way of life for us but also a sign of salvation for the world. So a lawfully structured religion is not only something we need, but also it is something we owe our brethren outside the community for whom

---

[242] Cf. *Dogmatic Constitution on the Church*, Ch. II, *art.* 9.

[243] *Pastoral Constitution on the Church in the Modern World*, Part. I, Ch. II, art. 32.

[244] *Declaration on Religious Freedom*, Ch. I, art. 3.

[245] Cf. THE AMERICAN HIERARCHY, *The Church in Our Day*: A Collective Pastoral of the American Hierarchy on the Mystery of the Church, on Her Nature and Function, Prepared in the Light of the Dogmatic Constitution on the Church Adopted by Vatican II and Certain Doctrinal Problems of the Hour (Washington 1968) 31.

we become a saving sign of the redeeming God, as well as something we owe God Himself, who wishes to share His life with us in the most intimate manner possible [246]. Applying these principles to the Catholic Church the American Bishops say:

> " The visible structuring of the Church is no less the Church than the invisible reality. The sacramental Church is the spontaneous result of grace, which like love, seeks visible expression and identifies with it. The grace of Christ in which the Church is created is not imprisoned in the visible structure of the Church, but neither is it independent of her. For the Church is sign or sacrament of grace. This means that the grace of the Lord, requiring visible presence among us (even as did He), is destined to triumph when time shall be no more and is expressed through the institutional structures of the Church and is inseparable from them. This is not to say that grace, salvation, or the Kingdom of God is found only *where* the organized Church is seen to be at work, but it is to say that all grace seeks to become manifest not only in the Incarnation of Christ, but also in those visible elements of His Church which are not merely human but sacramental in the fullest sense of the word " [247].

We cannot therefore agree with Radhakrishnan that the institutional elements in the Church are unwanted or are injurious to the spiritual life.

4) Since Radhakrishnan claims support for his view of a purely experiential religion from Jesus and argues that an organized religion is in direct contradiction to the will of Christ [248], we shall examine if Jesus was really against an organized form of religion.

According to Radhakrishnan the organizational elements in Christianity originated " when Christianity went to Rome and took over the traditions of Caesar " [249]. But a critical study will show that " already from the beginning of the world the foreshadowing of the Church took place " [250]. In the Old Testament there is remarkable preparation for the supernatural institution of a religion. God chose a people and made a covenant with them [251]. He did

---

[246] Cf. Ibid., p. 19.

[247] Ibid., p. 26.

[248] EWR, p. 58 f; ERWTh, p. 272.

[249] EWR, p. 58-59. Cf. also ERWTh, p. 273 f.

[250] Second Vatican Council, *Dogmatic Constitution on the Church*, Ch. I, art. 2.

[251] Cf. Ex. Ch. 19-24. For a brief treatise on the Church as existed

not communicate to each and every one of them directly, but sent His delegates to them with the authority to teach the doctrines which He revealed to them. The nature of this future religion was revealed in the Old Testament in various figures of speech. It is depicted as a flock of which God Himself is the shepherd [252]; it is the people of God and a holy nation foreshadowed by Israel [253].

Christ took up the Old Testament figures of the Church and clearly applied them to the religion which He instituted. The Church is a sheepfold whose one and necessary gate is Christ Himself [254]. She is the choice vineyard of the heavenly Vinedresser [255]. Such figures imply that the Church is something externally existing. Christ's attitude towards organization in religion is clear from the name He gave to His religion. The world 'Church' is the English equivalent of Greek ἠκκλησία which is a translation of the Hebrew *Qahal* (in Aramaic Qehilla). Qahal Yahweh, at the time of Jesus was an established community leading a holy life in the desert.

There is enough evidence in the Gospels to show that Christ founded a new spiritual society which He called *ecclesia,* the Church [256], and determined its basic organizational character. It is clear that He instituted a college of twelve [257], and sent them as His legates into the world [258] with the powers of teaching [259], sanctifying [260] and ruling [261]. Christ instituted also a supreme head in the new society [262]. He also revealed the doctrines which should be taught and believed in the new community [263] as necessary for eternal salvation [264].

The Apostles conceived the Church as an organized religion. The Church is the tract of land to be cultivated, the field of God [265]. On that ground grows the ancient olive tree whose holy roots were the Patriarchs and in which the reconciliation of Jew and Gentile had been and will be brought about [266]. The Church is an edifice

---

in the O. T. Cf. R. A. DYSON and A. JONES, *The Kingdom of Promise* (London 1951); HENRI DE LUBAC, *The Splendour of the Church,* trans. by Michael Mason (Glen Rock 1963) 37 ff.

[252] Cf. Is. 40, 11; Ez. 34, 11 ff.

[253] II Esd. 13, 1; Num. 20, 4; Dt. 23, 1. Cf. also Second Vatican Council, *Dogmatic Constitution on the Church,* Ch. II, art. 9.

[254] Cf. Second Vatican Council, *Dogmatic Constitution on the Church,* Ch. I, art. 6.

[255] Cf. Mt. 21, 33-43; Is. 5, 1 f.

[256] Cf. Mt. 16, 18; 18, 17 f. Cf. also KITTEL, ThWN, III, p. 58 ff.

of God [267] of which our Lord is the cornerstone [268]. On this cornerstone the Church is said to be built by the Apostles [269]. From this comes the durability and the solidity of the Church [270]. This figure shows at once the external organizational character and the inner spiritual nature of the Church. It shows also that these are not to be considered as two separate realities but as " one interlocked reality which is comprised of a divine and human element " [271]. Here is how St Paul puts it: " You are part of a building that has the apostles and prophets for its foundations, and Christ Jesus himself for its main corner stone. As every structure is aligned on him, all grow into one holy temple in the Lord " [272].

The idea of an externally structured Church is clearly expressed in the figure of " Jerusalem which is above " [273].

The organized character of the early Church is another undeniable indication that the organization of the Church owes its

[257] Cf. Mk. 3, 13 f; Lk. 6, 12 ff; Mt. 10, 1 ff; Jo. 6, 70.

[258] Cf. Jo. 17, 6 f. 14, 17 f; 10, 36; 20, 21.

[259] Cf. Mt. 10, 7. 27; Mk, 3, 14; 16, 15.

[260] By baptism, Cf. Jo. 3, 5; by Sacrifice, Cf. Lk 22, 19-20 and parallels; by absolving sins, Cf. Jo. 20, 22; Cf. also Mt. 18, 18.

[261] Mt. 16, 18-19; 18, 18; Jo. 21, 15-17.

[262] Cf. Jo. 21, 15-17.

[263] Cf. Mt. 28, 19 f; Mk. 16, 15; Lk. 24, 47.

[264] Cf. Mk, 16, 16; Cf. also Jo. 20, 31; Mt. 10, 32, 42; Lk, 10, 16.

[265] Cf. I Cor. 3, 9.

[266] Rom. 11, 13 ff. Cf. also Second Vatican Council, *Dogmatic Constitution on the Church,* Ch. I, art. 6.

[267] Cf. I Cor. 3, 9. This edifice is given various names in the sacred Scripture, all of which show the inner spiritual nature and the external structure of the Church (Cf. I Tim. 3, 15; Eph. 2, 19-22; Apoc. 21, 3). Cf. also Rom. 15, 20; I Cor. 3, 16; II Cor 6, 16; Gal. 4, 11 f; I Peter, 2, 5.

[268] Cf Eph. 2, 20; Mt. 21, 4 and parallels; Acts, 4, 11; I Peter, 2, 7; Ps. 118, 22.

[269] I Cor. 3, 11. Cf. also Second Vatican Council, *Decree on the Missionary activity of the Church,* Ch. I, art. 9; *idem, Dogmatic Constitution on the Church,* Ch. I, art. 6.

[270] *Cf. Second Vatican Council, Dogmatic Constitution on the Church,* Ch. I, art. 6.

[271] Cf. Second Vatican Council, *Dogmatic Constitution on the Church* Ch. I, art. 8: The Second Vatican Council has often made use of this figure (Cf. *Pastoral Constitution on the Church in the Modern World,* Part. I, Ch. 4, art. 40; Cf. also Ibid., Ch. II, art. 32; *Constitution on the Sacred Liturgy,* art. 2; *Decree on the Church's Missionary Activity,* Ch. I, art. 9).

[272] Eph. 2, 20-21.

[273] Cf. Gal. 4, 26. Cf. also Apoc. 12, 17; 21, 9-14.

origin to Christ. There was a centre which regulated the doctrines and disciplines in the Church to which cases of doubts were referred [274]. The need of approbation from the leaders of the centre was acknowledged even by St Paul [275]. The Apostles were always supervising the doctrines and disciplines of the various churches [276]. Thus it is beyond question that the religion which Christ instituted is an organized Church. The Second Vatican Council sums it up beautifully:

> " Christ, the one Mediator established and ceaselessly sustains here on earth His holy Church, the community of faith, hope and charity, as a visible structure. Through her He communicates truth and grace to all ... This is the unique Church of Christ which in the creed we avow as one, holy, catholic and apostolic. After His resurrection our Saviour handed her over to Peter to be shepherded (Jo. 21, 17) commissioning him and the other apostles to propagate and govern her (Cf. Mt. 28, 18ff). Her He erected for all ages as the " pillar and mainstay of the truth " (1 Tim. 3, 15). This Church, constituted and organized in the world as a society, subsists in the Catholic Church " [277].

The Council believes that the external structure of the Church is so important an instrument of salvation that it finds an analogy between the organization of the Church and the humanity of Christ:

> " Just as the assumed nature inseparably united to the divine Word serves Him as a living instrument of salvation, so, in a similar way does the communal structure of the Church serves Christ's Spirit, who vivifies it by way of building up the body " [278].

Therefore, from our discussion we conclude that not only Radhakrishnan's idea of religion as purely internal and experiential, but also his idea of organized religions as merely external systems and destructive of the spiritual life are one-sided and inadmissible.

---

[274] Acts, Ch. 15.
[275] Cf. Gal. 2, 5 ff.
[276] Cf. Acts, 8, 14; 9, 1 f. 22; Gal. 2, 2.
[277] *Dogmatic Constitution on the Church,* Ch. I, art. 8.
[278] Ibid.

v) *An Evaluation of Radhakrishnan's Rejection of Authority and Dogma in Religion*

The two fundamental reasons for Radhakrishnan's rejection of organized religions are their claim to authority and their dogmatic teaching of religious truths. He has constantly and untiringly attacked these two points in organized religions and has described them as the greatest evils in man's religious endeavours and the greatest obstacles to the realization of the world religion. Therefore we shall examine these points also.

a) *Why does Radhakrishnan Reject Infallible Authority and Dogmas in Religion?*

Radhakrishnan's rejection of infallible authority and dogmas is consequent upon his concept of divine revelation and its expression. As we have explained in the third chapter Radhakrishnan does not recognize genuine supernatural revelation, but identifies it with human intuition. He thinks that neither revelation (even when he admits it for argument's sake) nor intuition can ever be expressed infallibly, because the moment they are expressed, they get into the realm of duality and thus necessarily contract an element of untruth. Therefore no religion can lay claim to absolute truth valid for all; and there can be no binding authority in religion. Common sense guided by personal experience will be the supreme guide to the individual. Priests and hierarchy will find no important place in such a religious set up. Religion must then be tolerant towards different and even opposing doctrines. For, every doctrine at its best is only a way or theory of salvation. A special claim by any one religion can only be viewed, therefore, as arrogance and pride. But things change once we admit a supernatural religion.

b) *Supernatural Revelation Cannot be Denied A priori*

By supernatural revelation we mean the manifestation which God makes to men through speaking [279]; a manifestation which is unattainable by any natural power. More briefly, it is a free self-

---

[279] Cf. Heb. 1, 1; 2 Ch. 36. 15 f; Ex. 33, 11; Jo. 15, 14 f; The Second Vatican Council, *Dogmatic Constitution on Divine Revelation,* Ch. I, art. 2. 4. 6. By speaking we mean the direct and immediate manifestation of one's mind to another.

disclosure of God of His Being and Will to men, themselves unattainable by human effort [280].

Radhakrishnan's position, which is in the main the modern Hindu view of other religions, involves an a priori assumption that all religions are natural [281], because he really does not admit the supernatural in the strict sense. It also involves a presupposition that all religions are different expressions of a single underlying religion.

The common argument from the contradictory doctrines of different religions does certainly militate against the unity of all religions. But if we remember that Radhakrishnan and most of the Hindu theologians do not recognize doctrines as something essential to religion, and that they put forward experience as the only constitutive element of religion, then the above answer cannot be considered as the ideal one. The Hindu theologians would see the argument as false, because there is a transition from the accidentals (doctrines) to the essential (experience). A better reply to Radhakrishnan's a prioristic rejection of a supernaturally instituted religion is as follows:

"Such a position, as we see clearly, is inadmissible, because their a priori assertion itself implies a judgment of value, or rather begging the question. To assert a priori the fundamental equality of all religions it would be necessary to occupy a 'metaphysical locus' which would be above God who grants revelation and above man who receives it and such a perspective higher than the creator-creature polarity is obviously inconceivable and illusory because there exists absolutely nothing outside this polarity. Besides a Christian does not begin by passing judgments on other religions but just takes his religious experience as the phenomenon to start with and analyses it objectively and tries to grasp its meaning [282].

---

[280] Cf. KARL RAHNER, Theological Investigations, trans. by Karl Kruger V (London 1966) 469.

[281] According to Radhakrishnan " religion is the natural outcome of the human mind" (Cf. ERWTh, p. 184); "all religions are human attempts to reach the Ultimate Reality" (OSW, October 1952 - February 1959, p. 377). Cf. also STEPHEN NEILL, Christian Faith and Other Faiths (London 1961) 83. This is the basic but preconceived principle of all those who defend relativity and unity of all religions (Cf. BEDE GRIFFITHS, in "Clergy Monthly Supplement" VII (1964-1965) 151.

[282] M. DHAVAMONY, Christian Experience and Hindu Spirituality, in "Gregorianum" 48 (1967) 778.

We cannot question God's capability or deny Him the right to intervene in His world in the way He wants, even though we may not understand fully His manner of working, or some may refuse to acknowledge His authority. " He came to His own domain and His own people did not accept Him " [283].

It is rather unfortunate that Radhakrishnan in all his life-long career as an explorer of religious truths has never approached religion from any angle other than that of his own religion. Nowhere in his writings do we find critical research into the possibility and suitability of a supernatural religion.

c) *Divine Revelation is Possible*

There is nothing to make divine revelation metaphysically impossible [284]. If God is omnipotent, He has the capability and the means to reveal His being and mind to us; otherwise He would not be omnipotent. The Psalmist asks, " Is the inventor of the ear unable to hear! the creator of the eye unable to see " [285]. A free communication implies a state of act, of perfection and not imperfection. God is goodness; and goodness is self-communicating. There is, therefore, no metaphysical impossibility in God revealing Himself, and on the part of man it is desirable that God reveals Himself, without in any way denying the gratuitousness of such revelation. In fact He has taken the initiative and has revealed His economy of salvation. Since the object of intellect is being as such, man can certainly accept and understand revealed truths. Man is a person endowed with autonomous reason. But this autonomy is not such that it remains closed within itself but is open to truth. Even if a particular revealed truth was already known to man, God's revelation gives the highest possible certainty to our assent to it.

It seems that Radhakrishnan does not deny categorically all divine revelations. He admits divine revelation as a human intuition of divine truth by the seer. But what he categorically denies is man's capacity to give an infallible expression to the revealed Truth of God, to the truth visioned by the seer, and with that he denies authority and dogmas in religion [286]. In other words, according to Radhakrishnan a revelation given in time cannot escape the relativism inherent in history.

---

[283] Jo. 1, 11.
[284] First Vatican Council, Sess. III, Cf. D 1807, D 1808.
[285] Ps. 94, 9.
[286] Cf. *The Brahma Sūtra*, p. 112 f; Pr. Ups, p. 22 f.

This, indeed, is a serious difficulty. But one should not forget that God who revealed had foreseen such a difficulty and has solved it:

a) God prepared the human mind to receive His words by electing and preparing a people and even by purifying the concepts which would serve to express His divine message.

b) The fullness of revelation came to us through the unique medium of the Word Incarnate. Incarnation offers a solution to the difficulty posed by Radhakrishnan. Rene Latourelle explains this: " Christ is Man-God, perfectly connatural to human language as well as divine thinking. As Creator He dominates men and is familiar with all his psychological make up and his every human resource; He dominates history and knows all its ins and outs. And it is He, the Man-God, who chooses the analogies which can serve as likenesses to the divine mystery " [287]. The union of natures and the unity of person authorizes the transfer from the divine milieu to the human and at the same time assures the fidelity of the transmission [288].

c) Christ did not leave His doctrine to the chance of history and individual interpretation. He protects it first by handing it down through a charism of *inspiration,* and secondly, He entrusts it to a Church which He fortifies with charism of *infallibility* to preserve, defend, propose, and authentically interpret revelation [289]. Without this special divine assistence and divinely established authority no doctrine can escape the fluctuations of history.

d) *Revealed Truths Can Be Expressed Infallibly*

If God could really assume human nature and be God-man and express Himself concretely on earth, at a definite point in space and time, then there can be no reason why He cannot help His representatives express truths conceptually yet absolutely infallibly. The Second Vatican Council teaches:

> " In His gracious goodness, God has seen to it that what He had revealed for the salvation of all nations would abide perpetually in its full integrity and be handed on to all generations " [290].

---

[287] R. LATOURELLE, *Theology of Revelation* (New York 1967) 355.
[288] Cf. Ibid., p. 365.
[289] Ibid., p. 355.
[290] *Dogmatic Constitution on Divine Revelation,* Ch. II, art. 7.

And again,

> " Inspired by God and committed once for all to writing,
> they (Sacred Scripture and Tradition) impart the word of
> God Himself without change and make the voice of the Holy
> Spirit resound in the words of the prophets and apostles " [291].

Thus the doctrines expressed are no longer fallible, but divine
and absolutely infallible. They are the " words of God expressed
in human language " [292]. That is why St Paul could say: " if
anyone preaches a version of the Good News different from the
one we have already preached to you, whether it be ourselves or
an angel from heaven, he is to be condemned " [293].

Therefore Radhakrishnan's greatest objection to the infallible
and absolute nature of dogmas and to authority, namely : that since
dogmas, as conceptual expressions of truth, are necessarily fallible
and therefore there can be no binding authority in religion, is
invalid and unacceptable save on the presupposition of relativism
of truth. The idea of religion as a mere seeking after the Absolute and the belief in the incapacity of the intellect to attain to
absolute truth have actually landed Radhakrishnan in the relativism
of truth and finally in religious relativism.

Relativism of truth, whatever basis it may afford for tolerance
in religion, is logically untenable. For it holds that the truths
which man knows are valid only in the context of a particular
finite system, that is, the world of the individual's own sensibility,
whereas there are other systems differing from it or even opposing
it, yet equally sound. Often it appears to succeed very easily in
reconciling differing or even contradictory religious and theological
systems. But this theory implies an assertion of its own universal
validity and therefore contradicts itself. Karl Rahner and Herbert
Vorgrimler condemn the theory of relativism in these words:
" This relativism (as the assertion of its own universal validity)
is nonsense for the simple reason that such an assertion contradicts
itself : relativism in the context of any particular system can be
rejected as false by that system " [294].

Though we defend the absolute character of revealed truth

---

[291] Ibid., Ch. VI, art. 21. Cf. also Ibid., Ch. III, art. 11; Ch. V, art.
18; Jo. 20, 31; II Tim. 3, 16; II Peter, 1, 19-21; 3, 15-16.

[292] Ibid., Ch. III, art. 13.

[293] Gal. 1, 8.

[294] K. RAHNER and H. VORGRIMLER, *Theological Dictionary* (New York
1968) 398.

18

and dogma, we are not defending the absolute nature of its expression.   St Augustine had pointed out that the reference to time
is a changeable factor in a statement of faith.   St. Thomas explained it by saying that statements of faith exclude a changeable-
ness which is essential, but not one which is accidental [295].   Theologians now commonly agree that " since the doctrine is expressed
by means of the conceptions of a given era, it is necessary to
distinguish truth itself from its mode of presentation " [296].   The
mode of presentation must not be confused with the reality itself.
The terminological material available to present the reality is limited,
historically conditioned and changeable.   But the reality referred
to by this historically conditioned expression is of infinite fullness.   It can be said to be properly known only " when it is
grasped as something infinite and incomprehensible — as a per-
manent mystery — in the very act of taking hold of its finite concept " [297].   This mystery is announced in history through limited
materials of expression.   But it receives its real binding presence
in history, because " the original statement of faith ", as K. Rahner
points out, " already includes that moment of genuine human reflection which makes it legitimate and necessary and which continues to be effective and to unfold itself in later theology " [298].

e) *The Need of Authority in Revealed Religion*

God can treat man only as he is, as a free social being.   Therefore man must certainly be able to retain his liberty even when he
assents to revealed truth, and he must get sufficient assistance to
be able to communicate without change to others what he has seen
in the light of grace.   If we take our social nature seriously, we
have to agree that it is more expedient for God that He communi-
cates to us through His ministers who are given further assistance
to express His message to us and to preserve it for ever in its
purity.   This is the economy of man's salvation.   " If God wished
to preserve publicly throughout the ages without change the original
meaning of the revealed deposit, oral as well as written, there was
only one way to do this : it was to accompany publicly throughout
the ages the revealed deposit with an interpretation which had
God's help.   This He has done.   When Christ sent the eleven into

295 III Sent., *dis. 24, art.* 1. Q 2 ad 5.
296 RENE LATOURELLE, *Theology of Revelation,* p. 355; Cf. also CHAR-
LES JOURNET, *What Is Dogma?* p. 42.
297 KARL RAHNER, *Theological InvestigationsV* (London1966) 58.
298 Ibid., p. 61.

the world He told them: 'All authority in heaven and on earth has been given to me; you, therefore, must go out, making disciples of all nations. And behold I am with you all through the days that are coming, until the consummation of the world'" [299]. "Upon this authority rests, by divine mandate, the duty of going out into the world and preaching the Gospel to every creature" [300]. This authority was not to expire with the death of the last Apostle. It subsists in the lawful successors of the Apostles, it subsists in the Catholic Church.

The word of God is so profound and our capacity to understand it varies so much from man to man that we need an authoritative interpreter, who enjoys God's assistance to interpret infallibly, so that we may find the true original message of God. This "task of authentically interpreting the word of God, whether written or handed on, has been entrusted exclusively to the living teaching office of the Church" [301].

This is the point which Radhakrishnan constantly and strongly attacks. He accuses Christianity of exclusivism, of pride and arrogance. The best answer to such a charge comes from Pope Paul VI. He reminds all such accusers that Christianity is not a privilege for some but a gift for all. The Church is not a particular sect, but the spiritual family of humanity — God's revealed programme for the world [302]. The authority of the Church is not pride or arrogance but a continuous act of obedience to the will of God and service to the people of God.

Radhakrishnan's stand against dogmas and authority, we believe, is due to a confusion between 'dogmas' and 'authority' in Hinduism and dogmas and authority in Christianity. Even though he claims that Hinduism is the most elastic of all religions, we know (and perhaps he also) that the truth is the opposite. Hinduism has also its own dogmas, unchangeable traditions which are often plainly untenable, and belief in the authority of the sacred Scriptures. Immediately after asserting that "in our allegiance to

---

[299] CHARLES JOURNET, *What is Dogma?* (London 1964) 50-51.

[300] Second Vatican Council *Declaration on Religious Freedom.* Ch. II, art. 13.

[301] Second Vatican Council, *Dogmatic Constitution on the Divine Revelation,* Ch. II, art. 10. Cf. also Ibid., Ch. IV, art. 14.

[302] Cf. Sermon on the Feast of the Epiphany, 1960, given in *The Mind of Paul VI on the Church and the World,* ed. by James Walsh, trans. by Archibald Colquhoun (London 1964) 55. Cf. also CARDINAL F. KÖNIG, *Finding Peace Through the Light and Strength of Religion,* in *Man and Religion,* ed by Walter Leifer (München 1967) 18.

dogmas, we overlook the claims of truth", Radhakrishnan says,
"when the question of the abolition of *sati* arose in India, the
fundamentalists turned to scriptures and quoted texts and did not
concern themselves about human life and misery "[303]. This is
the concept of dogma which Radhakrishnan got from his own
religion. Naturally, he understood the dogmas of every other religion in this way, which led him to attack dogmas wherever he
found them and the authority which insisted on dogmatic teachings.

But if Radhakrishnan is willing to subordinate human authority to divine authority, to put the credibility of divine revelation
above that of human insight, as necessarily every true seeker of
truth must do, then he will see the obligation to accept the divine
revelation. He will then, and then only, distinguish between fanatical teachings and the dogmas of revealed religion based on divine
authority.

When a Christian accepts dogmas, he is not doing so on any
created authority but on the authority of God who reveals Himself
to us[304]. To subordinate ourselves to the authority of God is not
servility or bartering away one's freedom for ease, but to situate
oneself in relation to the universe of men and God[305]. It is a
paramount instance of the right use of freedom. "The act of
faith is of its very nature a free act. Man, redeemed by Christ
the Saviour and through Christ Jesus called to be God's adopted
son, cannot give his adherence to God revealing Himself unless the
Father draws him[306] to offer to God the reasonable and free submission of faith "[307]. The acceptance of dogmas, which is *ipso*

---

[303] RR, p. 29.

[304] Cf. CHARLES JOURNET, *What is Dogma?*, p. 106.

[305] C. HERVE CARRIER, *The Sociology of Religious Belonging* (London
1965) 299.

[306] Cf. Jo. 6, 44.

[307] Second Vatican Council, *Declaration on Religious Freedom*, Ch. II,
art. 10. Because the act of faith of its very nature must be free, the Church
has always strictly forbidden the use of force in matters religious, no matter of whatever totalitarianism she is accused by her critics. Christ bore
witness to truth but He refused to impose the truth by force on those who
spoke against it (Cf. Ibid., Ch. II, art. 11). The way of Christ became the
way of the Apostles. "It is one of the major tenets of the Catholic doctrine that man's response to God in faith must be free" (Cf. Ibid., Ch. II,
art. 10); "The Church strictly forbids forcing any one to embrace the
faith or alluring or enticing people by unworthy techniques" (Second Vatican Council, *Decree on the Missionary Activity of the Church.* Ch. II,
art. 2, n. 13), teaches the Second Vatican Council. Cf. also cic. cc. 752,
1351.

facto the acceptance of the authority of the Church and ultimately of God, is hence an encounter of two spiritual liberties — the liberty of God in freely bestowing His grace, and the liberty of man in freely accepting it. It is the most intimate and personal meeting that we can think of. Thus the belief in the dogmas and authority of the Church gives us assurance of the deepest spiritual experience that is possible for a human being [308].

---

[308] Cf. M. DHAVAMONY, *Christian Experience and Hindu Spirituality*, in "Gregorianum" 48 (1967) 787.

CONCLUSION

The passionate appeal of Radhakrishnan to approach the problems of life from a religious angle is unquestionably admirable. His vision of an emerging world community with a world religion, of a world which is the household of God is high and noble. War and preparations of war sum up a good part of world history; materialism and Marxism are gaining ground everywhere. To such a world Radhakrishnan's message means much.

The fundamental principles of Radhakrishnan can be said to be partially sound; but his use of them often baffles the unbiased reader. Even though we are told that the intellect is not opposed to intuition, but is related to intuition as between what is less perfect and more perfect, and that personality is denied to God "only in the interests of super-personality" [309], to intellectual values no ultimate value is given and God is spoken of as impersonal. In spite of his own principle that whatever is conceptually expressed contains an element of untruth, he, nonetheless, takes "*tat tvam asi*" as absolutely valid, without any element of untruth. This basic assumption leads him to argue that the world is an emanation from the Absolute and man a particle of It — panentheism becomes unavoidable. Everything that is not the Absolute can only alienate us from the Absolute. Even God's revelations are not to be absolutely relied upon. Man is left alone; his salvation is in solitary interiority. He has to discover his identity with the Absolute. Man is thus advised to do something which is feigned, that is, to consider himself the Absolute and realize it.

From this aprioristic assumption Radhakrishnan criticizes every other religion which seeks salvation through inter-personal interiority. At times his criticism of other religions becomes so hard and obviously intolerant that even his own principles regarding the manner of approach to other religions are in jeopardy. Very often the target of his attack is Christianity, and he repeats

---

[309] ERWTh, p. 292.

many of the accusations of her determined enemies. His rejection
of authority and dogmas in religion is resolute.

Had he been true to his own principle that intellect is not
opposed to intuition, then he would have found a personal God and
could have recognized divine revelation as more credible than human
intuition. His theology would have then avoided some of the
insoluble difficulties of his position.

Radhakrishnan's insistence on the Divine in man is a challenge
to us to meet Christ not only in the tabernacles where He is
really present, but also in the innermost depths of our own and
our neighbour's beings, where He is spiritually present through
grace. This encounter with Christ should not be merely at the
interior level alone, but must shine forth in all our actions. In
other words, our life itself must be a witness to Christ indwelling
in our souls. Although our study compels us to reject Radhakrishnan's accusations of externalism, of formalism, of authoritarianism and of dogmatism in Christianity, such accusations must
make us reflect and see if we have failed to bear eloquent witness
to Christ. The Second Vatican Council observes:

> " For although the Catholic Church has been endowed with
> all divinely revealed truth and with all means of grace, her
> members fail to live by them with all the fervour they should.
> As a result the radiance of the Church's face shines less
> brightly in the eyes of our separated brethren and of the
> world at large and the growth of God's kingdom is retarded.
> Every Catholic must therefore aim at Christian perfection
> and, each according to his station, play his part so that the
> Church ... may daily be more purified and renewed " [310].

To live a life of witness to Christ is an inalienable obligation of
all Christians. The same council reminds us:

> " Wherever they live, all Christians are bound to show forth,
> by the example of their lives, and by the witness of their
> speech that new man which they put on at baptism, and that
> power of the Holy Spirit by whom they were strengthened
> at confirmation. Thus other men, observing their good
> works, can glorify the Father and can better perceive the
> real meaning of human life and the bond which ties the
> whole community of mankind together " [311].

---

[310] *Decree on Ecumenism,* Ch. I, art. 4.
[311] *Decree on the Missionary Activity of the Church,* Ch. II, art. 11.

Just as Christ proclaimed the kingdom of His Father by the testimony of His life and the power of His words [312], so too the Christian must spread abroad a living witness to Christ [313]. A living answer to this great call of the Second Vatican Council, "the testimony of a life resplendent in faith, hope and charity" [314] will be the best possible reply to Radhakrishnan as well as to many other critics of Christianity [315].

---

[312] *Dogmatic Constitution on the Church,* Ch. IV, art. 35.

[313] *Ibid.,* Ch. II, art. 12. Here it is generally asserted of all Christians. The same Council asks also in particular the Bishops (Cf. *Pastoral Constitution on the Church in the Modern World,* P. I, Ch. IV, art, 43), the priests (Cf. *Dogmatic Constitution on the Church,* Ch. V, art. 41. Cf. also Ch. III, art. 28), the religious (Cf. *Decree on the Appropriate Renewal of the Religious Life,* art. 25), and the laity (Cf. *Decree on the Apostolate of the Laity,* Ch. I, art. 3; *Dogmatic Constitution on the Church,* Ch. IV, art. 31; Ibid., art. 38; *Pastoral Constitution on the Church in the Modern World,* P. I, Ch. IV, art. 43) to be witnesses to Christ.

[314] *Dogmatic Constitution on the Church,* Ch. IV, art. 31.

[315] For the urgency of a testimony of life, Cf. RENÉ LATOURELLE, *La testimonianza della vita segno di salvezza,* in VINCENZO D'AGOSTINO (ed.), *Laici sulle vie del Concilio* (Assisi 1966) 348 ff.

BIBLIOGRAPHY

1) THE WORKS OF DR RADHAKRISHNAN

The Ethics of the Vedanta and its Metaphysical Presuppositions. His Thesis for the M. A. Degree from Madras University, Madras, The Guardian press, 1908.

Karma and Free Will, in "Modern Review" III (1908) 424-428.

Indian Philosophy, The Vedas and the six Systems, in "Madras Christian College Magazine" VIII (1908) 22-35.

"Nature" and "Convention" in Greek Ethics, in "Culcutta Review" CXXX (1910) 9-23.

Egoism and Altruism - The Vedanta Solution, in "East and West" IX (1910) 626-630.

Morality and Religion in Education, in "Madras Christian College Magazine" X (1910-11) 233-239.

The Ethics of the Bhagavadgītā and Kant, in "International Journal of Ethics" XXI (1911) 465-475.

The Essentials of Psychology, London, Oxford University Press, 1912.

The Ethics of the Vedanta, in "International Journal of Ethics" XXIV (1914) 168-193.

The Vedanta Philosophy and the Doctrine of Māyā in "International Journal of Ethics" XXIV (1914) 431-451.

A View from India on the War-I, in "Asiatic Review" VI (1915) 369-374. (The second part did not appear owing to censoring).

The Vedanta-Approach to Reality, in "The monist" XXVI (1916) 200-231.

Religion and Life, in "International Journal of Ethics" XXVII (1916) 91-106.

Bergson's Idea of God, in "The Quest" VIII (1916) 1-8.

The Philosophy of Rabindranath Tagore-I, in "The Quest" VIII (1917) 457-477.

The Philosophy of Rabindranath Tagore-II, in "The Quest" VIII (1917) 592-612.

Is Bergson's Philosophy Monistic?, in "Mind" XXVI (1917) 329-339.

The Philosophy of Rabindranath Tagore, London, Macmillan and Co., 1918.

James Ward's Pluralistic Theism-I, in "Indian Philosophical Review" II (1918) 97-118.

James Ward's Pluralistic Theism-II, in "Indian Philosophical Review" II (1918) 210-232.

Bergson and Absolute Idealism-I, in "Mind" XXVIII (1919) 41-53.

Bergson and Absolute Idealism-II, in "Mind" XXVIII (1919) 275-296.

The Reign of Religion in Contemporary Philosophy, London, Macmillan and Co., 1920.

The Metaphysics of the Upanishads-I, in "Indian Philosophical Review" III (1920) 213-235.

The Metaphysics of the Upanishads-II, in "Indian Philosophical Review" III (1920) 346-362.

Review of: Bosanquet's *Implications and Linear Inference,* in "Indian Philosophical Review" III (1920) 301.

The Future of Religion, in "Mysore University Magazine" IV (1920) 148-157.

Gandhi and Tagore, in "Culcutta Review", Third Series I (1921) 14-29.

Religion and Philosophy, in "Hibbert Journal" XX (1921) 35-45.

Tilak as an Orientalist, in "Indian Review" XXII (1921) 737.

The Heart of Hinduism, in "Hibbert Journal" XXI (1922) 5-19. (Reprinted in *Heart of Hindustan,* pp. 1-22).

The Hindu Dharma, in "International Journal of Ethics" XXXII (1922) 1-22.

Contemporay Philosophy, in "Indian Review" XXIII (1922) 440.

Indian Philosophy I, Published in The Muirhead Library of Philosophy, London, Allen & Unwin, 1923 (Revised second ed. 1929; Indian ed. 1940).

Islam and Indian Thought, in "Indian Review" XXIV (1923) 665 ff. (Reprinted in the *Heart of Hindustan,* pp. 53-72).

Religious Unity, in "Mysore University Magazine" VII (1923) 187-198.

The Philosophy of the Upanishads. Reprinted from *Indian Philosophy* I with a forward by Rabindranath Tagore and an introduction by Edmond Holmes, London, Allen & Unwin, 1924. (Revised second ed. 1935).

Hindu Thought and Christian Doctrine, in "Madras Christian College Magazine" XXIV (1924) 18-24.

The Hindu Idea of God, in "The Quest" XV (1924) 289-310.

The Hindu View of Life, London, Allen & Unwin, 1927. (Radhakrishnan's Upton Lectures delivered at Manchester College, Oxford, in 1926. Reprinted ten times. Unwin Books ed. 1960.

Indian Philosophy — Some Problems, in "Mind" XXXV (1926) 154-180.

The Role of Philosophy in the History of Civilisation, in E. S. BRIGHTMAN, (ed.), *Proceedings of the sixth International Congress of Philosophy,* New York, Longmans, Green & Co., 1927, pp. 543-550. (Reprinted in D. S. ROBINSON, [ed.], *Anthology of Recent Philosophy,* New York 1929, pp. 55-63).

The Doctrine of Māyā: Some Problems, in E. S. BRIGHTMAN, (ed.), *Proceedings of the sixth International Congress of Philosophy,* New York, Longmans, Green & Co., 1927, pp. 683-689.

Indian Philosophy II, Published in The Muirhead Library of Philosophy, London, George Allen & Unwin, 1927 (Revised 2nd ed. 1931, Indian ed. 1940).

Presidential Address at the Third Indian Philosophical Congress, Bombay University in December 1927. Published in *Proceedings of the III Indian Philosophical Congress,* Culcutta 1927, pp. 19-30.

The Religion We Need, London, Ernest Benn, 1928.

The Vedanta according to Sankara and Ramanuja, London, George Allen & Unwin, 1928. (A reprint from *Indian Philosophy II*).

Indian Philosophy — Notes, in "Mind" XXXVII (1928) 130-131.

Evolution and its Implications, in "New Era" (1928) 102-111.

Kalki or the Future of Civilisation, London, Kegan Paul & Co., 1929, (2nd ed. 1948).

Indian Philosophy: Encyclopaedia Britannica 14th ed. XII (1937) 247-253.

Review of: JOHN BAILLIE, *Interpretation of Religion — An Introductory Study of Theological Principles,* Edinburg 1929, in "Hibbert Journal" XXVIII (1930) 740-742.

Forward to A. K. MAJUMDAR, *The Sāmkhya Conception of Personality,* Culcutta 1930.

The Hindu Idea of God, in "The Spectator", May 1931. (Reprinted in *The Heart of Hindusthan,* pp. 46-52).

Intuition and Intellect, in *The Golden Book of Tagore,* Culcutta 1931, pp. 310-313.

Forward to Dr N. K. BRAHMA, *The Philosophy of Hindu Sadhana,* London 1932.

An Idealist View of Life, London, Allen & Unwin, 1932 (2nd ed. 1937). Presidential Address at VIII Indian Philosophical Congress, Published in *Proceedings of the VIII Indian Philosophical Congress,* Culcutta, 1932, pp. v-xvi.

Sarvamukti (Universal Salvation), in *Proceedings of VIII Indian Philosophical Congress,* Culcutta 1932, pp. 314-318.

East and West in Religion, London, George Allen & Unwin, 1933, (A collection of five lectures).

Intellect and Intuition in Sankara's Philosophy, in "Triveni" VI (1933).

The Teaching of the Buddha, published by The Public Trustee of Ceylon, 1933.

The Teaching of the Buddha by Speech and by Silence, in "Hibbert Journal" XXXII (1934) 342-356.

Freedom and Culture, Madras, G. A. Natesan & Co., 1936, (A collection of addresses at various occasions).

Contemporary Indian Philosophy, edited jointly with J. H. Muirhead, London, George Allen & Unwin, 1936, (2nd ed. 1952).

The Heart of Hindusthan, Madras, G. A. Natesan & Co., 1936.

The Supreme Spiritual Ideal: The Hindu View. An address delivered at the World Congress of Faiths at Queen's Hall, London, on July 1936. Published in "Hibbert Journal" XXXV (1936) 26-39. Included also in *Eastern Religions and Western Thought,* pp. 35-57.

Religion and Religions. A lecture delivered at the World Congress of Faiths on July 8, 1936. Published in Proceedings of the World Congress of Faiths, London, 1936, pp. 104-115. (Discussion on this lecture, Ibid., pp. 116-119. Reply, Ibid., pp. 119-121.

Foreword to *The Philosophy of Yoga Vaśiṣṭha* By B. L. Atreya, Madras 1936.

Spiritual Freedom and New Education. A lecture delivered on August 3, 1936, at the Seventh World Conference of the New Education Fellowship, Published in "New Era" XVII (1936) 233 ff.

The Spirit in Man, in *Contemporary Indian Philosophy,* pp. 257-289. (In the 2nd edition pp. 475-505).

Progress and Spiritual Values. A lecture delivered at the Evening meeting of the British Institute of Philosophy, January 19, 1937. Published in "Philosophy" XII (1937) 259-275.

Hinduism, in G. T. GARRETT (ed.), *The Legacy of India,* Oxford, 1937, pp. 256-286.

My Search for Truth, in VERGILIUS FERM (ed.), *Religion in Transition* New York 1937, pp. 11-59. (A separate off-print of this essay was brought out by Shiva Lal Agarwala & Co. Agra in 1946.

The Failure of the Intellectuals, in "Indian Review" XXXVIII (1937) 737 ff.

Education and Spiritual Freedom, in "Triveni" X (1937). Also in *Education, Politics, and War,* pp. 91-110.

Introduction to *The Cultural Heritage of India I,* Calcutta 1937. (Reproduced in 2nd edition, Culcutta 1958, pp. xxiii-xxxvi).

Foreword to Dr S. K. DAS, *A Study of the Vedanta,* Calcutta 1937.

Gautama the Buddha, in *Proceedings of the British Academy,* London 1938. (Reprinted by Humphrey Milfored, London 1938. Reprinted also by Hind Kitabs, Bombay. 2nd edition 1946).

Foreword to T. M. P. MAHADEVAN, *The Philosophy of the Advaita,* London 1938.

Eastern Religions and Western Thought, London, Oxford University Press, 1939. (Revised 2nd edition 1940).

Mahatma Gandhi: Essays and Reflections on his Life and Work, (editor) London, George Allen and Unwin, 1939. (Introduction is by Radhakrishnan. 2nd edition 1949).

Foreword to S. K. GEORGE, *Gandhi's Challenge to Christianity,* London 1939.

Presidential Address at the Fifteenth All India Federation of Educational Associations' Conference, Lucknow in December 1939. Published in the Proceedings of the Conference, Allahabad 1939, pp. 100-105.

Hinduism and the West, in O'MALLEY (ed.) *Modern India and the West* Oxford 1941, pp. 338-353.

General Preface to G. JHA, *The Pūrva Mīmāṁsā in its Sources,* Benares 1942.

The Cultural Problem, in *Oxford Pamphlets on Indian Affairs* I, Oxford 1942, pp. 41-50.

India's Heritage. Welcome Address to the XII All India Oriental Conference, 1943-44. Published in the *proceedings and Transactions of XII Session of the All India Oriental Conference,* pp. 1-5. (Reprinted in *Education, Politics, and War,* pp. 176-186).

Silver Jubilee Address to the Bhandarkar Oriental Research Institute on January 4, 1943. Published in *Annals of the Bhandarkar Oriental Research Institute* XXIV (1943) 1-8.

India and China, Bombay, Hind Kitabs, 1944. (2nd. ed. 1947).

Education, Politics, and War, Poona, International Book Service, 1944. (A collection of Lectures).

Foreword to D. S. SARMA, *The Renaissance of Hinduism,* Benares 1944.

Foreword to SWAMI NIRVEDĀNANDA, *Hinduism at a Glance,* Calcutta 1944.

Is This Peace? Bombay, Hind Kitabs, 1945.

Foreward to SWAMI AVINĀSĀNANDA, *Gītā Letters,* Bombay 1945.

Moral Values in Literature, Address delivered at the P. E. N. Conference at Jaipur in September 1945. Published in the *The Proceedings of the P. E. N. Conference,* Bombay, International Book House, 1945, pp. 86-105.

Introduction to DILIP KUMAR ROY, *Among the Great,* Bombay 1945.

Foreword to R. K. PRABHU and U. R. RAO, *The Mind of Mahatma Gandhi,* Bombay 1945.

P. E. N. Dinner Speech on February 6, 1946. Published in "P. E. N. News", (1946) 142, pp. 8-11.

Broadcast Speech in the B.B.C.'s Overseas Service on December 4, 1946. Published in *Records of the General Conference, UNESCO,* 1946, pp. 27 f.

Bhagavān Srī Ramana, in *Golden Jubilee Souvenir,* Srī Ramanashram, Tirvannamalai, 1946.

Religion and Society, London, George Allen & Unwin, 1947. (2nd ed. 1948).

Science and Religion, in *Art and Thought,* A volume in honour of the late Dr. Ananda Coomaraswamy, London 1947, pp. 180-185.

The Spirit of Asia, Government of India Information Service, 1947. Address before the Second Session of the UNESCO on November 8, 1947. Published in *Records of the General Conference, UNESCO,* 1947, pp. 58-62.

The Bhagavadgītā, With an Introductory Essay, English translation and Notes, London, George Allen & Unwin, 1948. (2nd ed. 1949. Translated in French, Swedish, Italian, German, Hindi, Marathi and Kannada).

Mahātmā Gāndhi, Address delivered in the All Souls College, Oxford, on February 1, 1948. Published in "Hibbert Journal" XLVI (1948) 193-197. Address at the third General Session of the UNESCO, published in *Records of the General Session, UNESCO,* 1948, pp. 56-59.

Indian Culture, Address at the opening session of the UNESCO in Paris. Printed in *The Reflections on our Age,* London 1948, pp. 115-133.

General Statement in CLARA URQUHART (ed.), *Last Chance, eleven Questions on Issues Determining our Destiny Answered by 26 Leaders of Thought of 14 Nations,* Boston 1948, pp. 46-54.

Hinduism, in HUTCHINSON (ed.), *Twentieth Century Encyclopedia,* p. 522.

Great Indians, Bombay, Hind Kitabs, 1949. (The introductory Essay is on Radhakrishnan by D. S. Sarma).

Report of the University Education Commission I, Jointly with James Duff and others. New Delhi, 1949.

Address at the fourth General Session of the UNESCO (Paris). Published in *General Records of the UNESCO,* 1949, pp. 44-45; 58-60.

Foreword to R. R. DIWAKAR, *The Upanishads in Story and Dialogue,* Bombay 1949.

A Clean Advocate of Great Ideals, in *The Nehru Birthday Book,* Delhi 1949, pp. 93-96.

Goethe, in *Goethe,* UNESCO Publication No. 411, Paris 1949, pp. 99-108.

The Dhammapada, With English translation and Notes. London, Oxford University Press, 1950.

Speech at the fifth General Session of the UNESCO in Florence in 1950. Published in *General Records of the UNESCO* 1950.

UNESCO and World Revolution, in "The New Republic" (1950) 15-16.

Religion and the World Unity, in "Hibbert Journal" L (1951) 218-225.

The Nature of Man, in BARBARA WAYLEN, (ed.), *Creators of the Modern Spirit,* London 1951, pp. 64-66.

Religion and the World Crises, in CHRISTOPHER ISHERWOOD, (ed.), *Vedanta for Modern Man,* 1951, pp. 338-341.

The Religion of the Spirit and the World's Need: Fragments of a Confession, in PAUL ARTHUR SCHILPP, (ed.), *The Philosophy of Sarvepalli Radhakrishnan,* New York, Tudor Publishing Company, 1952, pp. 5-82.

Reply to Critics, in PAUL ARTHUR SCHILPP (ed.), *The Philosophy of Sarvepalli Radhakrishnan,* New York, Tudor Publishing Company, 1952, pp. 787-842.

History of Philosophy, Eastern and Western. Edited by Radhakrishnan. London, George Allen and Unwin, 1952, v. I, 1953, v. II.

Vedānta- The Advaita School, in *History of Philosophy, Eastern and Western.* I, pp. 272-284.

Epilogue, in *History of Philosophy, Eastern and Western* II.

The Principal Upanishads. Edited by Radhakrishnan with Introduction, English translation and Notes, London, George Allen & Unwin, 1953.

East and West, Some Reflections, London, George Allen & Unwin, 1955.

Recovery of Faith, World Perspective Series, New York, Harper & Brothers, 1955. (London, George Allen & Unwin, 1956).

Occasional Speeches and Writings, October 1952 - January 1956, Delhi, The Publication Division, Ministry of Information and Broadcasting, Government of India, 1956.

Occasional Speeches and Writings, February 1956 - February 1957, Delhi, The Publication Division, Ministry of Information and Broadcasting, Government of India, 1957.

A Source Book in Indian Philosophy. Edited jointly with Charles A. Moore. London, Oxford University Press, 1957.

The Religion of the Spirit and the World's Need, in WHIT BURNETT (ed.), *This Is My Philosophy,* London 1958, pp. 344-366.

The Concept of Man, edited Jointly with P. T. Raju, London 1960.

The Brahma Sūtra: The Philosophy of Spiritual Life, London, George Allen & Unwin, 1960.

Occasional Speeches and Writings, October 1952 - February 1959, Delhi, The Publication Division, Ministry of Information and Broadcasting, Government of India, 1960.

Fellowship of the Spirit, Cambridge, Massachusetts, The Centre for the Study of World Religions, Harvard Divinity School, 1961.

Occasional Speeches and Writings, July 1959 - May 1962, Delhi, Publications Division, Ministry of Information and Broadcasting, Government of India, 1963.

President Radhakrishnan's Speeches and Writings, May 1962 - May 1964, Publications Division, Ministry of Information and Broadcasting, Government of India, 1965.

On Nehru, Delhi, Publications Division, Ministry of Information and Broadcasting, Government of India, 1965. (A collection of speeches on Nehru).

Mahatma Gandhi and One World. Edited Jointly with others. Delhi, Publications Division, Ministry of Information and Broadcasting, Government of India, 1966.

Religion in a Changing World, London, George Allen & Unwin, 1967.

Speech on the occasion of confering Nehru Award to U Thant, on April 12, 1967, New Delhi. Published in *Times of India* (Bombay, Delhi), April 14, 1967, p. 1.

New Motto of " Service at any Cost ". Speech to the Indian Nation on the eve of his retirement from the Presidency. Published in *Times of India* (Bombay, Delhi), May 14, 1967, pp. 1 and 9.

Religion and Culture, Delhi, Hind Pocket Books, 1968.

Radhakrishnan: an Anthology, edited by A. N. Marlow, London, George Allen & Unwin, 1952.

The Present Crisis of Faith, An Orient Paperback, Delhi, 1970.

2) WORKS ON DR RADHAKRISHNAN

ARAPURA, J. G., *Radhakrishnan and Integral Experience: The Philosophy and World Vision of Sarvepalli Radhakrishnan,* London 1966.

ATREYA, J. P. (Managing Editor), *Dr. S. Radhakrishnan Souvenir Volume,* Moradabad 1964. (A collection of 76 articles by different authors).

BENZ, ERNST, *Einführung zu: S. Radhakrishnan, Wissenschaft und Weisheit,* München 1961.

BÜRKLE, HORST, *Dialog 'mit dem Osten: Radhakrishnans neuhinduistische Botschaft im Lichte christlicher Weltanschauung,* Stuttgart 1965.

DATTA, D. M., *The Chief Currents of Contemporary Philosophy,* Calcutta 1952. (deals also with Radhakrishnan).

—, *Radhakrishnan and Comparative Philosophy,* in PhSR, pp. 659-685.

DUTT, K. I., (ed.), *Sarvepalli Radhakrishnan,* New Delhi 1966.

FALLON, P., *Ramakrishna, Vivekananda and Radhakrishnan,* in R. DE SMET, *Religious Hinduism: A Presentation and Appraisal,* 2nd. ed., Allahabad 1964, pp. 283-291.

GATHIER, E., *Un aspect de l'Hinduisme moderne: Radhakrishnan,* in *Studia Missionalia,* Rome 1953, No. 53, pp. 369-390.

GNANAPRAKASAM, IGNATIUS, Dr. *Radhakrishnan and Jñāna, an Essay on the Metaphysical Aspects of a Spiritual Wisdom,* Shembaganur 1959.

HACKER, P., *Ein Prastanatraya - Kommentar des Neuhinduismus: Bemerkungen zum Werk Radhakrishnans,* in " Orientalische Literaturzeitung " 56 (1961) 565-576.

HEINMANN, BETTY, Review of *The Philosophy of Sarvepalli Radhakrishnan* in "' Philosophy " 29 (1954) 181 ff.

HINMAN, E. L., *Modern Idealism and the Logos Teaching: Radhakrishnan,* Bombay 1951.

—, " Radhakrishnan and the Sung Confucianism ", in PhSR, pp. 607-632.

—, Review of *The Reign of Religion in the Contemporary Philosophy,* in " Philosopphical Review " 29 (1920) 582-586.

INGE, W. R.. et al. (eds), *Radhakrishnan: Comparative Studies in Philosophy presented in Honour of His sixtieth Birthday,* London 1951.

—, *Radhakrishnan and the Religion of the Spirit,* in PhSR, pp. 323-332.

JOAD, C. E. M., *Counter Attack from the East: Philosophy of Radhakrishnan,* London 1933. (Bombay 1951).

KLOSTERMAIER, K., *Some Aspects of the Social Philosophy of Dr Sarvepalli Radhakrishnan,* in " Religion and Society " XIV (1967) 32 f.

KRAEMER, HENDRIK, *Religion and the Christian Faith,* London 1956, (part II, pp. 97-136, deals with Radhakrishnan).

KRÄMER, A., *Christus und Christentum im Denken des modernen Hinduismus*, Bonn 1958, pp. 91-100.

MASCARENHAS, ANTONIO, *A Critique of Sir S. Radhakrishnan's Basis for Human Fellowship*, Lisboa 1959.

MELZER, F., *Radhakrishnan- Der Hinduismus auf dem Wege zum Westen*, in "Evangelisches Missionsmagazin" (1936) 211-220.

—, Review of *Indische Philosophie II, Die Systeme des Brahmanismus*, in "Theologische Literaturzeitung" 82 (1957) 846-847.

MOSES, D. G., *Professor Radhakrishnan and a Parliament of Religions*, in *The Claim, Content and Context of Christian Evangelism*, Indian Research Series, No. 2, Madras 1950.

NARAVANE, V. S., *Modern Indian Thought*, Bombay 1964, pp. 230-264.

NEILL, STEPHEN. *Christain Faith and other Faiths*, London 1961, pp. 81-86.

NEUNER, J., *Gespräch mit Radhakrishnan*, in "Stimmen der Zeit" No. 4 (1961-62) 241 ff.

RAJU, P. T., *Idealistic Thought of India*, London 1953, pp. 331-350.

—, *Radhakrishnan's Influence on Indian Thought*, in PhSR, pp. 513-539.

RYLE, G., Review of *The Philosophy of Sarvepalli Radhakrishnan*, in "Mind" 53 (1954) 417-419.

SAMARTHA, S. J., *Introduction to Radhakrishnan: the Man and his Thought*, New Delhi 1964.

SANTOSH KUMAR, RAY, *The Political Thought of President Radhakrishnan*, Calcutta 1966.

SARMA, D. S., *Studies in the Renaissance of Hinduism in the nineteenth and twentieth Centuries*, Benares 1944, pp. 585-634.

SCHARMA, C., *P. C. Ray and Sir S. Radhakrishnan*, London 1941.

SCHILPP, PAUL ARTHUR (ed.), *The Philosophy of Sarvepalli Radhakrishnan*, New York 1952. (A collection of 23 essays by different authors and an Introduction and a Reply to the Critics by Radhakrishnan.)

SCHWARZ, W., *Hoffnung im Nichts. Radhakrishnan, Gebser und der westöstliche Geist*, Krailling bei München 1961.

SING, CHRIST KUMAR, *Die Mystik bei Radhakrishnan und die Offenbarungstheologie*, Berlin 1966.

SING, RAJENDRA PAL, *Radhakrishnan: The Portrait of an Educationist*, Delhi 1967.

SING, SURJIT, *Preface to Personality. Christology in Relation to Radhakrishnan's Philosophy*, in Indian Research Series, No. 9, Madras 1952.

VARADACHARI, K. C., *What is Intuition according to Tagore, Radhakrishnan and Aurobindo*, in "The Arian Path", Bombay August 1935.

VOGEL, H., *Die Mystik Radhakrishnans und das Evangelium von Jesus Christus*, in "Evangelische Theologie" XXI (1961) 387-407.

WOLFF, OTTO, *Radhakrishnan*, Göttingen 1962.

—, *Christus unter dem Hinduismus*, Güterloh 1965, pp. 167-186.

YOUNGHUSBAND, FRANCIS, *Down in India*, London 1930. (Chap. xvii).

3) MODERN HINDUISM

BHATTACHARYA, HARIDAS (ed.), *The Cultural Heritage of India*, IV, 2nd. ed. Calcutta 1956.

DEVANANDAN, P. D., *The Renaissance of Hinduism: A Survey of Hindu History from 1800-1950*, in "Theology Today" (1955) 189-205.

FARQUHAR, J. N., *Modern Religious Movements in India*, London 1924.

GANDHI, M. K., *My Religion*, compiled and edited by B. Kumarappa, Ahamedabad 1955.

GLASENAPP, H. V., *Der Hiduismus; Religion uund Gesselschaft in heutigen Indien*, München 1922.

—, *Religiöse Reformbewegungen im heutigen Indien*, Leipzig 1928.

GRISWOLD, H. H., *Insights into Modern Hinduism*, New York 1934.

HACKER, P., *Der Dharma-Begriff des Neuhinduismus*, in "Zeitschrift für Missionswissenschaft und Religionswissenschaft" (1958) 1-15.

MELZER, F., *Indien greift nach uns: West-östliche Begegnung mit modernen Hinduismus*, Stuttgart 1962.

NEUNER, J., *Religiöse Strömungen im heutigen Indien*, in "Stimmen der Zeit" (1953) 415 ff.

ROY, B. G., *Contemporary Indian Philosophers*, Kitabistan 1947.

SARMA, D. S., *Studies in the Renaissance of Hinduism*, Benares 1944.

SAVARIMUTHU, S. V., *Zur gegenwärtigen Lage in Indien*, in *Die Unordnung der Welt und Gottes Heilsplan* II, Zürich 1948, pp. 195-205.

TAGORE, RABINDRANTH, *The Religion of Man*, London 1931.

4) ADVAITA

DAS GUPTA, SURENDRA NATH, *Indian Idealism*, Cambridge 1962.

GUPTA, KALAYAN CHANDRA, *Monism: A Critical Survey*, Calcutta 1954.

HACKER, P., *Untersuchungen über Texte des frühen Advaitavada, I: Die Schüler Sankaras*, Mainz-Wiebaden, 1950.

LACOMBE, O., *L'Absolu selon le Védânta*, Paris 1937.

MAHADEVAN, T. M. P., *Gaudapāda, A Study in Early Advaita*, Madras 1952.

—, *The Philosophy of Advaita*, Madras 1957.

MURTHY, K. S., *Revelation and Reason in Advaita Vedanta*, Watair 1959.

NARAIN, K., *A Critical Study of Madhva-criticism of Sankara*, Allahabad 1961.

RAJU, P. T., *The Inward Absolute and the Activism of the Finite Self*, in *Contemporary Indian Philosophy*, London 1952.

—, *Idealistic Thought of India*, London 1953.

SANKARACHARYA, *Self-Knowledge*, trans. by Swami Nikhilananda, New York 1946.

SRINIVASACHARYA, P. N., *Advaita and Visistādvaita*, London 1961.

VARMA, P. M., *The Role of Vedanta as Universal Religion and the Science of Self-Realization*, Vishva Bharata Series, Allahabad 1960.

5) HINDUISM IN GENERAL

ANANDA ACHARYA. *Brahmadarsanam, An Introduction to the Study of Hindu Philosophy*, New York 1917.

AUROBINDO, SRI, *The Life Divine*, 3rd. ed., 2 Vols, Calcutta 1947.

—, *Supramental Manifestation upon Earth*, Pondicherry 1952.

BARTH, A., *The Religion of India*, trans. by J. Wood, 6th ed., London 1932.

BON MAHARAJ, B. H., *Origin and Escatology of Hindu Reilgion*, Vrindaban 1960.

BOUQUET, A. C., *Hinduism*, London 1948.

BENNET, ALLAN, *The Wisdom of the Aryans*, London 1923.

BHATTACHARYA, HARIDAS, *The Cultural Heritage of India*, Calcutta 1956-1962.
BLOOMFIELD, MAURICE, *The Religion of the Veda, The Ancient Religion of India* (from Rig Veda to Upanishads), New York 1908.
CARPENTER, JOSEPH ESTLIN, *Theism in Medieval India*, London 1921.
DAS, BHAGAVAN, *The Essential Unity of All religions*, Benares 1939.
—, *Kṛṣhṇa, a Study in the Theory of Avatāras*, Adyar 1929.
DAS GUPTA, S. N., *Indian Philosophy*, 4 Vols, Cambridge 1951.
DEUSSEN, PAUL, *Allgemeine Einleitung und Philosophie des Veda bis auf die Upanishads*, Leipsig 1894.
—, *Die Philosophie der Upanishads*, Leipzig 1899.
—, *Das System des Vedanta*, Leipzig 1921.
DHAVAMONY, M., *Indian Philosophy*: New Catholic Encyclopedia VII (1967) 458-461.
—, *The Mystery of God according to the Bhakti mystics of modern Hiduism*, in *La Réalité Suprême dans les Religions non-chrétiennes*, Studia Missionalia XVII (1968) 147-168.
EIDLITZ, W., *Die Indische Gottesliebe*, Freiburg 1955.
—, *Der Glaube und die heiligen Schriften der Inder*, Freiburg 1957.
ELIOT, SIR CHARLES, *Hinduism and Buddhism*, 3 Vols, London 1948.
EATON, GAI, *The Richest Vein, Eastern Tradition and Modern Thought*, London 1949.
FARQUHAR, J. N., *An Outline of the Religious Literature of India*, London 1920.
GUÉNON, RÉNE, *Introduction générale à l'étude des doctrines hindoues*, Paris 1921.
GONDA, JAN, *Notes on Brahman*, Utrecht 1950.
—, *The Concept of a personal God in ancient Indian religious thought*, in *La Réalité Suprême dans les Religions non-chrétiennes*, Studia Missionalia XVII (1968) 111-136.
HEIMANN, B., *Facets of Indian Thought*, London 1964.
HARRISON, MAX HUNTER, *Indian Monism and Pluralism*, London 1932.
JACOBI, HERMANN, *Entwicklung der Gottesidee bei den Indern*, Bonn 1923.
MAITRA, S. K., *The Spirit of Indian Philosophy*, Benares 1947.
LEMAITRE, S., *L'Hinduisme*, Paris 1957.
MACNICOL, NICOL, *Indian Theism from the Vedic to the Mohammedan Period* London 1915.
MAHADEVAN, T. M. P., *Time and the Timeless*, Madras 1953.
MEHTA, ROHIT, *The Intuitive Philosophy*, Adyar 1950.
MORGAN, K. W., *The Basic Beliefs of Hinduism*, Calcutta 1955.
—, *The Religion of the Hindus*, New York 1953.
MUKERJI, A. C., *The Nature of the Self*, Allahabad 1938.
MÜLLER, F. MAX, *The Sacred Books of the East*, 51 Volf, Oxford 1879-1910.
OLDENBERG, HERMANN, *Die Lehre der Upanishaden und die Anfänge des Buddismus*, Göttingen 1915.
PAPALLI, C. B., *Hinduismus*, 2 Vols. Roma 1953-1960.
PRATT, JAMES BISSETT, *India and Its Faiths*, Boston, New York 1915.
QUEGUINER, M., *Introduction à l'Hinduisme*, Paris 1958.
RENOU, L., *L'Hinduisme*, Paris 1951.
RUBEN, W., *Geschichte der indischen Philosophie*, Berlin 1954.
SARMA, D. S., *What is Hinduism*, Madras 1945.
—, *Hinduism through the Ages*, Bombay 1956.

SCHWEITZER, A., *Die Weltanschauung der indischen Denker*, München 1935.
SEN, K. M., *L'Hinduisme*, Paris, Payot 1962.
SHARMA, C., *A Critical Survey of Indian Philosophy*, London 1960.
SINHA, J., *The Foundations of Hinduism*, Calcutta 1955.
VIDYARTHI, L. P., *Aspects of Religion in Indian Society*, Meerut 1961.
ZACHARIAS, O. C. D., *An Outline of Hinduism*. Alwaye 1956.
ZIMMER, H., *Philosophie und Religion Indiens*, Zürich 1960.
For further Bibliography of Hinduism:
MAHAR, MICHAEL, J., *India: A Critical Bibliography*, Arizona, The University of Arizona Press, 1966.

6) COMPARATIVE RELIGION

ALTHAUS, P., *Höhen ausser christlicher Religionen*, in *Die Welt Religionen und das Christentum*, München 1928.
ANDERSEN. W., *Auf dem Wege zu einer Theologie der Mission*, Gütersloh 1957
ANDREWS, C. F., *The Hindu View of Christ*, in " The International Review Missions" (1939) 259 ff, 264 ff.
ANTOINE et al, *Religious Hinduism: A Presentation and Appraisal*, 2nd ed., Bombay 1964.
APPASAMY, A. J., *Christianity as Bhakti Marga: A Study in the Mysticism of the Johannine Writings*, Madras 1930.
—, *The Christian Tasks in Independent India*, London 1951.
—, *The Gospel and India's Heritage*, New York 1942.
ASIRVATHAN, EDDY, *Christianity and the Indian Church*, Calcutta 1955.
BENZ, E., *Indische Einflüsse auf die frühchristliche Theologie*, Wiesbaden 1958.
BHATTY, E. C., *Evangelism in a Revolutionary India*, in " National Christian Council Review" (1959).
BIANCHI, U., *Problemi di Storia delle religioni*, Roma 1958.
BOUQUET, A. C., *Comparative Religion*, London 1956.
—, *Sacred Books of the World*, London 1954.
—, *The Christian Faith and Non-Christian Religions*, London 1958.
BULCKE, C., *Catholic Approach to Hinduism*, in " Clergy Monthly Supplement" VI (1962-63) 279-282.
BÜRKLE, H., *Christus, das Ende der Geschichte und die Mission*, in " Evangelische Missionszeitschrift" (1962) 57-69.
—, *Der Christus der Geistgemeinschaft*, in " Evangelische Missionszeitschrift » (1963) 161-170.
CHENCHIA, P., *Religion in Contemporary India*, In *Rethinking Christianity in India*, Madras 1938.
COOKE, G., *As Christians Face Rival Religions*, New York 1962.
CUTTAT, JACQUES ALBERT, *Encounter of Religions*, New York 1960.
DANIELOU, J., *Introduction to the Great Religions*, Notre Dam 1964.
DEVASAHAYAM, D. M. and SUDARISANAM, A. N., (eds), *Rethinking Christianity in India*, Madras 1938.
DEUSSEN. P., *Über die innere Verwandschaft der indischen Religion mit der christlichen*, in *Verhandlungen des 2. Internationalen Kongress für Religionsgeschichte*, Basel 1905, pp. 77 ff.
DEVANANDAN, P. D., *Christian Concern in Hinduism*, Bangalore 1961.

—, *The Gospel and Renascent Hinduism*, London 1959.

Dhavamony, M., *Hinduism and Christianity, The Christian Encounter: 4*, in "Theology" LXX (1967) 156-165.

—, *Christian Experience and Hindu Spirituality*, in "Gregorianum" 48 (1967) 776-791.

—, *La Chiesa e l'Induismo*, in "Via, Verita e Vita", No. 21, XVII (1969) 42-51.

Eliade, M., *Patterns in Comparative Religion*, trans. R. Sheed, New York 1958.

—, and Kitagawa, J. M., (eds), *The History of Religions; Essays in Methodology*, Chicago 1959.

Frick, H., *Vergleichende Religionswissenschaft*, Berlin 1928.

—, *Das Evangelium und die Religionen*, Basel 1933.

Fuchs, Stephen, *Rebellious Prophets: A Study of Messianic Movements in Indian Religions*, London 1965.

Grant, John Webster, *God's People in India*, Toronto 1959.

Griffiths, Bede, *Christ in India: Essays towards a Hindu-Christian Dialogue*, New York 1967.

Heiler, F., *Christlicher Glaube und indisches Geistesleben*, München 1926.

Hirschman, E., *Phönomenologie der Religion: Eine historisch-systematische Untersuchung*, Würzburg-Aumühle, 1940.

Hogg, A. G., *The Christian Message to the Hindu*, London 1947.

Jordan, L. H., *Comparative Religion, Its Adjuncts and Allies*, Oxford 1916.

Karrer, O., *Das Religiöse in der Menschheit und das Christentum*, Freiburg 1934.

Kraemer, Hendrik, *Religion and the Christian Faith*, London 1956

—, *Christian Message in a Non- Christian World*, 3rd ed., London 1953.

Krämer, A., *Christus und Christentum im Deken des modernen Hinduismus*, Bonn 1958.

Kulandran, S., *Grace, A Comparative Study of the Doctrine in Christianity and Hinduism*, London 1964.

Leo Tigga, et al., *Hinduism, Studia Missionalia* XIII, Rome 1963.

Macquarrie, J., *Twentieth Century Religious Thought*, New York 1963.

Manikam, R. B., *Christianity in the Asian Revolution*, Methuen 1954.

Melzer, F., *Die Christusbotschaft in Indien*, Stuttgart 1948.

—, *Christus und die indischen Erlösungswege*, Tübingen 1949.

Mensching, G., *Vergleichende Religionswissenschaft*, Leipzig 1938.

Messenger, Ernest Charles, (general Editor) *Studies in Comparative Religion*, 5 Vols, London 1935.

Moses, D. G., *Religious Truth and the Relation between Religions*, Indian Research Series V, Madras, Bangalore, 1950.

Neill, Stephen, *Christian Faith and Other Faiths*, London 1961.

Ohm, Thomas, *Indien und Gott*, Salzburg 1932.

—, *Asia Looks at Western Christianity*, New York 1959.

Neuner, J. et al., *Hinduismus und Christentum*, Wien 1962.

Panikkar, R., *The Unknown Christ of Hinduism*, London 1964.

—, *Kerygma und Indien zur Heilsgeschichtlichen Problematik der christlichen Begegnung mit Indien*, Hamburg 1967.

—, *Kultmysterium in Hinduismus und Christentum: ein Beitrag zu vergleichenden Religionstheologie*, Freiburg, München 1964.

Parrinder, G., *Gītā and Bible*, London 1962.

PERRY, E., *The Gospel in Dispute: The Relation of Christian Faith to Other Missionary Religions*, New York 1958.
RUTHNASWAMY, M., *India after God*, Ranchi 1964.
SCHLETTE, H. R., *Towards a Theology of Religions*. London 1966.
SCHLUNK, M., *Die Weltreligionen und das Christentum*, Hamburg 1923.
SCHOMERUS, H. W., *Indien und das Christentum*, 3 Vols, Halle 1931, 1933.
SCHUMANN, F. K., *Das Christentum und die Weltreligionen*, Stuttgart 1938.
THOMÉ, J., *Es gibt viele Religionen: über die Absolutheit des Christentums*, Frankfurt 1953.
THOMPSON, E. W., *The Word of the Cross to Hindus*, Madras 1956.
VICEDOM, G. F., *Die Weltreligionen im Angriff auf die Christenheit*. 2nd ed., Münich 1957.
WACH, W., *The Comparative Study of Religions*, New York 1958.
WINSLOW, J. C., *The Christian Approach to the Hindu*, London 1958.
WITTE, J., *Die Christusbotschaft und die Religionen*, Göttingen 1936.
WOLF, O., *Christus unter den Hindus*, Gütersloh 1965.
ZACHARIAS, O. C. D., *Christianity and Indian Mentality*, Alwaye 1952.
ZAEHNER, R. C., *At Sundry Times*, London 1958.
—, (ed.). *The Concise Encyclopaedia of Living Faiths*, London. 1959.
—, *The Catholic Church and World Religions*, London 1964.

7) MYSTICISM

AULÉN, G., *Glaube und Mystik*, in "Zeitschript für systematische Theologie" II (1925) 268 ff.
BAUMGARDT, D., *Great Western Mystics*, New York 1961.
—, *Mystik und Wissenschaft*, Witten 1963.
BETH, K., *Frömmigkeit der Mystik und des Glaubens*, Leipzig, Berlin 1927.
BRUNNER, E., *Die Mystik und das Wort*, 2nd ed., Tübingen 1928.
BUTLER, DOM. C., *Western Mysticism*, London 1922.
DAS GUPTA, S. N., *Hindu Mysticism*, (reprint from 1927), New York 1959.
RANADE, R. D., *Indian Mysticism: Mysticism in Maharastra*, Poona 1933.
HEILER, F., *Die Bedeutung der Mystik für die Weltreligion*, München 1919.
—, *Die Mystik in den Upanishaden*, München 1925.
HÜGEL, F. V., *The Mystical Element of Religion*, 2 Vols, 2nd ed., London 1923.
INGE, W. R., *Christian Mysticism*. 7th ed., New York 1960.
—, *Mysticism in Religion*, Illinois 1948.
JONES, R. M., *Studies in Mystical Religion*, London 1909.
KNOX, R. A., *Enthusiasm*, New York 1961.
MILBURN, R. GORDON, *The Religious Mysticism of the Upanishads*, London 1924.
MOUROUX, JEAN, *L'experience chrétienne*, Paris 1952.
POULAIN, A. F., *The Graces of Interior Prayer*, trans. by L. L. York Smith, St. Louis 1950.
RAVIER, A. et al., *La Mystique et les mystiques*, Paris 1965.
OTTO, RUDOLF, *West-östliche Mystik*, Gotha 1929.
SCHLÖTERMANN, H., *Mystik in den Religionen der Völker*, München, Baden 1956.
SCHWEITZER, A., *Die Mystik des Apostel Paulus*, 2nd ed., Tübingen 1954.
SHARPE, A. B., *Mysticism: Its True Nature and Value*, St. Louis 1910.

SIRCAR, M., *Hindu Mysticism according to the Upanishads*, London 1934.
SPENCER, S., *Mysticism in World Religion*, Baltimore 1963.
STACE, W. T., *Mysticism and Philosophy*, New York 1960.
THOROLD, A., *An Essay in Aid of the Better Appreciation of Catholic Mysticism*. London 1900.
TYCIAK, J., *Morgenländische Mystik*, Düsseldorf 1949.
ZAEHNER, R. C., *Mysticism Sacred and Profane*, Oxford 1957.
—, *Hindu and Muslim Mysticism*, London 1960.

8) RELIGION

ALLPORT, G. W., *The Individual and His Religion*: *"A Psychological Interpretation"*, London 1951.
ALTHAUS, PAUL, *Die Christliche Wahrheit*, 5th ed., Gütersloh 1959.
ANDERSON, G. H. (ed.), *The Theology of the Christian Mission*, New York 1961.
SANTAYANA, GEORGE, *Interpretations of Poetry and Religion*, New York 1957.
ARGYLE, M., *Religious Behaviour*, London 1958.
ASHBY, PHILIP, *History and Future of Religious Thought*: *Christianity, Hinduism, Buddhism, Islam*, Englewood Cliffs, 1963.
BALTHASAR, HANS URS VON, *Science, Religion and Christianity*, trans. by Hilda graef, Westminster 1958.
BERGSON, H., *The Two Sources of Morality and Religion*, trans by Audra *et al.*, New York 1935.
BÉVENOT, M., *Tradition, Church and Dogma*, in "Heythrop Journal" I (1960) 34-47.
BILLOT, L., *De Ecclesia Christi*, 3rd., Roma 1927.
BOULARD, F., *An Introduction to Religious Sociology*, London 1960.
BOUILLARD, H., *Human Experience as Starting Point for Fundamental Theology*, in "Concilium» VI (1965) 32-42.
CAILLOIS, R., *Man and the Sacred*, Chicago 1939.
CAPERAN, L., *Le problème du salut des infidèles*, 2 Vols, Toulouse 1934.
CARRIER, HERVÉ, *The Sociology of Religious Belonging*, London 1965.
CHRISTIAN, W. A., *Meaning and Truth in Religion*, Princeton 1964.
CLARK, E. T., *Non-Theological Factors in Religious Diversity*, in "Ecumenical Review" III (1951) 347-356.
CLARK, GORDON H., *Religion, Reason and Revelation*, Philadelphia 1961.
DAWSON, CHRISTOPHER H., *Progress and Religion, an Historical Enquiry*, London 1929.
—, *Religion and Culture*, London 1948.
DEVOLDER, N., *Inquiry into the Religious Life of Catholic Intellectuals*, in "Journal of Social Psychology 28 (1948) 39-56.
EBELING, G., *Das Wesen des christlichen Glaubens*, Tübingen 1959.
ELIADE, M., *Das Heilige und das Profane*, Hamburg 1957.
EMINYAN, M., *The Theology of Salvation*, Boston 1960.
FERRE, N. F. S.. *Reason in Religion*, London, Edinburg 1963.
GRAFTON, T. H., *Religious Origins and Sociological Theory*, in "American Sociological Review" X (1945) 726-738.
GROOT, DE J. F., *Conspectus Historiae Dogmatum*, 2 Vols, Romae 1931.
GUARDINI, R., *Religion und Offenbarung*, Würzburg 1958.

GÜNTHER, G. (ed.), *Die Grossen Religionen*, Göttingen 1961.

HARNACK, A., *Dogmengeschichte*, 3 Vols, 4th ed., Tübingen 1910.

HOWELLS, J., *A Comparative Study of those who Accept as against those who Reject Religious Authority*, in "Studies in Character" No. 167, II (1928) 1-80.

HOCKING, W. E., *The Coming World Civilization*, New York 1956.

HOULT, T. F., *The Sociology of Religion*, New York 1958.

JAMES, E. O., *The Ancient Gods*, New York 1960.

JAMES, WILLIAM, *The Varieties of Religious Experience*, London 1915.

JOURNET, CHARLES, *What Is Dogma?*. London 1964.

JURJI, E. J. (ed.), *The Great Religions of the Modern World*, 5th Impr. London 1953.

KARRER, OTTO, *Religions of Mankind*, trans. by E. I. Watkin, London 1936.

KITAGWA, J. M. (ed.), *Modern Trends in World Religions*, La Salle 1959.

KITAY, P. M., *Radicalism and Conservatism toward Conventional Religion*, New York 1947.

LATOURELLE, R., *La Révélation et sa transmission selon la Constitution "Dei Verbum"*, in "Gregorianum" XLVII (1966) 5-40.

LEEUW, G., VAN DER, *La Religion dans son essence et dans ses manifestations*, Paris 1955.

LEIFER, WALTER, *Man and Religion*, München 1967.

LEWIS, H. D., *Philosophy of Religion*, London 1965.

MALINOWSKI, B., *Magic, Science and Religion*, Boston 1948.

MONTINI, GIOVANNI BATTISTA (Pope Paul VI), *Man's Religious Sense: a Pastoral to the Ambrosian Diocese*, Westminster 1961.

NICOLAU, M., *De revelatione christiana sive de vera religione*, in *Sacrae Theologiae Summa* I, Madrid 1958. (All the manuals of Theology gives a treatise on Religion).

OTTO, R., *The Idea of the Holy*, trans. by John W. Harvey, London 1925.

RAHNER, K., "Belonging to the Church according to the Encyclical *Mystici Corporis*", in *Theological Investigations* II, London 1963.

—, "What is a Dogmatic Statement"? in *Theological Investigations* V, London 1966.

—. "History of the World and Salvation-History", Ibid.

REARDON, B. M. G., *Religious Thought in the Nineteenth Century*, Cambridge 1966.

RIESE, HUBER, *Der anonyme Christ nach Karl Rahner*, in "Zeitschrift für Katholische Theologie" (1964) 286-303.

RÖPPER, A., *Die anonymen Christen*, Mainz 1963.

SCHILLING, H. K., *Science and Religion*, New York 1962.

SCHMIDT, W., *The Origin and Growth of Religion: Facts and Theories*, trans. by H. J. Rose, 2nd ed., London 1935.

SHEEN, F. J., *Philosophy of Religion: the Impact of Modern Knowledge on Religion*, New York 1948.

TOYNBEE, A. J., *An Historian's Approach to Religion*, New York 1956.

VISSERT, HOOFT, W. A., *No Other Name*, London 1965.

WACH, J., *Types of Religious Experience, Christian and Non-Christian*, Chicago 1951.

WEBER, O., *Grundlage der Dogmatik*, 2 Vols, Neunkirchen 1959, 1962.

WERNER, M., *Die Entstehung des christlichen Dogmas. Problem-geschichtlich dargestellt*, Tübingen 1953.